D1269455

BEYOND MAYFIELD: MEASUREMENTS OF NEST-SURVIVAL DATA

Stephanie L. Jones and Geoffrey R. Geupel
Associate Editors

Studies in Avian Biology No. 34

A PUBLICATION OF THE COOPER ORNITHOLOGICAL SOCIETY

Front cover photographs: top left—Brown-headed Cowbird (*Molothrus ater*) and Western Tanager (*Piranga ludociviana*) by Colin Woolley, top right—Dickcissel (*Spiza americana*) by Ross R. Conover, bottom—Sandwich Terns (*Thalasseus sandvicensis*) and Royal Terns (*Thalasseus maxima*) by Stephen Dinsmore.
Back cover photographs: top left—Brown-headed Cowbird (*Molothrus ater*) by Amon Armstrong, middle left—Black Skimmer (*Rynchops niger*) by Stephen Dinsmore, bottom left—Allen's Hummingbird (*Selasphorus sasin*) by Dennis Jongsomjit, top right—Chipping Sparrow (*Spizella passerine*), by Colin Woolley middle right—Dusky Flycatcher (*Empidonax oberholseri*) by Chris McCreedy, bottom right—Chestnut-collared Longspur (*Calcarius ornatus*) by Phil Friedman.

STUDIES IN AVIAN BIOLOGY

Edited by

Carl D. Marti
1310 East Jefferson Street
Boise, ID 83712

Spanish translation by
Cecilia Valencia

Studies in Avian Biology is a series of works too long for *The Condor*, published at irregular intervals by the Cooper Ornithological Society. Manuscripts for consideration should be submitted to the editor. Style and format should follow those of previous issues.

Price $18.00 including postage and handling. All orders cash in advance; make checks payable to Cooper Ornithological Society. Send orders to Cooper Ornithological Society, % Western Foundation of Vertebrate Zoology, 439 Calle San Pablo, Camarillo, CA 93010

ISBN: 9780943610764

Library of Congress Control Number: 2007925309
Printed at Cadmus Professional Communications, Ephrata, Pennsylvania 17522
Issued: 9 May 2007

CONTENTS

LIST OF AUTHORS

ANDREW B. COOPER
Department of Natural Resources
Institute for the Study of Earth, Oceans and Space
Morse Hall 142
University of New Hampshire
Durham, NH 03824

J. SCOTT DIENI
Redstart Consulting
403 Deer Road
Evergreen, CO 80439

JAMES J. DINSMORE
Department of Natural Resource Ecology and Management
Iowa State University
Ames, IA 50011-1021

STEPHEN J. DINSMORE
Department of Wildlife and Fisheries
Mississippi State University
Mississippi State, MS 39762
(Current Address: Department of Natural Resource Ecology and Management, Iowa State University, Ames, IA 50011-1021)

MATTHEW A. ETTERSON
Smithsonian Migratory Bird Center
National Zoological Park
(Current address: U.S. Environmental Protection Agency, Mid Continent Ecology Division, 6201 Congdon Boulevard, Duluth, MN 55804)

BRIAN R. GRAY
U. S. Geological Survey
Upper Midwest Environmental Sciences Center
2630 Fanta Reed Road
La Crosse, WI 54603

RUSSELL GREENBERG
Smithsonian Migratory Bird Center
National Zoological Park
Washington, DC 20008

GEOFFREY R. GEUPEL
PRBO Conservation Science
3820 Cypress Drive #11
Petaluma, CA 94954

DENNIS M. HEISEY
U. S. Geological Survey
National Wildlife Health Center
6006 Schroeder Road
Madison, WI 53711

SHARYN L. HOOD
Department of Wildlife and Fisheries
Mississippi State University
Mississippi State, MS 39762
(Current address: Florida Fish and Wildlife Conservation Commission, 8535 Northlake Boulevard, West Palm Beach, FL 33412-3303)

DOUGLAS H. JOHNSON
U. S. Geological Survey
Northern Prairie Wildlife Research Center
200 Hodson Hall
1980 Folwell Avenue
Saint Paul, MN 55108

STEPHANIE L. JONES
U.S. Fish and Wildlife Service, Region 6
P.O. Box 25486 DFC
Denver, CO 80225

MELINDA G. KNUTSON
U. S. Geological Survey
Upper Midwest Environmental Sciences Center
La Crosse, WI 54603
(Current Address: U.S. Fish and Wildlife Service, 2630 Fanta Reed Road, La Crosse, WI 54603)

MARK LINDBERG
Department of Biology and Wildlife and Institute of Arctic Biology
University of Alaska
Fairbanks, AK 99775

JOHN D. LLOYD
Ecostudies Institute
512 Brook Road
Sharon, VT 05065

MELISSA S. MEIER
U. S. Geological Survey
Upper Midwest Environmental Sciences Center
2630 Fanta Reed Road
La Crosse, WI 54603

TIMOTHY J. MILLER
Large Pelagics Research Center
Department of Zoology
University of New Hampshire
Durham, NH 03824

BRIAN OLSEN
Smithsonian Migratory Bird Center
National Zoological Park
Washington, DC 20008
(Current address: Department of Biological Sciences, Virginia Polytechnic Institute and State University, Blacksburg, VA 24060-0406)

JAY J. ROTELLA
Ecology Department
Montana State University
Bozeman, MT 59717

ROBIN E. RUSSELL
Department of Ecology
Montana State University
Bozeman, MT 59715
(Current Address: USDA Forest Service, Rocky Mountain Research Station Bozeman, MT 59717)

Terry L. Shaffer
U. S. Geological Survey
Northern Prairie Wildlife Research Center
8711 37th Street SE
Jamestown, ND 58401

Scott Stephens
Ecology Department
Montana State University
Bozeman, MT 59717
(Current Address: Ducks Unlimited, Inc., 2525 River Road, Bismarck, ND 58503)

Rodney X. Sturdivant
Department of Mathematical Sciences
223 Thayer Hall
United States Military Academy
West Point, NY 10996

Mark Taper
Ecology Department
Montana State University
Bozeman, MT 59717

Joshua J. Tewksbury
Biology Department
University of Washington
Seattle, WA 98115

Frank R. Thompson, III
USDA Forest Service
North Central Research Station
University of Missouri
Columbia, MO 65211

Gary C. White
Department of Fishery and Wildlife Biology
Colorado State University
Fort Collins, CO 80523

PREFACE

Recent broad-scale declines in bird populations have resulted in an unprecedented level of research into the factors that limit bird populations. While surveys based on bird counts can measure changes in distribution and trends in abundance, these measurements have limited value in identifying factors that directly regulate populations. In addition, measures of abundance can be poor assessments of habitat quality or habitat selection. Investigations of parameters such as productivity, survivorship, and recruitment, as well as factors affecting these parameters, are required for baseline research and successful conservation efforts.

Productivity, perhaps the most variable and important demographic parameter, is measured in both direct and indirect ways. The most common approach is to measure nest survivorship (nest success), where a successful nest is a nest that fledged at least one host young. This approach is one of the best quantifiable measurements of productivity that can be applied at multiple scales. Furthermore, estimates of nest success are commonly used to model population growth and viability, and to develop and evaluate habitat management prescriptions and other conservation actions. Accordingly, interest in estimating and identifying factors influencing nest success has never been greater (Johnson, *chapter 1 this volume*).

Nests of altricial birds are notoriously difficult to locate and typically require a systematic, labor-intensive effort to find. Formerly, one would simply take the number of nests found as the sample size, and using the number of successful nests, calculate the proportion of successful nests, termed apparent nest success. However, the majority of nests are found and monitored after clutch completion, which causes bias in the estimates of nest survivorship—nests that fail prior to discovery generally do not contribute to the dataset—while nests that are found during later stages of nesting are more likely to survive (i.e., have less opportunity to fail). In 1961, Harold P. Mayfield addressed this bias by estimating daily survival based on the numbers of days that a nest was under observation (Mayfield 1961, 1975). Mayfield's simple, yet ingenious solution of treating nest-success data has been widely used in avian demographic studies ever since and has evolved into many of the analytical approaches currently used (Johnson, *chapter 1 this volume*).

A major dilemma with the Mayfield method is that it cannot be used to build models that rigorously assess the importance of a wide range of biological factors that affect nest survival, nor can it be used to compare competing models. Many novel and powerful analytical methods to isolate factors influencing nest survivorship were introduced in the last several years. Accordingly, this has left many biologists confused about which analytical approach should be used and if changes in study design need to be considered. Thus, we hosted a workshop in conjunction with the 75th annual meeting of the Cooper Ornithological Society (15–18 June 2005, Arcata, California) to bring the statistical and biological communities together to evaluate and discuss the uses and assumptions of these new methods in order to reduce confusion and improve applications.

The primary goal of this workshop was to familiarize field biologists with the calculations and appropriate uses of the most recent methods, ensuring that appropriate data that meet the assumptions of the methods of analysis are collected. We also hoped to familiarize the biostatisticians with some of the issues in field data collection. This volume contains some of the key papers from this symposium and a few other invited manuscripts that we felt provided excellent examples on the use of these approaches.

We hope that this volume will underscore the value of consulting statisticians prior to the onset of fieldwork. More importantly, we hope that with the dissemination of the approaches described, we can begin to understand and act on the multitude of factors that limit bird populations.

ACKNOWLEDGMENTS

The contributions of many people led to the success of the symposium and production of this volume. We thank John E. Cornely and the USDI Fish and Wildlife Service Region 6 Migratory Bird Coordinator's Office for financial and logistical support. We also thank Matt Johnson and T. Luke George for inviting us to participate in organizing this symposium, and Doug Johnson, Jay Rotella, and J. Scott Dieni for their insights and advice; and Carl Marti for this opportunity and for his leadership as editor. We are grateful to Tom Martin for inspiring many to use systematic nest monitoring across the continent as part of the BBIRD program. Manuscripts benefited tremendously from the helpful suggestions of the many reviewers, including B. Andres, J. Bart, J. F. Bromaghin, A. B. Cooper, J. S. Dieni, S. J. Dinsmore, J. Faaborg, K. G. Gerow, M. P. Herzog, A. L. Holmes, W. H. Howe, D. M. Heisey, D. H. Johnson, W. A. Link, J. D. Lloyd, J. D. Nichols, N. Nur, D. L. Reinking, J. J. Rotella, J. A. Royle, J. M. Ruth, J. A. Schmutz, T. L. Shaffer, S. Small, B. D. Smith, J. D. Toms,

K. S. Wells, G. C. White, M. Winter, and M. Wunder. We are particularly indebted to the statistical reviewers who worked hard to explain difficult concepts to us. We thank A. L. Holmes, S. K. Davis, M. P. Herzog, T. L. McDonald, J. R. Liebezeit, T. A. Grant, S. J. Kendall, P. D. Martin, N. Nur, C. B. Johnson, C. Rea, D. C. Payer, S. W. Zack, and S. Brown for contributions to papers presented in the symposium. We thank the following for monetary support of the publication of this volume: USDI Fish and Wildlife Service, Region 6; U.S. Environmental Protection Agency, Mid-Continent Ecology Division; U.S. Geological Survey, Northern Prairie Wildlife Research Center; Iowa State University, Department of Natural Resource Ecology and Management; Mississippi State University, Department of Wildlife and Fisheries; University of New Hampshire, Department of Natural Resources; USDI Fish and Wildlife Service, Upper Midwest Environmental Sciences Center; U.S. Geological Survey, National Wildlife Health Center; Ducks Unlimited, Great Plains Regional Office; Montana State University, Ecology Department. This is PRBO contribution # 1535.

We dedicate this volume to L. Richard Mewaldt (1917–1990) and G. William Salt (1919–1999) for their inspiration; their students are still striving to meet their standards of excellence. And, of course, to Harold F. Mayfield, who died at age 95 in January 2007. One of the giants in 20th-century ornithology, Mayfield was truly a gifted amateur ornithologist, publishing more than 300 scholarly papers (see Johnson, *chapter 1 this volume*). The paper that inspired this volume (Mayfield 1961) described a major advance in the estimation of nest survival rates. We all are very grateful for the opportunity to work in his shadow in the same field, to advance his work. He will be missed.

Stephanie L. Jones
Geoffrey R. Geupel

Studies in Avian Biology No. 34:1–12

METHODS OF ESTIMATING NEST SUCCESS: AN HISTORICAL TOUR

Douglas H. Johnson

Abstract. The number of methodological papers on estimating nest success is large and growing, reflecting the importance of this topic in avian ecology. Harold Mayfield proposed the most widely used method nearly a half-century ago. Subsequent work has largely expanded on his early method and allowed ornithologists to address new questions about nest survival, such as how survival rate varies with age of nest and in response to various covariates. The plethora of literature on the topic can be both daunting and confusing. Here I present a historical account of the literature. A companion paper in this volume offers some guidelines for selecting a method to estimate nest success.

Key Words: history, Mayfield estimator, nest success, survival.

MÉTODOS PARA LA ESTIMACIÓN DE ÉXITO DE NIDO: UN RECORRIDO HISTÓRICO

Resumen. La cantidad de artículos metodológicos en la estimación de éxito de nido es muy grande y está creciendo, y refleja la importancia de este tema en la ecología de aves. Harold Mayfield propuso hace cerca de medio siglo el método mayormente utilizado. Subsecuentemente se ha expandido ampliamente su trabajo partiendo de su método, permitiendo así a los ornitólogos encausar nuevas preguntas respecto a la sobrevivencia de nido, tales como la forma en la qual la tasa de sobrevivencia varía con la edad del nido y en respuesta a varias covariantes. El exceso de literatura en el tema puede ser tanto desalentador como confuso. Aquí presento un recuento histórico de la literatura. Algún otro artículo en este volumen ofrece las pautas para seleccionar un modelo para estimar el éxito de nido.

Ornithologists have long been fascinated by the nests of birds. To avoid predation, many species of birds are very secretive about their nesting habits; thus locating nests may become a real challenge. Curiosity about the outcome often drives the biologist to check back later to see if the nests had been successful in allowing the clutches to hatch and young birds to fledge. If enough nests are found, one can calculate the percentage of nests that were successful. Such nest-success rates are very convenient metrics of reproductive success and have been used to compare species, study areas, habitat types, management practices, and the like. Certainly, nest-success rates are incomplete measures of reproduction since they do not account for birds that never initiated nests, birds that renested after either losing a clutch or fledging a brood, and the survival of eggs and young. Nonetheless, nest success is a valuable index to reproductive success and for most populations is a critical component of reproductive success (Johnson et al. 1992, Hoekman et al. 2002). For these reasons it is important that measures of nest success be accurate.

In this chapter, I review the history of methods developed to estimate nest success. The number of these methods is surprisingly large, reflecting both the interest in and importance of the topic, as well as a lack of awareness of what others had done previously. Some wheels have been invented repeatedly. Being a historical perspective, this account will be largely chronological. I do not review methodological papers that discuss how to find nests (Klett et al. 1986, Martin and Geupel 1993, Winter et al. 2003) nor how to treat nesting data (Klett et al. 1986, Manolis et al. 2000, Stanley 2004b), although these topics clearly are important in their own right. This historical overview is complementary to Johnson (*chapter 6, this volume*), which provides some guidelines for selecting a method to use.

THE HISTORY

The measure mentioned above, the ratio of successful nests to total nests in a sample, has come to be known as the apparent estimator of nest success, and has a history that spans decades, if not centuries. It is straightforward and easy to calculate. That it can be biased, often severely, was not widely recognized in the scientific literature until 1960. Harold F. Mayfield, an amateur ornithologist (see sidebar), was compiling a large amount of information on the breeding biology of the Kirtland's Warbler (*Dendroica kirtlandii*) for a major treatise on the species (Mayfield 1960). In that book he pointed out the bias in the apparent estimator and proposed what became known as the Mayfield estimator as a remedy. Recognizing the general need for such a treatment of nesting data, Mayfield (1961) focused specifically on the methodology.

FIGURE 1. Harold F. Mayfield in 1984.

Harold F. Mayfield (Fig. 1) is perhaps best known among ornithologists as the developer of a method for estimating nest success, a method that now bears his name. Mayfield's seminal 1961 paper on the topic is the most-frequently cited ever to appear in the *Wilson Bulletin*. His ornithological credentials, however, are much greater than that single, albeit highly valuable, contribution to our science. His monograph on the Kirtland's Warbler won the Brewster Award, the top scientific honor granted by the American Ornithologists' Union. He has often trekked to the Arctic; one product of those trips was a monograph on the life history of the Red Phalarope (*Phalaropus fulicaria*). These represent just two of his approximately 300 published papers in ornithology.

Mayfield also has the distinction of being the only individual to have served as president of all three major North American scientific ornithological societies: the American Ornithologists' Union, Cooper Ornithological Society, and Wilson Ornithological Society. Among his other honors are the Arthur A. Allen award from the Cornell Laboratory of Ornithology, the Ridgway award from the American Birding Association, and the first-ever Lifetime Achievement award from the Toledo Naturalists' Association.

What may be most surprising is that Mayfield is not a professional ornithologist; he is an amateur in the true sense of the word, someone who does something out of love, not for compensation. His paying profession was in personnel management. He is accomplished in that field, too, having published more than 100 papers in its journals. Mayfield in fact traces the roots of the Mayfield method to his background in industry, where safety was measured in terms of incidents per worker-day exposure.

When I most recently visited Harold and his wife Virginia in 1995, at their home in Toledo, he was still intellectually active at age 85. To illustrate, he had come up with a new hypothesis to explain the migration path of Kirtland's Warblers.

More personally, Harold Mayfield has been a gracious supporter of my own work on the topic of estimating nest success. When I developed the maximum likelihood estimator that allowed for an uncertain termination date (Johnson 1979), I thought it would be useful to compare estimates from that method with estimates Mayfield had obtained with his method. When I wrote to state an interest in obtaining the data he used, he generously provided his original data on Kirtland's Warblers. Further, he continued to write to me, encouraging me, and expressing his satisfaction that someone was taking a more rigorous look at the topic. His enthusiastic support continued to his death in 2006.

In hindsight, but hindsight only, his method was simple and the need for it obvious. A nest that is found, say, 1 d prior to hatching has a high probability of success, because it has to survive only one more day. Conversely, a nest found early in its lifetime has to survive many more days to succeed, and its chances of success are lower. So the fates of a sample of nests found at different ages are not likely to represent the likelihood of a nest surviving from initiation until hatching. The problem, in statistical jargon, is one of length-biased sampling. That is, the chance that a unit (nest, in this case) is included in a sample depends upon the length of time it survives. One way to overcome this bias is to use in the analysis only nests found at the onset, but in most studies this restriction would result in the omission of many nests. Mayfield (1960, 1961) suggested that the time that a nest is under observation be considered; he termed this period the exposure. He further suggested the nest-day as the unit of exposure. Then, the number of nest failures observed divided by the exposure provides an estimate of the daily mortality rate, which when subtracted from one yields a daily survival rate (DSR). To project DSR to the length of time necessary for a nest to succeed yields an estimate of nest success. When nests fail between visits, Mayfield assumed the failure occurred midway between visits and assigned the exposure as half the length of that interval. He acknowledged his assumption of constant DSR throughout the period. Also key is the assumption that DSR does not vary among nests.

It can be noted (Gross and Clark 1975) that Mayfield's estimator is the maximum likelihood estimator of the daily survival rate under the geometric model, the discrete analog of the exponential model, both of which assume a constant hazard rate.

Other investigators too had noted the bias in the apparent estimator. For example, Snow (1955) observed that nests nest found at an advanced stage of the nesting cycle will bias the percentage in favor of success if included in the analyses. He alluded to a rather laborious mathematical procedure to compensate for the bias and indicated an intention to deal fully with the mathematical procedure in a forthcoming paper (Snow 1955). In a 1996 letter to me (D. W. Snow, pers. comm.), he indicated that the paper never was published.

Coulson (1956) also recognized the bias and suggested a remedy. He reasoned that, on average, a failed nest would be under observation for only half the period necessary to succeed, so the chance of finding a failed nest would be only half the chance of finding a successful one. Thus, the actual number of failed nests would be twice the number observed. So, whereas the apparent estimator of nest success is 1 – failed/(failed + hatched), Coulson generated an estimate of 1 – (2 × failed)/(2 × failed + hatched). This ad hoc procedure seemed to receive little use (but note Peakall 1960) and did not closely approximate Mayfield's estimator of nest success rate in some example data sets (D. H. Johnson, unpubl. data).

Hammond and Forward (1956) also recognized a problem with the apparent estimator—neglecting to consider the length of time nests are under observation as compared with the total period they are exposed to predation would lead to a recorded success higher than that actually occurring (Hammond and Forward 1956). Note that they used the term exposed, much as Mayfield did. Hammond and Forward (1956), in fact, developed a Mayfield-like estimator of nest-survival rate, and scaled it to a mortality rate per week. In their data set, they noted (Hammond and Forward 1956) for 2,543 nest-days observation of group (1), the predation rate was 10.8% destroyed per week as compared with 6.7% for 728 nest-days observation of group (2) nests. They also projected the rate to the term of nesting. It is interesting that the Hammond-Forward method was used little if at all, despite being essentially the same as the Mayfield method and published 4 yr earlier than Mayfield's article. Possibly if Hammond and Forward (1952) had presented a paper focused directly on the methodology, as did Mayfield, we might today be referring to the Hammond-Forward estimator, rather than the Mayfield estimator.

Peakall (1960) identified two problems associated with the apparent estimator. First, it does not account for failed nests that were not found; this is the same length-biased sampling concern noted above. He recommended Coulson's (1956) adjustment as a solution to this problem. Second, he indicated that it is easier to determine the fate of nests that fail than those that succeed, because successful nests last longer and the observer may not be persistent enough to learn their fate. Peakall (1960) proposed a new method, which is akin to the Kaplan-Meier method (Kaplan and Meier 1958). It can use only nests found at onset, however. For the example he cited, the apparent estimate was 52.6% and his estimate was 44.6%. It should be noted that if only nests found at initiation are used, then the apparent estimator itself is unbiased.

Gilmer et al. (1974) and Trent and Rongstad (1974) each used Mayfield-like estimators, although without citing Mayfield, in applications to telemetry studies. Gilmer et al. (1974) defined a daily predation rate as the number of predator kills per duck tracking day. They projected the DSR (1 minus the daily predation rate) to a 120-d breeding season. Trent and Rongstad (1974) also presented confidence limits for the survival-rate estimate, based on treating days as independent binomial variates, and approximating the binomial distribution with a Poisson distribution. Trent and Rongstad (1974) identified the key assumptions: (1) each animal day was an independent trial, and (2) survival was constant over time (and, unstated among animals). They similarly projected DSR, and its confidence limits, to a 61-d period.

Mayfield (1975) revisited the issue, because many studies were ignoring the difficulty he raised, and he often was being asked for guidance in applying his method. He noted that not every published report shows awareness of the problem and that some people have difficulty with details (Mayfield 1975). He mentioned that, no field student is happy to see a simple concept like nest success made to appear complicated (Mayfield 1975). That paper had other interesting observations. Mayfield commented on the effect of visitation on nest survival by alluding to a biological uncertainty principle whereby any nest observed is no longer in its natural state (Mayfield 1975). And, wisely, he cautioned against pooling data even if differences are not significant, a mistake many professional scientists still make.

Mayfield's method began to draw some critical attention 15 yr after first publication. Göransson and Loman (1976) tested the validity of the assumption that the hazard rate is constant with a study of simulated Ring-necked Pheasant (*Phasianus colchicus*) nests. They found that mortality was low for the first day, high for the next 3 d, then low for the rest of the period. They concluded that the Mayfield method in that situation would not be suitable for the laying period.

Green (1977) suggested that Mayfield's estimator would be biased if DSR was not constant. He argued that such heterogeneity would bias the estimator downward. Later, Johnson (1979) pointed out that Green's (1977) concern would manifest itself only if all nests were found at initiation, and that the bias would be in the opposite direction under the usual conditions that nests are found later in development.

Dow (1978) argued that Mayfield's (1975) test for comparing mortality rates between periods—based on a chi-square contingency table test between days with and without losses—is inappropriate. Dow (1978) proposed an analogous test that used nests rather than nest-days as units. Johnson (1979) pointed out that Dow's (1978) test is inappropriate in general unless the lengths of the periods are the same.

Miller and Johnson (1978) drew attention to the Mayfield method by illustrating its applicability to waterfowl nesting studies Townsend (1966) was noted as the only other waterfowl study to use Mayfield's method. They observed that the Mayfield method had not been widely adopted (Miller and Johnson 1978) and provided a detailed illustration of the bias associated with the apparent estimator and an explanation of the Mayfield method. A figure in Miller and Johnson (1978) illustrated the length-biased nature of the sampling problem. They also demonstrated the importance of the bias of the apparent estimator even for comparing treatments, with an example of Simpson's paradox (Simpson 1951).

Miller and Johnson (1978) suggested that the midpoint assumption of Mayfield was too generous in assigning exposure for the examples they considered—which were waterfowl nests typically visited at intervals of 14–21 d—and proposed that intervals with losses contribute only 40%, rather than 50%, of their length to exposure calculations. They supported this recommendation by calculating the expected exposure under a variety of scenarios. That estimator became known as the Mayfield-40% estimator.

Miller and Johnson (1978) further indicated how an improved estimate of the number of nests initiated could be made, by dividing the number of successful nests by the estimated success rate. Because the number of successful nests is the number of nests initiated times the nest-success rate, an estimator of the number of nests initiated is the number of successful nests divided by the nest-success rate. This estimator is more accurate than just the number of nests found because it is often feasible to accurately determine the total number of successful nests, since such nests persist for rather long times.

Johnson (1979) demonstrated that the Mayfield estimator is in fact a maximum likelihood estimator under a particular model, one that assumes that DSR is constant and that the loss of a nest occurs exactly midway through an interval between visits to the nest. As a maximum-likelihood estimator, it possesses certain desirable properties. Johnson (1979) developed an estimator of the standard error of Mayfield's estimator. He further explored the midpoint assumption and found that, for intervals averaging up to about 15 d and for moderate daily mortality rates, Mayfield's assumption was reasonable. For long intervals—such as were common with waterfowl studies—the midpoint assumption assigns too much exposure to destroyed nests, as Miller and Johnson (1978) had indicated.

Johnson (1979) also developed a model for which the actual time of loss was unknown and determined a maximum likelihood estimator for DSR under that less restrictive model. Iterative computation was required, which, at that time limited its applicability. Further, a comparison of the new estimator with Mayfield's and the Mayfield-40% estimators suggested that the new one most closely matched the original Mayfield values if intervals between visits were short, and was closer to the Mayfield-40% values if intervals were long. Johnson (1979) recommended routine use of the Mayfield or Mayfield-40% estimators because of their computational ease.

Johnson (1979) also considered variation, due either to identifiable or to non-identifiable causes, in the DSR. He calculated separate estimators for different stages of the nesting cycle and used t-tests to compare them statistically. He considered heterogeneity in general and suggested a graphical means for detecting it and exploiting it if it exists. This has been called the intercept estimator; it does, however, require that detectability of nests not vary with nest age.

Willis (1981) credited Snow (1955) and others with noting the bias of the apparent estimator. Mistakenly, he suggested that Mayfield's estimator would be biased because it allotted a full day of exposure to a nest destroyed during a day. Willis (1981) suggested that only a half-day be assigned in such a situation. That recommendation was later withdrawn, but only in an easily overlooked corrigendum (Anonymous 1981).

Hensler and Nichols (1981) proposed a model of nest survival based on the assumption that nests are observed each day until they succeed or fail. The maximum-likelihood estimator under that model turned out to be the same as Mayfield's. The standard error they computed was also the same as that derived by Johnson (1979) for Mayfield's model. Hensler and Nichols (1981) incorporated encounter probabilities, representing the probability that an observed nest was first found at a particular age. These turned out to be irrelevant to the estimator, although they may contain information that could be exploited. Hensler and Nichols (1981) provided some sample size values needed for specified levels of precision.

Klett and Johnson (1982) explored the key assumption of the Mayfield estimator, that daily survival is constant with respect to age and to date. They examined the variation in daily mortality rate, using waterfowl nests in their examples. Klett and Johnson (1982) found that the daily mortality rate tended to decline with the age of nest. Seasonal variation also was evident. They developed a product estimator that accounted for such variation by taking the product of individual age-dependent survival probabilities. The stratification necessary for the product estimator required detailed allocation of losses and exposure days to categories of age and date. In their example, the product estimator, based on age-specific survival rates, did not differ appreciably from the ordinary Mayfield estimator. Klett and Johnson (1982) also computed intercept estimators (Johnson 1979) for their data. They found that the Mayfield estimator was robust with respect to mild variation in DSR. They further doubted that pure heterogeneity existed in their data sets; the intercept estimators were not useful. Klett and Johnson (1982) also provided some sample-size recommendations.

Bart and Robson (1982) also developed maximum-likelihood estimators, giving guidance for iteratively solving them. They also used power analysis to generate some sample-size requirements.

Johnson and Klett (1985) clearly demonstrated the bias of the apparent estimator, being greater when the survival rate is low to medium or when nests are found at older ages. They proposed a shortcut estimator of nest success, which uses the apparent rate and the average age of nests when found. The approximation is made by assuming that all nests were found on that average day. Several examples indicated that the shortcut estimator was closer to Mayfield values and Johnson (1979) maximum likelihood values than was the apparent estimator.

Hensler (1985) developed estimators for the variance of functions of Mayfield's DSR, such as the survival rate for an interval that spans multiple days.

Goc (1986) proposed estimating nest success by constructing a life table from the ages of nests found. He indicated that the frequency of clutches recorded in consecutive age groups would correspond to the survival of clutches to the respective ages (Goc 1986). Stated requirements for the method were: (1) large sample sizes (300–500 nest checks), (2) sampling to occur throughout the season, and (3) detectability of nests being equal for nests of all ages. Goc (1986) did not address the need for independence of nest checks, which would seem necessary and which would make the data requirements very demanding. Further, in most situations the detectability of nests varies rather dramatically by age of the nest. The influence of such variation on survival estimates based on this method bears scrutiny.

A nice mathematical property of the constant-hazard (exponential) model is its lack of memory. This lack-of-memory property means that no additional information is gained by knowing the nest's age, which is extremely appealing because many nests are difficult to age. But constant-hazard models are often unrealistic, and all other models require some consideration of age, usually in the form of age-specific discovery probabilities. Age-specific discovery probabilities were introduced but turned out to be irrelevant in the Hensler and Nichols (1981) model, a consequence of the very special lack-of-memory property of their model. Pollock and Cornelius (1988) apparently were the first to address the issue of estimating age-dependent nest survival in the situation where nest ages are not known exactly but for which bounds were known. Their estimator allowed the survival rate to vary among stages (age groups). In addition to survival parameters, their model requires the estimation of discovery parameters. Because their estimator basically treated all nests in a stage as if they were found at the beginning of the stage, it has the same problem, but at a smaller scale, as the apparent estimator; it was shown to be biased high by Heisey and Nordheim (1990).

Green (1989) suggested a transformation of the apparent estimator to reduce its bias. The fundamental idea is that the numbers of nests found at a particular age should be proportional to the numbers surviving to that age. Its validity depends on the detectability of nests being constant over age of the nests, which is unlikely in most situations (Johnson and Shaffer 1990). It also requires that the observed nests be but a small fraction of the nests available for detection or that nest searches are infrequent relative to the lifetime of successful nests.

Johnson (1991) revisited Green's (1989) procedure and noted that it involved a mixture of a discrete-time model and a continuous-time model of the survival process. By example, Johnson (1991) clarified the distinction between the two modeling approaches. This has been a source of confusion in some published papers (Willis 1981). Johnson (1991) proposed a new formulation that was consistent in its reliance on the discrete-time approach. It turned out to be slightly more complicated than Green's (1989) original method in that it required separate specification of the daily survival rate and the length of the interval a clutch must survive in order to hatch. Johnson's (1991) modification always produces slightly higher estimates of nest success than the original Green (1989) version. A comparison of several estimators with both actual and simulated data sets indicated the Johnson (1979) or Mayfield method to be preferred, but if exposure information is not available, the Johnson-Klett (1985), Green (1989), or Johnson-Green (Johnson 1991) estimators performed similarly.

Johnson (1991) also indicated that the assumptions of Green's (1989) estimator could be checked by plotting the log of the number of nests found at each age against age. Based on this relationship, one could estimate the DSR solely from the age distribution of nests when found (cf. Goc 1986).

Johnson and Shaffer (1990) considered situations in which the daily mortality rate is likely to be severely non-constant, specifically when destruction of nests occurs catastrophically. The Mayfield estimator, with its assumption of constant DSR, was shown to be inaccurate in such situations. Apparent estimates were satisfactory when searches for nests were frequent and detectability of nests was high. Johnson and Shaffer (1990) specifically considered island nesting situations, which often differ from those on mainland due to: (1) generally high survival of nests, and therefore lower bias of the apparent estimator, (2) greater synchrony of nesting, which facilitates finding nests early and thereby reduces the bias of the apparent estimator, (3) catastrophic mortality being more likely on islands, due to extreme weather events or the sudden appearance of a predator, therefore violating the key assumption of the Mayfield estimator, and (4) destroyed nests being more likely to be found, again reducing the bias of the apparent estimator.

Johnson and Shaffer (1990) also described conditions under which apparent and Mayfield estimates of nest success led to reasonable estimates of the number of nests initiated. Mayfield estimates were better in situations with constant and low mortality rates. When mortality was high and constant, or catastrophic, the apparent estimator led to acceptable estimates of number of nests initiated only when many searches were made and detectability of nests was high.

Johnson and Shaffer (1990) observed that, if detectability is independent of age of clutch, then a plot of the logarithm of the number of nests found at a particular age against age should be linear aand decreasing. In the Blue-winged Teal (*Anas discors*) example they cited (Miller and Johnson 1978), the pattern was increasing, indicating that detectability of nests in fact varied by age.

Johnson (1990) justified a procedure that he had used for some time to compare daily mortality rates for more than two groups. It extended the two-group t-test of Johnson (1979) to more than two groups by showing that multiple mortality rates could be compared by using an analysis of variance on the rates, with exposure as weights, and referring a modified test statistic to a chi-square table. The original publication contained a typographical error, which was corrected in the Internet version (Johnson 1990)

Bromaghin and McDonald (1993a, b) developed estimators of nest success based on encounter sampling, in which the probability of a nest being included in a sample depends on the length of time it survives and on the sampling plan used to search for nests. Bromaghin and McDonald (1993a) presented the framework for a general likelihood function, with component models for nest survival and nest detection. This general model uses the information about the age of a nest that is contained in the length of time a nest is observed, e.g., a successful nest is known to have survived the entire period and a nest observed for k days is known to be at least k-days old. They provided two examples based on the Mayfield model and demonstrated that the models of Hensler and Nichols (1981) and Pollock and Cornelius (1988) are special cases of their more general model. Bromaghin and McDonald (1993b) presented a second model employing systematic encounter sampling and Horvitz-Thompson (Horvitz and Thompson 1952) estimators. Unique features of this model are that no assumptions about nest survival are required and that additional parameters, such as the total number of nests initiated, the number of successful nests, and the number of young produced, can be estimated.

Bromaghin and McDonald's (1993a, b) methods are innovative but require more complex estimation procedures than many other estimators. They assume that the probability of detecting a nest is the same for all nests and for all ages, although this assumption could be generalized. As noted above, the length-biased sampling feature associated with most nesting studies leads to a severe bias of the apparent estimator. Incorporating detection probabilities into the estimation process essentially capitalizes on the problem associated with length-biased sampling. Also, Bromaghin and McDonald (1993a, b) treated the nest, rather than the nest-day, as the sampling unit. Their methods are not appropriate for casual observational studies, but rather require field methods to be carefully designed and implemented so that detection probabilities can be estimated.

Heisey and Nordheim (1995) addressed the same basic problem as Pollock and Cornelius (1988)—estimating age-dependent survival when nest ages are not known exactly. Their goal was to avoid the bias issues of Pollock and Cornelius (1988) by constructing a likelihood that more accurately represented the actual exposure times of the discovered nests. Their approach simultaneously estimated age-dependent discovery and survival parameters using almost-nonparametric, stepwise hazard models. The likelihood was relatively complicated and much of the paper focused on numerical methods for obtaining maximum likelihood estimates via the expectation-maximization (EM) algorithm (Dempster et al. 1977). The calculation by Miller and Johnson (1978) of the expected time of failure anticipated the application of EM; it is essentially an E-step. Heisey (1991) extended the method to accommodate effects of covariates (including time) on both discovery and survival rates. Because of its complexity and lack of available software, the Heisey-Nordheim method (Heisey and Nordheim 1995) has received little application by ornithologists. Using the basic likelihood structure they had proposed, however, Stanley (2000), He et al. (2001), and He (2003) later explored computationally more tractable approaches to estimation.

Aebischer (1999) clearly articulated the assumptions of the Mayfield estimator. He also developed tests to compare daily survival rates based on the deviance, in particular one comparing more than two groups (cf. Johnson 1990). Aebischer (1999) showed that Mayfield models can be fitted within the framework of generalized linear models for binomial trials. Based on this latter result, he indicated that Mayfield models can be fitted by logistic regression where the unit of analysis is the nest, the response variable is success/failure, and the number of binomial trials is the number of exposure days. The same method had been used somewhat earlier by Etheridge et al. (1997). Hazler (2004) later re-invented Aebischer's (1999) method and demonstrated in her examples its robustness to uncertainty in the date of loss, when nest visits were close together.

Although not explicitly stated, strict application of Aebischer's (1999) method requires that the date of loss is known exactly (Shaffer 2004). Nonetheless, like the original Mayfield estimator, it performs well when one assumes the date of loss to be the midpoint between the last two nest visits, especially if nest visits are fairly frequent. Aebischer (1999) did not indicate how to treat observations for which the midpoint is not an integer, as is typically required for logistic regression. Some users of the method round down and round up alternate observations. That device may induce a bias, however, if nests are not analyzed in random order, so Aebischer (pers. comm.) recommends making a random choice between rounding down and rounding up. A slightly more complicated procedure, but one that should perform better, would be to include two observations in the data set for any nest for which the midpoint assumption results in a non-integral number of days. One observation would have its exposure rounded down, the other, rounded up. Each observation would be weighted by one-half. More accurate weights (Klett and Johnson 1982) could be computed, but they likely would offer negligible improvement.

Natarajan and McCulloch (1999:553) noted that constant-survival models can seriously underestimate overall survival in the presence of heterogeneity. They described random-effects modeling approaches to analyzing nest survival data in the presence of either intangible variation (pure heterogeneity) or tangible variation (reflecting the effects of covariates) among nests. They also assumed the absence of confounding temporal factors. In the first of their two approaches, Natarajan and McCulloch (1999) allowed for pure heterogeneity among survival rates of nests. That is, each nest has its own DSR, which remains unchanged with respect to age (or any other factor). It is assumed that values of DSR follow a beta distribution with parameters α and β. Estimates of α and β, as well as of nest survival itself, can be obtained numerically. In their second approach, Natarajan and McCulloch (1999) outlined a method to incorporate heterogeneity associated with measured covariates (explanatory variables). They did this by allowing DSR values to be logistic functions of the covariates. In both of their approaches, Natarajan and McCulloch (1999) discussed situations in which all nests are found immediately after initiation. They relaxed that assumption to some degree by considering a systematic sampling scheme (Bromaghin and McDonald 1993a), in which the probability of detecting a nest is assumed to be constant across nests and ages.

Farnsworth et al. (2000) applied Mayfield and Kaplan-Meier methods to a data set involving Wood Thrushes (*Hylocichla mustelina*). They found essentially no difference between the methods in the estimated success rates; they also noted no variation in DSR with age and no evidence of pure heterogeneity.

Stanley (2000) developed a method to estimate nest success that allowed stage-specific variation in DSR. The underlying model was similar to that of Klett and Johnson (1982), but Stanley (2000) addressed the problem through the use of Proc NLIN in SAS, instead of the cumbersome method used by Klett and Johnson (1982). Stanley's (2000) method requires that the age of the nest be known; Stanley (2004a) relaxed that assumption. Stanley (2004a) assumed that nests found during the nestling stage would be checked on or before the date of fledging. Armstrong et al. (2002) used Stanley's (2000) method but encountered occasional convergence problems with the computer algorithm.

Manly and Schmutz (2001) developed what they termed an iterative Mayfield method, which they indicated was a simple extension of the Klett and Johnson (1982) estimator. The extension primarily involved the way that losses and exposure days are allocated to days between nest visits—Klett and Johnson (1982) assumed a constant DSR for this allocation, whereas Manly and Schmutz (iteratively) used DSRs that varied by age or date.

By assigning prior probabilities to the discovery and survival rates, He et al. (2001) and He (2003) developed a Bayesian implementation of the likelihood structure used by Heisey and Nordheim (1995). He et al. (2001) consider the special case of daily visits, while He (2003) generalized it to intermittent monitoring. He (2003) used the Bayesian equivalent of the EM algorithm for incomplete data problems, which involves the introduction of auxiliary, or latent, variables—so-called data augmentation. Both approaches, the EM algorithm and data augmentation, iteratively replace unknown exact failure times (including failure times of nests that were never discovered because they failed before discovery) by approximations; the procedure is then repeatedly refined. The advantage of a Bayesian-Markov chain Monte Carlo approach is that it allows the fitting of high-dimensional (many-parameter) models that would be intractable in a maximum likelihood context. This benefit comes at the cost of potentially introducing artificial structure via the assumed prior distributions. In examples with simulated data, the Bayesian estimator was closer to the known true daily mortality rates (and nest success rates) than was the Mayfield estimator. The method, however, often produces biased estimates for the survival rate of the youngest age class unless some nests were found at initiation and ultimately succeeded (Cao and He 2005). Cao and He (2005) suggested three ad hoc remedies that appeared to resolve the difficulty.

Williams et al. (2002) reviewed several of the approaches to modeling nest survival data including models with nest-encounter parameters and traditional survival-time methods such as Kaplan-Meier and Cox' proportional-hazards models. They also offered some guidelines for designing nesting studies.

A new era of nest survival methodology arrived with the new millennium, with three sets of investigators working more or less independently. Dinsmore et al. (2002) were the first to publish a comprehensive approach to nest survival that permitted a variety of covariates to be incorporated in the analysis. They allowed the DSR to be a function of the age of the nest, the date, or any of a variety of other factors. Survival of a nest during a day then was treated as a binomial variable that depended on those covariates. Analysis was performed using program MARK (White and Burnham 1999). Data files can become large and cumbersome, especially for long nesting seasons and numerous individual or time-dependent covariates (Rotella et al. 2004). This approach is discussed more fully in Dinsmore and Dinsmore (*this volume*).

Stephens (2003, also see Stephens et al. 2005) developed SAS software to analyze nesting data with the same model developed by Dinsmore et al. (2002). He further allowed for random effects to be included in models.

Shaffer (2004) applied logistic regression to the nest-survival problem. Others had attempted to do so before, but they had used fate of a nest as a binomial trial, either ignoring differences in exposure or incorporating exposure as an explanatory variable; neither approach is justified. Like the method of Dinsmore et al. (2002), Shaffer's (2004) logistic-exposure method is extremely powerful and accommodates a wide variety of models of daily nest survival.

The primary difference among the new methods is the use of program MARK (Dinsmore et al. 2002) versus the use of a generalized linear-model program (Shaffer 2004, Stephens et al. 2005). Another difference that may sometimes be relevant involves covariates that vary across an interval between nest checks, such as the occurrence of weather events. The effects of such covariates would be averaged over the interval in Shaffer's (2004) method but assigned to individual days in Dinsmore et al.'s (2002) method. Rotella et al. (2004) compared and contrasted the methods of Dinsmore et al. (2002), Stephens (2003), and Shaffer (2004). They also provided example code for various analyses in program MARK, SAS PROC GENMOD, and SAS PROC NLMIXED.

McPherson et al. (2003) developed estimators of nest survival and number of nests initiated based on a model involving detection probabilities and survival probabilities. The former component is comparable to the encounter probabilities of Pollock and Cornelius (1988), incorporating the daily probabilities of detection and survival. The second component, survival, is basically a Kaplan-Meier series of binomial probabilities. The McPherson et al. (2003) method assumes that nests were searched for and checked daily, which may be applicable to the telemetry study to which their method was applied but is generally unrealistic and excessively intrusive in most nesting studies. Their estimator of number of nests initiated was a modified Horvitz-Thompson estimator (Horvitz and Thompson 1952) and was a generalized form of that used by Miller and Johnson (1978). In the example given, the new estimate was virtually identical to that of Miller and Johnson (1978) but had a smaller standard error. The McPherson et al. (2003) survival model allowed for age-related, but not date-related, survival. In their example, they found very little variation due to age. McPherson et al. (2003) indicated it was essential to follow some nests from day one. They also noted that estimates of survival are expected to be robust with respect to heterogeneity in the actual survival rates (analogous to mark-recapture studies).

Jehle et al. (2004) reviewed selected estimators of nest success, focusing on the Stanley (2000) and Dinsmore et al. (2002) estimators in comparison to the apparent and Mayfield estimators. In the several data sets on Lark Buntings (*Calamospiza melanocorys*) examined, they found results of Mayfield, Stanley, and Dinsmore methods to be very similar; the apparent estimator was much higher, as expected. The authors emphasized that nest visits were close together, however, being generally only a day or two apart near fledging.

Nur et al. (2004) showed how traditional survival-time (or lifetime or failure-time) analysis methods could be applied to nest success estimation. They included Kaplan-Meier, Cox' proportional hazards, and Weibull methods in their discussion. Critical to such methods is the need to know the age of the nest when found and age when failed.

Etterson and Bennett (2005) approached the nest-survival situation from a Markov chain perspective. By doing so, they were able to explore the effect on bias and standard errors of Mayfield estimates due to variation in discovery probabilities, uncertainties in dates of transition (e.g., hatching and fledging), monitoring schedules, and the number of nests monitored. They found that the magnitude of bias increased with the length of the monitoring interval and was smaller when the date of transition was known fairly accurately. The assumption that transition always occurs at the same age did not appear to induce any consequential bias in estimates of DSR.

CAUSE-SPECIFIC MORTALITY RATES

Some investigators have sought, not only to estimate mortality rates of nests, but to estimate rates of mortality due to different causes. In the survival literature this topic is referred to as competing risks; I will deal only briefly with it here. Heisey and Fuller (1985) indicated how Mayfield-like estimators could be adapted to estimate source-specific mortality rates when the cause of death can be determined. Their context involved radio-telemetry studies, but the method would more generally apply to nesting studies. Etterson et al. (in press) modified the Etterson and Bennett (2005) approach to incorporate multiple causes of nest failure while relaxing the assumption that failure dates are known exactly. Johnson et al. (1989)

related daily mortality rates (due to predation) on nests of ducks to indices of various predator species. They found associations that were consistent with what was known about the foraging behavior of the different predators.

LIFE-TABLE APPROACHES

Goc (1986) evidently was the first to suggest that nest success could be estimated by constructing a life table from the ages of nests found. Critical to that approach is the assumption that nests are equally detectable at all ages. Johnson (1991) noted that that assumption could be verified by plotting the log of the number of nests found at each age against age. Based on this relationship, one could estimate the DSR from the age distribution; that line should have slope equal to the logarithm of DSR. Johnson and Shaffer (1990) showed that the crucial assumption that detectability does not vary with age was not met in their example.

LIFETIME ANALYSIS

A wealth of literature on survival estimation was developed largely in the biomedical and reliability fields (see Williams et al. [2002] for a review from an animal ecology perspective). Well-known methods such as Kaplan-Meier and Cox regression have been applied only rarely to nest-survival studies, and it is reasonable to ask why. As noted above, however, the Mayfield estimator of DSR is in fact the maximum-likelihood estimator under a geometric-survival model, the discrete counterpart of exponential survival. The critical assumption of the geometric and exponential models, like Mayfield's, is that the daily mortality rate (hazard rate, in survival nomenclature) is constant. A valuable and distinctive feature of the exponential (or geometric) model is that, because DSR is independent of age, it is not necessary to know the age of the nest to estimate survival. More general models of survival, such as Kaplan-Meier, Cox' proportional hazards, and Weibull, require knowledge of the age. In nesting studies, this means it is essential to know both the age of a nest when it is found and when it failed. Knowing the age of a nest of course is useful when using any other method if interest is in age-specific survival rates. It is not necessary for most methods if one is solely concerned with estimating nest success, although estimates based on constant daily survival may be biased if that assumption is severely violated.

Several investigators, beginning with Peakall (1960), have applied Kaplan-Meier methods to nesting or similar data (Flint et al. 1995, Korschgen et al. 1996, Farnsworth et al. 2000, Aldridge and Brigham 2001). The method proposed by McPherson et al. (2003) likewise incorporated a Kaplan-Meier model for daily survival.

Nur et al. (2004) brought the survival methodology to the attention of ornithologists by applying Kaplan-Meier, Cox' proportional-hazards, and Weibull models to a data set involving Loggerhead Shrikes (*Lanius ludovicianus*). They further demonstrated how to incorporate covariates such as laying date, nest height, and year in an analysis.

OBSERVER EFFECTS

Several authors considered the effect of visitation on survival of nests. See Götmark (1992) for a review of the literature on the topic. Bart and Robson (1982) proposed a model in which the daily mortality rate for the day following a visit differed from the rate on other days. They identified a major problem that arises when checks of surviving nests are not recorded—investigators might note that a nest is still active and try to avoid disturbance. Nichols et al. (1984) found no difference in survival of Mourning Dove (*Zenaida macroura*) nests visited daily versus those visited 7 d apart. Sedinger (1990) regressed survival rate during an interval against the length of the interval, so that departures of the Y-intercept from 1 would reflect the short-term effect of a visit at the beginning of the interval. He found the method to be imprecise. Sedinger (1990) also visited nests and revisited them immediately after the pairs had returned, again to document short-term effects; he found a negligible effect. Rotella et al. (2000) explored essentially the same model proposed by Bart and Robson (1982) and noted that observer-induced differences that were difficult to detect statistically nonetheless could have major effects on estimated survival rates. More generally, Rotella et al. (2000) demonstrated how a covariate reflecting a visit to a nest could be incorporated into an analysis of DSR.

Willis (1973) knew enough about the breeding biology of the species he was studying so that he could ascertain the status of a nesting attempt without visiting the nest. He concluded that visits to nests seemed to accelerate destruction of easily discovered nests, but had little effect on the number of nests that finally succeeded.

ESTIMATING THE NUMBER OF NEST INITIATIONS

Just as the apparent estimator of nest success typically overestimates the actual nest success rate, the number of nests found in a study underestimates the number that were actually initiated. In most situations, short-lived nests are unlikely to be found. Evidently the first to use improved estimates of nest success to account for these undiscovered nests were Miller and Johnson (1978). They proposed simply dividing the number of successful nests—virtually all of which can be found in a careful nesting study—by the estimated nest success rate. The method could be applied to the number of nests that attain any particular age, as long as virtually all the nests that reach that age can be detected. Johnson and Shaffer (1990) considered the situation in which the Mayfield assumption of constant DSR is severely violated; in such situations the apparent number of nests initiated is better than the Miller-Johnson estimator but is accurate only with repeated searches and high detectability. Horvitz-Thompson approaches (Horvitz and Thompson 1952) to estimating the number of initiated nests have been taken by Bromaghin and McDonald (1993b), Dinsmore et al. (2002), McPherson et al. (2003), Grant et al. (2005), and, while advising caution, Grand et al. (2006).

DISCUSSION

It should be noted that the primary objective of estimating nest success has been transformed by most of the methods described into an objective of estimating DSR. Mathematically, these objectives are equivalent, as long as the time needed from initiation to success is a fixed constant. The influence of variation in transition times (egg hatching and young fledging) has received little attention (but see Etterson and Bennett 2005).

Although this has been a largely chronological accounting of published papers that addressed the topic of estimating nest success, some themes recurred; the notion of encounter probabilities arose frequently. Several of the methods incorporated these probabilities, which measure the chance that a nest will be first detected at a particular age. Hensler and Nichols (1981) used them in the development of their model. Those probabilities turned out to be unnecessary, because their new estimator was equivalent to Mayfield's original one, but others have suggested that observed encounter probabilities might contain useful information. Pollock and Cornelius (1988) used the same parameters in their derivation. Bromaghin and McDonald (1993a, b) exploited the relationship between the lifetime of a nest and the probability that the nest is detected through the use of a modified Horvitz-Thompson estimator (Horvitz and Thompson 1952). More recently, McPherson et al. (2003) employed a model of nest detection in their method to estimate nest success and number of nests initiated.

Encounter probabilities are intriguing measures. They reflect both the probability that a nest survives to a particular age—which typically is of primary interest—as well as the probability that a nest of a particular age is detected—which reflects characteristics of the nest, the birds attending it, the schedule of nest searching, and the observers' methods and skills. Some inferences about survival can be made by assuming detection probabilities are constant with respect to age, but that is a major and typically unsupported assumption (Johnson and Shaffer 1990). Intriguing as they are, encounter probabilities confound two processes, and their utility seems questionable unless some fairly stringent assumptions can be met.

Most of the nest-survival-estimation methods require more information than the apparent estimator does. At a minimum, the Mayfield estimator requires information about the length of time each nest was under observation. Many methods require knowledge of the age of a nest when it was found.

Several investigators have proposed methods to reduce the bias of the apparent estimator without nest-specific information. Coulson's (1956) procedure simply doubles the number of failed nests when computing the ratio of failed nests to failed plus successful nests. Hence, it can be calculated either from the apparent estimator and the total number of nests, or from the numbers of failed and successful nests. The shortcut estimator of Johnson and Klett (1985) also falls into this category. It uses the average age of nests when found to reduce the bias of the apparent estimator. Green's (1989) transformation is another such method; it requires no additional information beyond the apparent estimates, but relies on some questionable assumptions, such as detectability not varying with age of nest. Johnson's (1991) modification of Green's estimator behaves similarly.

Such methods for adjusting apparent estimates have potential utility for examining extant data sets, for which information needed to compute more sophisticated estimators is not available. For example, Beauchamp et al. (1996) used Green's (1989) transformation of the apparent estimator to conduct a retrospective comparison on nest success rates of waterfowl by adjusting the apparent estimates, which were all that were available from the older studies, to more closely match the Mayfield estimates that were used in more-recent investigations.

CONCLUSIONS

Any analysis should be driven by the objectives of the study. In many situations, all that is needed is a good estimate of nest success. In other cases, insight into how daily survival rate varies by age of nest is important; a large number of methods have addressed that question. Often information is sought about the influence on nest survival of various covariates. Assessment of those influences can be made with many of the methods if nests can be stratified into meaningful categories of those covariates; for example, grouping nests according to the habitat type in which they occur. If covariates are nest- or age-specific, however, the options for analysis are more limited; the recent logistic-type methods (Dinsmore et al. 2002, Shaffer 2004, Stephens et al. 2005) are well-suited to these objectives. Guidelines for selecting a method to analyze nesting data are offered in Johnson (*chapter 6, this volume*).

Despite the numerous advances in the nearly half-century since the Mayfield estimator was developed, it actually bears up rather well. Johnson (1979) wrote that the original Mayfield method, perhaps with an adjustment in exposure for infrequently visited nests, should serve very nicely in many situations. Others (Klett and Johnson 1982, Bromaghin and McDonald 1993a, Farnsworth 2000, Jehle et al. 2004) have made similar observations. Etterson and Bennett (2005) suggested that traditional Mayfield models are likely to provide adequate estimates for most applications if nests are monitored at intervals of no longer than 3 d. McPherson et al. (2003) drew a parallel to mark-recapture studies by suggesting that estimates of survival are expected to be robust with respect to heterogeneity in the actual survival rates. Johnson (pers. comm. to Mayfield) stated that the Mayfield method may be better than anyone could rightly expect.

The seemingly simple problem of estimating nest success has received much more scientific attention than one might have anticipated. Many of the recent advances were due to increased computational abilities of both computers and biologists. Can we conclude that the latest methods—which allow solid statistical inference from models that allow a wide variety of covariates—will provide the ultimate in addressing this problem? As good as the new methods are, I suspect research activity will continue on this topic and that even-better methods will be developed in the future.

ACKNOWLEDGMENTS

I appreciate my colleagues who over the years have worked with me on the issue of estimating nest success: H. W. Miller, A. T. Klett, and T. L. Shaffer. H. F. Mayfield has been supportive of my efforts from the beginning. Thanks to S. L. Jones and G. R. Geupel for organizing the symposium and inviting my participation. This report benefited from comments by J. Bart, G. R. Geupel, S. L. Jones, M. M. Rowland, and T. L. Shaffer. I appreciate comments provided by authors of many methods I described, including N. J. Aebischer, J. F. Bromaghin, S. J. Dinsmore, M. A. Etterson, R. E. Green, K. R. Hazler, C. Z. He, G. A. Jehle, B. F. Manly, C. E. McCulloch, R. Natarajan, J. J. Rotella, C. J. Schwarz, T. R. Stanley, S. E. Stephens, and especially D. M. Heisey. Each author helped me learn more about the methods they presented.

Studies in Avian Biology No. 34:13–33

THE ABCS OF NEST SURVIVAL: THEORY AND APPLICATION FROM A BIOSTATISTICAL PERSPECTIVE

Dennis M. Heisey, Terry L. Shaffer, and Gary C. White

Abstract. We consider how nest-survival studies fit into the theory and methods that have been developed for the biostatistical analysis of survival data. In this framework, the appropriate view of nest failure is that of a continuous time process which may be observed only periodically. The timing of study entry and subsequent observations, as well as assumptions about the underlying continuous time process, uniquely determines the appropriate analysis via the data likelihood. We describe how continuous-time hazard-function models form a natural basis for this approach. Nonparametric and parametric approaches are presented, but we focus primarily on the middle ground of weakly structured approaches and how they can be performed with software such as SAS PROC NLMIXED. The hazard function approach leads to complementary log-log (cloglog) link survival models, also known as discrete proportional-hazards models. We show that cloglog models have a close connection to the logistic-exposure and related models, and hence these models share similar desirable properties. We raise some cautions about the application of random effects, or frailty, models to nest-survival studies, and suggest directions that software development might take.

Key Words: censoring, complementary log-log link, frailty models, hazard function, Kaplan-Meier, left-truncation, Mayfield method, proportional-hazards model, random effects, survival.

EL ABC DE SOBREVIVENCIA DE NIDO: TEORÍA Y APLICACIÓN DESDE UNA PERSECTIVA BIOESTADÍSTICA

Resumen. Consideramos como estudios de sobrevivencia de nido se ajustan a la teoría y métodos que han sido desarrollados para el análisis bioestadístico de datos de sobrevivencia. En este marco, la visión adecuada de fracaso de nido es la de un continuo proceso del tiempo, la cual pudiera ser observada solo periódicamente. La sincronización en la captura del estudio y observaciones subsecuentes, así como suposiciones respecto al proceso de tiempo continuo subyacente, únicamente determina el análisis apropiado vía la probabilidad de los datos. Describimos cómo los modelos continuos de peligro del tiempo forman una base natural para este enfoque. Son presentados enfoques no paramétricos y paramétricos, sin embargo nos enfocamos principalmente en el término medio de enfoques débilmente estructurados, y de cómo estos pueden funcionar con programas computacionales tales como el SAS PROC NLMIXED. El enfoque de función peligrosa dirige a modelos de vínculos de sobrevivencia complementarios log-log (cloglog), también conocidos como modelos discretos proporcionales de peligro. Mostramos que modelos cloglog tienen una conexión cercana a modelos de exposición logística y relacionados, y por lo tanto estos modelos comparten propiedades similares deseadas. Brindamos algunas precauciones acerca de la aplicación de modelos de efectos al azar o de falla, a estudios de sobrevivencia de nido, y sugerimos hacia donde pudiera dirigirse el desarrollo de programas computacionales.

A strong interest in nest survival has resulted in numerous papers on potential analysis methods. Recent papers by Dinsmore et al. (2002), Nur et al. (2004), and Shaffer (2004a) have presented methods for modeling nest survival as functions of continuous and categorical covariates and have spawned questions about how the approaches relate to one another. Rotella et al. (2004) and Shaffer (2004a) showed that the Dinsmore et al. (2002) method (which can be implemented in either program MARK or SAS PROC NLMIXED) and Shaffer's (2004a) method are very similar, but how these approaches relate to the Nur et al. (2004) approach is less obvious. In this paper we provide an overview of biostatistical survival analysis. We show how first principle considerations lead to a new nest-survival analysis method based on the complementary log-log link that has practical and theoretical appeal. We focus on techniques designed for grouped or interval-censored data: continuous-time events that are observed in discrete time. We use SAS software (SAS Institute Inc. 2004) for illustration although other environments could be used as well. We discuss and illustrate how current methods used for modeling nest survival relate to methods used in biostatistical applications.

Survival analysis is the branch of biostatistics that deals with the analysis of times at which events (e.g., deaths) occur, and is sometimes referred to as event time analysis. Bradley Efron, inventor of the bootstrap and a leading figure in statistics, described biostatistical survival analysis as a wonderful statistical success story (Efron 1995). Time is just a positive random variable, apparently qualitatively no different than say weights, which must also be positive. But no large branch of statistics is devoted exclusively to the analysis of weights—what is so special about event times? The answer is how times are observed, or more accurately, how they are only incompletely observed. For example, the classical survival analysis problem is how to estimate the survival distribution from a sample of subjects in which not all subjects have yet reached death; such subjects are said to be right-censored. All we know about right-censored subjects is that their event times are in the future sometime after their last observation. Information on the failure times of these subjects is incomplete. Although perhaps initially counterintuitive, hatching (or fledging) is actually a censoring event because it prevents the subsequent observation of a nest failure. The goal of survival analysis is to extract the maximum amount of information from incomplete observations, which requires a good way of representing incomplete information.

Biostatistical survival analysis has been a relatively specialized domain that has focused mostly on human medical applications. Although some survival-analysis procedures, such as Kaplan-Meier (Kaplan and Meier 1958) and Cox (1972), are fairly widely known beyond biostatistics, the general breadth of survival analysis is not fully appreciated outside of biostatistics. As we discuss, Kaplan-Meier and Cox approaches are seldom well suited to nest-survival analyses and more specialized procedures are generally needed. Our goal here is to show how most nest survival studies can be handled conveniently within the broad framework of modern biostatistical survival analysis theory.

Events in time, such as nest failures, may be incompletely observed in many ways. Two general mechanisms that occur in most nesting studies are left-truncation (resulting from delayed entry) and censoring (exact failure age unknown). Given the various ways in which observations can be incomplete, how can one be assured that the maximum amount of information is being recovered from each observation? This is where the data-likelihood function is important. A correctly specified data likelihood describes the precise manner in which observations are only partially observed. Loosely speaking, the likelihood principle and the related principle of sufficiency imply that the data-likelihood function captures all of the information contained in a data set (Lindgren 1976). No analysis can be better than one based on a correctly specified likelihood.

The likelihood principle says that the data likelihood is the only thing that matters. In some cases, identical likelihoods arise from apparently very different types of data. For example, likelihoods that arise from event-time data are quite frequently identical to likelihoods that result from discrete-count data. By recognizing such equivalences, it is possible to use software to perform event-time analyses even if the software was originally designed for other applications such as Poisson or logistic regression of discrete-count data (Holford 1980, Efron 1988).

Once the data likelihood is constructed, the rest of the analysis follows more or less automatically. Two factors solely determine the data likelihood: data-collection design, and biological structure. Data-collection design refers to how the data are observed and collected, and determines the macro-structure of the likelihood. Biological structure reflects the assumptions or models the researcher is willing to make or wants to explore with respect to the nest-failure process. Biological assumptions and models are usually formulated in terms of the instantaneous-hazard function, and the hazard function in turn determines the micro-structure of the likelihood. Together, the data collection design and biological structure fully specify the data likelihood which forms the foundation of analysis. The need to correctly construct the appropriate data likelihood does not depend on whether one is taking a Bayesian or classical (maximum likelihood) approach to estimation and inference; both approaches are based on the same data likelihood. Here we focus on the maximum likelihood (ML) method which underlies both the classical frequentist approach as well as the recently popularized information-theoretic approach of Burnham and Anderson (2002). We focus on ML methods primarily because of tradition and readily accessible software.

Once the data are collected, the macro-structure of the likelihood is essentially set. The researcher has little or no discretion with respect to structuring this portion of the likelihood once the data are in hand. From the data-collection design it is usually clear what macro-structure is needed. The only reason to use an analysis that is not based on the exact macro-structure is because it is exceedingly inconvenient. In such cases, researchers can try analyses with likelihood macro-structures corresponding to data-collection designs that they hope are close enough to give good approximations. Mayfield's (1961, 1975) method, including Mayfield logistic regression (Hazler 2004), is an example of an analysis that is based on an approximate macro-structure as a result of the unrealistic assumption that failure dates are known to the day (i.e., Mayfield's midpoint assumption). Johnson (1979) and Bart and Robson (1982) derived an exact analysis for the problem considered by Mayfield, but these methods have received relatively little use because software was not readily available at the time. Because it is difficult to say when an approximate likelihood is close enough, one should always strive for a likelihood as accurate as possible. The consequences of such assumption violations can range from negligible errors to completely invalid results, affecting both estimation and testing.

The researcher has much more freedom with respect to the biological structure, and this is the aspect of nest-survival analysis that requires some creativity and judgment. In biostatistical survival analyses, so-called nonparametric procedures such as the Kaplan-Meier estimator (KME) and the Cox partial likelihood approach enjoy great popularity because of the perception that they can be applied almost unconsciously on the part of the researcher. However, things are often not so simple with nest-survival data. In fact, many nest-survival data sets cannot support fully nonparametric approaches because of left-truncation and interval-censoring, which will be described later. Indeed, nonparametric is a misnomer; nonparametric survival approaches actually require the estimation of many more parameters than typical parametric analyses (Miller 1983), which is why they are not a panacea in nest-survival studies.

Due to the low data-to-parameter ratio in fully nonparametric procedures, the resulting survival estimates typically have large variances. The primary appeal of fully nonparametric procedures is that under some circumstances the estimates can be counted on to be relatively unbiased and moderately efficient (although left-truncation and interval-censoring, common features of nest survival studies, may result in exceptions; Pan and Chappell 1999, 2002). The situation is reversed for so-called parametric approaches. The survival estimates from parametric survival models typically have small variances because few parameters must be estimated. However, this can be at the price of large biases. In statistics in general, it has long been recognized that the best estimators are those that achieve a balance between variance and bias, which is measured by the mean squared error. Thus, in many survival-analysis situations, including nest survival, the best approach is the middle ground between fully nonparametric approaches and traditional parametric models; this middle ground is often referred to as weakly structured models, which we will explore in the nest-survival context.

Our intention is to present practical ideas that will be useful in the analysis of real data. To facilitate this, we use an example data set throughout the paper to illustrate how particular ideas translate specifically into analyses. All programs used for the analyses are given in the Appendices.

PROBABILITY BASICS

Symbolic Representation of a Nest Record

We will use T to represent the actual age at which a nest fails. In most cases, this quantity will not be observed exactly or at all, but we can always put bounds on it. A nest record needs to describe two things: (1) the age observation starts (discovery), and (2) what bounds we can put on the failure age T. For example, suppose we discover a nest at age r, and follow it until age t. Suppose age t is the last we observed the nest, at which point it was still active. Symbolically, we will describe such a nest observation as $T > t \mid T > r$, which means starting at age r (conditional on being active at r), the nest was observed until age t, and had not yet failed. Another nest, discovered at age r, still active at age x, but failed by age t would be described as $x < T < t \mid T > r$.

Nest Record Probabilities

The data likelihood gives the probability of the observed data. It is constructed by first computing the survival probability (or survival probability density in some cases) corresponding to each nest record, and then multiplying all of these nest-likelihood contributions together. The age of nest failure T is a random variable that is characterized by its probability distribution. For the record described by $T > t \mid T > r$, $\Pr(T > t \mid T > r)$ is its probability. This is the probability of the nest surviving beyond age t conditional on it being active at age r. It is often more convenient to write this using the shorthand $S(t \mid r) = \Pr(T > t \mid T > r)$. A very important special case occurs when the record starts at the origin (nest initiation) $S(t \mid 0) = \Pr(T > t \mid T > 0)$; this is referred to as the survival function, and is often represented as just $S(t)$. The general goal of survival analysis is often to estimate and characterize $S(t)$. Even if one is only interested in an interval survival such as a monthly rate, $S(t)$ is the means to that end; for example, if age is in days, $S(30)$ is the monthly survival rate.

A very fundamental property of conditional survival probabilities is that they multiply. So for ages $a < b < c$, then $S(c \mid a) = S(b \mid a)S(c \mid b)$. In particular $S(t) = S(1 \mid 0)S(2 \mid 1)...S(t \mid t - 1)$ (of course assuming age t is an integer). The importance of this multiplicative law of conditional survival in survival analysis cannot be overemphasized.

Suppose we discovered a nest at initiation (age 0), and visited it periodically. We observe that it failed between ages x and t. This observation is described as:

$$x < T < t \mid T > 0,$$

and it should seem reasonable that

$$\Pr(x < T < t \mid T > 0) = S(x) - S(t).$$

From the multiplicative law

$$S(t) = S(x)S(t \mid x),$$

so this can also be written as

$$\Pr(x < T < t \mid T > 0) = S(x)(1 - S(t \mid x)).$$

The term $1 - S(t \mid x)$ is especially important in survival analysis, and is referred to as the conditional interval mortality. It is the probability of failing in the age interval x to t, given one starts the interval alive at age x. We can represent this as

$$\Pr(x < T < t \mid T > x) = 1 - S(t \mid x) = M(t \mid x).$$

LIKELIHOODS

Data-collection Designs—Likelihood Macro-structure

Nest-study data-collection designs, which determine the likelihood macro-structure, can be broadly categorized into three general cases, given below. In a certain sense, the macro-structure is not scientifically interesting, although it must be accommodated to get the right answer. It reflects how the data were collected and is not directly influenced by biology. By interval monitoring, we mean that some interval of time elapses between visits to the nest; the inter-visit intervals need not all be of the same duration. If a nest fails, the failure time is known only to have been sometime during that interval. Without going into the details, under continuous monitoring the contribution of a failed nest to the likelihood is technically a probability density rather than a probability per se.

Case I: Known age, continuous monitoring:
  Discovered at age r:
    Last observed active at age t:
      $\Pr(T > t \mid T > r) = S(t \mid r)$
    Observed failure at exactly age t:
      $\Pr(t < T < t + dt \mid T > r) \approx S(t \mid r)h(t)dt$;
      $h(t)$ is a hazard function.

Case II: Known age, interval monitoring:
  Discovered at age r:
    Last observed active at age t:
      $\Pr(T > t \mid T > r) = S(t \mid r)$
    Observed failure between ages x and t:
      $\Pr(x < T < t \mid T > r) = S(x \mid r)(1 - S(t \mid x))$.

Case III: Unknown age, continuous or interval monitoring:
  Age at discovery known only to be between r_y (youngest possible) and r_o (oldest possible):
    Last observed active time d after discovery:
      $\Sigma p(r)S(d + r \mid r)$;
      $r_y \leq r \leq r_o$
      $p(r)$ is the probability of discovery at age r
    Observed failure between z and d days after discovery ($z < d$)
      $\Sigma p(r)S(z + r \mid r)(1 - S(d + r \mid z + r))$
      $r_y \leq r \leq r_o$

Case I allows for left-truncation (delayed discovery) and right-censoring (some failures never observed) and is very important in human biomedical applications, but is seldom appropriate in nesting studies. Case II allows for left-truncation, interval-censoring (failure time known only to an interval), and right-censoring. Case III allows for left-truncation and general double-censoring (Heisey and Nordheim 1995). While Case III is the most general, it is not yet straightforward in application due to software issues. We focus most of our attention on Case II—known-age, interval monitoring.

The Geometric Interpretation of Likelihood Contributions

The basics of the macro-structure likelihood contributions become clear by considering the Lexus diagram (Fig. 1). The Lexus diagram has a long history in survival analysis (Anderson et al. 1992), and is extremely useful for visualizing the likelihood contributions in complex situations involving delayed discovery and interval-censoring, especially in the most general case when survival can vary both by age and calendar time, which we briefly consider later. The Lexus diagram displays the known history of a nest in the calendar time/nest age plane. One can imagine a probability density spread over this two-dimensional surface. To determine the likelihood contribution, one has to first determine the region on the time/age plane that is being described by the nest record. One then collects the appropriate probability over this region.

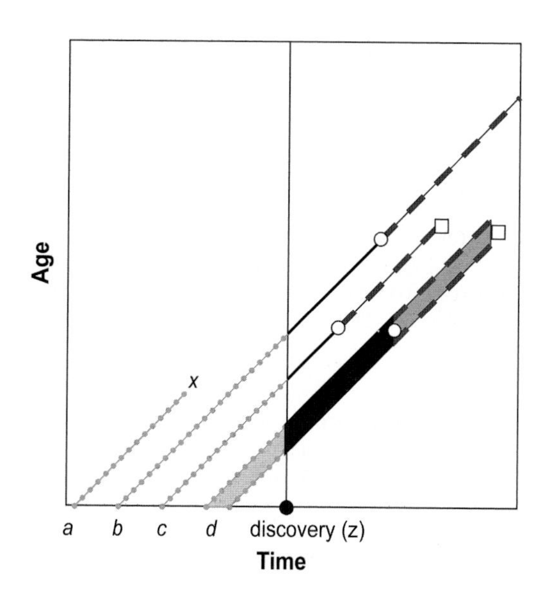

FIGURE 1. Lexus diagram showing some possible observational outcomes for four nests in a typical survival study. The nests are indicated as *a*, *b*, *c*, and *d*. We will also let *a*, *b*, *c*, and *d* indicate the dates of nest initiation. A hollow circle indicates the last visit during which the nest was known to be active, and the hollow square indicates the first visit at which the nest was known to have failed. We assume nests were searched for on only one day, say *z*. Nest *a* is an example of a hypothetical nest that failed before discovery on day *z*, and hence was unobservable (left-truncated). Nests *b* and *c* are examples of nests that were discovered on day *z* and determined to be exactly $z - a$ and $z - b$ days old. Nest *b* went on to hatch, so its hypothetical failure time can be thought as being sometime during the infinite interval after hatching. Nest *c* was observed to fail sometime during the indicated interval. The likelihood contributions mirror this structure. Nest *d* could not be aged exactly, so its date of initiation can only be bounded. Such unknown ages result in a two-dimensional region over which probability density must be collected, which is why Case III likelihood contributions are sums.

The histories of four nests are shown (Fig. 1). For simplicity of illustration, nests were searched for on only one day, labeled discovery on the *x*-axis. The day of discovery is the so-called truncation limit; nests that do not survive until that day are truncated from the potential sample and their existence is never known. Nest *a* is an example of a truncated nest. If we had discovered the remnants of nest *a*, this would constitute a left-censored observation; failure occurred to the left of the first observation. We do not deal with such problematic observations in this paper. Nests *b*, *c*, and *d* are examples of discovered nests. The ages of both nests *b* and *c* were determined exactly at the time of discovery, so their records are known to lie on a line in the time/age plane. The hollow circle indicates the last visit at which the nest was active, and the hollow square indicates the first visit when the nest was known to have failed. The solid line to the right of discovery indicates when the nest is known to have been active, and the broken line is the region in which the nest could have failed. Nest *c* was observed to fail in an interval (say between *x* and *t*), after first surviving for an interval from *r* to *x*. This history is described as $(x < T < t \mid T > r)$, with corresponding probability:

$$\Pr(x < T < t \mid T > r) = S(x \mid r)(1 - S(t \mid x)).$$

Nest *b* was never observed to fail (right censored), but the geometry of its observation can be viewed in exactly the same manner as nest *c*. We assume nest *b* would hypothetically fail sometime between the last observation and infinity, so its record is $(t < T < \infty \mid T > r)$. The corresponding probability statement is $\Pr(t < T < \infty \mid T > r) = S(t \mid r)(1 - S(\infty \mid t))$. Of course the probability of surviving forever is 0, $S(\infty \mid t) = 0$, so the likelihood contribution for a right-censored observation reduces to $\Pr(T > t \mid T > r) = S(t \mid r)$, as given before. This shows that right-censoring is just a special case of interval-censoring where the upper bound is infinity.

Nest *d* illustrates the case where a nest's age at discovery could only be bounded. The black polygon indicates time/age points when the nest could have been active, and the grey polygon indicates time/age points when the nest could have failed. The Case III likelihood contributions reflect the sums over these two-dimensional regions.

In the Lexus diagram nest age and calendar time are continuous variables. This is realistic; a nest can fail at any time day or night. In almost all cases it is appropriate to think of the event of nest failure as a continuous-time event, even if it is not observed or recorded in continuous time. This continuous-time event framework is the framework on which most of modern biostatistical survival analysis theory rests. Its power lies in its ability to accurately represent how data are incompletely observed under a diversity of circumstances as suggested by the Lexus diagram. Failure to accurately represent the continuous time region in which the observation may have occurred is likely to result in biases. An obvious example of this is the well-known issue of apparent survival versus the Mayfield estimator; Heisey and Nordheim (1990) give a more complex example.

Example

We now introduce an example that we will use throughout this paper for illustration. It is a sample (N = 216) of Blue-winged Teal (*Anas discors*) nests taken in 1976 reported by Klett and Johnson (1982). Nests in the sample were obtained by searching right-of-way habitat along Interstate 94 in south-central North Dakota. The macro-structure of the data set is classic general Case II—aged nests discovered sometime after initiation with periodic re-visitation (Fig. 2). Few of the nests were discovered on or near the time of initiation, so as suggested by Fig. 2 the data contain very little survival information with respect to the youngest ages. On Fig. 2, a solid black line segment indicates an age span during which it is known that the nest survived. A black segment going from age r to age t contributes the term $\Pr(T > t \mid T > r) = S(t \mid r)$ to the likelihood. A dashed-line segment indicates an age span during which it is known that the nest failed. Such a segment going from age x to t contributes: $\Pr(x < T < t \mid T > x) = 1 - S(t \mid x)$ to the likelihood. These are the correct likelihood contributions for the observational design of the study, and in addition to demonstrating appropriate approaches, one of our goals will be to examine the consequences of using less appropriate analyses.

The data file contains five variables. One variable is the nest identifier nestid. The variables firstday and lastday are the first and last days of a visitation interval; the days on which visits occurred. The variable success indicates whether the subject survived the interval (1) or not (0). The variable distance gives the distance to the road shoulder. A nest often had multiple records, one for each inter-visitation interval. However, no loss of information occurs by combining all consecutive successful intervals for a nest and treating them as a single interval. This follows since: $S(b \mid a)S(c \mid b) = S(c \mid a)$.

Continuous-time Events, Hazard Functions, and the Daily Survival Rate

The hazard function $h(t)$ is the key to representing survival probabilities in continuous time; it is the basic structure on which all else rests in survival analysis. It links the probability surface over the Lexus diagram to interesting biological models. The best way to think of $h(t)$ is as the conditional interval mortality scaled per unit time,

$$h(t) \approx \frac{M(t+dt \mid t)}{dt}$$

i.e., the instantaneous failure rate. It is formally defined as the limit of this relationship as dt goes to 0. Hazard functions are particularly suitable for regression modeling. The hazard function uniquely determines the survival function through the rather opaque relationship:

$$S(t \mid r) = \exp\left[-\int_r^t h(u)du\right] \qquad (1)$$

The specific form of this relationship should be viewed more-or-less as just math; relatively little intuition can be gained from studying it although it is a key mathematical relationship to know. The term

$$\int_r^t h(u)du$$

is very important in modern survival analysis, and is referred to as the cumulative interval hazard; we will represent it with the more convenient notation

$$\Lambda(t \mid r) = \int_r^t h(u)du$$

Just as conditional survival probabilities multiply, cumulative interval hazards add: $\Lambda(c \mid a) = \Lambda(b \mid a) + \Lambda(c \mid b)$. This additivity is quite convenient.

Usually nests will not be visited more than once daily and we assume that this is the case in this paper. This is convenient because we can assume age t is always an integer and use the daily cumulative hazard $\Lambda_t = \Lambda(t \mid t-1)$ as the basic building block and avoid showing integrals almost entirely (i.e., the integral in (1) is replaced by a sum). This now provides a firm theoretical underpinning for the traditional approach of using daily survival rate (DSR) in nest survival analyses. That is, if DSR_t is the daily survival rate for day t, $DSR_t = S(t \mid t-1) = \exp(-\Lambda_t)$. Thus, the cumulative daily hazard can be viewed as just a one-to-one transformation of the DSR, $\Lambda_t = -ln(DSR_t)$. By recognizing this relationship between the DSR and the cumulative daily hazard, DSR models can be constructed which have clear hazards-based interpretations.

In ordinary regression analysis, we are accustomed to parameters (slopes) having any possible value, negative or positive. But because hazard functions $h(t)$ must be non-negative, cumulative interval hazards such as Λ_t must be non-negative as well. We can get around this range restriction by using the log cumulative daily hazard $\gamma_t = ln(\Lambda_t)$ for modeling. The relationship of the log cumulative daily hazard to the DSR is then:

$$DSR_t = S(t \mid t-1) = \exp(-\exp(\gamma_t))$$

This can be rewritten as:

$$\gamma_t = ln(-ln(1 - DMR_t))$$

where DMR is the daily mortality rate 1 – DSR.

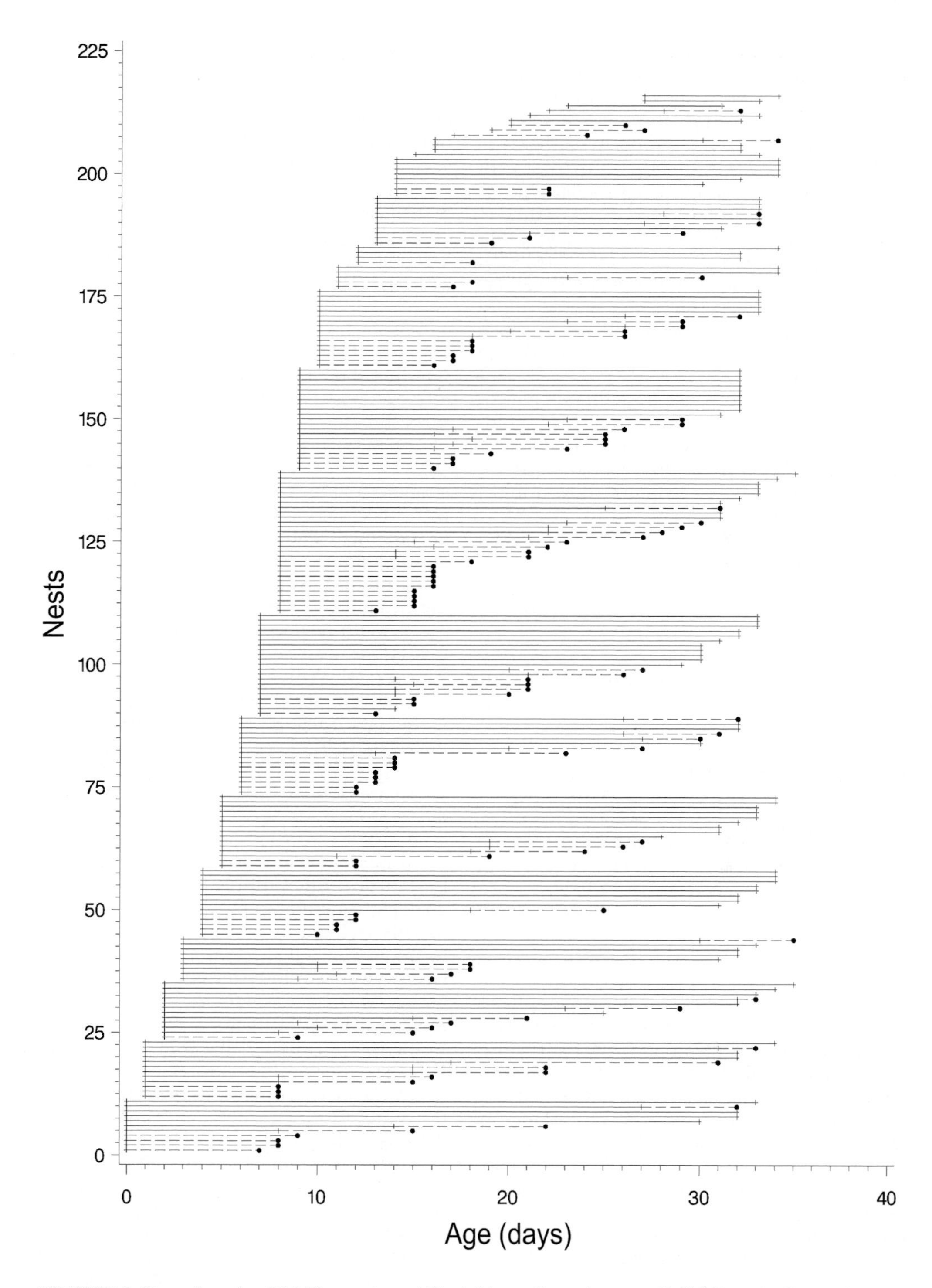

FIGURE 2. Raw data for 216 Blue-winged Teal (*Anas discors*) nests. Solid lines indicate times at which the nest was under observation and known to have survived. Dashed lines ending with a solid dot indicates intervals during which nests are known to have failed.

This important relationship is often referred to as the complementary log-log link model because it links the daily cumulative hazard to the mortality (or survival) function; it is also referred to as the discrete proportional-hazards model. We have been unable to discover with certainty why this model is traditionally given in its complementary form, i.e., in terms of DMR rather than DSR, but without going into the details we believe it is because $ln(-ln\ (1 - P))$ is quite similar to the logit model logit(P), while $ln(-ln\ (P))$ is not. On this scale, we can build familiar-appearing regression models, where the parameters have very clear hazards-based interpretations.

To summarize, for Case II likelihood contributions such as our example, the basic building block is the conditional interval survival, say $S(t \mid r)$. We will assume visits are at the beginning of a day, so visits on days i and j corresponds to the age span $i - 1$ to $j - 1$. Thus, $S(t \mid r) = DSR_{r+1}DSR_{r+2}...DSR_t$. This in turn can be expressed as:

$$S(t \mid r) = \exp(-(\Lambda_{r+1} + \Lambda_{r+2} + \ldots + \Lambda_t)), \quad (2)$$
and $\Lambda_s = \exp(\gamma_s)$.

Equation (2) can be expressed in pseudo-code as:

```
total_cumulative_hazard ← 0
for day = firstday to lastday - 1 do{
  daily_cumulative_hazard ←
    exp(gamma[day])
  total_cumulative_hazard ←
    total_cumulative_hazard +
    daily_cumulative_hazard
}
interval_survival ←
  exp(-total_cumulative_hazard);
```

Any Case II analysis will have this general structure at its core because this general structure accommodates the likelihood macrostructure. Most of the remainder of this paper focuses on various models for the vector gamma, which gives the micro-structure. The importance of (2) in general Case II applications is difficult to over emphasize. (Aside: time indexing for such analyses can be rather confusing. In the above pseudo-code, because visits are assumed to occur at the beginning of the day, the last full day survived is the day before the last visit, hence lastday-1.)

So the total data likelihood is a product of terms of the form $S(t \mid r)$ and $1 - S(t \mid r)$. In this respect, even though the random variable being modeled is actually the continuous variable age at failure, the likelihood appears exactly the same as one that would arise from binary or binomial data. This is very convenient because it allows us to use software intended for the analysis of discrete binary or binomial data. For our examples, we used SAS PROC NLMIXED specifying a binary model.

SURVIVAL ESTIMATION

The Simplest Example—General Case II, Constant Hazard

We start with the simplest (and most restrictive) possible model, which is under the assumption that the hazard does not vary with age, so $h(t) = \lambda$. When applied to general Case II data, this estimator corresponds to the generalization of the Mayfield model developed by Johnson (1979) and Bart and Robson (1982). Under the special circumstance of Case II data resulting from once-daily monitoring, Mayfield estimates are obtained. Under this model, all values of the vector gamma are the same, regardless of age (Program A-1; Appendix 1). The result of applying this model to the example data is shown on Fig. 3. With respect to the hazard function $h(t)$, this is the most restricted and smoothest possible model. With this as background, we next look at the least restricted and roughest possible models with respect to $h(t)$, so-called nonparametric models.

Case I and Special Case II—Nonparametric Survival Estimation

Nonparametric is a somewhat murky term in statistics with multiple meanings. In survival analysis, a nonparametric survival estimator is usually defined as one that converges exactly to the true survival function $S(t)$ as the sample size grows to infinity for any $S(t)$ (Kaplan and Meier 1958). The counterexample is a parametric survival estimator which will converge to the true $S(t)$ only if the true $S(t)$ happens to belong to the specified parametric family. For a nonparametric estimator to converge to $S(t)$ for every possible $S(t)$, such an estimator must be extremely flexible.

From a theoretical standpoint, a big difference exists between truly continuous monitoring (Case I) and almost continuous periodic monitoring (once daily monitoring—Special Case II). Theoretical justification of continuous-monitoring estimators typically involves rather sophisticated theoretical devices—this has to do with the fact that the probability of a continuous random variable ever assuming a specific value is 0. Kaplan and Meier (1958) achieved biostatistical fame primarily because of their

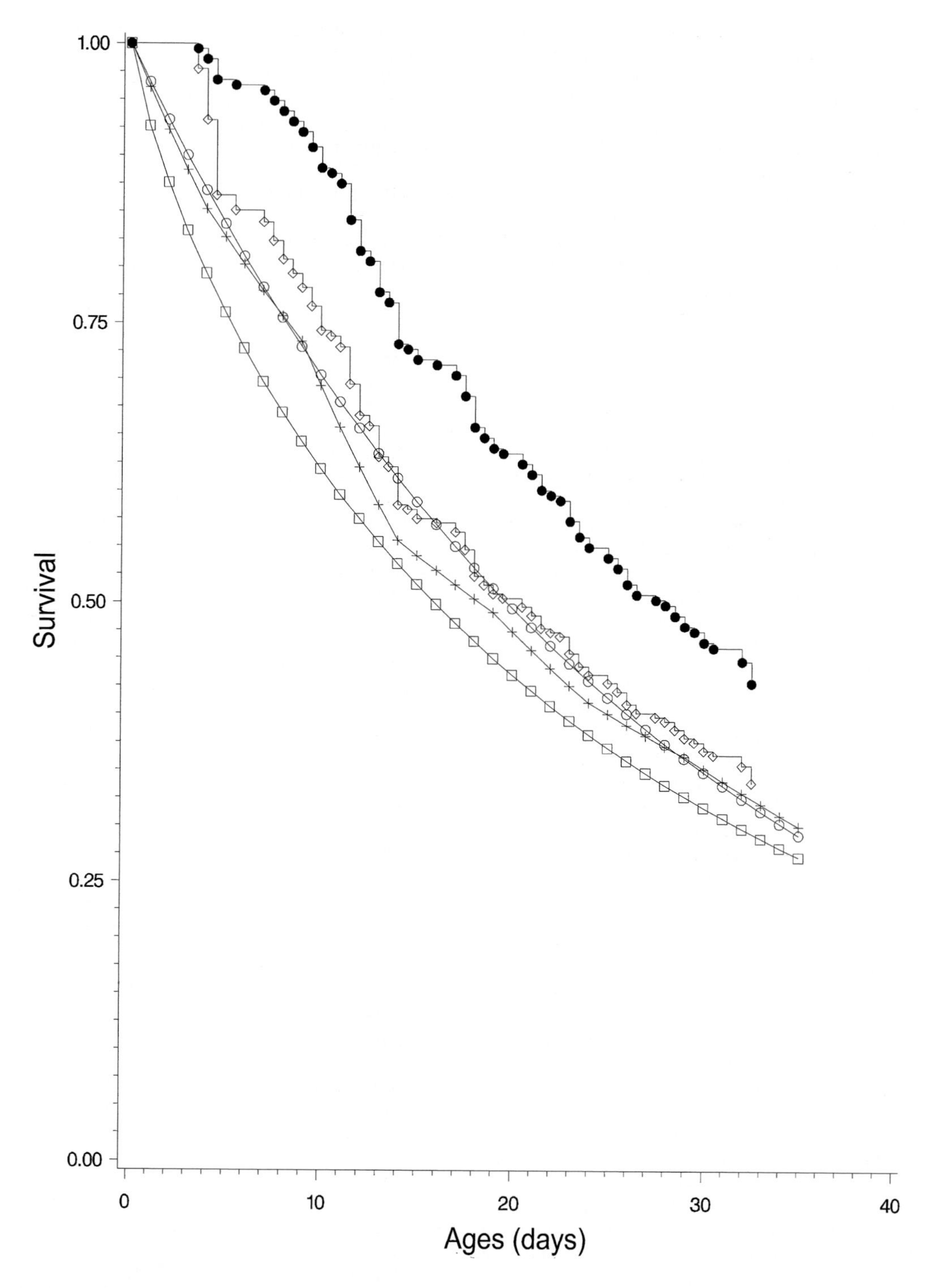

FIGURE 3. Estimated survival curves. The upper most curve (solid dots) is the usual Kaplan-Meier estimator (KME), which ignores the left-truncated (delayed entry) aspect of the data. The generalized Kaplan-Meier estimator (GKME) which accommodates left-truncation but not interval-censoring is the step function with hollow diamonds. The hollow circles correspond to the constant hazard model, the hollow squares to the Weibull model, and the crosses to the weakly structured model with a step-hazard model (steps every 5 d).

clever argument showing that the KME is the nonparametric maximum likelihood estimator (NPMLE) of $S(t)$ specifically under continuous monitoring. In application, this distinction is often not so important—for example, the KME for continuous monitoring and the life table (actuarial) estimator for frequent periodic monitoring are identical, so there seems little harm in referring to both as KMEs as is frequently done. In the following we focus on once-daily monitoring, and occasionally blur the distinction between continuous and once-daily monitoring a little to avoid tedious qualifications.

As noted, for a nonparametric estimator to converge to $S(t)$ for every possible $S(t)$, such an estimator must be extremely flexible. The manner in which nonparametric estimators typically achieve this is by allowing the empirical hazard to change whenever a failure is observed. Two popular approaches are the impulse-hazard model and the step-hazard model.

To justify the impulse-hazard model, it can be argued that it is reasonable to assume that on a day when no failures occur, the cumulative daily hazard Λ_t is 0. But on a day a failure occurs, Λ_t spikes up but then falls back down the next day if no failures occur. Under the step-hazard model, it can be argued that it is reasonable to assume the daily cumulative hazard Λ_t remains constant (and not necessarily 0) until after the next failure occurs, but that it might step up or step down at that point. Both of these models are extremely flexible, perhaps in some sense too flexible.

Either of these hazard models can be implemented relatively easily within our general framework outlined earlier. Let $t_{(1)}, t_{(2)}, \ldots$ indicate the days on which failures were observed. For the impulse-hazard model, the easiest approach is simply to discard any days on which no failures occurred and then allow γ_t to be different for each day $t_{(i)}$ on which failures were observed. To implement the step-hazard model, the γ_t of the gamma vector are constrained to be equal over the interfailure interval between the i-th and i + 1-th failure days (including the i + 1-th failure day): $\gamma_{t(i)+1} = \gamma_{t(i)+2} = \ldots = \gamma_{t(i+1)}$. This step model is a straightforward generalization of the simple constant hazard model we presented earlier. But the goal of the description here is primarily to show how nonparametric models fit into the bigger picture which we will be developing; we would generally not recommend that researchers use our SAS PROC NLMIXED approach to fit these nonparametric models. Very good special purpose software already exists that is perfectly satisfactory for fitting these models, or models that are close enough.

The impulse model corresponds to the KME or the generalized KME, or GKME. In modern usage the KME usually refers specifically to the version of Kaplan and Meier's (1958) estimator appropriate for untruncated data. As implemented in many programs such as SAS PROC LIFETEST, the KME does not allow for delayed entry (left-truncation). Hyde (1977) points out that a close reading of Kaplan and Meier (1958: 463, Eq. 2b) shows that they also explicitly treated left-truncation as well. Lynden-Bell (1971) appears to be the first to give a detailed consideration of nonparametric estimation of $S(t)$ in the presence of truncation (Woodroofe 1985), and presents the generalization of the KME, the GKME. The GKME has been reinvented numerous times from various perspectives; Pollock et al. (1989) popularized this estimator in wildlife telemetry studies.

As noted, Kaplan and Meier (1958) demonstrated that what they called the product limit estimator was the nonparametric maximum-likelihood estimator (NPMLE) of $S(t)$ for Case I observations. Although NPMLEs are of great theoretical interest, this does not imply that NPMLEs are in any sense best estimators. Nonparametric maximum likelihood is not the same thing as ordinary maximum likelihood. The optimality properties of ordinary maximum likelihood do not necessarily carry through to NPMLEs (Cox 1972, Anderson et al. 1992).

The step-hazard model is closely, and confusingly, related to another popular nonparametric survival estimator, the Breslow survival estimator. Indeed, the step-hazard model is sometimes called the Breslow hazard model. However, as Miller (1981) notes, Breslow (1974) extended his step-hazard structure to his survival estimator in a manner that does not appear to be consistent with equation (1), and the resulting Breslow survival estimator essentially appears to be based on an impulse-hazard model. Link (1984) fixed this, and developed a survival estimator that is directly consistent with Breslow's step-hazard model through equation (1); we will refer to this as the Breslow-Link model. We mention Breslow-Link only because it is the approach that is exactly consistent with our general development.

In practice GKME, Breslow, or Breslow-Link will usually give very similar answers, and no clear theoretical reason exists for preferring one over another if one has Case I or once-daily monitored Case II data. SAS PROC PHREG is a good software choice for either the GKME or the Breslow approach. We are not aware of an implementation of Breslow-Link, but either GKME or Breslow are fine substitutes. To accommodate the left-truncation, that is, entry after age $t = 0$, one must use the ENTRY = varname model statement option, where varname is the SAS variable giving the age at which the nest was discovered. Using a KME procedure such as SAS PROC LIFETEST that assumes entry at age $t = 0$ will result in a potentially biased results because early failures will be underrepresented (Tsai et al. 1987), much like the apparent estimator of nest success is biased. To obtain survival estimates in PROC PHREG, one specifies a null model without any covariates and includes a BASELINE statement. One can specify either the GKME model with the BASELINE METHOD = PL or the Breslow approach with BASELINE METHOD = CH.

Because of the requirement of continuous or near continuous monitoring, these procedures cannot be recommended for application to our general Case II example data. GKME or Breslow are not appropriate because the exact day of failure is not known due to interval-censoring. In addition, KME is not appropriate because it ignores the left-truncation. However, we applied these techniques to examine the consequences. For these analyses, if a failure was observed, we used the midpoint of the failure interval as the exact age at which the failure occurred. We used SAS PROC PHREG to obtain KME (Program B-1, Appendix 2) and GKME (Program B-2, Appendix 2) estimates. By not including the ENTRY statement, the resulting KME assumes all nests are discovered at age 0, (nest initiation), and as expected, this resulted in a substantial upward bias in the estimated survival curve (solid circles, Fig. 3). The GKME (hollow diamonds, Fig. 3) correctly accommodates the left-truncation (delayed entry), but the midpoint assumption appears to cause bias at the youngest ages because the relative long initial intervals prevent any imputed failure times near initiation. By the end of the nesting period, the GKME is not too dissimilar from the more appropriate estimators presented later. The problems observed with the KME and GKME are predictable consequences of the incorrectly specified likelihood macrostructures.

General Case II—Nonparametric Survival Estimation

Turnbull (1976) developed the general theory for obtaining NPMLE's of $S(t)$ for interval-censored and truncated data. Pan and Chappell (1999) later showed that Turnbull's estimator would not always work when the data are sparse, and provided a correction. Even when this approach works in the sense of giving consistent estimates, the estimates may be unstable (Lindsey and Ryan 1998). Generally speaking, Turnbull's and related NPMLE algorithms are seeking the points at which the hazard should have impulses similar to GKME. The goal of nonparametric maximum likelihood estimation is to find the maximum number of impulses that can be estimated, but this means the problem often teeters on the brink of over-parameterization. In the real world, it is usually unlikely that the hazard function swings wildly up and down from day to day (except from known events such as storms that can be accounted for), and the flexibility of a fully nonparametric estimator is, in general, wasted. By imposing a minimal amount of structure on the daily hazard rates, we can avoid the problems with instability yet still maintain flexibility. We explore this idea of weakly structured models next.

General Case II—Weakly Structured Survival Estimation

The simple solution to the problems of a fully nonparametric approach is to use the step-hazard model with fewer than the maximum number of possible steps, which preserves flexibility yet permits reliable estimation. This is an easy extension of the simple constant-hazard model $h(t) = \lambda$ we presented previously. We now break the time line into intervals at our discretion, and if age t falls into the κ-th interval, we have:

$$h(t) = \lambda_\kappa$$

which constrains all of the Λ_t's (or γ_t's) in interval k to be equal.

This form of the step-hazard model has a long history in biostatistics as a convenient weakly structured survival model (Oakes 1972; Holford 1976, 1980; Laird and Oliver 1980, Anderson et al. 1997, Kim 1997, Lindsey and Ryan 1998, Ibrahim et al. 2001), and it is the logical companion of the Breslow-Link nonparametric model. It has been referred to as semi-parametric (Laird and Oliver 1980) or loosely parametric (Cai and Betensky 2003). This model adapts well to interval-censored data (Kim 1997, Lindsey and Ryan 1998), who both present EM (expectation-maximization) algorithms for estimation in the untruncated setting. However, in our experience Newton-type maximization algorithms such as used by SAS PROC NLMIXED work fine as long as starting values are selected carefully. An effective strategy for step or piecewise models is to fit models with progressively more pieces, using the previous estimates as starting values in an obvious way. Lindsey and Ryan (1998) discuss strategies for positioning the steps.

We applied this approach to our example data with steps somewhat arbitrarily placed every 5 d (Program A-2, Appendix 1). The results suggest some irregularity in the age-specific survival, with a perhaps an inflection around day 15 (crosses in Fig. 3).

GENERAL CASE II—PARAMETRIC SURVIVAL ESTIMATION

We have already considered the simplest hazard model $h(t) = \lambda$, the constant or age-independent model which results in exponentially distributed failure times. In biostatistical survival analyses, many other popular parametric-hazard models correspond to different ideas about how the hazards change with age. An especially popular one is the Weibull (Kalbfleisch and Prentice 1980). The hazard function for the Weibull is given as $h(t) = \lambda\rho(\lambda t)^{\rho-1}$, which allows the failure hazard to change smoothly with age, either increasing or decreasing depending on the parameter ρ (the Weibull reduces to the exponential model when $\rho = 1$). Because our NLMIXED approach is based in the daily cumulative hazard rather than the hazard $h(t)$ directly, we need the daily cumulative hazard to obtain exact maximum likelihoods, which after a simple integration is found to be $\Lambda_t = \lambda^\rho[(t)^\rho - (t - 1)^\rho]$ (Kalbfleisch and Prentice (1980). In terms of γ_t, we have $\gamma_t = \rho\varphi + \log(t^\rho - (t-1)^\rho)$, where $\varphi = \log(\lambda)$ (Program A-3, Appendix 1). Figure 3 shows the Weibull fit to the example data (hollow squares) drops away more rapidly than the exponential model, and generally produces the lowest survival estimates of any of the procedures. In this example, the weakly structure estimates are bracketed by the exponential and Weibull although there is no reason to expect this in general. The Weibull shape parameter ρ was estimated to be 0.80 with 95% confidence intervals of 0.51–1.10, so on this basis it cannot be claimed that the Weibull is a significant improvement over the exponential. Indeed, as measured by Akaike's information criterion (AIC) (Burnham and Anderson 2002), the exponential model (AIC = 594.1) is as good as or better than the Weibull (AIC = 594.4) and better than the weakly structured model (AIC = 601.4). Some would no doubt argue that this shows the potential advantages of parametric models (Miller 1983), while others might not (Meier et al. 2004). At least in our example, it does not appear to matter much which hazard model is used but this of course cannot be counted on in general.

Many other parametric hazard models have been proposed (Kalbfleisch and Prentice 1980). Sometimes these are justified on the basis of some underlying theory that gives rise to their particular form, but they are frequently used in a less theoretical curve-fitting mode. For pure curve fitting, one could postulate a quadratic trend by specifying a hazard function $h(t) = \exp(a + bt + ct^2)$. With a little more programming, this curve-fitting approach could be extended to very flexible models such as polynomial splines (i.e., piecewise polynomial models that satisfy certain continuity constraints at the knots that join them). The most basic such piecewise polynomial spline model is the step-function model discussed previously.

If using parametric survival-analysis software such as SAS PROC LIFEREG, one must be careful that both the interval-censoring and left-truncation are appropriately handled. For example, LIFEREG can accommodate interval-censoring but not left-truncation. As with KME, ignoring left-truncation in parametric models can seriously bias survival estimates upward.

GENERAL CASE II—REGRESSION ANALYSIS

Proportional Hazards Analysis of Covariates

Within the above framework, regression analyses are easy. Let $\mathbf{X}$ be a row vector of covariates, and let β be a column vector of regression coefficients. The log-hazard function $ln\ (h(t))$ can assume any value from $-\infty$ to ∞, so it is natural to model it with a typical linear model $ln\ (h(t \mid \mathbf{X})) = \beta_0(t) + \mathbf{X}\beta$. This can also be expressed as the multiplicative model $h(t \mid \mathbf{X}) = h_0(t)\exp(\mathbf{X}\beta)$ which is the proportional-hazards (PH) model popularized by Cox (1972). The covariate-specific term $\exp(X_i\beta_i)$ is the hazard ratio, and scales the hazard function up or down. The unit hazard ratio $\exp(\beta_i)$ indicates how much a unit shift in X_i shifts the hazard function.

The baseline hazard function $h_0(t)$ is the value $h(t \mid \mathbf{X})$ assumes when all covariate values are 0 (when $\mathbf{X} = \mathbf{0}$, $\exp(\mathbf{X}\beta) = 1$). Under the proportional-hazards assumption, we have the relationship $ln\ \Lambda_t(\mathbf{X}) = \gamma_{0t} + \mathbf{X}\beta$, where the intercept γ_{0t} is the log baseline cumulative daily hazard. Covariates are easily included in any of the analyses illustrated above simply by adding $\mathbf{X}\beta$ to each element of the vector gamma.

The models presented here are essentially generalizations of Prentice and Gloeckler's (1978) grouped data PH model, generalized for left-truncation and overlapping intervals. Very useful background can found in Section 4.6 of Kalbfleisch and Prentice (1980). Our approach extends Lindsey and Ryan's (1998) piecewise treatment of interval-censored data to left-truncated data as well. When the above regression approach is applied to Case I or once-daily monitored Case II data, the result is the full-likelihood version of the Cox model. Cox invented the idea of partial likelihood, in which one can essentially ignore all of the likelihood except that portion that contains the covariates and their coefficients and thus avoid estimating the γ_t's. This has great computational benefits for large data sets but otherwise no reason is evident to prefer partial maximum-likelihood estimates. For Case I or once-daily monitored Case II data, it will generally be more convenient to use commercial software (e.g., SAS PROC PHREG) that accommodates delayed entry. However, we are not aware of a commercial program that correctly accommodates general left-truncated, interval-censored data that are typical of many nest-survival studies.

Alternative Regression Approaches (Advanced)

In addition to PH models, accelerated failure time (AFT) models and proportional discrete hazards odds (PDHO) models enjoy some popularity in survival analysis. AFT models that allow weakly structured modeling of the baseline have not been well developed and we will not consider them further. PDHO models can be traced to at least Cox's original 1972 paper; they are best suited to situations where the failure events are occurring in truly discrete time (Breslow 1974, Thompson 1977, Kalbfleisch and Prentice 1980: Eq. 2.23.). Truly discrete time-failure processes are relatively rare in nature, and require the event probability to be zero at almost all times except a countable number of instances. An example of a truly discrete time failure process is the repeated slamming of a car door in reliability testing (B. Storer, pers. comm.)

For example, assume that all failed nests fail at an instant before the end of the monitoring day. Then, the daily mortality probability for day t, $M(t \mid t-1)$ places all its probability mass at that single instant, which we will call $\delta_t = M(t \mid t-1)$, the discrete hazard function. In proportional daily discrete hazards odds (PDDHO) models, the daily odds

$$\theta_t(\boldsymbol{X})=\frac{\delta_t(\boldsymbol{X})}{1-\delta_t(\boldsymbol{X})}$$

takes the place of the cumulative daily hazard $\Lambda_t(\boldsymbol{X})$ in PH models. The log PDDHO model is then $ln\ \theta_t(\boldsymbol{X}) = \alpha_{0t} + \boldsymbol{X}\alpha$, where

$$\alpha_{0t}=\ln\left(\frac{\delta_t(0)}{1-\delta_t(0)}\right)$$

and α is the vector of log odds ratios. This posits a logistic regression model for daily failures. In terms of log daily cumulative hazards, the PDDHO model can be expressed as $\gamma_t = \log(\log(1 + \exp(\alpha_{0t} + \boldsymbol{X}\alpha)))$ which allows us to fit PDDHO models within our general hazards framework. When daily survival is moderately high, the PH and PDDHO will return similar results in most survival applications as long as the likelihood macrostructure is correctly represented (Thompson 1977). Efron (1988) illustrates the application of the PDHO model in what is essentially a once-monthly monitoring situation and relates it back to hazard functions. The approaches of Dinsmore et al. (2002), Rotella, at al. (2004), and Shaffer (2004a) are examples of general Case II nest-survival analyses with correctly specified PDDHO models. Given the similarity of results in most cases, the primary reason for preferring the PH approach over PDHO are theoretical rather than practical. The PDHO model for grouped data assumes that one has discovered the time interval at which the survival process acts in a proportional odds manner. If a process follows a PDHO process for a daily interval, it cannot obey a PDHO process for any other interval width and hence the interpretation of the regression coefficients α depends in the interval choice. The PH approach is interval invariant; $h(t \mid \boldsymbol{X}) = h_0(t)\exp(\boldsymbol{X}\beta)$, $\Lambda_t(\boldsymbol{X}) = \Lambda_t(\boldsymbol{0})\exp(\boldsymbol{X}\beta)$, and $S(t \mid \boldsymbol{X}) = S(t \mid \boldsymbol{X} = \boldsymbol{0})^{\exp(\boldsymbol{X}\beta)}$ are all equivalent representations of the PH model.

General Case II—Regression Example

For our example data set, nests in the sample were obtained by searching right-of-way habitat along Interstate 94 in south-central North Dakota. We examined whether distance to the road shoulder was associated with survival (Programs A-4, A-5, A-6; Appendix 1); the unit of distance measurement was meters. These data are summarized in Table 2 of Shaffer (2004a). Generally speaking, the effect of model misspecification in the regression analysis of survival data is to weaken the covariate association and that indeed appears to be consistent with what we observe (Table 1). The three models with correctly specified macro-structures give similar results regardless what hazard structure (constant, Weibull, step) was assumed, although increasing the flexibility of the baseline appears to slightly increase the variance (decrease the t-ratio). A hazard ratio of 1.016 means that for every meter away from the shoulder, the failure hazard $h(t)$ or $\Lambda(t)$ increases by a factor of 1.016. Thus, X meters from the shoulder the hazard ratio is $H(X) = 1.016^X$. In terms of age-specific survival, this means the survival of a nest distance X meters from the shoulder is $S(t \mid X) = S(t \mid X = 0)^{H(X)}$, where $S(t \mid X = 0)$ is the survival

TABLE 1. HAZARD AND ODDS RATIOS FOR MODELS FITTED TO THE BLUE-WINGED TEAL (*ANAS DISCORS*) DATA.

Model	Hazard ratio (t) [a]	Odds ratio (t)
Constant hazard (or odds)	1.016 (2.00)	1.016 (2.00)
Weibull hazard	1.016 (1.99)	–
Step-hazard (or odds)	1.015 (1.91)	1.016 (1.91)
Cox/GKME baseline	1.014 (1.76)	–
Cox/KME baseline	1.012 (1.52)	–

[a] The number in parentheses is the t-ratio for the log-hazard ratio: estimate/(SE).

immediately at the shoulder. The Cox-GKME approach (Program B-3, Appendix 2) fails to model the interval censoring, and results in a somewhat weakened covariate association. The Cox-KME (Program B-4, Appendix 2) approach which fails to model both the left-truncation and interval-censoring results in an even weaker association. No appreciable difference occurs between the hazard-ratio (PH) or odds-ratio (PDDHO) formulation (Programs A-7, A-8; Appendix 2). PDDHO models can be cast equally well in terms of mortality odds as we have done or survival odds as Shaffer (2004a) did, which accounts for why his log odds ratio for this example is the same as ours except for the sign.

TIME AND TIME-VARYING COVARIATES AND COEFFICIENTS (ADVANCED)

So far, the most general regression model we have considered is:

$$h(t \mid \mathbf{X}) = h_0(t)\exp(\mathbf{X}\beta),$$

where t is age. However, in its fullest generality we can have

$$h(t,c \mid \mathbf{X}(t,c)) = h_0\,(t,c)\exp(\mathbf{X}(t,c)\;\beta(t,c)),$$

where c refers to calendar time. This model incorporates three new features: (1) a bivariate calendar time/age baseline hazard function, (2) time and/or age varying covariates, and (3) time and/or age varying coefficients. We will describe each of these briefly. For sticklers, we note that we are appealing here to the mean value theorem for integrals to justify blurring the distinction between $h(t)$ and Λ_t, and we avoid the complication of integrating $h(t,c \mid \mathbf{X}(t,c))$ out over the day $t - 1$ to t.

Bivariate time/age baseline

Before, we constructed a piecewise step function for the age-specific hazard. We can take a similar approach for calendar time. This can be thought of as dividing the Lexus diagram into a patchwork of rectangles. Let k index the age intervals, and let m index the time intervals. Then for the resulting rectangle indexed by km, we can posit the log daily cumulative-hazard model $\gamma_k + \tau_m$. This log-linear model implies conditional independence of age and time (Bishop et al. 1975), as the daily cumulative hazard for each day is the product of a day term and a time term. An age-time interaction model is constructed by defining an individual term for each rectangle km. For this weakly structured age-time approach to work well, one must be judicious with respect to the number and position of the rectangles.

Time and age varying covariates

It is fairly easy to build time or age-varying covariates into the generic SAS PROC NLMIXED approach by using arrays that allow the covariate values to change as age or time changes. The use and interpretation of time-varying covariates requires care. Kalbfleisch and Prentice (1980) identify two general classes of time-varying covariates—external and internal. An internal covariate is something measured from the nest, such as the number of eggs or presence of parasitism and depends on the existence of the nest to be measured. As the name implies, an external covariate is one measured external to the nest, such as temperature or rainfall. Internal time-varying covariates are problematic with interval monitoring because the covariate values themselves will be interval-censored. The most common approach is to take the most recent value forward in time, although this is not without issues (Do 2002). Interpreting internal time-varying covariates can be problematic. For example, if parasitism is associated with nest failure, it is difficult to conclude directly whether parasitism is causal or simply associated with frail nests predisposed to fail regardless.

Even for a fixed covariate such as distance to the road, say X, we may be interested in whether its effect changes with age or time. We can model this as $(\alpha + \beta t)X$, where $\alpha + \beta t$ is viewed as a generalized regression coefficient of X that is a linear function of age t. We applied this to our example data using the weakly structured baseline model (Program A-9, Appendix 1);

no suggestion arose that the road effect varied with age (t-ratio = –0.24). Of course more flexible age-varying models could be specified as well. At the highest level of generality, one can have time/age-varying covariates with time/age-varying coefficients.

Frailty (Random Effects) and Spatial Models (Advanced)

In addition to allowing traditional fixed-effect regression models, some programs such as SAS PROC NLMIXED allow the inclusion of random effects. Such models are appealing because they allow a mechanism for modeling nests reasonably expected to have correlated fates. For example, for nests near an ephemeral pond, the fates of all nests may share some statistical association, if the pond dries up. We could reflect this by adding a random pond effect in the proportional hazards model, where z_j is the random effect of pond j, giving the mixed model $ln\ X_t(\mathbf{X}, j) = z_j + \gamma_t + \mathbf{X}\beta$.

Random effects in survival models require some special considerations. In survival-analysis, random-effects models such as just described are called shared-frailty models, with z_j being an unobserved frailty factor shared by all members in cluster j. Frailties have the effect of making the population (marginal) hazard decline over time because subjects with large frailties (large z_j) get eliminated first, and the remaining population becomes progressively shifted toward small z_j as time goes by. This is problematic in nest-survival studies because of left-truncation: the frailty distribution for discovered nests will be a function of the age of discovery as well as other covariates.

To clarify this, suppose it is possible to find all nests at the time of initiation. In this case, no nests would be overlooked, and we would be aware of all clusters. The typical assumption is that the cluster random effect z_j is normally distributed with mean 0 and variance σ^2, i.e., N(N, σ^2). If the discovery of nests is delayed, some nests will fail and be unavailable for discovery. In some cases, all the nests in a cluster will fail so the cluster cannot even be identified. Because the initial z_j influences the likelihood that all nests in the cluster will be destroyed and later unavailable for discovery, the z_j of the discovered clusters are a biased sample from N (0, σ^2), the mean of which will be shifted to the left toward the less frail. This will be most problematic in situations where some clusters have few nests initiated to begin with, and an especially troublesome scenario is when the random effect is associated with both the number of nests initiated in a cluster as well as survival in the cluster (i.e., birds should avoid nesting in habitat where success is likely to be low). Additional work is needed to better understand the practical significance of this issue and to develop strategies for addressing it.

Frailty models for left-truncated data have received relatively little attention in survival analysis (Huber-Carol and Vonta 2004, Jiang et al. 2005), and more work is needed before reasonable guidelines can be given on this. Natarajan and McCulloch (1999) present some models of heterogeneity for nest-survival data, but their approach appears to be difficult to relate to a standard hazards-based frailty approach. With the increasing interest in including spatial information into ecological analyses, this problem is especially urgent because spatial correlation in survival models is most conveniently accounted for with frailty models (Banerjee et al. 2003). Extending such analyses to left-truncated data is an important and challenging problem that should be a research priority.

Before leaving the topic of frailties, it is interesting to note their relationship with covariates. Suppose the failure process obeys the regression relationship:

$$ln\ (\Lambda_t) = \gamma + X,$$

where we assume the baseline γ does not depend on age and X is some continuous covariate. If we do not observe X and fit just a baseline model, we will observe that the baseline γ_t declines with age due to the frailty effect induced by X, despite the fact that an individual nest's hazard is not age-dependent. This points out the importance of allowing for flexible baselines as one explores different models.

ESTIMATION AND PREDICTION

We used the relationship

$$S(t) = \exp\left[-\sum_{i=1}^{t}\exp(\gamma_i)\right]$$

to obtain the estimates displayed on Fig. 3. The ESTIMATE statement in SAS PROC NLMIXED could be used to obtain standard errors as well. We now briefly consider what this is an estimate of, and what assumptions are involved. For the estimate of $S(t)$ to have meaning, the samples on which it was based must have been representative of some population of interest. The ideal situation would be to have a representative sample of all initiated nests, but delayed discovery and resulting left-truncation ensures this is usually unobtainable. But what we can hope for is that when we discover a nest at age r, it is representative of all initiated nests that then survive to age r. If this condition is met, a correctly specified likelihood takes care of the left-truncation issues.

What might cause a nest discovered at age r not to be representative of all initiated nests that survive to age r? This can occur whenever the discovery of active nests is also associated with covariates that affect survival. For example, suppose active nests are more easily discovered close to water, and suppose independently of this, nests close to the water have higher survival. Such enhanced discovery will bias the number of close water nests in the sample above and beyond the bias caused by their higher survivability alone. The result will be that the estimate of $S(t)$ is in turn biased high and not representative of all initiated nests.

On the other hand, the regression evaluation of covariates does not require that the sample be representative of the active nests and indeed sample collection may attempt to disproportionately obtain nests with particular covariate values for increased power.

This emphasizes the importance of carefully planned sampling designs that weigh the various goals of survival estimation versus covariate assessment.

A goal closely related to that of estimation is that of prediction. That is, if we observed that cover density, say X, is associated with nest survival, it would be interesting to predict how overall survival would respond if X were manipulated. This is a nontrivial problem, and involves estimating the distribution of X associated with the nests at the time of initiation. This problem is considered by Shaffer and Thompson (*this volume*). Extending these considerations to random effects models, which involves integrating over the random effects distribution, seems especially challenging.

DISCUSSION

Our primary goal was to embed nest survival into the biostatistical approach to survival analysis. This provides both a sound theoretical foundation as well as a large toolbox from which to choose techniques. Such a unified framework permits judging the strengths and weaknesses of recently proposed nest survival techniques, such as the logistic-exposure model (Shaffer 2004a) or Kaplan-Meier and Cox applications (Nur et al. 2004). From basic survival-analysis considerations, we propose a new class of nest-survival analyses based on the complementary log-log link function. This framework is well-suited for use with weakly structured hazard models, which combine the flexibility of nonparametric models with the stability of fully parametric procedures.

Given their immense popularity in human biostatistics, some readers may be surprised that we did not devote more attention to fully nonparametric procedures. Fully nonparametric approaches work remarkably well for untruncated and right-censored data (Meier et al. 2004), but the resulting enthusiasm should not be automatically conferred to the left-truncated and interval-censored situation. Indeed, unless at least a few nests are discovered on the day of initiation, left-truncation will even prevent the fully nonparametric estimation of the survival function. Weakly structured approaches, while not a panacea, ameliorate these problems to a large extent.

Many weakly structured procedures, including those presented here, can be thought of as attempts to approximate the hazard function with a piecewise polynomial spline function. Piecewise models such as we presented are the simplest example, and constitute a 0-order B-spline basis. Smoother approximations can be obtained by specifying more complex splines, but this comes at the cost of additional parameters to estimate. A very appealing solution would be to employ a penalized spline approach (Gray 1992, Cai and Betensky 2003), but software is unavailable.

Although some theoretical holes still exist (e.g., frailty models), in general nest-survival theory has progressed well beyond the readily available software. It would be nice to be able to avoid the arbitrariness of the piecewise hazard approach with either an optimally smoothed spline (Gray 1992, Heisey and Foong 1998) or Bayesian approach (He et al. 2001, He 2003), but user-friendly software that includes regression analysis is not yet available. Theoretical and practical work is needed to extend the ideas of model goodness-of-fit and residuals from the continuous monitoring situation (Therneau and Grambsch 2000) to interval-censoring. User-friendly software which would allow covariate analysis of both survival and discovery probabilities is needed for the general Case III situation (Heisey 1991).

ACKNOWLEDGMENTS

Special thanks are due to Stephanie Jones, who helped improve both the substance and form of this paper. Christine Bunck, Bobby Cox, Ken Gerow, and an anonymous reviewer provided many helpful comments and suggestions. Douglas Johnson and the late Albert T. Klett collected the data used in our examples.

APPENDIX 1. INTERVAL-CENSORED EXAMPLES.

```
libname local '';
options ls=75 ps=50;
data a;
  set local.bwteal;
  run;

/*
Variables in the data set are:
nestid   (nest id)
firstday (age on first day of interval)
lastday  (age on last day of interval)
success  (whether interval was survived(1) or not(0))
d2road   (covariate; distance to road)
*/

/* Basic macro used by all methods; corresponds to pseudo-code in text */

%MACRO CASE2ML;
  PROC NLMIXED DATA=A DF=99999;
   %INITPARM;
   ARRAY GAMMA {*} X1-X35;
   %GAMMAMOD;
   CUMHAZ = 0;
   DO DAY = firstday to lastday-1;
     DAYCUMHZ = EXP(GAMMA[DAY]);
     CUMHAZ = CUMHAZ + DAYCUMHZ;
   END;
   SURVIVE = EXP(-CUMHAZ);
   MODEL success~BINARY(SURVIVE);
   %ESTIMATE;
   RUN;
%MEND;

/* ------------------------------------------------------------ */

TITLE 'PROGRAM A-1: Constant hazard; Johnson-Bart-Robson model';

%MACRO INITPARM;
  PARMS g1=-3.3;
%MEND;

%MACRO GAMMAMOD;
  DO AGE = 1 TO 35;
   GAMMA [AGE] = g1;
  END;
%MEND;

%MACRO ESTIMATE;
  ESTIMATE 'DSR' EXP(-EXP(g1));
%MEND;

%CASE2ML;

/* ------------------------------------------------------------ */

TITLE 'PROGRAM A-2: Piecewise constant hazard; weakly structured';

%MACRO INITPARM;
  PARMS g1=-3 g2=-3 g3=-3 g4=-3 g5=-3 g6=-3 g7=-3;
%MEND;

%MACRO GAMMAMOD;
  DO AGE = 1 TO 35;
```

```
  IF   (AGE LE 5)    THEN GAMMA [AGE] = g1;
  ELSE IF(AGE LE 10) THEN GAMMA [AGE] = g2;
  ELSE IF(AGE LE 15) THEN GAMMA [AGE] = g3;
  ELSE IF(AGE LE 20) THEN GAMMA [AGE] = g4;
  ELSE IF(AGE LE 25) THEN GAMMA [AGE] = g5;
  ELSE IF(AGE LE 30) THEN GAMMA [AGE] = g6;
  ELSE GAMMA [AGE] = g7;
  END;
%MEND;

%MACRO ESTIMATE;
  ESTIMATE 'DAILY BASELINE, INTERVAL 1' EXP (-EXP (g1));
  ESTIMATE 'DAILY BASELINE, INTERVAL 2' EXP (-EXP (g2));
  ESTIMATE 'DAILY BASELINE, INTERVAL 3' EXP (-EXP (g3));
  ESTIMATE 'DAILY BASELINE, INTERVAL 4' EXP (-EXP (g4));
  ESTIMATE 'DAILY BASELINE, INTERVAL 5' EXP (-EXP (g5));
  ESTIMATE 'DAILY BASELINE, INTERVAL 6' EXP (-EXP (g6));
  ESTIMATE 'DAILY BASELINE, INTERVAL 7' EXP (-EXP (g7));
%MEND;

%CASE2ML;

/* ---------------------------------------------------------------- */

TITLE 'PROGRAM A-3: Weibull hazard';

%MACRO INITPARM;
  PARMS rho=1 loglam=-3;
%MEND;

%MACRO GAMMAMOD;
  GAMMA [1] = rho*loglam + LOG(1);
  DO AGE = 2 TO 35;
  GAMMA [AGE] = rho*loglam + LOG(AGE**rho - (AGE-1)**rho);
  END;
%MEND;

%MACRO ESTIMATE;
%MEND;

%CASE2ML;

/* ---------------------------------------------------------------- */

TITLE 'PROGRAM A-4: Constant hazard with covariate';

%MACRO INITPARM;
  PARMS g1=-3.3 beta=0;
%MEND;

%MACRO GAMMAMOD;
  DO AGE = 1 TO 35;
   GAMMA [AGE] = g1 + beta*d2road;
  END;
%MEND;

%MACRO ESTIMATE;
  ESTIMATE 'Hazard Ratio' EXP(beta);
%MEND;

%CASE2ML;

/* ---------------------------------------------------------------- */
```

```
TITLE 'PROGRAM A-5: Piecewise constant hazard with covariate';

%MACRO INITPARM;
  PARMS g1=-3 g2=-3 g3=-3 g4=-3 g5=-3 g6=-3 g7=-3 beta=0;
%MEND;

%MACRO GAMMAMOD;
  DO AGE = 1 TO 35;
  IF   (AGE LE 5)    THEN GAMMA [AGE] = g1;
  ELSE IF(AGE LE 10) THEN GAMMA [AGE] = g2;
  ELSE IF(AGE LE 15) THEN GAMMA [AGE] = g3;
  ELSE IF(AGE LE 20) THEN GAMMA [AGE] = g4;
  ELSE IF(AGE LE 25) THEN GAMMA [AGE] = g5;
  ELSE IF(AGE LE 30) THEN GAMMA [AGE] = g6;
  ELSE GAMMA [AGE] = g7;
  GAMMA [AGE] = GAMMA [AGE] + beta*d2road;
  END;
%MEND;

%MACRO ESTIMATE;
  ESTIMATE 'Hazard Ratio' EXP(beta);
%MEND;

%CASE2ML;

/* ------------------------------------------------------------ */

TITLE 'PROGRAM A-6: Weibull hazard with covariate';

%MACRO INITPARM;
  PARMS rho=1 loglam=-3 beta=0;
%MEND;

%MACRO GAMMAMOD;
  GAMMA [1] = rho*loglam + LOG(1) + beta*d2road;
  DO AGE = 2 TO 35;
  GAMMA [AGE] = rho*loglam + LOG(AGE**rho - (AGE-1)**rho) + beta*d2road;
  END;
%MEND;

%MACRO ESTIMATE;
  ESTIMATE 'Hazard Ratio' EXP(beta);
%MEND;

%CASE2ML;

/* ------------------------------------------------------------ */

TITLE 'PROGRAM A-7: Constant odds with covariate';

%MACRO INITPARM;
  PARMS t1=-3.3 alpha=0;
%MEND;

%MACRO GAMMAMOD;
  DO AGE = 1 TO 35;
   GAMMA [AGE] = log(log(1 + exp(t1 + alpha*d2road)));
  END;
%MEND;

%MACRO ESTIMATE;
  ESTIMATE 'Odds Ratio' EXP(alpha);
%MEND;

%CASE2ML;

/* ------------------------------------------------------------ */
```

```
TITLE 'PROGRAM A-8: Piecewise constant odds with covariate';

%MACRO INITPARM;
  PARMS t1=-3 t2=-3 t3=-3 t4=-3 t5=-3 t6=-3 t7=-3 alpha=0;
%MEND;

%MACRO GAMMAMOD;
  DO AGE = 1 TO 35;
  IF   (AGE LE 5)    THEN GAMMA [AGE] = log(log(1 + exp(t1 + alpha*d2road)));
  ELSE IF(AGE LE 10) THEN GAMMA [AGE] = log(log(1 + exp(t2 + alpha*d2road)));
  ELSE IF(AGE LE 15) THEN GAMMA [AGE] = log(log(1 + exp(t3 + alpha*d2road)));
  ELSE IF(AGE LE 20) THEN GAMMA [AGE] = log(log(1 + exp(t4 + alpha*d2road)));
  ELSE IF(AGE LE 25) THEN GAMMA [AGE] = log(log(1 + exp(t5 + alpha*d2road)));
  ELSE IF(AGE LE 30) THEN GAMMA [AGE] = log(log(1 + exp(t6 + alpha*d2road)));
  ELSE GAMMA [AGE] = log(log(1 + exp(t7 + alpha*d2road)));
  END;
%MEND;

%MACRO ESTIMATE;
  ESTIMATE 'Odds Ratio' EXP(alpha);
%MEND;

%CASE2ML;

/* ------------------------------------------------------------ */

TITLE 'PROGRAM A-9: Piecewise constant hazard with covariate';

%MACRO INITPARM;
  PARMS g1=-3 g2=-3 g3=-3 g4=-3 g5=-3 g6=-3 g7=-3 alpha=0 beta=0;
%MEND;

%MACRO GAMMAMOD;
  DO AGE = 1 TO 35;
  IF   (AGE LE 5)    THEN GAMMA [AGE] = g1;
  ELSE IF(AGE LE 10) THEN GAMMA [AGE] = g2;
  ELSE IF(AGE LE 15) THEN GAMMA [AGE] = g3;
  ELSE IF(AGE LE 20) THEN GAMMA [AGE] = g4;
  ELSE IF(AGE LE 25) THEN GAMMA [AGE] = g5;
  ELSE IF(AGE LE 30) THEN GAMMA [AGE] = g6;
  ELSE GAMMA [AGE] = g7;
  GAMMA [AGE] = GAMMA [AGE] + (alpha + beta * (AGE-15))*d2road;
  END;
%MEND;

%MACRO ESTIMATE;
%MEND;

%CASE2ML;
```

APPENDIX 2. KAPLAN-MEIER AND COX MODEL EXAMPLES.

```
libname local '';
options ls=75 ps=50;
data a;
  set local.bwteal;
  run;

/*
Variables in the data set are:
nestid   (nest id)
firstday (age on first day of interval)
lastday  (age on last day of interval)
success  (whether interval was survived(1) or not(0))
d2road   (covariate; distance to road)
*/

PROC SORT; BY nestid firstday;

DATA onerec;
  SET a;
  RETAIN entry;
  BY nestid firstday;
  IF first.nestid THEN entry = firstday - 1; /* visits at start of day */
  IF last.nestid THEN OUTPUT;

DATA onerec;
  SET onerec;
  IF success THEN time = lastday - 1;
  ELSE time = (firstday + lastday)/2 - 1;
  RUN;

TITLE 'Program B-1: KME model';
PROC PHREG data=onerec;
  MODEL time * success(1)=/;
  BASELINE OUT=out2 SURVIVAL=s2;
  RUN;

TITLE 'Program B-2: GKME model';
PROC PHREG data=onerec;
  MODEL time * success(1)=/ENTRY=entry;
  BASELINE OUT=out1 SURVIVAL=s1;
  RUN;

TITLE 'Program B-3: GKME model with covariate';
PROC PHREG data=onerec;
  MODEL time * success(1)=d2road/ENTRY=entry;
  RUN;

TITLE 'Program B-4: KME model with covariate';
PROC PHREG data=onerec;
  MODEL time * success(1)=d2road;
  RUN;
```

Studies in Avian Biology No. 34:34–44

EXTENDING METHODS FOR MODELING HETEROGENEITY IN NEST-SURVIVAL DATA USING GENERALIZED MIXED MODELS

Jay Rotella, Mark Taper, Scott Stephens, and Mark Lindberg

Abstract. Strong interest in nest success has led to advancement in the analysis of nest-survival data. New approaches allow researchers greater flexibility in modeling nest-survival data and provide methods for relaxing assumptions and accounting for potentially important sources of variation. The most flexible method uses linear-logistic models with a random-effects framework to both incorporate potential covariate effects and model remaining heterogeneity. With the goal of increasing the use of more flexible methods, we provide additional detail regarding linear-logistic mixed models and their implementation. We use an example dataset to (1) demonstrate data preparation for analysis in PROC NLMIXED of SAS, (2) describe the use of code for evaluating competing models, (3) illustrate implementation of models with and without random effects and that evaluate potential effects of observer visits to nests, and (4) present methods of obtaining estimates of nest-survival rate for various covariate conditions of interest. We also conduct Monte Carlo simulations to evaluate the performance of linear-logistic mixed models of nest-survival data. We present the results of evaluation for one scenario and show that the estimation procedure as implemented in PROC NLMIXED is effective and that simulation can be used to gain insights into the advantages and disadvantages of various study designs. We encourage the development of further advancements that will allow greater flexibility in modeling.

Key Words: generalized mixed model, nest survival, population dynamics, random-effects statistics.

AMPLIACIÓN DE MÉTODOS PARA MODELAR LA HETEROGENEIDAD DE DATOS DE SOBREVIVENCIA DE NIDO UTILIZANDO MODELOS GENERALIZADOS MEZCLADOS

Resumen. El fuerte interés respecto a al éxito de nido, ha llevado al avance del análisis de datos de sobrevivencia de nido. Nuevos enfoques permiten a los investigadores tener mayor flexibilidad en el modelaje de datos de sobrevivencia de nido, y proveer métodos para suavizar las suposiciones y el conteo de fuentes potenciales importantes de variación. El método más flexible utiliza modelos lineares logísticos con un marco de efectos al azar, tanto para incorporar efectos covariantes potenciales, como para modelar la heterogeneidad restante. Con el objeto de incrementar la utilización de métodos más flexibles, proporcionamos detalle adicional respecto a modelos lineares logísticos mezclados y su implementación. Utilizamos un ejemplo de conjunto de datos para (1) demostrar la preparación de datos para el análisis en PROC NLMIXED de SAS, (2) describir la utilización del código para evaluar modelos competentes, (3) ilustrar la implementación de modelos con o sin efectos al azar y que evalúan potenciales efectos de visitas observadas a nidos, y (4) presentar métodos de estimaciones obtenidos de tasas de sobrevivencia de nido para varias condiciones covariantes de interés. También condujimos simulaciones Monte Carlo para evaluar el desempeño de modelos lineares logísticos mezclados de datos de sobrevivencia de nido. Presentamos los resultados de la evaluación para un escenario y mostramos que el procedimiento de estimación como el implementado en PROC NLMIXED es efectivo, y que la simulación puede ser utilizada para aumentar la penetración en las ventajas y desventajas de varios diseños de estudios. Promovemos el desarrollo de futuros adelantos que permitan mayor flexibilidad en el modelaje.

Methods for estimating nest survival rate have received considerable attention (Mayfield 1961, Johnson 1979, Bart and Robson 1982, Natarajan and McCulloch 1999, Farnsworth et al. 2000, Dinsmore et al. 2002). Williams et al. (2002) provide a useful review of historical development, available approaches, and estimation programs. Information regarding how daily survival rates and overall nest success are calculated is provided by Dinsmore et al. (2002).

The Mayfield (1961) method, either in its original form or as expanded by Johnson (1979) and Bart and Robson (1982), requires the assumption of a constant daily survival rate for all nests in a sample over the time period being considered. However, heterogeneity in daily survival rates among members of the study population can cause estimates of nest success and, in some cases, daily survival rate to be biased (Farnsworth et al. 2000, Rotella et al. 2000).

To allow greater flexibility in modeling nest-survival data in the presence of heterogeneity, numerous publications have presented methods for relaxing assumptions and account for potentially important sources of variation

(Dinsmore et al. 2002, Rotella et al. 2004, Stanley 2004a). Most troubling has been the assumption of the absence of overdispersion. Overdispersion occurs when the variance of the response variable exceeds the nominal variance. Overdispersion can be caused by lack of independence among animals and heterogeneity in the probabilities beyond that specified by the model. Overdispersion in count-based models can have profound inferential consequences. If not adjusted for, overdispersed count data will lead to inter-related problems: (1) model-selection procedures selecting over-parameterized models, (2) hypothesis tests that are too liberal, and (3) parameter confidence intervals that are too short (Lebreton et al. 1992, Fitzmaurice 1997, Ennis 1998). Lebreton et al. (1992) introduced a quasi-likelihood-based adjustment of a generalized variance-inflation factor. This adjustment influences both model identification and parameter confidence intervals but not parameter estimates (Lebreton et al. 1992).

Quasi-likelihood is not the only device for coping with overdispersion. An alternative approach is to model explicitly the random effects generating the overdispersion (Hinde and Demetrio 1998, Lee and Nelder 2000). The most flexible methods explicitly for nest-survival analysis were linear-logistic models that use covariate-based fixed effects and random effects to incorporate overdispersion (Natarajan and McCulloch 1999). Their approach can also incorporate nest-encounter probabilities (Pollock and Cornelius 1988, Bromaghin and McDonald 1993a, McPherson et al. 2003).

Explicitly modeling fixed and random effects in a generalized mixed model is an attractive way of addressing overdispersion. First, because the random effects are estimated jointly with the fixed effects, there will be a reduction in bias of the estimated fixed effects. As with normal mixed models, this effect is generally small (Cox 1983, McCullagh and Nelder 1989), but on occasion, as with normal mixed models, more substantial differences can occur. Secondly, comparisons of models incorporating random effects in a variety of ways yield greater biological insight into the genesis of the overdispersion than does the calculation of a single overarching variance-inflation factor. Such insight may lead to the inclusion of further covariates in the fixed effects that reduce the overdispersion. Williams et al. (2002:349) concluded that the approach is a reasonable and natural way to view nest survival, but also noted that, at present, the complexity of the computations may limit the ability of many biologists to apply this approach. To date, this impairment appears real, because we are unaware of any published study that has implemented the full approach.

Despite the computational complexities of mixed models, several benefits can be gained from using mixed models when they are appropriate. In some situations, the precision of estimates will be increased. Incorporation of random effects can allow one to make broader inferences. For example, if a random effect of study site is present and mixed models are used, inferences can be made about the actual population of study sites from which samples were drawn. In contrast, if fixed-effects-only models were used and each study site were treated as a fixed effect, then inferences would be limited to only those specific sites used in the study. Finally, information about random effects can motivate thinking about the process underlying the structure of the data and missing covariates that could be measured in the future to explain the random effects.

Mixed models are appropriate if levels of some covariates represent all possible levels, or at least the levels for which inferences are desired (these are fixed factors), whereas for others covariates, the levels observed are only a random sample of a larger set of potential levels of interest (these are random factors; Breslow and Clayton 1993, Littell et al. 1996, Pinheiro and Bates 2000). Examples of covariates that might be treated as random effects are study site or individual. This is true because it will often be the case that the particular experimental units such as the sites or individuals studied are selected at random from the population of sites or individuals, which are of interest. Pinheiro and Bates (2000: 8) stated that they are random effects because they represent a deviation from an overall mean. Thus, the effect of choosing a particular site, year, or individual may be a shift in the expected response value for observations made on that experimental unit relative to those made on other experimental units experiencing the same levels for the fixed effects. In other words, multiple observations made on the same site, year, or individual may be correlated, and if so, this should be accounted for in the analysis.

In a broad discussion of data analysis, Littell et al. (1996) stated they believe that valid statistical analysis of most data sets requires mixed-model methodology. Given the potential utility of such an approach, our objective here is to provide further details of the method beyond those presented previously (Rotella et al. 2004, Shaffer 2004a, Stephens et al. 2005). Although some material presented here has been presented previously (Rotella et al. 2004), we repeat it here to provide a more coherent treatment of the subject. We also provide additional information of how to implement the technique by analyzing an example dataset. In so doing, we review the programming statements written that can be used with SAS (SAS Institute 2004) for conducting necessary computations for a suite of candidate models, and consider a variety of important aspects of interpreting the output from generalized mixed models of daily survival rates. Sturdivant et al. (*this volume*) developed a goodness-of-fit test for the nest-survival model reviewed here, and they illustrate its implementation with the same example dataset used here and in Rotella et al. (2004). We conclude by presenting alternative analysis approaches that could be used and by pointing out the need for future improvements.

A GENERALIZED LINEAR-MIXED-MODELS APPROACH FOR NEST SURVIVAL

The nest-survival model employed by Stephens et al. (2005) generalizes the model described by Bart and Robson (1982). The model employs a generalized linear-models approach (McCullagh and Nelder 1989) based on a binomial likelihood, where daily survival rates are modeled as a function of nest-, group-, and/or time-specific covariates. Daily survival rates can then be estimated from the resulting model and multiplied together, as appropriate, to estimate nest success.

To illustrate the model likelihood, let S_i (daily survival rate) denote the probability that a nest survives from day i to day i + 1. Consider a nest that was found on day k was active when revisited on day l, and was last checked on day m ($k < l < m$). Because the nest is known to have survived the first interval, its contribution to the likelihood for that interval is $S_k S_{k+1} \ldots S_{l-1}$. During the second interval, the nest either survives with probability $S_l S_{l+1} \ldots S_{m-1}$ or fails with probability $(1 - S_l S_{l+1} \ldots S_{m-1})$. The likelihood is thus proportional to the product of probabilities of observed events for all nests in the sample (Dinsmore et al. 2002).

A link function is used to characterize the relationship between daily survival rate and the covariates of interest. A variety of link functions can be used (White and Burnham 1999, Williams et al. 2002). Here, focus will be on use of the logit link (and the logistic inverse link) as it is the natural link for the binomial distribution (McCullagh and Nelder 1989). The logit link is frequently used in mark-resighting modeling, provides a flexible form, and bounds estimates of survival in the (0, 1) interval. Stephens et al. (2005) used the logit link in their work, and Lebreton et al. (1992) presented methods for estimating confidence intervals and back-transforming to model parameters and estimates of their variances and covariances when the logit link is used.

With the logit link, daily survival rate of a nest on day i is modeled as:

$$\frac{\exp(\beta_0 + \sum_j \beta_j x_{ji})}{1 + \exp(\beta_0 + \sum_j \beta_j x_{ji})}$$

where the x_{ji} (j = 1, 2, ..., J) are values for J covariates on day i and the are coefficients to be estimated from the data. Logit transformation of the above expression yields

$$\beta_0 + \sum_j \beta_j x_{ji}.$$

Thus, the relationship between the logit of S_i, i.e., $\ln(S_i/(1 - S_i))$, and the covariates is linear, whereas the relationship between S_i and the covariates is logistic or S-shaped. Once the are estimated, an estimate of the parameter(s) of interest (S_i) is generated by solving the regression equation and then back transforming the answer. Note that the above formulation allows daily survival rates to vary among groups of nests based on group-specific covariates, among individual nests based on nest-specific covariates, and among days based on time-specific covariates.

The parameters β_j of competing models are estimated iteratively by the method of maximum likelihood using computer code designed for generalized linear models. Accordingly, a variety of likelihood-based methods are available for evaluating competing models. Likelihood ratio tests can be used to formally test hypotheses about whether specific covariates are associated with variation in nest survival (but see Anderson and Burnham 2002). If a set of candidate models is used, then information-theoretic measures such as Akaike's information criterion (AIC) and AIC_c can be used to select which model or models to use for inference (Burnham and Anderson 2002). Model-selection inference will be most robust if the model set is selected a priori, but nevertheless, useful inferences of a weaker epistemic standing can still be made with a post hoc model set (Taper and Lele 2004).

Assumptions of the daily nest-survival model described here are: (1) homogeneity of daily survival rates as modeled (e.g., if the model contains nest age and no other covariates, then all nests of a given age are assumed to have the same daily survival rate), (2) nest fates are correctly determined on each visit after the first one, (3) nest discovery and subsequent nest checks do not influence survival (although see below for methods of modeling the effects of nest visits and relaxing this assumption), (4) nest fates are independent or sources of dependency are appropriately modeled, (5) all visits to nests are recorded, (6) the age of nests can be determined correctly so that the day of hatching, or fledging can be determined correctly, and (7) nest checks are conducted independently of nest fate. If data are available for more than one interval length, an extension of the model presented by Rotella et al. (2000) can be used to evaluate and possibly relax assumption three. Assumption one, by virtue of the fact that daily survival rates can be modeled as a function of group-, nest-, and time-specific covariates, is far less restrictive than is necessary for Mayfield's (1961) method. If nest age is to be considered in models of daily survival rate, then it is also assumed that the age of nests can be determined correctly when first found (Dinsmore et al. 2002). Although it is analytically possible to estimate age-specific daily survival rates for nests of all ages, logistical constraints may prevent this. If nests are rarely found early in the laying stage, then estimates may be lacking or very imprecise for this period. If visits to nests containing older nestlings commonly cause nestlings to leave their nest prior to the expected fledging age, then it may not be possible to estimate daily survival rates for nests beyond some threshold age. The method requires no assumptions about when nest losses occur during the interval between two nest visits.

DATA INPUT FORMAT

Each row of data input typically contains information for one observation interval for an individual nest as this allows a complete record of all nest observations and nest visits to be entered. An observation interval is the length of time (*t*; an integer, typically measured in days) between any two successive nest visits. Note that for a given nest, different observation intervals do not need to be of the same length. The minimum data that must be provided are the length of the interval (*t*) and the nest's fate for the interval (Ifate; 1 = successful, 0 = unsuccessful). In addition, individual and group- and time-specific covariates can be included. For example, the date (StartDate) and age of the nest (StartAge) at the start of the interval might be recorded. If each interval starts with an observer visit to the nest, and all visits involve similar activities by observers, then information about observer visits is not needed even if one is interested in estimating observer effects on daily survival rate (see below). However, if all intervals do not start with a nest visit such as when telemetry is used to remotely check nest status for many intervals, or, if activities during visits differ among occasions, then it may be useful to provide information about the nature of visits with a covariate (see below). Other individual covariates such as habitat measures associated with the nest site could be included. Covariates associated with a group of nests (group covariates) such as weather or year could also be included.

To illustrate the data format, we utilize an example dataset for Mallard (*Anas platyrhynchos*) nests that were monitored during 2000 in the Coteau region of North Dakota as part of a larger study (Stephens et al. 2005). The example dataset contains nest-, group- and time- specific covariates and contains information from 1,585 observation intervals for 565 nests monitored on 18 sites during a 90-d nesting season. Interval lengths ranged from 1–18 d and were most commonly 4, 5, or 6 d (frequencies of observations for interval lengths of 1, 2, 3, 4, 5, 6, 7, 8, 10, 11, 12, and 18 d were 50, 27, 150, 475, 542, 245, 63, 21, 4, 6, 1, and 1, respectively). Here, the following subset of the covariates measured by Stephens et al. (2005) was considered for each observation interval: (1) nest age at the start of the interval (Age, 1–35 d), (2) day of the nesting season at the start of the interval (Date, 1–90), (3) vegetative visual obstruction at the nest site (Robel et al. 1970), (4) the proportion of the study site (10.4 km^2) containing the nest that was in grassland cover (PpnGr), (5–7) the habitat type in which the nest was located (three dummy variables were used to distinguish among native grassland (NatGr), planted nesting cover (PlCov), wetland vegetation (Wetl), and roadside right-of-way (Road), (8) study site (Site), and (9) nest-visitation status on each day of the interval (Ob, a dummy variable coded as 1 on the day a nest was visited and 0 otherwise). Nest-visitation status did not appear in the original input file as this variable was created with programming statements during the analysis (see below).

Data were originally recorded in interval-specific form, and thus, each row of data contained information for one observation interval for an individual nest (Table 1). All analyses that appear below were conducted on this dataset and input format. However, it is possible to do a great deal of modeling with a reduced version of the dataset. If the possible observer effects on daily survival rates are not of interest, and, if nest age and date are the only nest-specific time-varying covariates to be considered, then the interval-specific data can be collapsed with no loss of information.

TABLE 1. INPUT FORMAT FOR INTERVAL-SPECIFIC NEST-SURVIVAL DATA.[A]

ID	Species	Site	Hab	Int	t	IFate	SDate	Sage	Robel	PpnGr
1	MALL	14	PlCov	1	5	1	1	1	4.50	0.96
1	MALL	14	PlCov	2	5	1	6	6	4.50	0.96
1	MALL	14	PlCov	3	4	1	11	11	4.50	0.96
1	MALL	14	PlCov	4	6	1	15	15	4.50	0.96
1	MALL	14	PlCov	5	5	1	21	21	4.50	0.96
1	MALL	14	PlCov	6	5	1	26	26	4.50	0.96
1	MALL	14	PlCov	7	4	1	31	31	4.50	0.96
2	MALL	14	PlCov	1	5	1	1	3	0.88	0.96
2	MALL	14	PlCov	2	5	1	6	8	0.88	0.96
2	MALL	14	PlCov	3	4	1	11	13	0.88	0.96
2	MALL	14	PlCov	4	6	0	15	17	0.88	0.96
2,206	MALL	16	Road	1	4	1	73	13	6.00	0.80
2,206	MALL	16	Road	2	5	1	77	17	6.00	0.80
2,206	MALL	16	Road	3	4	1	82	22	6.00	0.80
2,206	MALL	16	Road	4	3	1	86	26	6.00	0.80

[a] (ID—nest number, Species—species code, Site—study site, Hab—habitat code, Int—observation interval, t—interval length (d), Ifate—nest fate for the interval, SDate—date at the start of the interval, SAge—nest age at the start of the interval, Robel—vegetative visual obstruction at nest site, and PpnGr—proportion of grassland cover on the 10.4-km² study site.

The critical information to retain for each nest consists of (1) the age of the nest when it was found, (2) the day the nest was found, (3) the last day the nest was checked alive, (4) the last day the nest was checked, and (5) the fate of the nest (successful or unsuccessful) on the last visit. For successful nests, the dates in items (3) and (4) above will be equal, and the entire set of re-visit intervals can be collapsed into one interval (one row of data with Ifate = 1). For unsuccessful nests, the dates in items (3) and (4) above will be different, and data may need to be presented as one or two rows of data depending on the timing of nest failure. For nests that fail by the end of the first re-visit interval, the relevant data are contained in a single row of data (with Ifate = 0). For nests that fail after the end of the first re-visit interval, two rows of data are required: one row of data will consist of a successful interval (Ifate = 1) starting on the day the nest was found (item 2 above) and ending on the last day the nest was checked alive (item 3 above); a second interval (with Ifate = 0) will start on the last day the nest was checked alive (item 3 above) and end on the last day the nest was checked (item 4 above). Analysis of data in this reduced format will not be considered further here but can be accomplished with the methods described below. It is worth noting that data in this reduced format do prevent the evaluation of possible visit effects on nest fate.

GENERALIZED MIXED MODELS IN PROC NLMIXED

Because interval lengths typically are >1 d, it is necessary to use programming statements from within NLMIXED to iteratively do the logit survival value for each of the days in an interval (see below). Through programming statements, covariates such as date and age that vary across an interval in a predictable fashion can be included in each day of an interval.

Consider a model that includes (1) a covariate x_1 that does not vary by time, (2) nest age, and (3) date. This method models a nest's fate for a given interval as:

$$Ifate_i = \prod_{k=0}^{t-1} \left(\frac{\exp(\beta_0 + \beta_1 x_{1i} + \beta_2(StartAge_i + k) + \beta_2(StartDate_i + k)}{1 + \exp(\beta_0 + \beta_1 x_{1i} + \beta_2(StartAge_i + k) + \beta_2(StartDate_i + k)} \right).$$

Applying this model to a 2-d observation interval that started on the 20th day of the nesting season for a nest that was 15-d old at the start of the interval and whose value for covariate x_1 was 10 would yield:

$$\left(\frac{\exp(\beta_0 + \beta_1 10 + \beta_2 15 + \beta_2 20)}{1 + \exp(\beta_0 + \beta_1 10 + \beta_2 15 + \beta_2 20)} \right) \left(\frac{\exp(\beta_0 + \beta_1 10 + \beta_2 16 + \beta_2 21)}{1 + \exp(\beta_0 + \beta_1 10 + \beta_2 16 + \beta_2 21)} \right)$$

Because the method allows covariates to be specified differently on different days within an interval, observer effects on nest survival can be modeled in a straightforward manner. Specifically, an index variable (visit) is created with programming statements such that it takes on a value of one for the first day of an interval (day the nest was visited) and zero otherwise. This variable can then be used to evaluate whether variation in daily survival rates was associated with observer visits. If additional covariates contain information on the nature of a nest visit, these covariates can be allowed to interact with the visit variable to test for their potential influence on survival rate. To illustrate, consider a 2-d interval and a model that includes the effect of an observer visit and a single covariate (x_1) on daily survival rate.

$$Ifate_i = \left(\frac{\exp(\beta_0 + \beta'_0\, visit + \beta_1 x_{1i})}{1 + \exp(\beta_0 + \beta'_0\, visit + \beta_1 x_{1i})} \right)$$

$$\left(\frac{\exp(\beta_0 + \beta_1 x_{1i})}{1 + \exp(\beta_0 + \beta_1 x_{1i})} \right)$$

Thus, procedures in SAS allow for examination of a rich collection of models for nest-survival data.

As stated earlier, the NLMIXED procedure also allows models to include random effects (associated with a single factor) as well as fixed effects; hence, it allows mixed models (SAS Institute 2004). The random effects are assumed to follow normal distributions, typically with zero mean and unknown variances. In the NLMIXED procedure, all random effects must be associated with a single factor (termed the subject variable in PROC NLMIXED) for which multiple observations made at the same level of the factor may be correlated. For example, study site might be considered as a factor having random effects on nest survival because fates of nests on the same site (same factor level) might be correlated to some degree.

Multiple random effects can be modeled in PROC NLMIXED as long as they are all associated with a single factor, and we now consider some of the mixed models that may be of interest in studies of nest survival. When presenting mixed models below, we follow a common convention (Littell et al. 1996) of using Greek symbols to refer to regression coefficients that are assumed to be fixed effects and using Latin symbols to refer to those that are random. Because random effects in PROC NLMIXED are assumed to follow normal distributions, typically with zero mean and unknown variances, it is appropriate to consider them as a random sample of deviations from some population regression model (Littell et al.1996). Thus, random effects can be used to model deviations in one or more of the fixed-effect coefficients (various combinations of the intercept and slope terms) associated with different levels of the random factor being considered.

To illustrate, consider a 1-d interval and a model that includes the effect of a single covariate (x_1) on daily survival rate. A model that also includes a random effect of study site on the model's intercept term would be:

$$Ifate_{ij} = \left(\frac{\exp((\beta_0 + b_{0j}) + \beta_1 x_{1i}}{1 + \exp((\beta_0 + b_{0j}) + \beta_1 x_{1i}} \right),$$

where b_{0j} represents the random effect on the intercept term that is associated with the jth study site. Alternatively, a model with

$$Ifate_{ij} = \left(\frac{\exp(\beta_0 + (\beta_1 + b_{1j}) x_{1i}}{1 + \exp(\beta_0 + (\beta_1 + b_{1j}) x_{1i}} \right)$$

could be used to include a random effect on the model's slope term, (b_{1j}), or both types of random effects could be considered:

$$Ifate_{ij} = \left(\frac{\exp((\beta_0 + b_{0j}) + (\beta_1 + b_{1j}) x_{1i})}{1 + \exp((\beta_0 + b_{0j}) + (\beta_1 + b_{1j}) x_{1i})} \right).$$

PROC NLMIXED will estimate the values for each of the elements of the variance-covariance matrix of the random effects that are specified in the model. For example, if the model included both b_{0j} and b_{1j}, the variance of each random effect and the covariance between b_{0j} and b_{1j} would be estimated.

In the NLMIXED procedure, mixed models are fit by maximizing an approximation to the likelihood that is integrated over the random effects (SAS Institute 2004). Accordingly, calculations may take some time and convergence is not guaranteed. Starting values are not required for PROC NLMIXED but may be helpful, and the procedure has tools for implementing a variety of starting values. The procedure has a variety of integral approximations and alternative optimization techniques available, and these may be helpful in some cases. Finally, it may be useful to run fixed-effects models prior to mixed models to obtain reasonable starting values for the fixed-effects parameters of mixed models.

PROC NLMIXED also enables one to calculate user-specified functions of the parameters and to compute the approximate standard errors using the delta method (Seber 1982). This is useful for estimating daily survival rate and nesting success from the parameter estimates by back-transformation through the inverse or logistic link function (Lebreton et al. 1992). If the user specified function only involves parameters representing fixed effects, the calculation can be made in SAS with an ESTIMATE statement. If on the other hand, the specified function includes random effects, either alone or in combination with fixed effects, a PREDICT statement must be used (SAS Institute 2004).

EXAMPLE ANALYSIS OF NEST-SURVIVAL DATA IN PROC NLMIXED

Here, we use the example Mallard dataset and a brief model list to illustrate the implementation of the methods described here using PROC NLMIXED and simple programming statements (Rotella et al. 2006). We analyzed a set of 10 fixed-effects models and two mixed models using PROC NLMIXED, where study site was considered a random effect in the mixed models (Table 2). Models included various combinations of nest-, group-, and time-specific covariates. This list included simple models that have been commonly employed in past studies of nest survival. The simplest model was an intercept-only model that held S_i constant for all groups, nest ages, dates, and habitat conditions, and which is similar to that of Johnson (1979) and Bart and Robson (1982). A model that allowed S_i to vary among groups (nests in different habitat types in this example) was analogous to (but more efficient than) conducting a stratified analysis with methods of Johnson (1979) and Bart and Robson (1982) and testing for homogeneity among group-specific survival rates with methods of Sauer and Williams (1989). For a more thorough analysis of the full data set from which this example was extracted, see the analysis and results presented by Stephens et al. (2005).

Of the 12 models considered, the two most parsimonious models both included a random effect of site (Table 2): the site-to-site process variance (Burnham et al. 1987) was estimated as 0.089 (SE = 0.052) by the better of these two models. Stephens et al. (2005) provided possible explanations for the presence of the random effect in these data, e.g., differing predator communities among sites. The second-most parsimonious model (ΔAIC_c = 0.33) provided some evidence of a negative effect of observer visits on daily survival rate for the day of a nest visit = ($\hat{\beta}$ = -0.844, SE = 0.629). The point estimate indicates that the effect was potentially of a size that is of interest, but the lack of precision makes inference difficult. For example, on a site with 50% grassland cover, daily survival for a 15-d old nest would be predicted as 0.911 (SE = 0.033, 95% CI = 0.842–0.981) if it were visited and 0.960 (SE = 0.010, 95% CI = 0.939–0.981) otherwise, where the estimates were obtained using the ESTIMATE statement (one statement for each of the two scenarios) of PROC NLMIXED (Rotella et al. 2006). It is noteworthy that models that held daily survival rate constant or simply allowed it to vary by habitat type, which are the only model types that have been used in many recent publications on nest survival (see above), received no support when compared to the models discussed above ($\Delta AIC_c \geq 15.10$).

Once one has chosen an approximating model of daily survival rate, one is interested in using that model and its estimated parameter values to obtain estimates of survival over multiple days for various covariate conditions. For example, one might be interested in estimating the probability that a Mallard nest on a site with 85% grassland cover would survive the 35 d from nest initiation to hatching. To do so involves working with functions of random variables (the estimated coefficients of the approximating model). For a model that considers nest age and proportion grass on the site, one can calculate the probability that a nest would survival from age one through age 35 on a site with 85% grassland as follows:

$$\hat{S}_{35days} = \prod_{Age=1}^{35} \left(\frac{\exp(\hat{\beta}_0 + \hat{\beta}_1 Age + \hat{\beta}_2(0.85))}{1+\exp(\hat{\beta}_0 + \hat{\beta}_1 Age + \hat{\beta}_2(0.85))} \right),$$

where S_{35days} is the probability of surviving 35 days. To derive an estimate of the variance of the transformation of the three estimated

TABLE 2. SUMMARY OF MODEL-SELECTION RESULTS OBTAINED IN PROC NLMIXED (SAS INSTITUTE 2004) FOR FIXED-EFFECTS AND MIXED MODELS OF DAILY SURVIVAL RATE FOR MALLARD NESTS STUDIED BY STEPHENS ET AL. (2005) IN NORTH DAKOTA.

Model	K	AIC_c	ΔAIC_c	w_i
$\beta_0+\beta_1 \times$ Age+$\beta_2 \times$ PpnGr+$b_1 \times$ site	4	1,554.013	0.000	0.529
$\beta_0+\beta_1 \times$ Age+$\beta_2 \times$ PpnGr+$\beta_3 \times$ Ob+$b_1 \times$ site	5	1,554.340	0.327	0.449
$\beta_0+\beta_1 \times$ Age+$\beta_2 \times$ PpnGr+$\beta_3 \times$ Ob	4	1,562.265	8.252	0.009
$\beta_0+\beta_1 \times$ Age+$\beta_2 \times$ PpnGr	3	1,563.010	8.996	0.006
$\beta_0+\beta_1 \times$ Age	2	1,564.066	10.053	0.003
$\beta_0+\beta_1 \times$ Age+$\beta_2 \times$ Robel	3	1,565.906	11.892	0.001
$\beta_0+\beta_1 \times$ Age+β_2NatGr+$\beta_3 \times$ CRP+$\beta_4 \times$ Wetl	5	1,567.344	13.330	0.001
$\beta_0+\beta_1 \times$ PpnGr	2	1,567.368	13.355	0.001
β_0	1	1,569.117	15.103	0.000
$\beta_0+\beta_1 \times$ Robel	2	1,570.775	16.762	0.000
$\beta_0+\beta_1 \times$ Date	2	1,570.826	16.813	0.000
$\beta_0+\beta_1 \times$ NatGr+$\beta_2 \times$ CRP+$\beta_3 \times$ Wetl	4	1,571.957	17.944	0.000

coefficients (or random variables) in the equation above random variables, one could use the delta method (Seber 1982, Williams et al. 2002) or simulation methods such as bootstrapping.

MONTE CARLO SIMULATIONS IN PROC NLMIXED

Monte Carlo Simulation (MCS) offers an empirical approach to examining a variety of characteristics of estimation results from analysis procedures (Fan et al. 2003). Distributional characteristics of estimated regression coefficients, and their associated estimates of precision, are of interest here, especially for the random effects, as these methods have not been employed for nest-survival data previously. MCS is also useful for evaluating the consequences of violating assumptions and for evaluating different potential sampling schemes that may be used in future research. Thus, we developed computer code that creates nest-survival data for multiple sites in interval-specific form according to an underlying model of interest (Rotella et al. 2006). Nests can vary from one another in terms of their characteristics, and nest-visitation intervals can vary in length among the samples. Nest fates, which can be affected by both fixed effects and a single random factor, are obtained using random sampling techniques. The data are then analyzed using models of interest, key results are stored, the process is repeated many times, and summary statistics of interest are calculated. The code can be adjusted to accommodate different scenarios.

Here we provide the results for a scenario where survival for an interval was modeled as

$$Ifate_{ij} = \prod_{k=0}^{t-1}\left(\frac{\exp((\beta_0 + b_{0j}) + \beta_1 x_{1i})}{1+\exp((\beta_0 + b_{0j}) + \beta_1 x_{1i})}\right).$$

In the simulation, the true parameter values for the fixed effects were $\beta_0 = 2.0$ and $\beta_1 = 1.75$. The random effect of study site was normally distributed (mean = 0, variance = 0.25). The covariate x_1 was a uniformly distributed nest-specific covariate (range = 0–1.0). For each simulation, data were generated for 375 nests (25 nests per site for 15 different sites).

Summary statistics based on 1,000 simulations provide evidence that the method produces estimates with little bias and reasonable precision (Table 3), at least for the scenario described above. Coverage for 95% confidence intervals was close to the nominal level for each of the parameters estimated. We have reached similar conclusions for a variety of scenarios where the samples of nests are balanced across sites.

The design of samples and experiments in a mixed model context is a subject in need of both further research and communication. But, based on the results of our simulation work, it seems clear that the bare-minimum data requirements of the mixed-models approach described here are as follows: data from ≥five levels of the factor being modeled as a random effect and data from ≥20 nests per level of the random factor. These are not hard and fast rules. For example, if one were to have data from only five study sites, then it would likely be best to treat site as a fixed effect as information is likely available from too few sites to allow accurate inference to the universe from which study sites might have been selected. Further, although 20 nests per site may be adequate for estimating landscape-level parameters if a substantial number of sites are surveyed, 20 nests per site will not yield an accurate estimate of the random effect at any given site. If estimating daily survival rate at the specific sites surveyed is of interest, considerably greater sample sizes will be required.

Heisey et al. (*this volume*) provide an important caveat regarding estimation in the presence of random effects. In typical studies of nest survival, data are left-truncated because some nests that fail early are not included in the sample (Heisey et al., *this volume*). Under these circumstances, it is easy to imagine scenarios for which estimates of survival will be biased high to some extent because nests in the sample over-represent nests with higher underlying survival rates (Heisey et al., *this volume*).

TABLE 3. SUMMARY STATISTICS FOR 1,000[a] MONTE CARLO SIMULATIONS.

			95% confidence interval		
Parameter[b]	Mean estimate	Mean SE	Lower bound	Upper bound	Coverage
β_0	2.13	0.19	1.72	2.54	0.98
β_1	1.76	0.30	1.17	2.36	0.97
σ^2_{site}	0.24	0.12	–0.02	0.50	0.97

[a] The general convergence criterion of PROC NLMIXED was satisfied for 985 of the 1,000 datasets. The 15 problematic datasets were discarded, and results presented are for the remaining 985 datasets. However, based on our experience with this procedure, convergence would likely have been achieved for many, if not all, of the remaining 15 datasets had we changed features such as the number of iterations, starting values, etc. (SAS Institute 2004).

[b] True parameter values were 2.0, 1.75, and 0.25, respectively.

To illustrate, we use an example where study site is a factor that is treated as a random effect. Under such a situation, a sample of sites having the same values for covariates treated as fixed effects will still vary in terms of their underlying survival rates: the unmeasured fixed effects responsible for the random effect will cause some of these sites to be better than others. All else being equal (nest densities, and search effort), sample sizes will be larger for those study sites that are associated with higher survival rates because nests in such settings are expected to survive longer and thus, have a greater chance of entering the sample. When the sample sizes are positively correlated with survival rates, estimates of survival will be biased high to some extent because nests in the sample over-represent nests with higher underlying survival rates (Heisey et al., *this volume*).

Given this fact, we conducted additional simulations for a modified version of the scenario described above in which the model structure and values for the fixed and random effects remained the same but the sample sizes varied among sites. Specifically, sample size per site was a function of the fixed effect and the random effect for the site, which caused a site's sample size to be positively related to a study site's survival rate (number of nests per site varied from ~10 for the poorest sites to ~25 on the best sites). We then evaluated the performance of two models: the generating model (mixed model) and a fixed-effects only model, which did not model the random effect. In accordance with statements made by Heisey et al. (*this volume*), estimates from the mixed model were biased. For the scenario investigated, the estimated parameter values were biased such that estimated survival rates were too high and the variation associated with the random effect of site was too low (true β_0 = 2.0, estimated β_0 = 2.5 [SE = 0.19]; true β_1 = 1.75, estimated β_1 = 1.3 [SE = 0.33]; true $\sigma^2_{\text{random effect}}$ = 0.25, estimated $\sigma^2_{\text{random effect}}$ = 0.14 [SE = 0.10]).

We believe that this result should not be interpreted as calling into question the use of mixed models for nest-survival data. This point is made clearer by considering the estimates that were obtained from the fixed-effects model for these simulations. Parameter estimates from a fixed-effects-only model had the same level of bias as did the estimates from the mixed model, but these estimates were more precise. Thus, if one were to avoid the use of mixed models, the bias due to analyzing left-truncated data in the presence of random effects would still persist. But, the inferences about the estimates would be falsely made more confidently, and, because the random effect would not be estimated, there would be no opportunity to detect the presence of heterogeneity in the data above and beyond the fixed effects. The primary problem is whether random effects are in the data.

Clearly, if random effects might be present in left-truncated nest-survival data, the study design will have to be carefully considered. Simulation work completed to date indicates that balanced designs (equal numbers of nests found across levels of the covariate being treated as a random factor) effectively deals with this potential problem. Given that one will not typically know prior to data analysis whether or not random effects will exist in the data, it seems prudent to adjust search effort such that balanced samples are achieved. The issue of bias from left truncation has received little attention, and more work is needed to determine the magnitude of the problem under typical sampling scenarios.

Optimal study design will, of course, depend upon the particulars of each study such as effect sizes for factors of interest, process variation in system, and complexity of models being considered. In planning a study, if one knows that great variation is likely among levels of the random factor, obtaining data from nests over many levels of that factor will be more useful than will be obtaining large numbers of nests per level of that factor. For example, data from many sites with fewer nests/site will be better than data from few sites with many nests/site. Simulations can be used to gain insights into the advantages and disadvantages of various study designs, especially if pilot data are available to guide the simulation, for example simulation code that can be readily modified to suit the specific circumstances of different studies is available (Rotella et al. 2006).

FUTURE DIRECTIONS

The methods reviewed above provide several advances over the typical analysis methods used for most studies of nest survival. We have provided examples of some of the utility of the approach, but other innovative uses of existing methods will likely be useful. For example, survival rates of individual young within nests could be investigated with individual nest treated as a random effect and covariates such as egg (or nestling) size and age considered as fixed effects. However, improvement is possible. In some studies, it will be desirable to examine the relationship between nest survival and multiple random factors. For example, in studies that are well replicated in space and time (>10 sites replicated for >10 yr), it will be of interest to estimate the variance components associated with the random effects of both study site and year.

Interest is growing in the consequences of individual variation in vital rates (Link et al. 2002), and results from models that incorporate heterogeneity indicate that the consequences on population dynamics can be substantial (Cam et al. 2002). Further, results show that sources of variation among individuals cannot always be sufficiently accounted for by age, year, or environmental conditions. That is, it may be necessary to allow each individual to have a unique mortality risk (Service 2000). One method of doing so is to use the methods described here to treat the individual as a random effect, but this cannot be done while also considering another random factor such as site or year. Thus, it is apparent that hierarchical models that permit multiple random factors are desirable.

Heisey et al. (*this volume*) raised an important issue regarding possible bias in estimates made from left-truncated data containing overdispersion due to random effects. We suggested above that balanced sampling designs may effectively deal with the problem. But, the issue of estimation bias from left truncation has received little attention, and more work is needed to (1) determine the magnitude of the problem under various sampling scenarios, (2) evaluate possible solutions that can be implemented during the analysis stage such as equal weighting of data from all levels of the random factor regardless of sample sizes, and (3) make recommendations regarding the appropriate interpretation of estimates from studies of nest-survival data when random effects may be present.

The methods presented here do not consider detection probability for nests with different characteristics as do some other methods (Pollock and Cornelius 1988, Bromaghin and McDonald 1993a, McPherson et al. 2003). Accordingly, these methods provide estimates that are conditional on the data set (Pollock and Cornelius 1988, Bromaghin and McDonald 1993a, McPherson et al. 2003). We note that the sample can also be non-representative of the entire population because the nature of the survey methods, birds, or both is such that nests can not be found until they are above some minimum age. For example, in some species it may be the case that nests can not be found prior to incubation because the birds spend little time on nests prior to incubation and the birds provide the cues used by researchers for finding nests. Or, for studies of species in which nest visits cause premature fledging, data may not be available for nests above some threshold age.

The methods presented here do not consider several other situations that may be encountered in nesting studies for some species. For some species, nest age will be a covariate of interest but be unknown for many nests (Stanley 2004a). Also, typical assumptions about the distributions of hatching and fledging events may be violated in some studies (Etterson and Bennett 2005). Under such circumstances, it will also be difficult to know the exact fledging date for nests and to time final nest checks such that nest fates can be unambiguously determined (Manolis et al. 2000). Given that these circumstances will occur regularly for some species of interest, it would be valuable to future studies of nest survival if methods for dealing with ambiguities in aging and determining fate (Manolis et al. 2000; Stanley 2000a, 2004; Etterson and Bennett 2005) could be incorporated into the methods presented here.

It seems clear that the analysis methods described here provide improvements but do not allow for complete evaluation of possible heterogeneity in nest-fate data. Analysis methods presented by Natarajan and McCullach (1999) provide conceptual solutions to the problem. However, exact solutions of the likelihoods presented are computationally intractable for modestly complex problems. An approach using accurate approximate solutions is essential, and extensions of work done by Lele and Taper (2002) may be useful in the future. Use of Markov Chain, Monte Carlo methods in a Bayesian approach (Link et al. 2002), may also prove useful for solving such complex problems with nest-survival data (He et al. 2001, He 2003). Bayesian alternatives to the approach described here can be implemented in readily available software packages such as program MARK (White and Burnham 1999) or WinBUGS (Lunn et al. 2000). Regardless of the approach used, we expect more complex hierarchical models to provide logical extensions to the concepts and analysis methods presented here. Of course, such analyses will require excellent data sets resulting from sound sampling designs.

The advances made by Mayfield (1961) and others (Johnson 1979, Bart and Robson 1982) are seminal and pivotal for continued improvement in the approaches that we use for analysis. Those historic approaches have some restrictive and potentially unrealistic assumptions that may cause biased estimates and misleading inferences if the investigator is not cautious about such pitfalls. Recent advancements in the analysis of nest-survival data and the availability of appropriate computer programs have raised the standards for assessing this important attribute of avian biology. Investigators that acquire nest-fate data collected from properly designed studies, which provide a representative sample of nests, should use these analysis tools to make reliable inference about nest survival. We therefore submit that analysis of nest-survival data in the framework provided by programs such as MARK (Dinsmore et al. 2002) or SAS (Stanley 2000, 2004a; Shaffer 2004a) should be a minimum level of analysis for modern, avian studies. We hope investigators with specific interests in the effects of heterogeneity on nest-survival estimates or those with specific questions about levels of process variation in their population will consider some of the advanced methods described here and elsewhere.

ACKNOWLEDGMENTS

We thank S. J. Dinsmore, T. L. Shaffer, T. R. Stanley, and G. C. White for comments on the analysis methods and G. C. White for helpful suggestions on SAS code and calculating effective sample size. S. J. Dinsmore, J. Bart, and an anonymous reviewer provided valuable comments on an earlier draft of the manuscript. Information provided by D. M. Heisey, D. H. Johnson, T. L. Shaffer, and G. C. White regarding random effects and left-truncated data helped improve this paper and is greatly appreciated. This work was funded by Ducks Unlimited, Inc., Great Plains Regional Office and Ducks Unlimited Canada, Institute for Wetland and Waterfowl Research. We thank D. Coulton, A. Fanning, M. Fillsinger, J. Mehlos, J. Olszak, and J. Walker for assistance in collecting field data used for the example data set and the staff of Ducks Unlimited, Great Plains Regional Office for extensive logistical support during the field-work.

Studies in Avian Biology No. 34:45–54

A SMOOTHED RESIDUAL BASED GOODNESS-OF-FIT STATISTIC FOR NEST-SURVIVAL MODELS

RODNEY X. STURDIVANT, JAY J. ROTELLA, AND ROBIN E. RUSSELL

Abstract. Estimating nest success and identifying important factors related to nest-survival rates is an essential goal for many wildlife researchers interested in understanding avian population dynamics. Advances in statistical methods have led to a number of estimation methods and approaches to modeling this problem. Recently developed models allow researchers to include a covariate that varies by individual and time. These techniques improve the realism of the models, but they suffer from a lack of available diagnostic tools to assess their adequacy. The PROC NLMIXED procedure in SAS offers a particularly useful approach to modeling nest survival. This procedure uses Gaussian quadrature to estimate the parameters of a generalized linear mixed model. Using the SAS GLMMIX macro, we extend a goodness-of-fit measure that has demonstrated desirable properties for use in settings where quasi-likelihood estimation is used. The statistic is an unweighted sum of squares of the kernel-smoothed model residuals. We first verify the proposed distribution under the null hypothesis that the model is correctly specified using the new estimation procedure through simulation studies. We then illustrate the use of the statistic through an example analysis of daily nest-survival rates.

Key Words: binary response, generalized linear mixed model (GLMM), goodness-of-fit, kernel smoothing, logistic regression, nest survival.

UNA ESTADÍSITICA BASADA EN AJUSTE DE CALIDAD RESIDUAL SUAVIZADA PARA MODELOS DE SOBREVIVENCIA DE NIDO

Resumen. Estimar el éxito de nido e identificar factores importantes relacionados a las tasas de sobrevivencia de nido es una meta esencial para muchos investigadores de vida silvestre interesados en el entendimiento de las dinámicas poblacionales de aves Avances en métodos estadísticos han dirigido a un número de métodos de estimación y acercamiento para modelar este problema. Recientemente, modelos que han sido desarrollados permiten a los investigadores incluir una covariante que varia por individuo y tiempo. Estas técnicas mejoran la realidad de los modelos, pero padecen de la falta de disponibilidad de herramientas de diagnóstico para valorar qué tan adecuadas son. El procedimiento PROC NLMIXED en SAS ofrece un acercamiento particularmente útil para modelar la sobrevivencia de nido. Este procedimiento utiliza cuadratura Gaussiana para estimar los parámetros de un modelo generalizado linear mezclado. Usando el SAS GLMMIX macro aumentamos la medida de calidad de ajuste, la cual ha demostrado propiedades deseables para utilizar en ajustes donde la estimación de probabilidad aparente es utilizada. La estadística es una suma no cargada de cuadrados de residuos del modelo suavizado kernel. Primero verificamos la distribución propuesta bajo la hipótesis nula de que el modelo está correctamente especificado, utilizando el nuevo procedimiento de estimación a través de estudios de simulación. Después ilustramos el uso de la estadística por medio de un ejemplo de análisis de tasas de sobrevivencia de nido diarias.

Dinsmore et al. (2002), Stephens (2003), and Shaffer (2004a) concurrently developed methods for modeling daily nest-survival rates as a function of nest, group, and/or time-specific covariates using a generalized linear model (McCullagh and Nelder 1989) with binomial likelihood (see Rotella et al. [2004] for review). All of the methods use the likelihood presented by Dinsmore et al. (2002) and extend the model of Bart and Robson (1982). As with the commonly used Mayfield estimate (Mayfield 1975), overall nest success is estimated by raising daily survival rates to the power of n, where n is the number of days in the nesting cycle.

The model likelihood involves the probability a nest survives from day i to i + 1, denoted S_i (the daily survival rate). As an example, consider a nest found on day k, and active when revisited on day l, and last checked on day m ($k < l < m$). The nest survived the first interval and therefore contributes $S_k S_{k+1} \ldots S_{l-1}$ to the likelihood. The probability the nest failed would be one minus the product so that the likelihood is proportional to the product of probabilities of observed events for all nests in the sample (Dinsmore et. al. 2002).

Using the logit link, the daily survival rate of a nest on day i is modeled:

$$\text{logit}(\pi_i) = \log\left(\frac{\pi_i}{1-\pi_i}\right) = \beta_0 + \sum_k \beta_k x_{ik} \quad (1)$$

where we let π_i denote the daily probability of nest survival and the x_{ik} are values of the K covariates. The outcome is modeled as a series of Bernoulli trials, where the number of trials is t for a nest surviving an interval of t days, and one for a nest failing within the interval (Rotella et al. 2004). Stephens (2003) implements nest-survival models in PROC NLMIXED of SAS (SAS Institute 2004) using programming statements within the procedure to perform iterative logistic regression for each day in an interval. This implementation allows the modeler to include random as well as fixed effects, as do recent implementations (Dinsmore et al. 2002) of program MARK (White and Burnham 1999).

The random-effects logistic-regression model accounts for clustering structures inherent in the data. Variables whose observations can be thought of as random samples from the population of interest are candidates for inclusion into the model as random effects (Pinheiro and Bates 2000). Examples of covariates in nest-survival studies that might be treated as random effects are study site, year, or individual nest. In this case, with two levels, we might suppose that either or both coefficients (intercept and slope of the linear logit expression) vary randomly across groups. Suppose for simplicity that we have a single covariate. If we treat the intercept and slope as random, the logistic model of (1) becomes:

$$\text{logit}(\pi_{ij}) = \log\left(\frac{\pi_{ij}}{1-\pi_{ij}}\right) = \beta_{0j} + \beta_{1j}x_{ij} \qquad (2)$$

with $\beta_{0j} = \beta_0 + \mu_{0j}$, and $\beta_{1j} = \beta_1 + \mu_{1j}$. The random effects are typically assumed to have a normal distribution so that $\mu_{0j} \sim N(0, \sigma_0^2)$ and $\mu_{1j} \sim N(0, \sigma_1^2)$. Further, the random effects need not be uncorrelated so we have, in general, $\text{Cov}(\mu_{0j}, \mu_{1j}) = \sigma_{01}$.

Substituting the random effects into expression (2) and rearranging terms, the model is:

$$\text{logit}(\pi_{ij}) = \log\left(\frac{\pi_{ij}}{1-\pi_{ij}}\right) = (\beta_0 + \beta_1 x_{ij}) + (\mu_{0j} + \mu_{1j}x_{ij}) \qquad (3)$$

The model in (3) suggests a general matrix representation for the random effects logistic-regression model given by:

$$\mathbf{y} = \pi + \varepsilon$$

where $\mathbf{y}$ is an $N \times 1$ vector of the binary outcomes (survived or not), π the vector of probabilities, and ε the vector of errors.

The response is related to the data through the link function:

$$\text{logit}(\pi) = \mathbf{X}\beta + Z\mu \qquad (4)$$

Here, $\mathbf{X}$ is a design matrix for the fixed effects. For the model given in expression (4) this is an $N \times 2$ matrix with first column of ones and the second column the vector of values for the predictor variable x_{ij}. The vector β is the corresponding $p \times 1$ vector of parameters for the fixed portion of the model. In our example this is the 2×1 vector $(\beta_0, \beta_1)'$. Under the $BIN(\pi)$ assumption (BIN referring to the binomial distribution), the vector of level-one errors, ε, has mean zero and variance given by the diagonal matrix of binomial variances: $\text{Var}(\varepsilon) = \mathbf{W} = \text{diag}[\pi_{ij}(1 - \pi_{ij})]$.

The term $Z\mu$ in (4) introduces random effects and represents the difference between the random effects and standard logistic-regression models. The matrix $\mathbf{Z}$ is the design matrix for the random effects. In the example in (3), $\mathbf{Z}$ is an $N \times 2J$ matrix as there are two random effects. The matrix is block diagonal, with the blocks corresponding to the groups in the hierarchy (in this example, the level two groups indexed from $j = 1$ to J). The vector μ is a $2J \times 1$ vector of coefficients corresponding to the random effects. The elements are the random intercept and random slope for each group in the hierarchy. The vector has assumed distribution $\mu \sim N(0, \Omega)$ with block diagonal covariance matrix.

Several methods are available for estimating the parameters of the hierarchical logistic-regression model (Snijders and Bosker 1999). The methods include numerical integration (Rabe-Hesketh et al. 2002), use of the E-M algorithm (Dempster et al. 1977) or Bayesian techniques to optimize the likelihood (Longford 1993), and quasi-likelihood estimation (Breslow and Clayton 1993).

By conditioning on the random effects and then integrating them out, an expression for the maximum likelihood is available. Although this integral is difficult to evaluate, estimation techniques involving numerical integration, such as adaptive Gaussian quadrature, recently have been implemented in many software packages including SAS PROC NLMIXED (SAS Institute 2004). These methods are computationally intensive and do not always result in a solution. As a result, in most cases, the technique cannot handle larger models (such as data with more than two hierarchical levels or a large number of groups or random effects).

In this paper, we wish to extend the goodness-of-fit measure introduced in the next section beyond the quasi-likelihood estimation approach (Breslow and Clayton 1993) used in its development and testing. Specifically, the SAS GLMMIX (SAS Institute 2004) macro was used in simulation studies to verify the theoretical distribution of the statistic (note that since that study, SAS has implemented the SAS GLMMIX procedure which can be used to obtain the same results). SAS GLMMIX implements a version of quasi-likelihood estimation which SAS refers to as PL or pseudo-likelihood (Wolfinger and O'Connell 1993). For the logistic-hierarchical model, a Taylor approximation is used to linearize the model. The estimation is then iterative between fixed and random parameters. These procedures suffer from known bias in parameter estimates (Rodriguez and Goldman 1995). In this paper, we extend the statistic to the less biased estimation approach of Gaussian quadrature available in PROC NLMIXED (SAS Institute 2004).

The Goodness-of-fit Measure

Various goodness-of-fit statistics are available for use in the standard logistic-regression setting, but none have been developed for use in the random effects version of the model. Recently, two approaches have been proposed that might extend to the nest-survival models discussed above. Pan and Lin (2005) suggest statistics to test each fixed effect and the link function in generalized linear mixed models (GLMM) which, taken together, would address overall model fit. Studying their approach in this setting is worthy of future research. The approach we examine here is a single statistic designed to measure overall model fit outlined by Sturdivant (2005) and Sturdivant and Hosmer (in press). They extend a residual based goodness-of-fit statistic used in standard logistic models to the case of the hierarchical logistic model. This statistic is based on the unweighted sum of squares (USS) statistic proposed by Copas (1989) for the standard logistic-regression model.

In the random effects logistic model, the statistic uses kernel-smoothed residuals. These smoothed residuals are a weighted average of the residuals given by:

$$\hat{\mathbf{e}}_{\mathbf{s}} = \mathbf{\Lambda}\hat{\mathbf{e}},$$

where Λ is the matrix of smoothing weights:

$$\Lambda = \begin{bmatrix} \lambda_{11} & & \lambda_{1n} \\ & \ddots & \\ \lambda_{n1} & & \lambda_{nn} \end{bmatrix} = \begin{bmatrix} \boldsymbol{\lambda}_1 \\ \\ \boldsymbol{\lambda}_n \end{bmatrix}.$$

The weights, λ_{ij}, produced using the kernel density are:

$$\lambda_{ij} = \frac{\mathbf{K}\left(\dfrac{|\hat{\pi}_1 - \hat{\pi}_j|}{h}\right)}{\sum_j \mathbf{K}\left(\dfrac{|\hat{\pi}_1 - \hat{\pi}_j|}{h}\right)} \qquad (5)$$

where K(ξ) is the Kernel density function and h is the bandwidth.

Previous research has explored three kernel-density functions commonly used in studies of standard logistic-regression models, and all three densities produced acceptable results (Sturdivant 2005, Sturdivant and Hosmer, in press). The uniform density used in a study of a goodness-of-fit measure in standard logistic regression (le Cessie and van Houwelingen 1991) is defined as:

$$K(\xi) = \begin{cases} 1 \text{ if } |\xi| < 0.5 \\ 0 \text{ otherwise} \end{cases}$$

A second choice used in standard logistic studies involving smoothing in the y-space (Hosmer et. al. 1997, Fowlkes 1987) is the cubic kernel given by:

$$K(\xi) = \begin{cases} 1 \text{ if } |\xi|^3 \text{ if } |\xi| < 1 \\ 0 \text{ otherwise} \end{cases}$$

The final choice was the Gaussian kernel density (Wand and Jones 1995) defined:

$$K(\xi) = \frac{1}{\sqrt{2\pi}} \exp\left(-\tfrac{1}{2}\xi^2\right)$$

The choice of kernel function is considered less critical than that of the bandwidth (Hardle 1990). The bandwidth, h, controls the number of observations weighted in the case of the uniform and cubic densities. The choice of bandwidth for the kernel-smoothed USS statistic is related, as well, to the number of subjects per cluster. Previous studies suggest a bandwidth weighting $0.5\sqrt{n}$ of the n residuals for relatively large clusters (>20 subjects) and weighting only $0.25\sqrt{n}$ for situations with smaller cluster sizes (Sturdivant 2005). For the Gaussian density, all observations are weighted. However, observations that are 2–3 SE outside of the mean effectively receive zero weight. The bandwidth then determines how many residuals are effectively given zero weight in the Gaussian case. Thus, the bandwidth choices for the Gaussian kernel place the selected number of observations within two standard deviations of the mean of the $N(0,1)$ density.

Regardless of the bandwidth criteria, a different bandwidth h_i is used for each $\hat{\pi}_i$ (Fowlkes 1987). The weights are then standardized so that they sum to one for each $\hat{\pi}_i$ by dividing by the total weights for the observation as shown in expression (5).

The goodness-of-fit statistic is then the USS statistic but using the smoothed rather than raw residuals:

$$\hat{S}_s = \sum_{i=1}^{n} \hat{e}_{si}^2 = \hat{\mathbf{e}}_\mathbf{s}{}' \hat{\mathbf{e}}_\mathbf{s}$$

The distribution of this statistic is extremely complicated due to the smoothing and the complexity of the hierarchical logistic model. Using an approach similar to that of Hosmer et. al. (1997), Sturdivant (2005) produced expressions to approximate the moments of the statistic. These moments are used to form a standardized statistic which, under the null hypothesis that the model is correctly specified, should have an asymptotic standard normal distribution:

$$Z_{\hat{S}} = \frac{\hat{S}_s - \mathrm{E}(\hat{S}_s)}{\sqrt{\mathrm{Var}(\hat{S}_s)}} \tag{6}$$

where:

$$\begin{aligned} E(\hat{S}_s) &= \mathbf{E[e'(I - \hat{M})'\Lambda'\Lambda(I - \hat{M})e} + \\ &\quad \mathbf{2\hat{g}'\Lambda'\Lambda(I - \hat{M})e + \hat{g}'\Lambda'\Lambda\hat{g}]} \\ &= \mathbf{trace\ [(I - \hat{M})'\Lambda'\Lambda(I - \hat{M})W]} + \\ &\quad \mathbf{\hat{g}'\Lambda'\Lambda\hat{g}} \end{aligned}$$

and:

$$\begin{aligned} \mathrm{Var}(\hat{S}_s) &= \sum_{i=1}^{n} \left[a_{ii}^2 w_i(1-6w_i)\right] + 2\,\mathrm{trace}\,\mathbf{(A\hat{W}A\hat{W})} + \\ &\quad \mathbf{b'\hat{W}b} + 2\sum_i a_{ii} b_i \pi_i (1-\pi_i)(1-2\pi_i) \end{aligned}$$

In these expressions $\mathbf{A} = \mathbf{(I - \hat{M})'\Lambda'\Lambda(I - \hat{M})}$, $\mathbf{b}' = \mathbf{2\hat{g}'\Lambda'\Lambda(I - \hat{M})}$, $\mathbf{M} = \mathbf{WQ[Q'WQ + R]^{-1}Q'}$ and $\mathbf{g} = \mathbf{WQ[Q'WQ + R]^{-1}R\delta}$. Further, $\mathbf{Q} = [\mathbf{X} \quad \mathbf{Z}]$ is the design matrix for both fixed and random effects, and

$$\hat{\boldsymbol{\delta}} = \begin{pmatrix} \hat{\boldsymbol{\beta}} \\ \hat{\boldsymbol{\mu}} \end{pmatrix}$$

the vector of estimated fixed and random effects. The other matrix in the expression involves the estimated random-parameter covariances and is defined:

$$\mathbf{R} = \begin{bmatrix} \mathbf{0} & \mathbf{0} \\ \mathbf{0} & \hat{\boldsymbol{\Omega}}^{-1} \end{bmatrix}$$

While complicated, the matrix expressions are easily implemented in standard statistical software packages using output of the random effects estimation (Sturdivant et al. 2006; Appendix 1).

To test model fit, the moments are evaluated using the estimated quantities from the model where necessary in expression (6). The standardized statistic is compared to the standard normal distribution. A large (absolute) value leads to rejecting the null hypothesis and calls into question the correctness of the specified model.

The asymptotic distribution is complicated but expected to be standard normal under a central-limit-theorem argument. Previous simulations studies have shown that the distribution holds under the null distribution not just for large samples, but for smaller samples likely to occur in practice (to include small cluster sizes) (Sturdivant 2005, Sturdivant and Hosmer, in press).

Simulation Study Results

The proposed goodness-of-fit statistic was developed and tested in hierarchical logistic-regression models fit using penalized quasi-likelihood (PQL) estimation. Stephens (2003) implements nest-survival models in PROC NLMIXED (SAS Institute 2004) using programming statements within the procedure to perform iterative logistic regression for each day in an interval. Rotella et al. (2004) demonstrate the value of this approach as it accounts for the time-varying covariates, in essence performing a discrete-time survival analysis. In addition, the estimation uses the less biased Gaussian quadrature estimation approach (SAS NLMIXED procedure) rather than PQL estimation.

Before accepting the kernel-smoothed USS statistic for use in such models, we performed simulations to validate its use with the different estimation schemes and in models with time-varying covariates. Theoretically, a residual-based goodness-of-fit measure would not be affected by the form of the model or the estimation method. However, the complexity of the models and the statistic, particularly in the presence of random effects and clustering, leads to the need to validate the theory when using a different procedure.

We were interested in examining the rejection rates of the statistic in settings similar to those of nest survival data for which Rotella et al. (2004) propose using PROC NLMIXED (SAS Institute 2004). Previous extensive simulations using the GLMMIX macro have shown that the statistic rejects at the desired significance (Sturdivant 2005). Here, we wish to confirm that this continues in the new setting and estimation scheme.

The simulations involve models typical of those found in nest-survival studies. In particular, the simulated data included a standard continuous fixed effect as well as a time- varying fixed effect. For nest-survival models, a random intercept or, in some instances, a random slope for the time varying covariate may be deemed appropriate. Thus, we simulated both situations. In each case, we created 1,000 replicates using a data structure with 20 clusters (sites) each including 20 subjects (nests). The simulated time intervals between nest visits were 5–8 d (chosen at random from a uniform distribution). The kernel-smoothed statistic was calculated using the cubic kernel and a bandwidth weighting $0.5\sqrt{n}$ of the residuals (the choice of bandwidth is discussed in the section on the goodness-of-fit measure). In this case, with N = 400 subjects (20 clusters of 20 subjects), this bandwidth choice means that 10 observations were weighted to produce each smoothed residual value.

The estimated moments for the statistic from the two simulation runs approximate the observed moments of the simulated statistical values (Table 1). Further, the empirical rejection rates at the 0.01, 0.05, and 0.10 significance levels are similar. The 95% confidence regions for the rejection rates at these three significance levels are 0.6%, 1.4%, and 1.9%, respectively. Only in the case of the 0.01 significance level for the random-slope model is the observed rejection rate outside of this interval. In that instance, the statistic rejects slightly more often than expected.

The case where the statistic appears to reject slightly too often deserves several comments. First, when the results of the goodness-of-fit test indicate a lack of model fit, the analyst should be prompted to further investigate the data and model, and not necessarily reject the model outright. Therefore, the slightly higher than expected rejection rate merely results in periodically investigating model fit under circumstances when researchers might not ordinarily do so. Further, the actual number of models used in the simulation of the random-slope model was 470 (of the 1,000 replications)—the NLMIXED procedure failed to converge (a well documented issue with the Gaussian quadrature estimation scheme in practice and not related to the goodness of fit). Thus, it is possible that with more simulations the actual rejection rate would converge to a value within the confidence region. In fact, the 95% confidence interval with only 470 replications is wider (0.9%) so that the observed rejection rate is even less; for a very sensitive rejection rate (0.01).

We conclude that the simulation results reported here confirm earlier papers (Sturdivant 2005, Sturdivant and Hosmer, in press) and suggest that the change in estimation method and the inclusion of time-varying covariate does not hurt the performance of the kernel smoothed USS statistic.

EXAMPLE

To illustrate the use of the statistic in a fitted model, we use data for Mallard (*Anas platyrhynchos*) nests monitored in 2000 in the Coteau region of North Dakota (Rotella et al. 2004). The data set we used contains 1,585 observations of 565 nests collected as part of a larger study. Rotella et al. (2004) analyzed the data using various techniques to account for the time varying covariates, in essence performing a discrete-time survival analysis. They estimated parameters for random effects models using Gaussian quadrature in PROC NLMIXED (SAS Institute 2004). We fit the same models and produced the kernel-smoothed USS statistic to measure overall model fit (Sturdivant et al. 2006; Appendix 1). The fixed effects of interest here include: nest age (1–35 d) and the proportion of grassland cover on the site containing the nest. The clusters or groups in this case are the 18 sites monitored during a 90-d nesting season.

The best random-effects model (Rotella et. al. 2004) included both nest age (treated as time varying) and proportion of grassland cover with a random intercept. With 18 nest sites (clusters) and 1,585 total observations, the bandwidth weighting more observations ($\frac{1}{2}\sqrt{1585}$) is

TABLE 1. SIMULATION STUDY RESULTS USING PROC NLMIXED WITH TIME VARYING COVARIATES (N = 1,000 REPLICATIONS FOR RANDOM INTERCEPT AND 470 FOR RANDOM SLOPE) AND CUBIC KERNEL USS STATISTIC.

Model	Kernel-smoothed statistic		Moment estimates		Rejection rates [c]		
	Mean	SD [a]	EV [b]	SD [c]	0.01	0.05	0.10
Random Intercept	12.5	2.0	12.1.	1.8	0.013	0.047	0.105
Random Slope	2.3	0.8	2.3	0.7	0.021	0.045	0.085

[a] SD = standard deviation.
[b] EV = expected value.
[c] Significance levels.

preferred. Using this bandwidth and the cubic kernel, the calculated statistic and moments are as follows: $\hat{S}_s$ = 15.3, E($\hat{S}_s$) = 13.8, Var($\hat{S}_s$) = 1.8, $Z_{\hat{S}}$ = 0.80, and P-value = 0.423.

Comparing the statistic to the standard normal distribution, we fail to reject the hypothesis of model fit (P = 0.42). Thus, we can conclude that the overall model specification has no problems and that this model is reasonable in terms of goodness-of-fit. Clearly, other possible considerations are possible in fitting models (such as the best model). The goodness-of-fit statistic is useful as shown in this example when the model building exercise is complete and the analyst wishes to verify the appropriateness of the final model selected. Note that, if desired, the goodness-of-fit statistic can be used as one would any other such statistic. For example, one might use it to evaluate the fit of the global model—such a procedure is often recommended when using an information-theoretic approach to model selection, and especially when model-averaging is done, in which case there may not be a clear choice of the model for which fit should be evaluated (Burnham and Anderson 2002). As discussed by Burnham and Anderson (2004), goodness-of-fit theory about the selected best model is a subject that has been almost totally ignored in the model-selection literature. In particular, if the global model fits the data, does the selected model also fit? Burnham and Anderson (2004) explored this question and provide evidence that in the case of AIC-based model selection that the selected best model typically does fit if the global model fits. However, they also point out that results can vary with the information criterion used to select among models as well as other particulars of the study in question. The goodness-of-fit statistic provided here should prove useful to future development of goodness-of-fit theory with regards to nest-survival data.

DISCUSSION

Our results suggest that the kernel-smoothed USS statistic is a reasonable measure of overall model fit in random effects logistic-regression models involving time-varying covariates and using Gaussian quadrature for estimation. This work is an important extension demonstrating that the USS statistic is valid in settings beyond the PQL procedures used in its development. Further, no other available tools exist to assess overall model fit in models which offer great value to wildlife researchers modeling nest survival. This statistic is easily implemented in software packages and is currently available for use with PROC NLMIXED (SAS Institute 2004) as well as the GLMMIX macro (SAS Institute 2004).

The power of the USS statistic deserves further exploration (Sturdivant and Hosmer, in press); this statistic has reasonable power to detect issues of fixed-effect specification in the presence of random effects (Sturdivant and Hosmer, in press). However, exactly how much power and what sort of model misspecification is detected is an area of current research.

Goodness-of-fit measures are designed to warn of potential problems with the selected model. However in using our methods, if the model fit is rejected it is currently not clear what an analyst should do to address issues with the model. In practice, the analyst should re-examine the model and the data to identify reasons (such as outliers or inaccurate data) for why the null hypothesis of model fit was rejected. This exploration will often offer insights leading to a more appropriate model. The use of the statistic in studies which fit a variety of models will provide information regarding the causes of null hypothesis rejection, and allow researchers to develop methods for improving model fit.

ACKNOWLEDGMENTS

We thank D. W. Hosmer for his role in development in the methods presented here, the Northern Great Plains Office of Ducks Unlimited, Inc. for financial support, and W. L. Thompson for facilitating our application of the method to nest-survival data. We thank K. Gerow and G. White for helpful review comments on an earlier draft of this manuscript.

APPENDIX 1. SAS CODE FOR THE EXAMPLE DATA ANALYSIS USED IN THIS PAPER IS AVAILABLE (STURDIVANT ET AL. 2006).

```
* MACRO used to produce the USS kernel-smoothed statistic ;
%MACRO u1kern1 ;
PROC IML ;
   USE piest ;
      read all var {ifate} into yvec ;    * RESPONSE VARIABLE NAME HERE ;
      read all var {pred} into pihat ;
   CLOSE piest ;
   USE west ;
      read all var {pred} into wvec ;
   CLOSE west ;

   ehat = yvec-pihat ;
   what = diag(wvec) ;
   n = nrow(pihat) ;
   getwt =  ceil(0.5*sqrt(n))+1 ;    * SELECT THE BANDWIDTH HERE ;

*  KERNEL SMOOTH ROUTINE ;

   wtmat = J(n,n) ;
   rx=J(n,1) ;
   do i=1 to n ;
        x = abs(pihat[i] - pihat);
        rx[rank(x)]=x;
        bw = rx[getwt] ;
        if bw = 0 then do ;
               bw = 0.0000000000001 ;
        end ;
        wtmat[,i] = x / bw ;
   end ;
   * Get Kernel density values and weights;
     * UNIFORM (-a,a) ;
   ukern = t(wtmat<1) ;
   icolsum = 1/ukern[,+] ;
   uwt = ukern # icolsum ;

     * CUBIC  ;
   ctemp = 1 - (t(wtmat))##3 ;
   ckern = ukern # ctemp ;
   icolsum = 1/ckern[,+] ;
   cwt = ckern # icolsum ;

     * NORMAL ;
   nkern = pdf('norm',t(2*wtmat)) ;
   icolsum = 1/nkern[,+] ;
   nwt = nkern # icolsum ;

* MOMENTS and TEST STATISTICS;

   USE mall ;          * NAMES OF FIXED DESIGN MATRIX HERE and data set ;
     read all var{lv3 sage PctGr4} into x ;    * Note: here lv3 is all ones so
              used as int ;
     read all var {site} into groups ; * NAME OF LEVEL2 VARIABLE HERE ;
   CLOSE mall ;
   zmat = design(groups) ;
   Q = x||zmat ;

   USE betahat ;
     read all var {Estimate} into betahat ;
   CLOSE betahat ;
   USE Randeff ;
     read all var {estimate} into muhat ;
   CLOSE Randeff ;
```

```
  USE Sigmahat ;
    read all var {estimate} into cov2 ;
  CLOSE Sigmahat ;
  icov2 = 1/cov2 ;
  icov2d=diag(icov2) ;
  icov2a = BLOCK(icov2d,icov2d,icov2d) ;
  icovbl2 = BLOCK(icov2a,icov2a,icov2a,icov2a,icov2a,icov2a);
* BLOCKS SAME NUMBER AS GROUPS ;

  faketop = j(ncol(x),ncol(x)+ncol(zmat),0) ;
  fakeleft = j(ncol(zmat),ncol(x),0) ;
  comb1 = fakeleft||icovbl2 ;
  R = faketop//comb1 ;

  dhat = betahat//muhat ;

  * CREATE g vector and M matrix ;

  mymat = inv( t(Q)*what*Q + R ) ;

  g = what * Q * mymat * R * dhat ;
  M = what * Q * mymat * t(Q) ;

  * CALCULATE TEST STATISTICS;

  im = I(nrow(M))-M ;

  midunif = t(uwt)*uwt ;
  midcube = t(cwt)*cwt ;
  midnorm = t(nwt)*nwt ;

  aunif = t(im)*midunif*im ;
  acube = t(im)*midcube*im ;
  anorm = t(im)*midnorm*im ;

  bunif = 2*t(im)*midunif*g ;
  bcube = 2*t(im)*midcube*g ;
  bnorm = 2*t(im)*midnorm*g ;

  Tuni = t(ehat)*midunif*ehat ;
  Tc = t(ehat)*midcube*ehat ;
  Tn = t(ehat)*midnorm*ehat ;

  * CALCULATE EXPECTED VALUES ;
  eunif = trace( aunif*what) + t(g)*midunif*g ;
  ecube = trace( acube*what) + t(g)*midcube*g ;
  enorm = trace( anorm*what) + t(g)*midnorm*g ;

  * CALCULATE VARIANCE ;
  temp1 = wvec#(1-6*wvec) ;
  temp3 = pihat#(1-pihat)#(1-2*pihat) ;

  tempu = (vecdiag(aunif))##2 ;
  tempc = (vecdiag(acube))##2 ;
  tempn = (vecdiag(anorm))##2 ;

  v1unif = sum(tempu#temp1) ;
  v2unif = 2* trace(aunif*what*aunif*what) ;
  v3unif = t(bunif)*what*bunif ;
  v4unif = 2*sum( (vecdiag(aunif))#bunif#temp3 ) ;

  v1cube = sum(tempc#temp1) ;
  v2cube = 2* trace(acube*what*acube*what) ;
  v3cube = t(bcube)*what*bcube ;
  v4cube = 2*sum( (vecdiag(acube))#bcube#temp3 ) ;
```

```
   v1norm = sum(tempn#temp1) ;
   v2norm = 2* trace(anorm*what*anorm*what) ;
   v3norm = t(bnorm)*what*bnorm ;
   v4norm = 2*sum( (vecdiag(anorm))#bnorm#temp3 ) ;

   vunif = v1unif + v2unif + v3unif + v4unif ;
   vcube = v1cube + v2cube + v3cube + v4cube ;
   vnorm = v1norm + v2norm + v3norm + v4norm ;

   cubestat = (Tc-ecube)/sqrt(vcube) ;
   normstat = (Tn-enorm)/sqrt(vnorm) ;
   unifstat = (Tuni-eunif)/sqrt(vunif) ;

   punif = 2*(1-probnorm(abs(unifstat))) ;
   pcube = 2*(1-probnorm(abs(cubestat))) ;
   pnorm = 2*(1-probnorm(abs(normstat))) ;

   print Tc ecube vcube cubestat pcube ;
   print Tn enorm vnorm normstat pnorm ;
   print Tuni eunif vunif unifstat punif ;

quit ; run ;
%MEND ;

* NEST DATA ;

data Mall; set Nests.mall2000nd;
 LV3 =1 ;                                 * ADD A COLUMN OF ONES FOR INTERCEPT ;
 if ifate=0 then ness+1;
 else if ifate=1 then ness+t;
/* create indicator variables for different nesting habitats */
    if hab=1 then NatGr=1; else NatGr=0;                    /* Native Grassland */
    if hab=2 or hab=3 or hab=9 then CRP=1; else CRP=0;      /* CRP & similar    */
    if hab=7 or hab=22 then Wetl=1; else Wetl=0;            /* Wetland sites    */
    if hab=20 then Road=1; else Road=0;                     /* Roadside sites   */
run;

Proc Sort data=Mall;
by site; run;

* FIT MODEL USING PROC NLMIXED;

PROC NLMIXED DATA=Mall tech=quanew method=gauss maxiter=1000;
parms B0=2.42, B2=0.019, B4=0.38, s2u=0.1;
  p=1;
      do i=0 TO t-1;
      if i=0 then Ob=1;
      else Ob=0;
           logit=(B0+u)+B2*(sage+i)+B4*PctGr4 ;
         p=p*(exp(logit)/(1+exp(logit)));
      end;
model ifate~binary(p);
random u~normal(0,s2u) subject=site out=randeff;
predict p*(1-p) out=west;
predict p out=piest ;
ods output ParameterEstimates=betahat
      (where=(Parameter=:"B")) ;
ods output ParameterEstimates=sigmahat
      (where=(Parameter=:"s2")) ;
ods output ParameterEstimates=B0Hat
      (where=(Parameter='B0') rename=(Estimate=Est_B0));
ods output ParameterEstimates=B1Hat
      (where=(Parameter='B1') rename=(Estimate=Est_B1));
ods output ParameterEstimates=B2Hat
```

```
     (where=(Parameter='B2') rename=(Estimate=Est_B2));
ods output ParameterEstimates=s2uhat
     (where=(Parameter='s2u') rename=(Estimate=Est_s2u));
run ;

%u1kern1 ;  * CALL KERNEL SMOOTHED STATISTIC MACRO ;
```

Studies in Avian Biology No. 34:55–64

THE ANALYSIS OF COVARIATES IN MULTI-FATE MARKOV CHAIN NEST-FAILURE MODELS

MATTHEW A. ETTERSON, BRIAN OLSEN, AND RUSSELL GREENBERG

Abstract. In this manuscript we show how covariates may be included in Markov chain nest-failure models and illustrate this method using nest-monitoring data for Coastal Plain Swamp Sparrows (*Melospiza georgiana nigrescens*) from Woodland Beach Wildlife Area, Delaware. First, we explore hypotheses for nest failure as a single event class, which is the converse of modeling covariates to survival. We then generalize to consider separate covariates to two classes of nest failure—predation and flooding. Temporal variability, both within and between years, was the most important factor for describing daily nest failure probabilities, though percent cover around the nest also received strong support. The Markov chain estimators for a single class of failure are likely to be similar to other generalizations of the original Mayfield estimator. The estimators for modeling two or more classes of failure should prove useful, but must be employed with caution. They are sensitive to nest-fate classification errors and they can lead to a proliferation of models, which could result in over-fitting.

Key Words: competing risks, covariates, Mayfield Markov chain, *Melospiza georgiana nigrescens*, nest survival.

EL ANÁLISIS DE COVARIANTES EN MODELOS MULTI DESTINO MARKOV DE FRACASO DE NIDO EN CADENA

Resumen. En el presente manuscrito mostramos de qué manera las covariantes pueden ser incluidas en modelos Markov de fracaso de nido en cadena, y también ilustramos este método utilizando datos de monitoreo de nido para los Gorriones Pantaneros (*Melospiza georgiana nigrescens*) del Área Silvestre Woodland Beach, en Delaware. Primero exploramos hipótesis para fracaso de nido, como clase de evento separado, el cual es inverso al modelaje de covariantes para la sobrevivencia. Por ello generalizamos para considerar separar covariantes en dos clases de fracaso de nido —depredación e inundamiento. La variabilidad temporal durante y entre los años, fue el factor más importante para describir las probabilidades de fracaso de nido diarias, sin embargo, el porcentaje de cobertura alrededor del nido también recibió soporte fuerte. Los estimadores de cadena Marcov por una clase separada de fracaso suelen ser similares a otras generalizaciones del estimador original Mayfield. Los estimadores para modelar dos o más clases de fracaso deberían probar utilidad, sin embargo deben ser empleados con cautela. Son sensibles a errores de clasificación de destino de nido y pueden dirigir hacia la proliferación de modelos, lo cual podría resultar en un exceso en el ajuste.

Nest-survival analysis has developed beyond simple survival estimation. Current methodologies now allow scientists to hypothesize and model sources (e.g., ecological and natural history) of variation in nest survivorship (Natarajan and McCulloch 1999, Dinsmore et al. 2002, Rotella et al. 2004, Shaffer 2004a). Historically, studies of daily nest survival have sought to explain nest failure, focusing on predation as the major cause. Thus, modeling daily survival as functions of covariates identifies important correlates to the absence of the event(s) of interest. When failure is the simple complement of survival, then the approaches are conversely equivalent and the appropriate inference is easy to make. However, when more than one cause of nest failure is present, covariate models of survival may identify models that are difficult to interpret as to their importance for a given cause of failure. In such cases, if researchers are in a position to unambiguously determine the fate of nests, more insight may be gained by modeling the different causes of failure separately.

Recently, Etterson and Bennett (2005) introduced a simple non-stationary Markov chain likelihood estimator for daily survival that allows incorporation of age-specific transition probabilities (hatching and fledging) in nest survival modeling. This Mayfield-Markov chain can be further generalized to incorporate multiple categories of nest failure while relaxing the requirement that nests are visited daily (Etterson et al., in press). This formulation is ideal for considering multiple simultaneous risks to nests because, when iterated, it correctly adjusts the probabilities of failure due to one cause conditional on failure due to another cause not occurring. The need for such discounting methods, typically referred to as competing risks, has long been recognized in human demography and actuarial science (Chiang 1968). In ecology, Royama (1981) and Carey (1989) have analyzed competing risks in insect demography using multiple decrement life-table analyses. Below we show how Markov chain models of competing risks may be applied toward a greater understanding of cause-specific avian nest failure by incorporating covariates thought to influence risk of nest failure.

Coastal Plain Swamp Sparrows (*Melospiza georgiana nigrescens*) breed in tidal marshes and, along with other tidal-marsh breeding birds, face two major challenges to successful reproduction (Greenberg et al., 2006)—predation and inundation due to tidal and storm-caused flooding. Nest failures from these two causes account for >95% of the total nest loss in Coastal Plain Swamp Sparrows (Greenberg et al., 2006). Predation and loss to flooding are likely to select for different nest-placement strategies, and therefore a trade-off may exist between behaviors that help protect against one factor or the other. For example, nests placed higher in the vegetation may help reduce the chance of flood loss, but at the same time increase the vulnerability of the nest to aerial predators. Therefore, it is quite plausible that in this subspecies the two major causes of failure may be negatively correlated via important covariates, if, to extend the above example, construction of the nest lower in the vegetation or over areas of deeper water deters nest predators. If such a trade-off exists, then female sparrows are faced with an optimization problem in where they place their nests.

Based on extensive studies of nest location and phenology, the basic natural history of nest placement can be summarized. Coastal Plain Swamp Sparrows are most common in high marsh (at or above the mean high-tide line). In this zone they tend to anchor their nests on shrubs or reed-like grasses at a fairly consistent height (approximately 30 cm above the substrate) where they can be covered in tussocks of salt hay (*Spartina patens*). Nests are found disproportionately in areas of high surface heterogeneity where water wells up forming moats around the nest plant. The salt hay cover dies back in the winter and re-grows relatively slowly in the spring. The nesting season is relatively long, beginning in mid-May and ending in late July to mid-August. Nest cover increases between mid-May (when the first nests are constructed) and the summer months (R. Greenberg, unpubl. data).

In this manuscript we use nest-monitoring data for Coastal Plain Swamp Sparrows to show how the Markov chain models can be adapted to incorporate age-, time-, and nest-specific covariates when estimating daily failure probabilities.

Markov Chain Nest-Survival Models

Before describing how to incorporate covariates into the Markov chain model, we briefly review the previously published Markov chain formulations, emphasizing the known limitations of those models. As in previous publications, our development of the likelihood functions will provide the kernel of the likelihood for an arbitrary exposure interval bounded by two visits on which the state of the nest was determined. The likelihood for a sequence of observations on a single nest or a collection of nests is generated by taking the product of the likelihoods over all such intervals. The simplest Markov chain model is:

$$\mathbf{M} = \begin{bmatrix} s & 0 \\ 1-s & 1 \end{bmatrix} \quad (1)$$

where s = daily probability of survival. The likelihood of an observation beginning in state $\mathbf{X}_n$, lasting d_n days, and ending in state $\mathbf{X}_{n+1}$ is:

$$l(s \mid \mathbf{X}_n, \mathbf{X}_{n+1}, d_n) \propto \mathbf{X}_{n+1}^{\mathrm{T}} \mathbf{M}^{d_n} \mathbf{X}_n \quad (2)$$

where n indexes the sequential visits to the nest, T is the transpose operator, and $\mathbf{X}_n$ and $\mathbf{X}_{n+1}$ are column vectors describing the observed states of the nest (Etterson and Bennett 2005):

$\mathbf{X}^{\mathrm{T}} = [1 \quad 0] \leftrightarrow$ nest is still active

$\mathbf{X}^{\mathrm{T}} = [0 \quad 1] \leftrightarrow$ nest has failed

The estimator (2) is closely related to the original Mayfield (1961, 1975) estimator and formulations by Johnson (1979), Hensler and Nichols (1981), and Bart and Robson (1982).

Etterson and Bennett (2005) extended (1) to incorporate stage-specific survival (Stanley 2000, 2004a) and transition (hatching and fledging) probabilities:

$$\mathbf{M}(a,b) = \begin{bmatrix} \sim H(a)s_1 & 0 & 0 & 0 \\ H(a)s_1 & \sim F(b)s_2 & 0 & 0 \\ 0 & F(b)s_2 & 1 & 0 \\ 1-s_1[\sim H(a)+H(a)] & 1-s_2[\sim F(b)+F(b)] & 0 & 1 \end{bmatrix} \quad (3)$$

In (3), s_1 = daily probability of survival during laying and incubation, s_2 = daily probability of survival during the nestling phase, a = age (in days) since the first egg was laid, b = age (in days) since hatching, $H(a)$ is the probability of hatching at age a, and $F(b)$ is the probability of fledging at age b ($\sim H(a)$ and $\sim F(b)$ are the probabilities of not hatching or fledging at the respective ages). With equation (3) there are four corresponding state vectors:

$\mathbf{X}^T = [1 \quad 0 \quad 0 \quad 0] \leftrightarrow$ eggs present, but not yet hatched,
$\mathbf{X}^T = [0 \quad 1 \quad 0 \quad 0] \leftrightarrow$ nestlings have hatched, but not yet fledged,
$\mathbf{X}^T = [0 \quad 0 \quad 1 \quad 0] \leftrightarrow$ nestlings fledged, and
$\mathbf{X}^T = [0 \quad 0 \quad 0 \quad 1] \leftrightarrow$ nest failed.

While simple in theory, equation (3) is difficult to apply empirically for several reasons. First, the hatching and fledging probabilities are typically not known because the distributions observed in field data are joint probabilities of survival and hatching or fledging (Etterson and Bennett 2005). Second, the use of transition probabilities requires knowledge of age, and the likelihood based on (3) is sensitive to errors in age-estimation, especially when temporal heterogeneity occurs in survival probability (Etterson and Bennett 2006). Third, equation (3) presumes that the state of a nest is determined unambiguously at each visit. This assumption may not be true for states three and four, i.e., when the nest is scored as either fledged or failed if determination of fate was made upon finding the nest empty and the nestlings were sufficiently developed to have fledged during the interval. Stanley (2004b) recommended discarding such observations, in which case (3) could be simplified to:

$$\mathbf{M}(a) = \begin{bmatrix} \sim H(a)s_1 & 0 & 0 \\ H(a)s_1 & s_2 & 0 \\ 1 - s_1[\sim H(a) + H(a)] & 1 - s_2 & 1 \end{bmatrix} \quad (4)$$

Equation (1) can also be extended to incorporate multiple classes of failure:

$$\mathbf{M} = \begin{bmatrix} s & 0 & 0 \\ m_p & 1 & 0 \\ m_f & 0 & 1 \end{bmatrix} \quad (5)$$

subject to the constraints $0 < s, m_p, m_f < 1$ and $s + m_p + m_f = 1$. Under this formulation, there are three state vectors:
$\mathbf{X}^T = [1 \quad 0 \quad 0] \leftrightarrow$ nest active,
$\mathbf{X}^T = [0 \quad 1 \quad 0] \leftrightarrow$ nest failed due to cause 'p' (predation in our example), and
$\mathbf{X}^T = [0 \quad 0 \quad 1] \leftrightarrow$ nest failed due to cause 'f' (flooding in our example).

The likelihood function incorporating (5) is:

$$l(m_p, m_f \mid \mathbf{X}_n, \mathbf{X}_{n+1}, d_n) \propto \mathbf{X}_{n+1}^T \mathbf{M}^{d_n} \mathbf{X}_n',$$

where m_p = daily probability of failure due to cause 'p', m_f = daily probability of failure due to cause 'f', and other terms are as defined above.

With this manuscript we combine (4) and (5) into a Markov chain with temporal heterogeneity and multiple causes of failure. We apply the resulting model to Coastal Plain Swamp Sparrow data with two main objectives. First, we develop and demonstrate methods for analysis of covariates in ecologically interesting models using the Markov chain formulation. To begin we demonstrate an application in which a single class of failure is modeled as a function of covariates to produce results similar to other current methods (Dinsmore et al. 2002, Shaffer 2004a). Next, we re-analyze the data in the first example, considering two classes of failure (predation and flooding) and use the results to discuss potential benefits and pitfalls of such analyses. Our second objective was to perform preliminary analyses of available Coastal Plain Swamp Sparrow data to help focus the allocation of ongoing field efforts for understanding the breeding ecology of this unique subspecies.

METHODS

A Markov chain incorporating temporal heterogeneity and two states of failure can be formulated as equation (6). The failure probabilities ($m_p(t)$, $m_f(t)$, $m_p(b,t)$, $m_f(b,t)$) are expressed as functions of time (t = Julian date relative to 1 May in our example), and age (b = age of nestlings in days since hatching). Because eggs were neither floated nor candled, we did not have reliable knowledge of age of eggs for most nests unless they hatched, so we chose not to model age-specific failure probabilities for eggs. Thus equation (6) specifies age- and time-specific failure for nestlings, but only time-specific failure for eggs. In a more general formulation (Etterson and Bennett 2005) the treatment of age (b) must handle cases in which age surpasses the maximum empirical fledging age, but this was not necessary here because the data were truncated prior to the minimum fledging age, after Stanley (2004a).

$$\mathbf{M}(a,b,t) = \begin{bmatrix} \sim H(a)(1 - m_p(t) - m_f(t)) & 0 & 0 & 0 \\ H(a)(1 - m_p(t) - m_f(t)) & (1 - m_p(b,t) - m_f(b,t)) & 0 & 0 \\ [\sim H(a) + H(a)]\, m_p(t) & m_p(b,t) & 1 & 0 \\ [\sim H(a) + H(a)]\, m_f(t) & m_f(b,t) & 0 & 1 \end{bmatrix} \quad (6)$$

To express the failure probabilities as functions of covariates, we used the multinomial logit:

$$m_i = \frac{\exp(\beta_i Y_{in})}{1 + \sum_i \exp(\beta_i Y_{in})}$$

where β_i is a row-vector of structural parameters and Y_{in} is a column-vector linking the covariates for observation n (on nest k, not subscripted) to failure due to fate i. In all models presented below, the first element of Y_{in} is reserved for a global intercept. Then, the likelihood of an arbitrary observation with initial state $\mathbf{X}_n$ and final state $\mathbf{X}_{n+1}$ and two states of failure can be written:

$$l(\beta_p, \beta_f \mid t_n, a_n, b_n, \mathbf{X}_n, \mathbf{X}_{n+1}, d_n, Y_{pn}, Y_{fn}) \propto \mathbf{X}_{n+1}^T \left[\prod_{d=1}^{d_n} \mathbf{M}(a_n + d, b_n + d, t_n + d) \right] \mathbf{X}_n \quad (7)$$

As above, the likelihood over all observations on all nests is the product of the likelihoods of each observation on each nest.

For the Swamp Sparrow models considered below, we found the maximum likelihood estimates (MLEs) of the β_i by numerically maximizing equation (9) using Matlab 7.04 (Mathworks 2004). All continuous covariates were standardized to improve convergence. Using the value of the likelihood function at the MLEs and formulae for effective sample size provided by Rotella et al. (2004), we compared models using Akaike's information criterion corrected for small sample sizes (AIC_c) and associated model weights (Burnham and Anderson 2002). Following the recommendation of Stanley (2004b) we censored all observations for which the nest was found empty and the nestlings in the nest could have been old enough to fledge (≥8 days since hatching, a conservative estimate) to avoid misclassification of success versus failure. Classification of failed nests into failure classes is described below.

Study Site and Field Methods

The data used in this manuscript are from an ongoing study of Coastal Plain Swamp Sparrows in two ~15 ha plots on the State of Delaware's Woodland Beach Wildlife Area. The plots are found on upland tidal salt marsh in a matrix of farmland and wetland forest along the Smyrna River, and they represent a wide range of mid-Atlantic marsh vegetation, Coastal Plain Swamp Sparrow densities, and flooding periodicity.

Nests were discovered primarily using nest-departure calls (Greenberg 2003). After discovery, nests were monitored every 2–3 d (2002) or almost daily (2003–2005) until failure or fledging. Most failed nests failed due to predation, with evidence ranging from observations of the predation event to broken eggshells, and torn up nests. However, some nests are known to have failed due to inundation during exceptionally high tides combined with storm surges in 2004 and 2005. These tides typically occur at night during a full or new moon and cause the synchronized failure of a subset of nests (or all active nests in 2004) with identical failure evidence. Flooded nest-sites show high water marks on the vegetation above the nest; eggs typically are floated out of the dish but otherwise unharmed; and chicks are killed without external evidence of injury. Abandonment was rare (six nests in the data analyzed below), and all such nests were combined in the class of depredated nests.

Covariates included in our models included a wide array of factors (Table 1) from vegetation characteristics, to spatial arrangement, to specific descriptions of nest placement. All represent possible influences on nest survival and are accompanied by specific hypotheses as to their effect. Some measures (e.g., nest height) attempt to explain flooding, while others attempt to explain predation (e.g., percent cover) and others may impact both (e.g., hummock index). Not all covariates were measured at all nests so the analyses presented here include the largest subset of nests for which all covariates were measured (Table 1).

Swamp Sparrow Nest-Failure Models

We modeled Coastal Plain Swamp Sparrow nest failure as a single class of failure using equation (4) generalized to include temporal and age heterogeneity. Daily failure probability was linked to covariates using a binomial logit. We included an intercept-only model for historical reasons, and to see how traditional estimators (Bart and Robson 1982) would perform over the same data. The Markov chain for this model is equivalent to equation (1) above. For the intercept only model, we computed 95% confidence intervals around the failure rate on the logit scale and report them on the probability scale. More realistically, we suspected that temporal heterogeneity would be important and we modeled it in two ways. First, we modeled variation due to year as a classification variable. The Markov chain for this model is:

TABLE 1. COVARIATES USED FOR SWAMP SPARROW ANALYSES.

Abbreviation	Name	Definition	Hypothesized relationship with failure
dte	Julian date	Chronological date after 1 May in each respective year	Positive (typical relationship in open-nesting passerines).
yr	Year	–	Random.
cov	Percent cover	Percent of nest hidden by vegetation when viewed from above	Negative.
ht	Nest height	Distance from lip of nest dish to the substrate	Negative for flooding, positive for predation.
pat5	Patens	Percent of ground cover within 5 m occupied by *Spartina patens*,which is the primary nest material, and often used for cover	Negative.
iva5	Iva	Percent of ground cover within 5 m occupied by *Iva frutescens*, which is a common nest anchor and often used for cover	Negative.
salt	Salinity	Salinity (parts per thousand) within 1 m of nest: salinity tolerance in Swamp Sparrows is low compared with other salt marsh passerines	Positive.
hmk	Hummock index	Difference between the water depth below the nest and at the deepest point within 1 m of the nest at high tide	Negative for predation, positive for flooding.
edg	Distance to edge	Straight-line distance from each nest to the nearest terrestrial habitat, which is wetland forest in both plots.	Negative for predation, positive for flooding.
stg	Developmental stage	Phase of nesting cycle, divided into two stages: laying and incubation vs. nestling	No prediction.
age	Nestling age	Days post-hatch	No prediction.

$$\mathbf{M} = \begin{bmatrix} 1 - m\{\text{yr}\} & 0 \\ m\{\text{yr}\} & 1 \end{bmatrix} \quad (8)$$

with 2002 effects lumped within the global intercept and yr functioning as an indicator variable with three levels (corresponding to 2003, 2004, and 2005; Table 1). Second, we modeled variation due to year (again as a class variable), but with an additional slope parameter, constrained to be equal across all years, describing changes in failure rate with Julian date. The choice to use a single slope parameter across years was made both for ecological reasons (to determine whether a general trend of increasing versus decreasing probability of failure occurs as the season progresses) and for reasons of parsimony (separate slopes would require the estimation of three additional parameters). The Markov chain for this model is:

$$\mathbf{M} = \begin{bmatrix} 1 - m\{\text{yr} + \text{dte}\} & 0 \\ m\{\text{yr} + \text{dte}\} & 1 \end{bmatrix} \quad (9)$$

with yr defined as above, and dte indicating a single slope parameter constrained to be equal across years (Table 1).

All models except the intercept only model contained one of the two above versions of temporal effects. The two temporal effects models were considered individually and were also crossed with seven additional ecological covariates (above, Table 1), each added as a single additional main effect. An example of the Markov chain for one of these models (the percent cover model) could be written as:

$$\mathbf{M} = \begin{bmatrix} 1 - m\{\text{yr} + \text{dte} + \text{cov}\} & 0 \\ m\{\text{yr} + \text{dte} + \text{cov}\} & 1 \end{bmatrix} \quad (10)$$

The two temporal-effects models were also combined with each of two models of nest development: a stage-specific model and a model that included age of nestlings nested within the stage effect. The Markov chain for the model of failure as a function of age of nestlings nested within the stage effect can be expressed in equation (11).

This resulted in 20 models plus the intercept only model, giving a total of 21 models. All models included a global-intercept parameter.

To model Coastal Plain Swamp Sparrow nest failure in two categories we used the above 20 models (excluding the intercept-only model) as models of nest predation. To save space, we do not present the Markov chains for each model, though the Markov chain for the most complicated model is presented at the end of this paragraph. Because the sample size for flooding was small, we did not include temporal effects within season. However, we did wish to explore whether the placement of flooded nests might place them at greater risk of failure to flooding. Thus we chose three covariates related to placement of the nests: distance to the edge of the marsh, nest height above ground, and the hummock index (Table 1). We combined the three placement variables with a year variable and an intercept-only model to produce five basic models of inundation probability—intercept only, year, distance to edge, height, and hummock index (Table 1). Each of these five flooding models was combined with the 20 predation models described above to give 100 models. Covariates were linked to the failure probabilities via structural parameters using the multinomial logit. The Markov chain for the temporal and age-specific predation model combined with the yearly flooding model is expressed in equation (12). Because of the short monitoring interval employed, we assumed that all nests that failed, having last been observed in incubation, had not hatched prior to failure, and, for nests that hatch, hatch date is inferred from the age of nestlings. In this case, the function $H(a)$ is greatly simplified because it is set to 1 on hatch date and zero otherwise (Etterson and Bennett 2005). Again, for historical reasons, we include an intercept-only model (i.e., equation 5 above), this time containing two parameters: an intercept for each category of failure. Thus, we had 101 models for the two causes of failure.

$$\mathbf{M} = \begin{bmatrix} \sim H(a)[1 - m\{\text{yr} + \text{dte}\}] & 0 & 0 \\ H(a)[1 - m\{\text{yr} + \text{dte}\}] & 1 - m\{\text{yr} + \text{dte} + \text{age(stg)}\} & 0 \\ m\{\text{yr} + \text{dte}\} & m\{\text{yr} + \text{dte} + \text{age(stg)}\} & 1 \end{bmatrix} \quad (11)$$

$$\mathbf{M} = \begin{bmatrix} \sim H(a)(1 - m_p\{\text{yr} + \text{dte}\} - m_f\{\text{yr}\}) & 0 & 0 & 0 \\ H(a)(1 - m_p\{\text{yr} + \text{dte}\} - m_f\{\text{yr}\}) & (1 - m_p\{\text{yr} + \text{dte} + \text{age(stg)}\} - m_f\{\text{yr}\} & 0 & 0 \\ [\sim H(a) + H(a)]\, m_p\{\text{yr} + \text{dte}\} & m_p\{\text{yr} + \text{dte} + \text{age(stg)}\} & 1 & 0 \\ [\sim H(a) + H(a)]\, m_f\{\text{yr}\} & m_f\{\text{yr}\} & 0 & 1 \end{bmatrix} \quad (12)$$

RESULTS

Of 476 Swamp Sparrow nests discovered between 2002 and 2005, survival data and the full complement of seven ecological covariates were collected at 192. Of these, 110 were depredated, 63 fledged young, 13 failed due to flooding, and six were abandoned. The earliest observed active nest was on 12 May 2004 and the latest active nest was last seen active on 30 August 2005. For the 192 nests analyzed here, the mean interval between nest visits was 1.12 ± 0.054 days and all observations together accounted for an effective sample size of 1,697 exposure days.

When Swamp Sparrow failure was modeled as a single fate, the best model included annual variation, seasonal variation, and percent cover around the nest (Table 2). All of the models containing seasonal variation in addition to annual variation scored higher than models with simple annual variation (Table 2). The best model containing simple annual variation (i.e., no seasonal effects) also contained percent cover (Table 2). Both models that included percent cover estimated an increasing probability of failure with increasing percent cover around the nest. For the intercept-only model, the estimated constant daily failure probability was 0.077, with upper and lower 95% confidence intervals estimated as (0.065–0.091). However, it was by far the worst of the 21 models, scoring over 17 AIC_c units worse than the best model (Table 2).

When the same data were modeled using two classes of failure, the best model of predation was also the annual variation, seasonal variation, and percent cover model (Table 3). The best model of flooding failure was the intercept-only model, though model uncertainty with respect to flooding is large as can be seen in the relatively similar performance provided by the five best models (Table 3), all of which differ in their parameterization of flooding effects. As above, the two parameter intercept-only model was the worst model considered, scoring 16.8 AIC_c units worse than the best model. It gave an estimated constant daily failure probability due to predation of 0.069 (0.057–0.082) and an estimated daily failure probability due to flooding of 0.009 (0.006–0.016). As above, all models containing percent cover as a covariate predicted increasing probability of failure with increasing cover.

All models of seasonal variation predicted increasing failure probabilities later in the season, with as much as a three-fold difference over the course of the season (Fig. 1). Removing the effects of flooding had little impact on the shape of the failure curve for the best models of failure (Fig. 1), with the single-fate curve being 10–15% higher, depending on year. None of the covariates aside from percent cover received much support either in the single-failure-class models or in the predation models in the dual-class models. Neither developmental stage, nor nestling age received much support in either the single- or dual-class estimators.

TABLE 2. AIC_c STATISTICS FOR 21 MODELS OF SWAMP SPARROW NEST SUCCESS, TREATING FAILURE AS A SINGLE CLASS.

Model[a]	Parameters	AIC_c	ΔAIC_c	Weight
m{ yr + dte + cov}	6	869.63	0.00	0.49
m{ yr + dte}	5	873.02	3.40	0.09
m{yr + dte + edg}	6	873.47	3.84	0.07
m{yr + dte + hmk}	6	873.92	4.29	0.06
m{yr + dte + ht}	6	874.61	4.98	0.04
m{yr + dte + salt}	6	874.68	5.05	0.04
m{yr + dte + age(stg)}	6	874.76	5.13	0.04
m{yr + dte + pat5}	6	874.87	5.24	0.04
m{yr + dte + stg}	6	874.88	5.25	0.04
m{yr + dte + iva5}	6	874.92	5.30	0.03
m{yr + cov}	5	875.83	6.20	0.02
m{yr}	4	877.4	7.78	0.01
m{yr + edg}	5	877.44	7.82	0.01
m{yr + ht}	5	877.78	8.15	0.01
m{yr + salt}	5	878.61	8.99	0.01
m{yr + hmk}	5	878.77	9.15	0.01
m{yr+pat5}	5	879.13	9.50	0.00
m{yr + age(stg)}	5	879.28	9.66	0.00
m{yr + iva5}	5	879.31	9.69	0.00
m{yr + stg}	5	879.36	9.73	0.00
m{.}	1	886.88	17.25	0.00

[a] In single class of failure models *m*{...} indicates model of overall failure for which covariates are contained within brackets. Covariate abbreviations follow Table 1.

TABLE 3. TEN BEST DUAL-FAILURE-CLASS MODELS FOR COASTAL PLAIN SWAMP SPARROW NEST FAILURE.

Model[a]	Parameters	AIC_c	ΔAIC_c	Weight
m_p\{yr + dte + cov\}m_f\{.\}	7	965.55	0.00	0.21
m_p\{yr + dte + cov\}m_f\{edg\}	8	966.52	0.96	0.13
m_p\{yr + dte + cov\}m_f\{yr\}	8	966.74	1.19	0.12
m_p\{yr + dte + cov\}m_f\{ht\}	8	967.38	1.82	0.09
m_p\{yr + dte + cov\}m_f\{hmk\}	8	967.57	2.02	0.08
m_p\{yr + dte\}m_f\{.\}	6	969.91	4.36	0.02
m_p\{yr + dte + edg\}m_f\{.\}	7	970.51	4.95	0.02
m_p\{yr + dte + hmk\}m_f\{.\}	7	970.56	5.00	0.02
m_p\{yr + dte\}m_f\{edg\}	7	970.89	5.34	0.01
m_p\{yr + dte\}m_f\{yr\}	7	971.09	5.54	0.01

[a] In dual class of failure models m_p\{...\} indicates model of predation for which covariates are contained within brackets. m_f\{...\} indicates models of flooding probability.

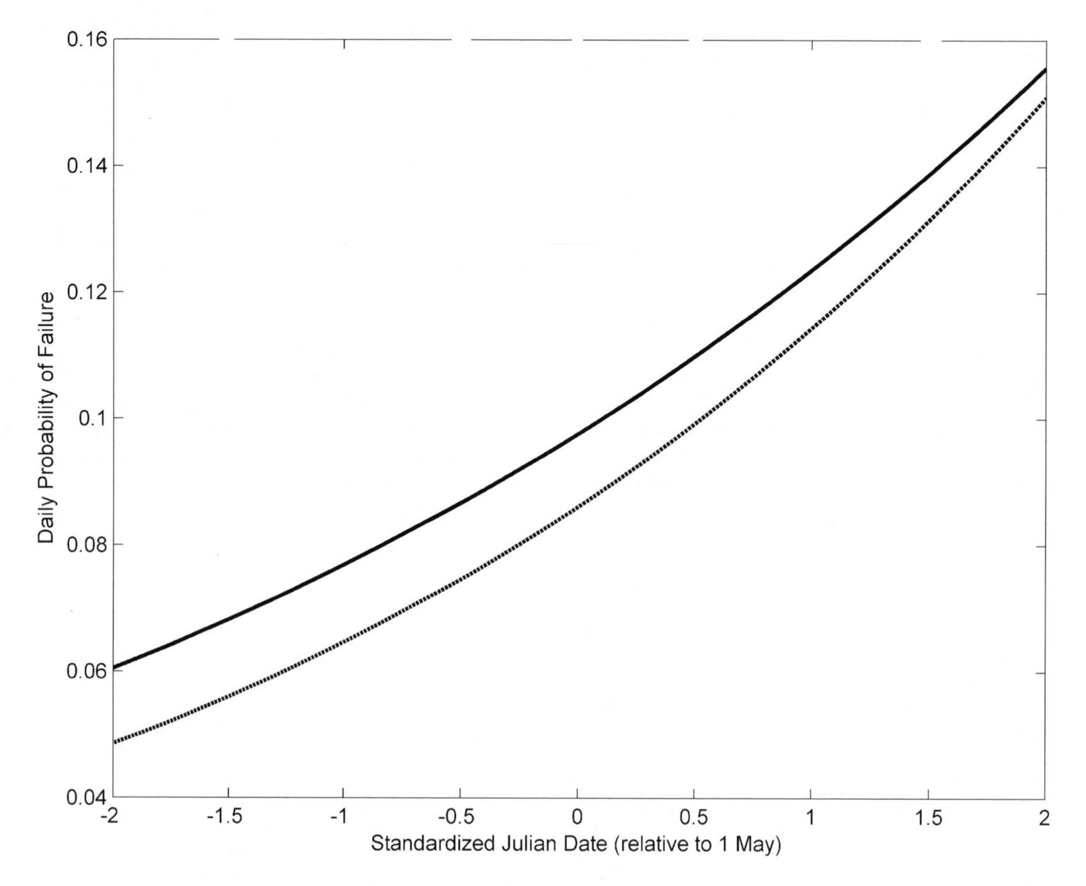

FIGURE 1. Representative patterns of within season nest failure showing change in daily failure rate with Julian date (standardized) in 2005 for best single-fate model and for predation component of best dual-fate model. For these analyses, modeling flooding failure separately simply reduces overall daily failure attributable to predation, without changing the seasonal pattern of failure.

DISCUSSION

Clearly, temporal variation, both within and between years, is critical for understanding Coastal Plain Swamp Sparrow nest failure. This temporal variation makes it difficult for us to decide conclusively the importance of the other ecological effects measured because of the relatively large number of estimated parameters that were required to describe temporal variation. With more data it may be possible to estimate such effects while controlling for temporal variation, as for example, percent cover appears to be an important factor explaining swamp sparrow nest failure, albeit in a surprising direction.

The increased predation rate with percent cover may be partly confounded with the within-season effect because available cover in this habitat increases as the season progresses. However, the selection of both variables as important for describing overall fate, and predation in particular, suggests that each contributes unique information to understanding nest failure. The increase in failure rates with increasing cover may be attributable to the foraging habits of the small mammals that constitute the primary nest predators. Heavy predation on these small mammals from both nocturnal and diurnal raptors may prevent serious foraging bouts in open areas. Avian nest predation in the study plots is low. Neither Blue Jays (*Cyanocitta cristata*) nor Fish Crows (*Corvus ossifragus*) are seen on the plots and all observed avian nest-predation events occurred as holes in eggs or nestling necks on territories that neighbored those of Marsh Wrens (*Cistothorus palustris*). Territory location may therefore play a larger role than nest camouflage in these failure events. Relatively few nests, however, completely lack cover, and the question remains why sparrows would place such a large proportion of their nests in deep cover if it is a reliable predictor of failure. Thus, it seems likely that nest cover is correlated with an additional factor that we failed to identify.

Other analyses of age-specific nest failure have shown age to be an important predictor of failure probability. For example, Dinsmore et al. (2002) showed that the daily probability of failure decreased with age in Mountain Plovers (*Charadrius montanus*). Conversely, Natarajan and McCulloch (1999:558) showed increasing daily probability of failure with age for another wetland passerine, the Red-winged Blackbird (*Agelaius phoeniceus*). In our analyses, the fitted age-specific model suggested decreasing probability of failure with age, though the model was not competitive with the better models described above (Table 2). However, age of eggs was not included as a covariate because many nests were discovered after clutch completion and we did not attempt to determine age through candling or flotation. Thus, we were only able to assess age effects for nestlings. Stanley (2004b) cautioned that the right-censoring we performed here might result in failure to detect age-specific heterogeneity if failure probabilities change substantially just prior to fledging. We do not think such effects were present in our data for two reasons. First, the terminal exposure intervals that were censored were usually only 1 d, and never more than 2 d, so little information would have been lost from censoring those observations. Second, in other analyses where we did not right-censor the data, the age-specific models also did not perform well. In fact, the minimal truncation had little effect on model performance for any of the models we considered.

The ability to include covariates in the Markov chain models will make this class of models more useful to ecologists and managers for determining causes of nest failure. The close relationship between the basic likelihood (equations 1 and 2) of the Markov chain model and that of Johnson (1979) and Bart and Robson (1982) suggests that the Markov chain model will give similar results to other generalizations of those estimators (Dinsmore et al. 2002, Shaffer 2004a), when similar covariate models are analyzed. However, there are some important differences. The Markov chain model has not yet been extended to allow the incorporation of random effects, as can be done in the SAS implementation of the logistic-exposure model (Rotella et al. 2004, Shaffer 2004a). In contrast, the incorporation of stage-transition probabilities (Etterson and Bennett 2005) cannot currently be done in MARK or in the logistic-exposure model, though Stanley's (2000, 2004a) model does provide this capability using SAS. Similarly, while multiple-fate nest-survival models can be implemented in SAS (Thompson and Burhans 2004), they require the assumption that the dates on which failure events occur are known precisely. The Markov chain model we present here relaxes that assumption. Other differences will occur due to the way in which time- and age-specific covariates are handled. In the analyses presented here, we allowed time and age to progress within exposure intervals, as did Dinsmore et al. (2002), whereas Shaffer (2004a) used the mean age of a nest during an exposure interval as a covariate to the entire interval. In practice, given the short monitoring interval for these data, the two methods would be virtually identical.

As suggested by Greenberg et al. (2006), flooding does not appear to be a major cause of nest failure for Coastal Plain Swamp Sparrows. Furthermore, little evidence exists in our data supporting hypotheses that flooding risk is related to any of the nest-placement variables we considered, though this result may be due to small sample size for flooding. The lack of correlates with ecological variables may also be due to the nature of flooding events, which, although rare, tend to destroy most or all active nests. Finally, the removal of flooding effects, in these data, has little effect on the shape of the resulting model for predation effects. Thus, it would appear that fitting the more complex model offers little benefit for these analyses, but this may not always be the case. Furthermore, even in this case, we have confirmed our previous belief that flooding effects are of relatively minor importance.

For now, the choice to use a multi-fate model such as the one we present here must ultimately be a subjective one, depending on the goals of the study, the interpretation one wishes to place in the failure parameters, and the confidence with which nests are classified. If the goal of research is to assess the importance of nest predation and to explore the ecological conditions that result in increased predation pressure, then it is sensible to model fates separately, assuming they are known with confidence. Our analyses suggest that the risk of failure due to predation is 10–15% lower than the overall risk of failure for Coastal Plain Swamp Sparrows. In fact, this difference is actually >10–15% because some nests that failed due to abandonment were also classified with depredated nests.

The latter observation highlights the need for the development of methods for controlling and reducing probabilities of classification error. To date, we know very little about the effects of such error because they cannot be estimated under typical monitoring protocols. In our opinion, this remains the largest obstacle to the use of competing risks nest-survival analyses. Some authors have begun to consider the importance and interpretation of ancillary evidence at nests (Manolis et al. 2000), and we think this is a promising direction for further research.

Another potential drawback to multiple-fate nest-failure modeling is the proliferation of models that can occur when a small set of models for one fate is combined with a small set of models for another fate. In our example, we had relatively simple sets of models for each fate, yet ended up with 101 models! If we had considered more main effects and interactions between ecological variables we could easily have conceived >1,000 plausible models describing the two fates. Thus, careful a priori consideration of models and objectives will be absolutely necessary to avoid over fitting.

The data we used for this demonstration were ideal. The short monitoring interval resulted in very well-characterized hatching dates; the unequivocal evidence available for determining whether a nest was destroyed due to flooding allowed us to apply the dual-fate model without much risk of classification error (but note that we still confounded abandonment and nest predation). In most cases data will be somewhat less ideal and the decision of appropriate modeling framework will require judgment on the part of the researcher. Our models also currently require a greater degree of attention to programming details than, for example, the nest-survival module in MARK (Dinsmore et al. 2002) or the logistic-exposure method (Shaffer 2004a) implemented in SAS. Nevertheless we believe the Markov chain framework will continue to prove itself a flexible template for the development of sophisticated nest failure models and for testing interesting ecological hypotheses about avian nest failure.

ACKNOWLEDGMENTS

This manuscript benefited greatly from comments by J. D. Nichols and J. F. Bromaghin. Field work conducted as part of this study was funded by grants from the Delaware Division of Fish and Wildlife, the Maryland Ornithological Society, the Smithsonian Institution's Abbot Fund, the Washington Biologists' Field Club, the Explorer's Club: Washington D.C. Group, the Eastern Bird Banding Association, Virginia Tech, and a Smithsonian Institution Graduate Fellowship. Field work was conducted in part by the following technicians: J. Wang, M. Powell, K. Murabito, J. Kolts, K. Callaway, A. Wessel, J. Adamson, B. Augustine, B. Beas, K. Heyden, and J. Felch.

Studies in Avian Biology No. 34:65–72

ESTIMATING NEST SUCCESS: A GUIDE TO THE METHODS

DOUGLAS H. JOHNSON

Abstract. A field biologist interested in analyzing data on the nest success of birds faces a bewildering array of literature on the topic. Methods proposed to treat these data range from the simple and easily calculated, to the complex and computationally challenging. Many methods have received little use, so it is difficult to assess how well they perform in the real world. The apparent estimator, the fraction of nests found that ultimately succeed, is seldom applicable. The Mayfield estimator, despite its extremely restrictive assumption that the daily survival rate is the same for all nests and all days, has fared surprisingly well in many applications. A few methods are too demanding to warrant routine use; for example, they might require daily visits to nests, which are rarely practical and may markedly influence the outcome of a nesting attempt. Many methods require that the age of each nest be known; other methods need this information only if age-related variation in daily survival rate is a concern, or is marked enough to require age-specific estimates to generate a satisfactory overall estimate. The use of survival-time methods is questionable because of their limited ability to handle left truncation and interval censoring.

Key Words: guide, Mayfield, nest success, recommendations, survival.

ESTIMANDO ÉXITO DE NIDO: UNA GUÍA PARA LOS MÉTODOS

Resumen. Un biólogo de campo interesado en el análisis de datos de éxito de nido enfrenta un desconcertante acomodo en la literatura respecto a este tema. Métodos han sido propuestos para tratar estos datos, los quales van desde lo simple y fácilmente calculado, hasta lo complejo y retador en términos computacionales. Muchos métodos han sido poco utilizados, por lo que es difícil valorar qué tan bien funcionan en el mundo real. El estimador aparente y la fracción de nidos encontrados que finalmente tuvo éxito es raramente aplicada. El estimador Mayfield, a pesar de su supuesto extremadamente restrictivo de que la tasa diaria de sobrevivencia es la misma para todos los nidos y todos los días, ha resultado sorpresivamente buena en muchas aplicaciones. Pocos métodos son lo suficientemente demandantes como para autorizar su uso rutinario; por ejemplo, quizás requieran visitas diarias a los nidos, lo cual es raramente práctico y quizás influyan de manera muy marcada los resultados del intento de anidación. Muchos métodos requieren que la edad de cada nido sea conocida; otros métodos requieren esta información solo si la variación relacionada con la edad en la tasa de sobrevivencia diaria es una preocupación, o es suficientemente marcada para requerir estimaciones específicas de edad para generar estimaciones totales satisfactorias. La utilización de métodos de sobrevivencia de tiempo es cuestionable debido a su limitada habilidad para manejar el redondeo de izquierda y examinadores de intervalo.

It is widely recognized that nest success is a major factor in the dynamics of bird populations and one that contributes substantially to the viability of those populations. Although other aspects of the life cycle (e.g., adult survival, propensity to nest and renest, clutch size, and survival of young birds) certainly influence population size, most of them pale in comparison to the effect of nest success (Johnson et al. 1992, Hoekman et al. 2002). Furthermore, in many situations nest success is more amenable to management than many of the other components and is more readily measured than most other critical components of population dynamics.

As a partial testament to the value of information on nest success, the literature on the topic of estimating nest success of birds is large and still growing. By my count, 44 articles have been published on this topic, all in the past half-century. Perhaps surprisingly, the rate of publication has been increasing, especially in the past few years (Fig. 1). This trend suggests that issues related to the topic are not settled, and that certain questions remain unresolved. To a field biologist seeking to analyze data on nest success, the volume of literature can be perplexing—what method should be used? Until about 1960, the decision was easy, as was the analysis. If you found and monitored, say, 50 nests, and 30 of them produced young, you estimated nest success as 60%.

Eventually, some problems associated with this simple method (which came to be known as the apparent estimator) were revealed, and most knowledgeable investigators adopted the method proposed by Mayfield (1961), which required keeping track of how many days each nest was under observation. By summing those values across all nests and dividing into the

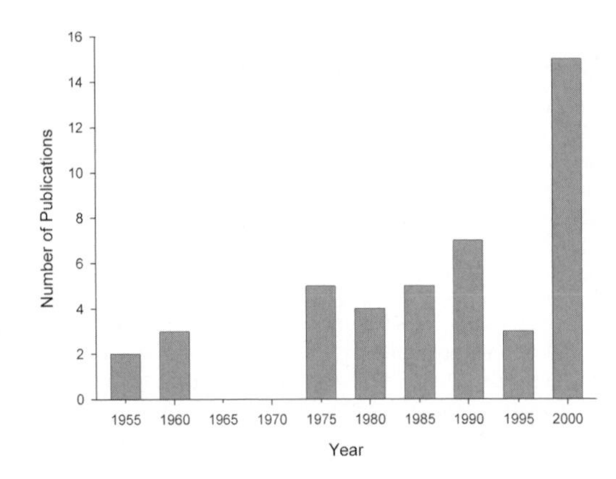

FIGURE 1. Number of methodological papers on estimating nest success published, by 5-yr period.

number of losses recorded, one could estimate a daily mortality rate for the sample of nests. Subtracting that result from one gave a daily survival rate (DSR), which could then be projected to the entire lifetime of a nest to estimate nest success. The Mayfield estimator is a somewhat more complicated procedure but one with much less bias than the apparent estimator; it has received a great deal of use by biologists, especially after standard errors for the estimator were developed (Johnson 1979).

Not content with the Mayfield method, investigators continued to develop new techniques for analyzing nest success information, especially to account for age-related variation in DSR. Few of these other methods received much use by practicing biologists, however. Then in the past few years, several papers were published that offered greater flexibility in the analysis of nesting data (reviewed by Johnson, *chapter 1, this volume*). The new methods were based on more sophisticated statistical models and required more computational abilities, leaving biologists to wonder if the new methods are worth the greater time and effort and, if so, which of them should be used.

The major objective of this paper is to offer guidance to biologists on how to select a method to analyze nesting data. First, I describe the major assumptions and requirements of the various methods and note their advantages and disadvantages. From that information, I develop guidelines for choosing a method, based on the objectives of the nesting study, features that characterize the study, and properties of the resulting data.

A generalized description of nesting studies is as follows. (see Klett et al. [1986] and Manolis et al. [2000] for more details on waterfowl and passerine studies, respectively). An investigator searches for the nests of birds, finding them by any of a variety of methods. Typically, nests are not discovered at their initiation, but are found only after they have progressed for some time. In some studies, nests that fail before nest searching begins, or are initiated but fail between nest visits, can be found, but in most studies such nests are hard to detect. Nests that failed early and thus are not included in the sample represent an example of left truncation, in the terminology of survival analysis (Heisey et al., *this volume*).

For virtually all methods (except life-table methods), nests must be monitored subsequent to their detection. Nests may be checked daily, but visits to nests usually are less frequent, partly because of logistic constraints and partly to reduce the effect of visitation on the fate of the nest (Götmark 1992). If nests are not visited daily, and a nest fails between two visits, the exact date of loss usually is uncertain. Analytic methods vary in how they treat such interval-censored data; the visitation frequency needed for a method varies from none to daily. Sometimes nests are not followed until termination—they may not have been relocated, or field work might have ended. Such nests are right-censored, in that the ending date is not known. Note that this definition of right-censoring differs from the usual definition in survival analysis; in that context, a nest that succeeds would be considered right-censored because its failure had not occurred when monitoring ceased.

Nesting studies differ in their objectives. Many studies seek only an estimate of the overall nest success rate. Others may focus on how DSRs vary by age of the nest. Some studies may address the influence on nest survival of other variables, such as date within the nesting season, habitat type, distance from various features, etc. Such covariates may be either group-specific (e.g., applying to all nests within a certain habitat type) or nest-specific (having individual values for each nest). Others may be time-specific (e.g., age of nest or date within season). Analytic methods differ in their abilities to accommodate these various objectives.

Some of the methods assume no variation in the DSR, by age, date, or nest. Others can accommodate various types of heterogeneity in DSR. By stratification, any method can accommodate variation among groups of nests, such as those in one type of habitat versus those in another type. Such stratification requires large sample sizes, however, so that nest success within each group can be estimated with adequate precision. The type of variation most commonly incorporated is that associated with the age of a nest. Certain methods, especially the more recently developed ones, allow a wider variety of influences on DSR, including age-specific, date-specific, and nest-specific covariates. In some situations it may be necessary to account for the effects of explanatory variables such as nest age to estimate nest success accurately (Grant et al. 2005).

Another consideration is the computational ease with which estimates of nest success can be calculated. Some estimators can be computed easily by hand. Others require only some fairly basic data processing. Some estimators demand knowledge of sophisticated software. Yet others need custom-designed programs that may not be generally available or well supported.

Virtually all the methods treat the survival process as discrete. That is, the process being modeled is whether a nest survives or not during a discrete time period, usually a day. In actuality, survival of nests is a continuous process, because deaths can occur at any time during a 24-hr period (Heisey et al., *this volume*). The discrete model is appropriate, however, for the observations resulting from the survival process, because nests are generally not under continuous observation. In most nesting studies, nests are checked daily or usually less frequently, so a finer resolution than a day is not feasible. And nests generally are checked at approximately the same time each day, consistent with the 24-hr period of a discrete model.

I am not considering the assumptions that are required for all the methods, such as the nests being a random or representative sample from the population to which inferences are to be drawn (but see Shaffer and Thompson [*this volume*] for use of model-based rather than design-based estimators to overcome non-representative samples); or that fates of nests are independent of one another (unless random effects are included); or that ages, if needed, are assigned correctly; or that fates are accurately determined; or that survival from day to day is conditionally independent (that is, DSRs can be multiplied). All methods assume that the monitoring process does not affect the fate of the nest, although several investigators (Bart and Robson 1982, Nichols et al. 1984, Sedinger 1990, Rotella et al. 2000) have addressed estimation or adjustment for the effects of observers on nest fate.

Table 1 briefly describes how various methods of estimating nest success accommodate particular features of the data. Included are the objectives of the study, whether or not a method satisfactorily deals with the exclusion of nests that were destroyed before they could be discovered, and the ability of a method to handle nests for which the age is unknown. Certain methods require that the age of the nest at discovery be known; others need that information only if age-specific analysis is desired. Many methods can use age to estimate the date of hatching, if nests are not visited daily. Although techniques for estimating the age of a nest sometimes can be employed, accurate aging often is a problem, especially for nests that ultimately fail and cannot be aged by counting backward from the date of hatching or fledging. Also Table 1 indicates whether or not the method accommodates right censoring—e.g., if it uses data from nests that could not be relocated or were still active after the study terminated, interval censoring—in which losses occur on an unknown day between visits to a nest, the types of heterogeneity in DSR that a method is designed to accommodate, and the relative effort needed in the field to provide data necessary for analysis with the method. In many cases this feature is closely tied to the ability of a method to handle uncertain failure dates and thereby the need for daily checks on nests.

In Table 2, I present the computational ease for the same methods, which indicates whether commonly available and easy-to-use software is available to apply the method. Results presented in Tables 1 and 2 lead to the guidelines offered in Table 3. There a researcher can respond to a few questions about the study and resulting data, and narrow down the choice of most appropriate methods. The questions involve the objectives of the study, the visitation schedule, whether or not the age of a nest when found is known, and whether or not failed nests are as detectable as active nests.

For example, if interest lies in the effect of some group covariate, say habitat type, then the choice narrows to methods 1–3, 5–7, 12, 13, and 18–22. If nests can be revisited only periodically and not on a rigid schedule, method 13 is eliminated from consideration. If nests cannot be aged accurately, we eliminate methods 7, 18, 19, and probably 20. Method 1 will not work if destroyed nests are less likely to be detected than active ones. That reduces the possibilities to methods 2, 3, 5, 6, 12, 21, and 22. Methods 2, 3, 5, and 6 require the estimation of DSR for each group (and hence large sample sizes) and subsequent comparisons. Methods 12, 21, and 22 can incorporate the group effect directly in the analysis. Method 12 relies on a midpoint approximation when nests are not visited daily.

CONCLUSIONS

The 23 methods of estimating nest success, outlined in Tables 1 and 2, offer a bewildering choice to a biologist posing a rather simple but important question—what is the success rate of a group of nests? Only a few of the methods

TABLE 1. THIS TABLE SUMMARIZES THE METHODS OF ESTIMATING NEST SUCCESS, THE OBJECTIVES EACH METHOD ADDRESSES, WHETHER OR NOT VARIOUS FEATURES OF NESTING DATA ARE ACCOMMODATED, AND THE DEGREE OF FIELD EFFORT REQUIRED TO OBTAIN DATA APPROPRIATE FOR THE METHOD. ID IS AN IDENTIFICATION NUMBER; METHOD IS EITHER A NAME COMMONLY ASSOCIATED WITH THE METHOD OR AN ORIGINAL REFERENCE TO THE METHOD; OBJECTIVES ADDRESSED IS WHETHER THE METHOD CAN ADDRESS THE EFFECT OF VARIOUS COVARIATES ON SURVIVAL. ACCOMMODATES INDICATES WHETHER THE METHOD SATISFACTORILY DEALS WITH: LEFT TRUNCATION—THE EXCLUSION OF NESTS THAT WERE DESTROYED BEFORE THEY COULD BE DISCOVERED; UNKNOWN AGE, NESTS FOR WHICH THE AGE IS UNKNOWN; UNCERTAIN FATE, RIGHT CENSORING; UNCERTAIN FAILURE DATE, INTERVAL CENSORING; AND VARIATION IN DSR—THE TYPES OF HETEROGENEITY IN DSR THAT THE METHOD IS DESIGNED TO ACCOMMODATE. FIELD EFFORT REQUIRED DESCRIBES THE RELATIVE EFFORT NEEDED IN THE FIELD TO PROVIDE DATA NECESSARY FOR ANALYSIS WITH THE METHOD.

			Accommodates					
ID[a]	Method	Objectives addressed	Left truncation	Unknown age	Uncertain fate	Uncertain failure date	Variation in DSR	Field effort required
1	Apparent	Nest success; group effects	No[b]	Yes	No	Yes	All[c]	Very easy
2	Mayfield (1961, 1975)	Nest success; group effects	Yes	Yes	Yes	Yes (but by assumption only)[d, e]	By group[f]	Easy
3	Johnson (1979)	Nest success; group effects	Yes	Yes	Yes	Yes	By group	Easy
4	Intercept (Johnson 1979)	Nest success	Yes	No	Yes	Yes	Heterogeneity; also age-related	Easy
5	Hensler and Nichols (1981)	Nest success; group effects	Yes	Yes	Yes	No[d]	By group	Easy
6	Bart and Robson (1982)	Nest success; group effects	Yes	Yes	Yes	Yes	By group	Easy
7	Product (Klett and Johnson 1982)	Nest success; age or group effects	Yes	No	Yes	Yes	Age, date, or any identifiable characteristic	Easy
8	Life table (Goc 1986)	Nest success; age effects	Yes	No	Yes	Yes	Age	Very easy; no checks needed
9	Pollock and Cornelius (1988)	Nest success; age effects	Yes	No	No	No	Age group	Easy
10	Bromaghin and McDonald (1993a, b)	Nest success	Yes	Yes	No	Yes	No assumptions made	Visits to nests regularly spaced
11	Heisey and Nordheim (1995)	Nest success; age effects	Yes	Yes	Yes	Yes	Age	Easy
12	Aebischer (1999)	Nest success; effects of covariates	Yes	Yes	Yes	Yes (but by assumption only)[d]	Age, date, or any identifiable characteristic	Easy
13	Natarajan and McCulloch (1999)	Nest success; heterogeneity; effects of covariates	Basic model assumes nests are found at initiation; generalization seems to assume no losses before discovery	Yes	No	Not an issue since nests need to be visited daily	Heterogeneity (nest-specific DSR); any identifiable variable, including nest- and time-specific ones	Assumes nests are visited daily or that detectability is constant

TABLE 1. CONTINUED.

			Accommodates					
ID[a]	Method	Objectives addressed	Left truncation	Unknown age	Uncertain fate	Uncertain failure date	Variation in DSR	Field effort required
14	Stanley (2000)	Nest success; age effects	Yes	No	Yes	Yes	Stage	Visits frequent enough to not miss any stage
15	Stanley (2004a)	Nest success; age effects	Yes	Yes	Yes	Yes	Stage	Visits frequent enough to not miss any stage
16	He et al. (2001)	Nest success; age effects	Yes	Yes	No	No	Age	Daily visits to nests
17	He (2003)	Nest success; age effects	Yes	Yes	No	Yes	Age	Frequent visits to nests
18	Survival time, (Aldridge and Brigham 2001, Nur et al. 2004)	Nest success; effects of covariates	No[g]	No	Yes	No[d]	Any identifiable variable, including nest- and time-specific ones	Frequent visits to nests
19	Manly and Schmutz (2001)	Nest success; age or group effects	Yes	No	Yes	Yes	Age (or date)	Easy
20	Dinsmore et al. (2002)	Nest success; effects of covariates	Yes	No[h]	Yes	Yes	Any identifiable variable, including nest- and time-specific ones	Easy
21	Stephens (2003)	Nest success; effects of covariates	Yes	Yes	Yes	Yes	Any identifiable variable, including nest- and time-specific ones	Easy
22	Shaffer (2004)	Nest success; effects of covariates	Yes	Yes	Yes	Yes	Any identifiable variable, including nest- and time-specific ones	Easy
23	McPherson et al. (2003)	Nest success; age effects	Yes; assumes some nests are found at Day 1	No	Yes	No	Age	Daily visits to nests

[a] Identification number.
[b] Unless successful and failed nests are equally likely to be found.
[c] Variation in DSR is accommodated implicitly but not specifically identified.
[d] Robust with respect to uncertainty in failure dates, as long as intervals between searches are short.
[e] Miller and Johnson (1978) modified the method for longer intervals between searches.
[f] Robust to variation among groups if variation in DSR is modest.
[g] See Heisey et al. (*this volume*).
[h] Method seems not to require known age but program MARK does.

TABLE 2. METHODS OF ESTIMATING NEST SUCCESS, THE EASE WITH WHICH ESTIMATES CAN BE COMPUTED, AND ANY OTHER DISTINGUISHING FEATURES.

ID	Method	Computational ease[a]	Other
1	Apparent	Hand	Failed and active nests must be equally detectable.
2	Mayfield (1961, 1975)	Hand	Assumes DSR is the same for all nests and nest-days in group (method is robust to modest variation); assumes losses between visits occurred at midpoint of interval.
3	Johnson (1979)	STATware	Same as Mayfield except midpoint assumption not needed.
4	Intercept (Johnson 1979)	STATware	Need to know age of nest when found; detectability must be the same for all ages and all nests; large sample required.
5	Hensler and Nichols (1981)	Hand	Same as Mayfield; also, strictly, requires exact failure date; in practice usually works with mid-point assumption when nest visits are not daily.
6	Bart and Robson (1982)	AUTHORware	Same as Mayfield except midpoint assumption not needed.
7	Product (Klett and Johnson 1982)	AUTHORware	Need to know age of nest when found.
8	Life table (e.g., Goc 1986)	STATware	Need to know age of nest when found; detectability must be the same for all ages and all nests; large sample required; must sample throughout season.
9	Pollock and Cornelius (1988)	AUTHORware	Generally produces biased estimators (Heisey and Nordheim 1990).
10	Bromaghin and McDonald (1993a, b)	AUTHORware	Detectability must be the same for all ages and all nests; rigid sampling design required.
11	Heisey and Nordheim (1995)	AUTHORware	
12	Aebischer (1999)	STATware	Strictly, requires exact failure date; in practice usually robust under mid-point assumption when nest visits are not daily.
13	Natarajan and McCulloch (1999)	AUTHORware	Random effects modeling; assumptions and properties not clear.
14	Stanley (2000)	AUTHORware	Need to know age of nest when found.
15	Stanley (2004a)	AUTHORware	No longer need to know age of nest when found.
16	He et al. (2001)	AUTHORware	Bayesian.
17	He (2003)	AUTHORware	Bayesian.
18	Survival time (Aldridge and Brigham 2001, Nur et al. 2004)	STATware	Need to know fairly precisely age when found and when lost. Care required to ensure that left truncation is properly handled by the software, and some nests need to be discovered at initiation (Heisey et al., *this volume*).
19	Manly and Schmutz (2001)	AUTHORware	An extension of Klett-Johnson (1982); need to know age of nest when found.
20	Dinsmore et al. (2002)	MARKware	
21	Stephens (2003)	STATware	Developed SAS code to perform method of Dinsmore et al. (2002); also allowed single random effect.
22	Shaffer (2004)	STATware	
23	McPherson et al. (2003)	AUTHORware	Requires daily checks of nests; some nests must be monitored from initiation.

[a] Hand—calculations can be done on a hand calculator or with simple spreadsheet, STATware—computations can be performed with general purpose statistical software such as SAS, MARKware—method requires special-purpose software that is readily available and well supported, AUTHORware—method uses specially written software available from the author and with limited support.

TABLE 3. A GUIDE TO SUITABLE METHODS OF ESTIMATING NEST SUCCESS AND EFFECTS OF ASSOCIATED VARIABLES, BASED ON THE OBJECTIVES OF THE STUDY, THE VISITATION SCHEDULE INVOLVED, WHETHER THE AGE OF A NEST AT DISCOVERY CAN BE DETERMINED, AND WHETHER OR NOT DESTROYED NESTS ARE AS READILY DISCOVERED AS NESTS THAT ARE ACTIVE.

Objective, if your objective involves:	Then consider methods:
Nest success only	Any
Age effects	7–9, 11–23
Group covariates	1, 2, 3, 5, 6, 7, 12, 13, 18–22
Individual covariates	12, 13, 18, 20–22
Visitation schedule:	
No revisit	8
Revisited after anticipated termination date	1, 8
Check only periodically	1–9, 11, 12, 18–22
Fairly rigid schedule	1–12, 14, 15, 17–22
Check daily	Any
Age of nest at discovery:	
Known	Any
Unknown	1, 2, 3, 5, 6, 10–13, 15–17, 21, 22
Detectability of failed nests:	
Same as successful	Any
Lower than successful	2–23

have received much use, beyond an example application in the paper that introduced the method. These little-used methods have not faced testing in the real world.

I think that the requirements of certain methods are too demanding to warrant frequent use. For example, methods 13, 16, and 23 require that nests be visited daily to meet their assumptions. Such a rigid schedule is hardly ever practical in field studies, and the effect on the fate of such intensive monitoring may be severe (Götmark 1992).

The apparent estimator (method 1) is reasonable only if destroyed nests can be detected as readily as active nests. Rarely is that condition met (Johnson and Shaffer 1990), so this estimator is seldom applicable. The apparent estimator seems largely to have fallen out of use, at least in North America, but Armstrong et al. (2002) recently indicated that it remains in common use in New Zealand.

Many methods (4, 7, 8, 9, 14, 18, 19, 23, and generally 20) require that the age of each nest be known. Other methods need this information only if age-related variation in DSR is an objective of the study, or is marked enough to require age-specific estimates to generate a satisfactory overall estimate (Grant et al. 2005). Ascertaining the age of nests accurately is fairly straightforward in some studies but nearly impossible in others.

Survival-time methods, which are widely used in many other applications, have been suggested for nest survival as well (Nur et al. 2004). Concerns about their suitability for routine use in nest-survival studies, remain, however, such as their ability to handle left truncation and interval censoring (Heisey et al., *this volume*).

The Mayfield estimator, despite its basis on what appears to be an extremely restrictive assumption (that DSR is the same for all days and all nests), has borne out rather well. In a number of comparisons with more sophisticated methods, it has proven competitive (Johnson, *chapter 1, this volume*). The Johnson (1979) variant, which obviates the need for Mayfield's midpoint assumption, likely will be useful in many situations, unless age-related variation in DSR is pronounced and sample sizes are large. Further, it can be readily calculated analogously to Shaffer's (2004) logistic-exposure method with a log link rather than a logistic link (T. L. Shaffer, pers. comm.). By doing so, biologists can compare the model with constant DSR to more complex models.

When more complex models are of interest, the choice usually is between the program MARK approach of Dinsmore et al. (2002)—or Stephens' version (2003) of that approach—and the logistic-exposure method of Shaffer (2004). The models are substantially similar, although program MARK generally requires that the ages of each nest be known. One difference arises when time-specific (or age-specific) covariates are included in the model. If visits to a nest are several days apart, the logistic-exposure method assumes the time-specific influence is the same on each day. In contrast, the program MARK approach allows the time-specific influence to vary day to day. It is unclear how frequently this difference will be appreciable. It should be noted that these approaches can be used with simple as well as complex models, and they lend themselves to addressing most common objectives. For example, if an objective is to estimate overall nest success, these methods can generate a pooled estimate that is comparable to, say, a Mayfield estimate. But, in addition, one can construct model-based estimators of nest success that can overcome biases resulting from the sample of nests being non-representative (Shaffer and Thompson, *this volume*).

Also, some methods, including those of Shaffer (2004) and Stephens (2003), readily permit random effects to be included in fitted models. Generally, the inclusion of random effects for factors such as study sites or years allows more appropriate inference to be made to the population of sites or years rather than merely to those sites and years that were sampled. The usual assumption that the mean of a random effect is zero is inappropriate for left-truncated data, however (Heisey et al., *this volume*), so the role of random effects in nest survival analysis is not yet clear.

Perhaps the greatest difference among the methods of Dinsmore et al. (2002), Stephens (2003), and Shaffer (2004) lies in the computer software requirements. To employ the first approach requires the user to be familiar with program MARK (White and Burnham 1999), a very powerful suite of software used to analyze mark-recapture data under a broad variety of models. The program and its documentation are freely available, but a substantial learning curve is involved. The latter two methods require the biologist to use generalized linear models software. Examples of such software include PROC GENMOD and PROC NLMIXED of SAS and the S function GLM. See Shaffer (2004) and Rotella et al. (2004) for further comparisons.

ACKNOWLEDGMENTS

Thanks to S. L. Jones and G. R. Geupel for organizing the symposium and inviting my participation. This report benefited from comments by S. L. Jones and T. L. Shaffer. I appreciate comments provided by authors of many methods I described, including N. J. Aebischer, J. F. Bromaghin, S. J. Dinsmore, R. E. Green, K. R. Hazler, C. Z. He, G. A. Jehle, B. F. Manly, C. E. McCulloch, R. Natarajan, N. Nur, J. J. Rotella, C. J. Schwarz, T. R. Stanley, S. E. Stephens, and especially D. M. Heisey. Each author helped me learn more about the methods they presented. C. J. Schwarz suggested the categorization of computation difficulty of the various methods.

Studies in Avian Biology No. 34:73–83

MODELING AVIAN NEST SURVIVAL IN PROGRAM MARK

STEPHEN J. DINSMORE AND JAMES J. DINSMORE

Abstract. Understanding the factors influencing nesting success is a primary goal of many studies. To do this effectively, more advanced tools than Mayfield's ad hoc estimator are needed. The recent development of a nest-survival model in program MARK provides a powerful and flexible tool for the study of avian nest survival that can incorporate seasonal variation in survival and nest-specific covariates. We briefly review the model and its development, illustrate how to include the effects of daily nest age and observer visits to nests, and conclude with an example analysis of Red-winged Blackbird (*Agelaius phoeniceus*) nest survival in Iowa. In this example, we found evidence for stage-specific differences in nest survival, seasonal patterns in nest survival that were best explained by a quadratic-time trend, and that survival differed between years. An exploration of several nest-specific covariates revealed that blackbird nest survival was positively affected by nest height, weakly affected by nest placement (nests placed in living vegetation may have experienced slightly higher survival), and unaffected by clutch size and within- and between-cell nest placement.

Key Words: *Agelaius phoeniceus*, nest survival, program MARK, Red-winged Blackbird.

MODELANDO SOBREVIVENCIA DE NIDO EN PROGRAMA MARK

Resumen. Entender los factores que influyen el éxito de anidación es una meta primordial para muchos estudios. Para lograrlo efectivamente se necesitan más herramientas avanzadas que las estimador ad hoc Mayfield. El reciente desarrollo del modelo de sobrevivencia de nido en el programa MARK es muy poderoso y flexible para el estudio de sobreviviencia de nidos de aves, el cual permite incorporar variación estacional en sobrevivencia y covariantes específicas de nido. Revisamos brevemente el modelo y su desarrollo, ilustramos cómo incluir los efectos de edad diaria de nido y visitas observadas de nidos, y concluimos con un ejemplo de análisis de sobrevivencia de nido de Tordo Sargento (*Agelaius phoeniceus*) en Iowa. En este ejemplo encontramos evidencia de diferencias de estado específicas y patrones estacionales en sobrevivencia de nido, los cuales fueron mejor explicados por una tendencia cuadrática de tiempo, y encontramos que la sobrevivencia difirió entre los años. Una exploración de varias covariantes específicas de nido reveló que la sobrevivencia de nido de tordos estaba positivamente afectada por la altura de nido, débilmente afectada por la colocación de nido (nidos colocados en vegetación viva quizás hayan experimentado una sobrevivencia ligeramente más alta), y no hayan sido afectadas por el tamaño de la nidada y dentro y entre colocación de nidos célula.

Ornithologists have long been interested in studies of avian reproductive success, and nest survival, is the metric most frequently measured. The terms nest success, nesting success, and nest survival are used interchangeably in the literature and refer to the probability that ≥one egg hatches (precocial species) or that ≥one young fledges (altricial species). We prefer the term nest survival because success can be attained on >one nesting attempt in a season. Furthermore, if the species is precocial, nest survival may include the nest building, egg-laying, and incubation stages. If the species is altricial, nest survival will include these three stages plus the nestling stage. Much of the nest-survival literature emphasizes estimating the probability that a nest is successful, although recently the focus has shifted more towards understanding factors that influence nest survival (Dinsmore et al. 2002, Rotella et al. 2004, Rotella 2005).

Approaches to estimating nest survival have until recently been rather simplistic. The early use of traditional estimates of apparent nesting success (the proportion of nesting attempts that are successful) was overshadowed by widespread acceptance of the Mayfield method (Mayfield 1961, 1975) by the 1970s. However, despite recent progress in the development of new approaches (Rotella et al. 2004) to modeling nest survival, the Mayfield estimator and its many variations (e.g., the Mayfield logistic approach; Hoover and Brittingham 1998, Aebischer 1999) are still widely used. The Mayfield approach, while intuitive and easy to compute, has several disadvantages that limit its use in investigating complex questions of avian nest survival: (1) survival is assumed to be constant over time, (2) the model cannot handle covariates in an efficient manner, and (3) the timing of losses must be known exactly. Given these deficiencies, alternate approaches to understanding avian nest survival were needed. This motivated the development of three similar approaches to modeling nest survival in a likelihood-based framework (Dinsmore et al. 2002, Stephens 2003, Shaffer

2004a) and a burgeoning interest in Bayesian approaches (He et al. 2001, He 2003).

Typically, ornithologists are interested in estimating nest survival for one of three primary reasons: (1) a desire to understand the processes that affect avian nest survival, (2) to provide best estimate(s) of nest survival, or (3) to incorporate estimates of nest survival into population-growth models. In this paper, we summarize the general approach to modeling avian nest survival in program MARK, introduce recent computational developments in MARK that will be useful to analyzing nest survival, comment on the application of this model to other types of studies, and provide a detailed example that illustrates our general modeling approach.

NEST-SURVIVAL MODEL

The nest-survival model described below (Dinsmore et al. 2002) is available in program MARK (White and Burnham 1999, Cooch and White 2005). This model is an extension of that described by Johnson (1979) and Bart and Robson (1982) and within the framework of MARK it offers a powerful and flexible tool for modeling nest survival. Many of the recent methods developed to analyze nest-survival data are similar, and the choice of a method probably depends more on the familiarity of the user with the software than with the details of the approach. MARK also offers the advantage of being menu driven, and minimizes the need for a user to be familiar with programming.

Here, the survival of a nest refers to the probability that a nest survives a specified time interval, typically 1 d. Briefly, the assumptions of this model are:

1. Nests are correctly aged when they are discovered.
2. Nest fates are correctly determined.
3. Nest discovery and subsequent nest checks do not influence survival.
4. Nest fates are independent.
5. Homogeneity of daily nest-survival rates.

Assumption 1 is the strongest, but in many studies the nest can be accurately aged using proven techniques such as candling or egg flotation (Westerkov 1956). Meeting assumption 2 is not often a problem if evidence at the nest can be used, e.g., the presence of eggshell fragments in the nest cup to infer hatching (Mabee 1997). Assumption 3 can be relaxed and modeled directly using the approach of Rotella et al. (2000). Assumption 4 can be a problem for analyses of aggregated species (e.g., colonial nesting birds), although violation of this assumption could be minimized by careful selection of nests for inclusion in the sample. Assumption 5 simply implies that estimated survival rates apply equally to all nests.

The nest-survival model in program MARK requires five pieces of information for each nest, and these are indexed by the letters in parentheses:

1. The day the nest was found (k).
2. The last day the nest was checked alive (l).
3. The last day the nest was checked (m).
4. The fate of the nest (0 = successful, 1 = unsuccessful) (f).
5. The number of nests with this encounter history. This will normally be 1 as most studies will include nest-specific covariates in the analysis.

Program MARK uses this information to construct an encounter history for each nest in live-dead (LDLD...) format. Examples of rules governing the coding of the triplet involving k, l, and m (where $k \leq l \leq m$) and the fate (f) can be found in the MARK help file.

In the nest-survival model, the encounter history is coded differently than in other models in program MARK. Basic nest information (k, l, m, and f) is entered in days by the analyst and then converted in MARK to an encounter history. The first step is for the analyst to convert calendar dates (the format in which field data are usually collected) to numerical days such that day 1 is the first date any nest in the sample was monitored. To illustrate this, suppose that in a 2-yr study the first nest was found on 5 May in year 1 and on 2 May in year 2. To convert dates to days, as required by MARK, 2 May would become day 1, 5 May would be day 4, etc. MARK then uses this information and the fate to construct the appropriate encounter history in LD format. Note that it is not necessary that time intervals between nest visits be equal, nor do they need to follow any consistent pattern between nests.

If appropriate, nests are assigned to groups using the following lines in the input file in program MARK:

```
Nest survival group = 1;
                     /* k  l   m f number */
/* 1994 33   */    13 15  15 0    1;
/* 1994 15   */    54 57  57 0    1;
/* 1994 39B  */    32 35  35 0    1;
/* 1994 29   */    13 15  15 0    1;
Nest survival group = 2;
/* 1994 33   */    15 24  26 1    1;
/* 1994 15   */    57 68  68 0    1;
/* 1994 16   */    17 20  24 1    1;
/* 1994 21   */    13 20  20 0    1;
    etc.
```

Groups will usually represent discrete subsets of the data such as nests monitored at different sites or in different nest stages. A comment field (the text between /* and */, ignored by MARK) can be used to reference nest-specific information of interest to the analyst, such as a nest identification number or nest stage.

The following illustrates the likelihood (L) function for the daily survival (S_i) from day i to day i+1 for a sample of n nests is:

$$L(S_i \mid k_j, l_j, m_j, f_j) \propto \prod_{j=1}^{n} \left[\left(\prod_{\substack{i=k \\ (k<l)}}^{l-1} S_i \right) \left(1 - \prod_{i=l}^{m-1} S_i \right)^{f} \left(\prod_{i=l}^{m-1} S_i \right)^{1-f} \right]$$

To illustrate how the model is parameterized, consider a nest that is found on day 1, is checked and still active on day 6, and is checked again on day 9 and found to be depredated. The fate of this nest is coded as 1 (f = 1, a failure).

Day								
1	2	3	4	5	6	7	8	9
↑					↑			↑
Found (k)					First check (l)			Last check (m)

This nest is known to have survived until day 6. The probability of surviving the first interval (from day 1 to day 6) is then

$$\prod_{\substack{i=k \\ (k<l)}}^{l-1} S_i = S_1 S_2 S_3 S_4 S_5$$

The nest was lost sometime between days 6 and 9. The three possible outcomes explaining this loss are: 1) the nest was lost between days 6 and 7 [$(1-S_6)$], 2) the nest survived until day 7 and was lost between days 7 and 8 [$S_6(1-S_7)$], and 3) the nest survived until day 8 and was lost between days 8 and 9 [$S_6S_7(1-S_8)$]. The probability of being lost any time during the interval between days 6 and 9 is then 1 minus the probability of surviving this interval, which can be written as

$$\left(1 - \prod_{i=l}^{m-1} S_i \right)^{f} = 1 - S_6 S_7 S_8$$

The third term in the model likelihood has a value of one. Thus, the overall probability of observing this encounter history is $S_1S_2S_3S_4S_5[1 - S_6S_7S_8]$.

Building models in program MARK is straightforward for those who are familiar with the program, have a basic understanding of generalized linear modeling, and possess an understanding of basic statistical methods. MARK offers a wide array of modeling options including the choice of a link function, the ability to provide initial parameter estimates to aid model convergence, and the ability to include functions in the design matrix (useful for modeling nest-age effects—see below), all of which are particularly useful for nest-survival analyses. Output options include estimates of real parameters (they can be exported to the spreadsheet Excel for easy construction of graphics) and the betas (necessary for generating predictive functions outside MARK), a variance–covariance matrix of the betas, and model averaging. The time needed to run models will vary depending on complexity. Using a fast computer with lots of memory (>512 MB of RAM), most model runs will take <1 min, unless you have a huge dataset with lots of individual covariates, which can take an hour or more to complete a single model run.

Modeling Considerations in MARK

The nest-survival model in program MARK offers a suite of modeling options, similar to other models in MARK. Once a set of candidate models is built in MARK, Akaike's information criterion (AIC; Akaike 1973) model selection is used to choose a model or models for inference (Burnham and Anderson 2002). Two features in MARK may be especially useful to users of the nest-survival model. First, the product function can be easily used to create non-linear relationships for covariates, as described in the MARK help file. Second, for those interested in incorporating a daily nest-age effect, a simpler approach than that of Dinsmore et al. (2002) can now be used. Consider an example where the nesting season is 10 d long and a nest is found at age 10 on day 1 and hatches (at age 15) on day 6. Under the old approach, a series of covariates, one for each day, was created to specify daily nest ages in the encounter history, as follows:

```
1  6  6  0  1      10 11 12 13 14 15
0  0  0  0;
```

Note that the first 5 numbers refer to k, l, m, f and nest frequency while the last 10 numbers are the daily nest age covariates. In MARK, the daily nest-age effect would be modeled in the design matrix by including a single column with a linear arrangement of daily covariates (Fig. 1a). Constructing the matrix of covariates using this approach can be cumbersome and is unnecessary. Instead, this encounter history could be constructed by replacing the daily

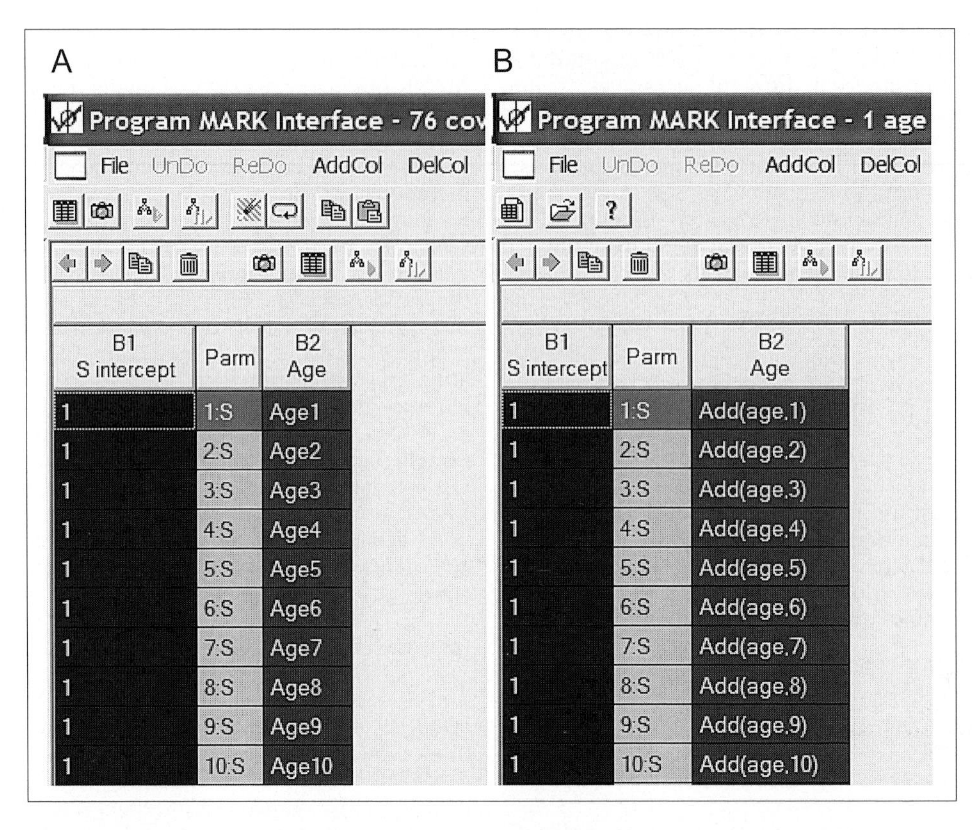

FIGURE 1. The design matrix in program MARK showing how age effects can be coded. In (a) the age effect is entered as a series of day-specific covariates in the input file while in (b) only a single age covariate is entered in the input file.

nest-age covariates with a single covariate for the age of the nest at discovery. The new encounter history would then be:

1 6 6 0 1 10;

Here, the same daily nest-age effect is modeled in MARK using the design matrix and a product function that increments the nest age daily until is succeeds or fails (Fig. 1b).

Some investigators may also be interested in modeling the possible effect on survival of observer visits to the nest (Rotella et al. 2000, Stephens 2003). The idea here is that survival may somehow be affected (usually negatively) for a short time period after the actual nest visit by the researcher. To model this in MARK, create a series of nest-specific covariates, one for each day that is coded as 1 for a nest visit and 0 otherwise. To run this observer-effect model, add a single column in the design matrix and fill it with the day-specific covariates (Fig. 2).

A few additional points are worth mentioning. As noted by Dinsmore et al. (2002), currently no method is available for estimating extra-binomial variation (over-dispersion) in typical nest-survival studies, and this is an area where additional research is needed (Rotella et al. 2004; Johnson, *this volume*). Also a formal goodness-of-fit test for nest-survival data is lacking, and the only way to minimize problems with lack of fit is to take care to meet model assumptions in the study design and data collection stages. Care must be given to the selection of nests to be included in a nest-survival analysis. Most studies will seek to infer the results to a larger population of interest, meaning that the sample must be representative of that larger population. This can best be assured by using consistent field methods. Nest searches should be allocated proportionally to available habitat and an effort should be made to avoid finding only easy nests, such as those most accessible to the researcher. And finally, the sample of nests must be sufficiently large to generate survival estimates with good precision. No rules exist for determining sample size because this will depend on the amount of information provided by each nest (number of exposure days) and the level of detail in the

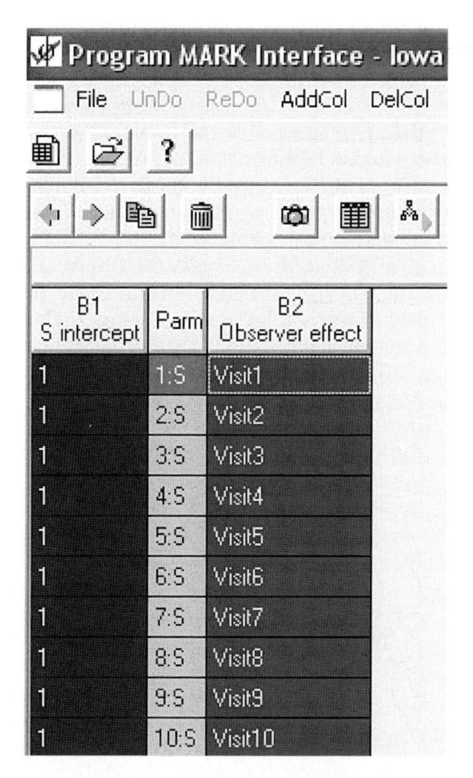

FIGURE 2. The design matrix in program MARK showing how an observer effect on nest checks can be coded. This design matrix codes for a simple model, S_{ObsEff}, where the observer effect in column two (B2) was modeled with a series of day-specific covariates called Visit1, Visit2, etc.

analysis (e.g., how many nest stages are being modeled). A related issue is the independence of nest-fates assumption, which makes studies of colonial birds problematic. In species where nests are aggregated, violation of this assumption could be minimized by study design considerations such as selecting nests from throughout the colony.

EXAMPLE—RED-WINGED BLACKBIRDS

To illustrate the use of program MARK for a nest-survival analysis, we present a detailed example below that includes a general modeling approach and presentation of select MARK output. This example is intended primarily as an illustration of a program MARK nest-survival analysis and not as a thorough biological analysis.

The Red-winged Blackbird (*Agelaius phoeniceus*) is a common and widespread breeding bird throughout much of North America where it breeds in a variety of wetland and upland habitats (Yasukawa and Searcy 1995). Information on its breeding biology is extensive (Beletsky 1996), and it is arguably one of the better studied North American breeding birds. The mating system is polygynous (Searcy and Yasukawa 1995, Beletsky 1996); eggs and young are brooded only by the female, although the male assists with feeding (Yasukawa and Searcy 1995). Apparent nesting success estimates ranged from 40–88% in a large study (Dyer et al. 1977). The causes of nest failure are varied, but most sources indicate that predation is the primary factor (Caccamise 1976, Yasukawa and Searcy 1995). Factors thought to influence nesting success are many and include weather, habitat type, habitat characteristics at the nest site, brood parasitism by Brown-headed Cowbirds (*Molothrus ater*), and age and experience of the tending adults (Yasukawa and Searcy 1995). Collectively, this information suggests several interesting hypotheses regarding the nest survival of the Red-winged Blackbird that can be easily tested in MARK.

METHODS

In 1994, JJD initiated a study of Red-winged Blackbird nest survival at a set of mesocosms on the Hinds Irrigation Farm near Ames, Iowa. The study continued through 2002, except that no data were collected in 2000. Mesocosms were constructed in 1989, and each consisted of a polyethylene tank 3.35 m in diameter and 0.91 m deep. The tanks were arranged in eight rows of six tanks each, spaced at 5.61 m intervals. Tanks were sunk into the ground so that the rims were just above ground surface. Each tank was filled with a three-inch layer of gravel covered with about 53 cm of sediment taken from another wetland. In fall 1989, cattail (*Typha* spp.) rootstocks were planted in the mesocosms (two plants per square meter, or about 15 plants per mesocosm). Cells were capable of holding water, and were seeded from wetland soils and the seed bank it contained. By fall 1991, the number of cattail shoots in the mesocosms ranged from 62–92 shoots per square meter, similar to shoot densities found in natural wetlands in north-central Iowa (Crumpton 1993).

Nests were located by systematically searching mesocosms at 2 or 3 d intervals. An observer walked the perimeter of each cell and carefully checked the vegetation for new nests. Red-winged Blackbirds vigorously defend their nest, making them relatively easy to locate. When a new nest was found the location of that nest within the cell was carefully noted. Because of the ease of locating nests and the frequency of searches, most (N = 162; 88% of total) nests were found during the nest building or egg-laying stages. Because of the small size of the cells, the contents of most nests could easily be viewed without entering the cell, either directly or with the use of a mirror attached to a pole. Only rarely was it necessary to enter the cell to view the contents of a nest.

A key assumption for our analyses is that the transition time between nest stages is known. If these are unknown, then the approach of Stanley (2000) can be used to estimate stage-specific nest survival rates. In our example, we visited nests frequently and were able to accurately assign transition times on the basis of one or more of the following pieces of evidence: (1) known nest-initiation date based on observation of egg-laying, (2) presence of both eggs and young in the nest on a single visit, or (3) presence of young in the nest that could be readily aged based on personal experience (Baicich and Harrison 1997). Based on published information, we assumed that Red-winged Blackbirds laid one egg per day, that incubation began with the laying of the second to last egg and lasted 11 d, and that the nestling period lasted 12 d (Yasukawa and Searcy 1995, Baicich and Harrison 1997). Lastly, we assumed that hatch day was the first day the nest contained ≥one nestling.

In our nest survival analysis, we were interested in understanding the possible influence of several factors on nest survival, many of them suggested in previous studies. These factors illustrate many of the advantages of modeling nest survival in MARK, and included:

1. Nest stage. We collected data during the egg-laying, incubation, and nestling stages for this analysis; some nests were observed during construction, but too few to incorporate into this analysis. We hypothesized that evidence of stage-specific differences in nest survival would be evident with survival being lowest during the nestling stage due to the increased activity at the nest (Caccamise 1978).
2. Nest position in mesocosms. We examined whether nest placement along the edge (E) or in the center (C) of the mesocosm had any influence on nest survival. We defined the edge as a ring that included the outer 1 m of each mesocosm; the remainder of the cell was considered the center. Because most nest losses in this species are thought to result from predation (Caccamise 1976, Beletsky 1996), we hypothesized that survival would be lower near the edge of the mesocosm because those nests were more accessible to nest predators, such as raccoon (*Procyon lotor*), mink (*Mustela vison*) (Knight et al. 1985, Sawin et al. 2003), American Crow (*Corvus brachyrhynchus*), and Common Grackle (*Quiscalus quiscula*).
3. Nest position among mesocosms. Given the arrangement of mesocosms, we investigated whether nests located in the outer (O), middle (M), or interior (I) band (24, 16, and 8 cells, respectively) had different nest-survival probabilities. We hypothesized that there might be slight differences in nest survival within these bands with survival generally being higher in interior nests due to decreased vulnerability to nest predators.
4. Nest height. We measured height of the nest above water (in centimeters) and hypothesized that higher nests would have increased survival because they were less accessible to raccoons and minks. For nests where height was not measured ($N = 8$), we assigned them the mean height (75 cm) of the entire nest sample.
5. Nest placement. Here, we were interested in the placement of the nest in live or dead vegetation. We hypothesized that nests in live vegetation were higher and offered better nest concealment, and would thus result in greater survival. Conversely, nests placed in dead vegetation were lower and more conspicuous and were expected to be more vulnerable to predation and experience lower survival. These hypotheses are generally consistent with other information suggesting that nests placed in live material are more successful (Yasukawa and Searcy 1995). We also note that seasonal variation in vegetation growth meant that a greater percentage of dead material occurred early in the nesting season while live material predominated later in the season.
6. Clutch size. We included clutch size as a covariate for all stages and for the nestling stage only, and reasoned that nests with larger clutches might be more vulnerable to predators because of increased activity at the nest (especially true during the nestling stage; Yasukawa and Searcy 1995). Caccamise (1976) reported that apparent nest success was lowest for small clutches, although this may have been the result of partial depredations and nest abandonment. That study also found that nests with a clutch of three eggs were the most successful while nests with four or five eggs experienced lower success.
7. Temporal patterns in survival within years. Other studies of avian nest survival (Klett and Johnson 1982) have found

evidence for within-year differences in nest survival. These patterns arise from a variety of factors including differences in nest timing between more and less experienced adults, temporal shifts in predator communities, weather patterns, and changes in the behavior of adults and young. For Red-winged Blackbirds, Caccamise (1976) showed that survival initially declined during the first 4 d of the incubation period, leveled off through the early nestling stage, and then dropped again until the young fledged.

8. Temporal patterns in survival between years. Others (Beletsky 1996) have noted that Red-winged Blackbird nest survival varied greatly from year to year with some years of almost total failure and other years with high nest survival. In some years, most nests were lost to predation, perhaps due to one or a few predators, while in other years most nests were successful.

We divided nests into three groups to correspond to different nest stages (egg-laying, incubation, and nestling). Thus, it was possible that a single nest could be a member of 1, 2, or 3 groups. For nests that were members of >one group, we censored the nest on the last day of observation for the first stage, and then initiated it on that day for the second stage. As an example, consider a nest from a two-stage (incubation and nestling periods) analysis that is found on day one and is in the incubation stage when it is discovered. Furthermore, suppose the nest is known to hatch on day 10, but then fails sometime between days 15 and 17 (before the young successfully fledge). This nest would be split into two encounter histories, one corresponding to each nest stage, and nest stages would be considered groups in the analysis. The encounter history for the incubation stage would be:

```
Nest survival group = 1;
    1    10    10    0    1;
```

The first three numbers are k, l, and m, the next number is fate, and the last column corresponds to the number of nests with this encounter history. Note that this stage is coded as a success (fate = 0) because it successfully transitioned into the nestling stage. The second encounter history for this nest would be:

```
Nest survival group = 2;
    10    15    17    1    1;
```

Notation is as above, except that this nest belongs in a different group (group 2 = nestling stage) and was unsuccessful (fate = 1, meaning the young did not fledge).

We combined year and nest stage effects into groups, resulting in $3 \times 8 = 24$ groups for our analysis. Note that in MARK it is possible to run the same analysis by coding the groups as covariates, although we prefer the use of groups. Other nest-specific covariates included nest height (continuous), clutch size (discrete), nest support (binary), nest placement within a mesocosm (binary), and nest position among mesocosms (discrete, three categories).

We used a hierarchical-modeling approach to build models to explain variation in the nest survival of Red-winged Blackbirds, mainly to keep the model set small with such a large number of covariates. Model building occurred in three steps:

1. We began by fitting five models to explain within and between year variation in nest survival. These models included constant survival, linear (T) and quadratic (TT) time trends, and year effects (year). We also chose to combine year effects with the best source of within-season temporal variation (constant, T, or TT) into an additive model. In our notation, a T denotes a linear temporal pattern, which can occur within a season or specific nest stage.
2. We next explored possible stage-specific differences by adding three sources of variation: (a) constant survival within each stage, (b) a linear time trend in survival within each stage, and (c) a quadratic time trend within each stage. For time trends, we considered models with separate trends for each stage and with a common trend across stages.
3. Finally, to the best model from step 2 we added the nest specific covariates singly. If >one individual covariate was represented in competing models (ΔAIC < 2), we then combined them in an additive fashion in a single model.

After the modeling was complete, we followed the general approach of Burnham and Anderson (2002) for making inference from our model set. Our results emphasized (1) understanding the factors influencing nest survival in Red-winged Blackbirds, and (2) using models to predict the influence of various factors on nest survival under a range of scenarios.

RESULTS AND DISCUSSION

Across the 8-yr study, we monitored a total of 184 nests (Table 1; 2,775 effective samples due to some nests being in >one group) during the period 8 May–20 August. Clutch size

TABLE 1. TOTAL NUMBER OF RED-WINGED BLACKBIRD (*AGELAIUS PHOENICEUS*) NESTS AND THE NUMBER BY NEST STAGE MONITORED NEAR AMES, IOWA, 1994–2002.

		No. by nest stage		
Year	No. nests	Egg-laying	Incubation	Nestling
1994	23	11	23	13
1995	26	26	26	15
1996	17	16	17	16
1997	53	48	50	28
1998	20	20	18	3
1999	14	14	14	10
2001	8	5	8	3
2002	23	22	23	14
TOTAL	184	162	179	102

ranged from two–five eggs, and the percent of the total for each clutch size was 2% (two eggs), 23% (three eggs), 69% (four eggs), and 6% (five eggs). We considered a total of 17 models in our analysis. Our results suggest that the nest survival of Red-winged Blackbirds was influenced by year, temporal variation within nest stage, nest height and support, clutch size, and between-cell placement of nests in the mesocosms (Table 2). All of the top models contained the effect of temporal variation within nest stage, with a separate quadratic trend for each stage. The quadratic trend performed slightly better than a linear trend within nest stage (ΔAIC difference of 1.04), and both of these were substantially better than other trend models (Table 2). Evidence for year effects on survival was strong. Compared to 2002, nest survival in 1996 was substantially greater (β_{1996} = 2.97 on a logit scale, SE = 1.09, 95% CI was 0.84, 5.11) while survival in 1998 was lower (β_{1998} = –1.72 on a logit scale, SE = 0.56, 95% CI was –2.81, –0.63). Survival in all other years did not differ from 2002.

The top model had weak evidence for an effect of nest height (β_{Height} = 0.23 on a logit scale, SE = 0.16, 95% CI was –0.08, 0.55), and it suggested that nests placed at a greater height experienced higher survival. The effect of nest support in the third best model was also weakly positive ($\beta_{Support}$ = 0.13 on a logit scale, SE = 0.15, 95% CI was –0.17, 0.43), hinting that nests placed in live material survived better. The effects of clutch size and within- and between-cell nest placement were weak, and the confidence intervals for those effects were nearly symmetrical around zero.

One of the advantages of the modeling approach used in program MARK lies in the predictive nature of the models. Given a model, meaningful values of the variables (e.g., a nest-specific covariate) can be input to illustrate how they influence nest survival. In this example, we were especially interested

TABLE 2. MODEL SELECTION RESULTS FOR RED-WINGED BLACKBIRD (*AGELAIUS PHOENICEUS*) NEST SURVIVAL NEAR AMES, IOWA, 1994–2002.

Model	AIC_c	ΔAIC_c	w_i	K	Deviance
Year+*TT* by stage+height	786.21	0.00	0.23	17	751.99
Year+*TT* by stage	786.26	0.05	0.22	16	754.07
Year+*TT* by stage+support	787.56	1.35	0.11	17	753.34
Year+*TT* by stage+height+support	787.87	1.66	0.10	18	751.62
Year+*TT* by stage+clutch	788.04	1.83	0.09	17	753.82
Year+*TT* by stage+between cell	788.16	1.95	0.08	17	753.94
Year+*TT* by stage+within cell	788.22	2.01	0.08	17	754.00
Year+*TT* by stage+clutch (nestlings only)	788.29	2.08	0.08	17	754.06
Year	830.82	43.01	0.00	8	813.97
TT by stage	834.90	48.69	0.00	9	816.83
T by stage	835.94	49.73	0.00	6	823.91
TT across stages	842.16	55.95	0.00	3	836.15
TT within stages	842.96	56.75	0.00	3	836.95
Nest stage	844.28	58.07	0.00	3	838.27
T within stages	855.68	69.47	0.00	2	851.67
T across stages	857.65	71.44	0.00	2	853.64
Constant survival	859.12	72.91	0.00	1	857.12

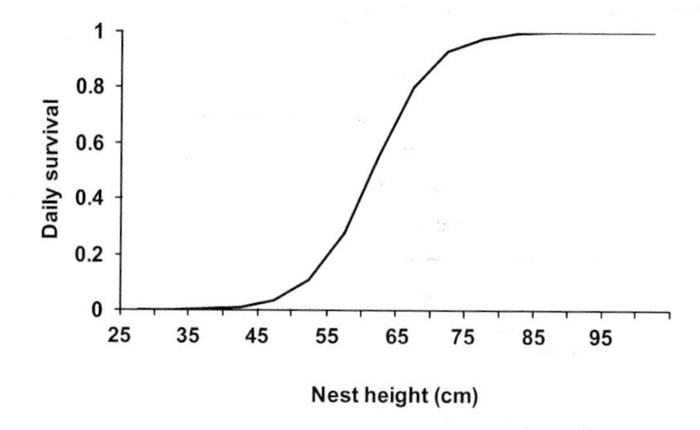

FIGURE 3. Predicted daily survival of Red-winged Blackbird (*Agelaius phoeniceus*) nests of differing heights during the 1995 incubation period. For illustrative purposes, survival is shown only for day one of the nesting season (2 May) across a range of nest height that approximates that seen during this study.

in understanding the influence of nest-specific covariates and nest stage on daily nest survival. To illustrate this, we first predicted the influence of nest height on the daily survival of 1995 nests in the incubation stage (Fig. 3). In this simple example, nest survival is predicted only for nests on day one of the study (2 May), although this could easily be extended to other days. Next, we predicted daily survival rates for each nest stage in what we considered a representative year (1995; Figs. 4–6), and further illustrated the influence of differing nest heights on survival. We chose to use values for the mean, 0.5 SD below the mean, and 1 SD above the mean to show that the influence of height was non-linear. Last, we show the predicted influence of nest support on Red-winged Blackbird nest survival (Fig. 7).

Our results confirm and add to what is known about patterns of Red-winged Blackbird nest survival. Our finding of stage-specific differences in survival is consistent with other literature on this species (Caccamise 1976, 1978), as are our within-stage temporal patterns except for the apparent increase at the end of the nestling stage. This result was unexpected and inconsistent with mechanisms explaining nest survival in altricial species, and we are at a loss to explain why we saw this pattern in our study. Strong year-specific differences in survival have been noted in other studies of this species (Beletsky 1996). Caccamise (1977) found that hatching success decreased with nest height whereas fledging success was not related to nest height. Among the habitat covariates we investigated, both nest height and support appeared to influence nest survival in ways consistent with other studies and published literature. We did not uncover any clear influence of nest placement within or among mesocosms, suggesting that either nest placement at this scale is unimportant or that we were unable to detect such an effect in our study. Clutch size did not appear to influence nest survival, even in the nestling stage, perhaps because our sample of nests included relatively few of extreme clutch sizes (one, two, or five eggs).

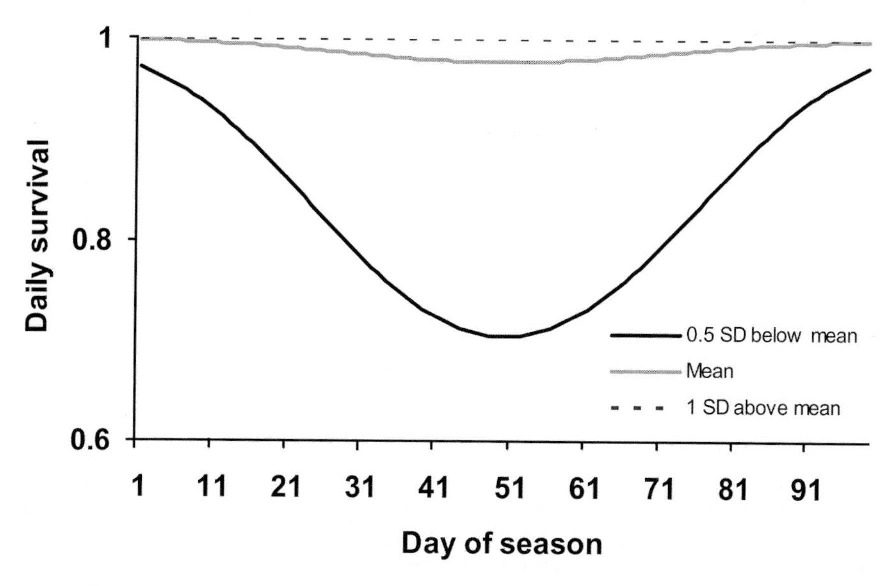

FIGURE 4. Predicted daily survival of Red-winged Blackbird (*Agelaius phoeniceus*) nests during the 1995 egg-laying period. Daily survival is illustrated for three scenarios of nest height: below average (0.5 SD below the mean), average (at the mean), and above average (1 SD above the mean).

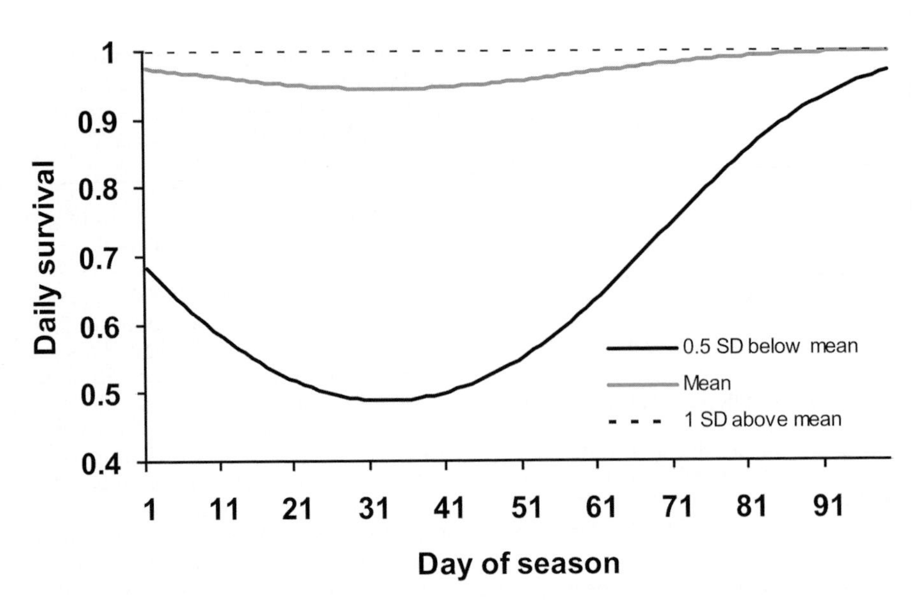

FIGURE 5. Predicted daily survival of Red-winged Blackbird (*Agelaius phoeniceus*) nests during the 1995 incubation period. Daily survival is illustrated for three scenarios of nest height: below average (0.5 SD below the mean), average (at the mean), and above average (1 SD above the mean).

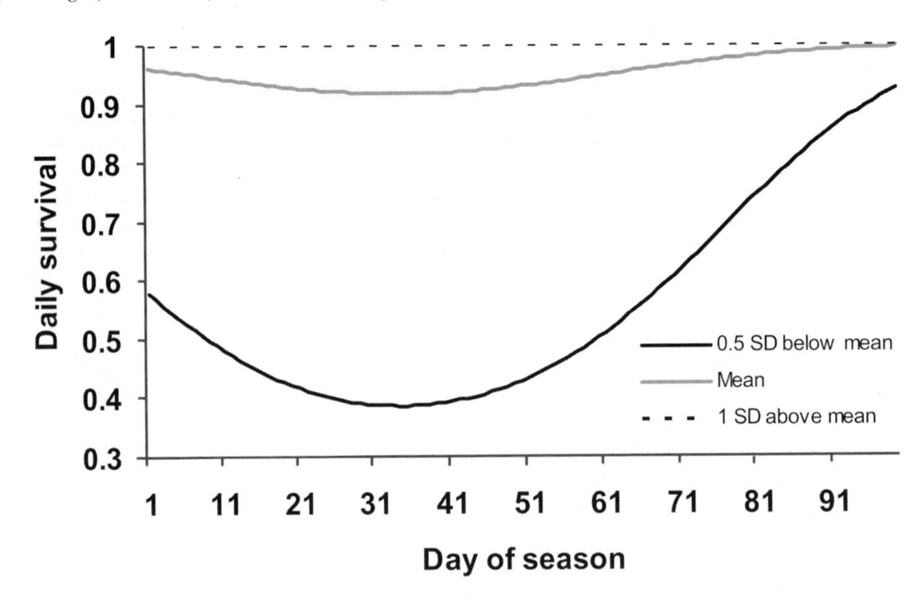

FIGURE 6. Predicted daily survival of Red-winged Blackbird (*Agelaius phoeniceus*) nests during the 1995 nestling period. Daily survival is illustrated for three scenarios of nest height: below average (0.5 SD below the mean), average (at the mean), and above average (1 SD above the mean).

RECOMMENDATIONS

Interest in studies of avian nest survival remains high, and researchers increasingly ask complicated questions in an attempt to better understand the processes affecting nest survival. This demand has promoted several recent developments which are rapidly gaining widespread use in the ornithological community. The long-standing Mayfield method and variations thereof are no longer accepted as the best approach for answering questions of avian nest survival.

The nest-survival model implemented in program MARK is one of these recent advances. Complete documentation for the model can be

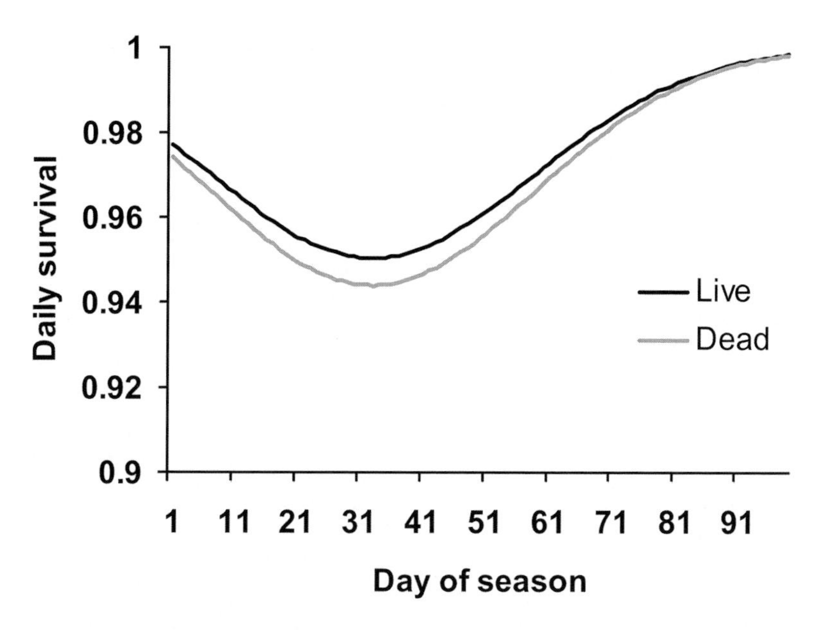

FIGURE 7. Predicted influence of nest support (live or dead material) on the daily survival of Red-winged Blackbird (*Agelaius phoeniceus*) nests during the 1995 incubation period.

found in Dinsmore et al. (2002). Additional support for program MARK is available through a detailed user's guide (Cooch and White 2005) and an on-line discussion group (http://www.phidot.org/forum/index.php). We hope that researchers conducting future studies of avian nest survival will find the nest-survival model implemented in MARK (or a similar model such as those mentioned in the introduction) appealing, and will recognize its many advantages.

ACKNOWLEDGMENTS

The mesocosms used in this study were established with primary funding from the Leopold Center for Sustainable Agriculture at Iowa State University. The College of Agriculture at Iowa State University provided funding for maintenance of mesocosms. William Crumpton provided access to the mesocosms, making this study possible. We also appreciate the field assistance of Tim Hanks and Sam Wickramasingh. This manuscript benefited from careful reviews by Mark Herzog and an anonymous referee.

Studies in Avian Biology No. 34:84–95

MAKING MEANINGFUL ESTIMATES OF NEST SURVIVAL WITH MODEL-BASED METHODS

TERRY L. SHAFFER AND FRANK R. THOMPSON III

Abstract. Model-based methods for analyzing nest survival can be used to investigate effects of continuous and categorical covariates and to produce less biased and more precise estimates of nest survival than design-based methods. Herein, we modeled avian nest survival using the logistic-exposure method, demonstrated how to make meaningful model-based estimates of nest survival, and provided examples using SAS. To produce estimates of nest survival with model-based methods, one first fits a model to the data and then uses that model to produce estimates for specific values of covariates in the model. Covariate values can be based on the sample (e.g., means for continuous covariates and proportions for categorical covariates), however, the sample of nests (and nest-days) is usually non-random and therefore may not be representative of the population of interest. Alternatively, nest-survival estimates can be based on covariate values that the investigator believes are more representative of the population to try and reduce bias resulting from non-random sampling. We discuss a general method that can be used to reduce bias by adjusting estimates for nests that were never observed. We illustrate the method with an example that involves estimating period survival when daily survival varies by date. When the survival model includes interactions among covariates, main effects can be misleading; it is therefore important to present survival estimates as functions of the interacting covariates. When support exists for multiple models, predictions should be generated from each model and then averaged to produce survival and precision estimates that account for model selection uncertainty. We offer some suggestions for presenting model-based results from studies of avian nest survival.

Key Words: design-based, estimation, logistic exposure, Mayfield method, model based, nest survival, population, sample, SAS.

HACIENDO ESTIMACIONES SIGNIFICATIVAS DE SOBREVIVENCIA DE NIDO CON MÉTODOS BASADOS EN MODELOS

Resumen. Métodos basados en modelos para el análisis de sobrevivencia de nido pueden ser utilizados para investigar efectos de covariantes continuas y categóricas, y para producir menos polarizaciones negativas y estimaciones de sobrevivencia de nido más precisas que los métodos basados en diseño. Además, modelamos sobrevivencia de nido utilizando el método de exposición logística, demostramos cómo hacer estimados basados en modelos significativos de sobrevivencia de nido, y proporcionamos ejemplos utilizando SAS. Para producir estimados de sobrevivencia de nido con métodos basados en modelos, primero se tiene que ajustar un modelo a los datos y después utilizar ese modelo para producir estimados para valores específicos de covariantes en el modelo. Los valores covariantes pueden estar basados en la muestra (ej., medias para covariantes contiguas y proporciones de covariantes categóricas), sin embargo, la muestra del nido (y días del nido) usualmente no es al azar, y por ello quizás no sea representativa para la población de interés. Alternativamente, las estimaciones de sobrevivencia de nido pueden ser basadas en valores covariantes los cuales el investigador crea sean más representativos de la población, para así tratar de reducir el sesgo causado por el muestreo de no azar. Discutimos un método general que puede ser utilizado para reducir el sesgo al ajustar estimaciones para nidos que nunca fueron observados. Ilustramos el método con un ejemplo que involucra período de estimación de sobrevivencia cuando la sobrevivencia diaria varía por día. Cuando el modelo de sobrevivencia incluye interacciones entre covariantes, efectos principales pueden ser engañosos; es por ello que es importante presentar estimaciones de sobrevivencia como funciones de covariantes interactuando. Cuando existe un soporte para modelos múltiples, las predicciones deben ser generadas de cada modelo y después ser promediadas para producir estimaciones de sobrevivencia y precisión que cuenten para la incertidumbre de selección del modelo. Ofrecemos algunas sugerencias para presentar resultados, basados en modelo para estudios de aves y sobrevivencia de nido.

Recent advances in techniques for modeling nest survival (Dinsmore et al. 2002, Rotella et al. 2004, Shaffer 2004a) provide new opportunities to examine nest survival in far greater detail than was previously possible with Mayfield's (Mayfield 1975) or similar methods (Johnson 1979). New methods allow daily survival to be rigorously modeled in terms of categorical, continuous, and time-dependent (e.g., nest age) explanatory variables. The new approaches can be used with simple or complex models and they can provide survival estimates that are comparable to past studies that used Mayfield's method, provided the investigator is willing to make the usual Mayfield assumptions that survival is constant nest to nest and day to day. A major advantage of the new techniques, however, is that they accommodate models in which daily survival rates vary among nests and among nest-days. These model-based estimators of nest survival are more realistic and precise, and less biased than Mayfield's estimator.

We used the logistic-exposure method (Shaffer 2004a) to model avian nest survival as a function of multiple explanatory variables and demonstrate how to make meaningful model-based estimates of survival. We describe various strategies for constructing model-based estimators and discuss circumstances under which one strategy may be more appropriate than another. We used the logistic-exposure method and provide examples using this method in SAS (SAS Institute 2004). However, the principles involved apply to other model-based methods as well (Dinsmore et al. 2002, Nur et al. 2004; Heisey et al., *this volume*). We provide SAS code that streamlines the process of generating model-based estimates when multiple models are involved and model-averaging is necessary. We offer suggestions for presenting model-based results.

EMPIRICAL VERSUS MODEL-BASED ESTIMATION

The properties of a sample are determined by the manner in which data are observed. For instance, if sample units are obtained completely at random then the sample mean provides an unbiased estimate of the population mean. Designs based on some form of random sampling lend themselves to design-based estimation because the design itself justifies the basic inference that results (Morrison et al. 2001). Design-based estimators, also known as empirical estimators, involve few assumptions, aside from the sample being representative of the population as a result of random sampling. A study of cavity nesting in artificial structures provides an example in which design-based inference is possible. In this situation, monitoring takes place on a sample of structures that can reasonably be assumed representative of a larger population of structures. Both successful and unsuccessful nests are easily detected, and therefore, the apparent estimator (number successful/number initiated) is an unbiased, design-based estimator of nest survival. Another situation in which design-based inference might be possible involves the use of radio telemetry to continuously monitor females for evidence of nesting.

Although design-based inference leads to estimators that are unbiased, those estimators can have large variances in comparison to model-based estimators. As their name implies, model-based estimators arise from the use of a model to exploit relationships between a response variable (Y) and predictor variables (X's), also known as covariates. For example, if Y is observed to vary linearly with X, then that relationship can be utilized in a model-based estimator of Y that will have smaller variance than the design-based estimator of Y, which ignores information about Y that is provided by X.

Non-random sampling is the norm in studies of nest survival because inactive nests do not have the same discovery probability as active nests. Therefore, design-based inference using the apparent estimator as illustrated above is usually not appropriate. Model-based methods can be used to increase precision when sampling is random, and they can help overcome issues resulting from certain types of non-random sampling. Mayfield's method is an example of a model-based estimator that addresses the issue of non-random sampling. Mayfield's model is somewhat simplistic in that it assumes that daily survival rates are constant within each stage of nesting and are the same for all nests. Mayfield's method treats the nest-day, rather than the nest, as the sampling unit. However, the sample of nest-days is itself non-random because nests are found at various ages and the probability of locating a nest is often a function of nest age. For example, newly initiated nests are irregularly attended by parents during laying and therefore are less likely to be found by nest searchers using methods that rely on flushing an adult near the nest; these nests are therefore underrepresented in samples. Mayfield's assumption of constant survival within stage was his way of dealing with this predicament. For instance, that assumption allows one to estimate the daily survival rate of a 1-d-old nest even if no 1-d-old nests are observed. Modern analysis tools, such as Shaffer's (2004a) logistic-exposure method, permit greater flexibility in addressing this and related issues. For example, Grant et al. (2005) used polynomial models to relax the assumption that survival was constant day to day and nest to nest and to generate model-based estimates of nest survival. Further complications resulting from uneven distribution of search effort across the breeding season, habitats, study areas, and years can also be addressed with model-based methods.

DAILY SURVIVAL VERSUS PERIOD SURVIVAL

We use the term daily survival to refer to the probability that a nest survives a given day, conditional on it being active at the beginning of that day. Similarly, we use the term period survival to refer to the probability of surviving a period of several days, conditional on being active at the beginning of that period. Period-survival estimates often are presented for the period beginning with the laying of the first egg through the day of fledging. Although modeling of nest survival is usually done in terms of daily survival rates, period-survival estimates are better-suited for some applications, such as when assessing population growth rates.

Perhaps the most widely used model-based estimator involves the estimation of period survival (*P*), which is simply the product of daily survival rates for each day in the period:

$$\hat{p} = \hat{s}_1, \hat{s}_2 \ldots \hat{s}_k$$

where the $\hat{s}_i$ are daily survival rate estimates and k is the number of days in the period. If a constant-survival model is used then $\hat{p} = \hat{s}^k$. Approximate lower and upper confidence bounds for P can be obtained by performing the same computations on the lower and upper bounds for the S_i.

FITTING A MODEL

The process of generating model-based estimates begins with development and selection of a nest-survival model (or models). The model expresses nest survival (typically daily survival rate) as some function of covariates, which can be either categorical or continuous and be measured on a group-, nest-, or unit-of-time (e.g., values can change daily) basis. The logistic-exposure method expresses the logit of daily survival rate as a linear combination of the covariates. We used the GENMOD procedure of SAS (SAS Institute 2004) to estimate parameters of our logistic-exposure models. We used the information-theoretic approach to rank models and assess their relative weights (Burnham and Anderson 2002). Model selection is an important topic that is beyond the scope of this paper.

Once a nest-survival model has been chosen and fitted, model-based estimates of survival are derived by substituting specific values for each covariate in the model. If no single model stands out as best, model-based estimates can be produced from each of the top models and the results averaged to arrive at a single estimate that reflects both sampling variability and model-selection uncertainty (Burnham and Anderson 2002).

ESTIMATING SURVIVAL

Model-based estimation differs from design-based estimation in that the investigator must choose values of covariates on which estimates will be based. The appropriate values for covariates will depend on the question being asked and what additional information the investigator may have about the population of interest. Two questions commonly addressed with model-based estimation are: what is the survival rate for a population of interest, and what is the effect of a covariate on nest survival? Categorical covariates often represent treatments, habitats, or years, whereas continuous covariates often reflect environmental factors, like precipitation, or temporal factors, such as nest age. Selection of covariate values to answer the first question could be based on values derived from the sample of nests or on additional knowledge about the population of interest. To answer the second question, values of categorical covariates are usually chosen to isolate a given treatment level or to provide an average across all levels of a treatment. Continuous covariates are usually evaluated at multiple levels that span the range of values in the sample or population of interest. We discuss and illustrate these approaches in detail below.

COVARIATE VALUES BASED ON THE SAMPLE

With this approach, covariate values are derived strictly from the data. A major limitation of this approach is that the sample of nests is usually non-random and therefore may not be representative of the population of interest. The sample mean (or median if the distribution is skewed) is the value usually used for a continuous covariate and the proportions of the sample represented by the various levels of a categorical covariate are used for a categorical variable.

We demonstrate how to produce an estimate of daily survival with SAS (SAS Institute 2004) based on a model that includes nest stage (laying, incubation, and nestling) and date as explanatory variables (Fig. 1). The value 172 following date in the ESTIMATE statement is the mean value of date in the sample, and values following stage represent the proportion of observations in the incubation, laying, and nestling stages, respectively. The estimate produced by the ESTIMATE statement is in the logit scale and needs to be back transformed to obtain an estimate of the daily survival rate. To do this

```
SAS code:

  proc genmod data=a descending;
    class stage;
    a=1/t;
    fwdlink link = log((_mean_**a)/(1-_mean_**a));
    invlink ilink = (exp(_xbeta_)/(1+exp(_xbeta_)))**t;
    model success = stage date/ dist=bin ;
    ods output Estimates=preddsr;
    estimate 'sample' intercept 1 stage .43 .07 .50 date 172;
  run;

  /*transform linear prediction to dsr*/
  data preddsr2; set preddsr;
    dsr=(exp(estimate))/(1+exp(estimate));
    dsrlow95 = (exp(lowercl))/(1+exp(lowercl));
    dsrup95 = (exp(uppercl))/(1+exp(uppercl));
  run;

  proc print; run;

  Output from proc print:

 Label Estimate  StdErr  Alpha   LowerCL  UpperCL   dsr   dsrlow95   dsrup95

Sample  2.8501   0.0875  0.05    2.6786   3.0216  0.945    0.936      0.954
```

FIGURE 1. SAS code and selected output illustrating use of the ESTIMATE statement in PROC GENMOD to estimate daily nest survival using the logistic-exposure method.

we output the estimate using an ODS output statement and do the transformation in a data step to produce the daily survival estimate (Fig. 1). Output from the ESTIMATE statement also includes the estimated standard error and 95% confidence limits for the logit. Although it is not possible to compute a standard error for the daily survival rate estimate from this output, we can produce a confidence interval for daily survival rate by back-transforming the logit confidence limits.

How should we interpret this model-based estimate of daily survival? Clearly it pertains to survival on day 172 (the average date in our sample), but the stage of the nesting cycle that this estimate reflects is less clear. Recall that we used the proportions of observations in the incubation, laying, and nestling stages to weight our estimate of daily survival rate. Because fewer nests are often found during egg-laying, our sample probably under represents the proportion of time spent in the laying stage and over represents the proportion of time spent in the incubation and nestling stages. An estimator that does not account for differences in nest encounter probabilities can give a biased view of the average daily survival rate across all stages of the nesting cycle. We provide a solution to this problem in the next section.

When might estimates based on means or proportions from the sample of nests be useful? Sometimes it may be reasonable to assume that the observed sample of nests is reflective of a larger population of nests. For example, a study examining nest survival of grassland passerines in relation to distance to edge could result in a sample of nests that approximated the unknown distribution of distances for all nests initiated in a field. If nest survival was found to vary with distance to edge, then one might want to base the estimate of survival of all nests on the average distance to an edge. A potential problem exists with using the mean value from the sample because the sample will be biased towards conditions that favor a nest being successful. Thus, if survival increases with distance to edge, the mean distance of sample nests will tend to overestimate the true mean. If the effect of distance on survival is not strong, then the bias may not be a big concern, but how one would objectively make that determination is unclear. We illustrate a procedure that can be used to correct for this type of bias in a later example.

Estimates based on covariate values derived from the sample may be sufficient when assessing treatment effects. Suppose in the above example that we wish to compare survival between managed and unmanaged grasslands. We must control for effects of distance to edge for this comparison to be meaningful. One way of doing that is to base the survival estimate for each treatment (unmanaged and managed) on the average value of distance calculated from the sample of all nests. This would be appropriate if the effect of distance was the same for both treatments (i.e., no treatment by distance interaction exists). However, no compelling reason exists to base the comparison on the mean value because the estimated treatment effect (i.e., difference in logit survival rates) is the same for all values of distance, unless treatment and distance interact. If treatment and distance are found to interact, then one should estimate treatment effects for a range of distance values (see below).

Covariate Values Based on the Target Population

Returning to our earlier example, suppose we desire an estimate of average daily survival rate that reflects the actual time allocated to each stage of nesting. We can produce such an estimate by specifying values of 0.19 (4/21) for laying, 0.48 (10/21) for incubation, and 0.33 (7/21) for the nestling stage. Here the proportions used for each stage are based on knowledge that laying, incubation, and nestling periods are 4, 10, and 7 d, respectively. This estimator gives equal weight to each day of the nesting cycle and theoretically produces an unbiased estimate of the average daily survival rate across all days of the nesting cycle. We say theoretically because the model must be correct to ensure that the estimator will be unbiased. This estimator utilizes information about the target population of nests (i.e., the length of each nest stage) that is not necessarily derived from the sample, and is an attempt to remove bias that results from the sample of nest-days being non-random. This estimator might be useful for comparing survival among species that had different age-related patterns in daily survival, or different durations in laying, incubation, or nestling periods.

Estimates that reflect the target population of nests are usually more desirable than those based on the sample. The target population might be defined as all nests initiated in a particular habitat block, all nests exposed to a particular treatment, or it can be somewhat nebulous as in the previous example. Consider an example in which the objective is to estimate nest survival in grass buffer strips surrounding wetlands in cropland. The target population is all nests initiated in buffer strips for some large cropland area. Suppose we choose a sample of five buffer strips to survey and that some of those strips are too large to be surveyed completely. Therefore we sample only a portion of the larger strips. Suppose the analysis indicates that survival varied among strips but was otherwise constant. A model-based estimator that gives equal weight to each buffer, regardless of the buffer size, will be a biased estimator of overall survival unless each buffer contained the same number of nests. In contrast, an estimator that weights each buffer by its area would be a reasonable estimator of overall survival if nest densities were similar among buffers. Issues like these require careful consideration on the part of the investigator to ensure that estimators are appropriate for the intended target population.

Interactions among Covariates

Model-based methods can be used to demonstrate the effect of a covariate while holding the effects of other covariates in the model constant, or to demonstrate interactions involving two (or more) covariates. To demonstrate this we fit a logistic-exposure model with covariates nest height and habitat (field or forest) and their interaction to data from Peak et al. (2004) on Indigo Buntings (*Passerina cyanea*). For ease of illustration we did not consider effects of nest stage or nest age. We held the effect of nest height constant by using the mean value of nest height from the sample (0.5 m) while producing an estimate for field and forest habitats (Figs. 2, 3a).

We also estimated daily survival across a range of nest heights for a population of nests split equally between field and forest habitats (Fig. 2, 3b). However, strong evidence indicated an interaction between nest height and habitat in these data. Thus, it was necessary to allow nest height and habitat to co-vary in order to obtain a clear understanding of the effect of each variable on survival (Fig. 2, 3c). This example clearly shows how main effects can be misleading when interactions are present.

Estimating Period Survival when Survival Varies with Date

Generating estimates that apply to the target population can be challenging because often we lack necessary information about that population. Earlier we discussed the desire to base the survival estimate on the mean covariate value (distance to edge) in the target population when the sample mean is a biased estimator. A similar situation occurs when daily survival varies with date and the objective is to estimate period

```
proc genmod data=indigo ;
    class hab;
    a=1/t;
    fwdlink link = log((_mean_**a)/(1-_mean_**a));
    invlink ilink = (exp(_xbeta_)/(1+exp(_xbeta_)))**t;
    model success = hab nestht*hab/ dist=bin ;

  /* estimate DSR by habtype while holding nestht = 0.5 */
    estimate 'field' intercept 1 hab 1 0 nestht .5 nestht*hab .5 0;
    estimate 'forest' intercept 1 hab 0 1 nestht .5 nestht*hab 0 .5;

  /* estimate DSR for 3 values of  nestht  giving equal weight to each habtype */
  estimate 'nesth0' intercept 1 hab .5 .5 nestht 0 nestht*hab 0 0;
  estimate 'nesth1' intercept 1 hab .5 .5 nestht 1 nestht*hab .5 .5;
  estimate 'nesth2' intercept 1 hab .5 .5 nestht 2 nestht*hab 1 1;

     /* estimate DSR by nestht and habtype to examine interaction */
    estimate 'field 0' intercept 1 hab 1 0 nestht 0 nestht*hab 0 0;
    estimate 'field 1' intercept 1 hab 1 0 nestht 1 nestht*hab 1 0;
    estimate 'field 2' intercept 1 hab 1 0 nestht 2 nestht*hab 2 0;
    estimate 'forest 0' intercept 1 hab 0 1 nestht 0 nestht*hab 0 0;
    estimate 'forest 1' intercept 1 hab 0 1 nestht 1 nestht*hab 0 1;
    estimate 'forest 2' intercept 1 hab 0 1 nestht 2 nestht*hab 0 2;
run;
```

FIGURE 2. SAS code to estimate daily survival rates by habitat type and nest height using the logistic-exposure method.

survival of all nests (P). The problem is easily seen when one considers the situation in which nests are classified as either early or late on the basis of nest initiation date. Let N_1 and N_2 be the numbers of initiated nests, and n_1 and n_2 the numbers of sample nests from the early and late periods. Let $N = N_1 + N_2$ and $n = n_1 + n_2$. Denote period-survival estimates for the two groups by $\hat{p}_1$ and $\hat{p}_2$. An intuitively reasonable estimator for P is $(N_1/N)\,\hat{p}_1 + (N_2/N)\,\hat{p}_2$. Because N_1 and N_2 are unknown, it is tempting to substitute n_1/n for N_1/N and n_2/n for N_2/N. However, if, for example, $P_1 > P_2$, then the expected value of n_1/n will be greater than N_1/N, and the estimator of P will be biased toward early nests.

Miller and Johnson (1978) proposed a solution to this problem in which they estimated N_i by dividing the number of successful nests by $\hat{p}_i$. Dinsmore et al. (2002) and Grant et al. (2005) used a related approach that is based on methods of Horvitz and Thompson (1952) and that incorporates information on both successful and unsuccessful nests. We provide an example (and SAS code; Shaffer 2004b) by considering the second-best model for Clay-colored Sparrow (*Spizella pallida*) from Grant et al. (2005). That model included cubic polynomial age effects and linear date effects:

$$\text{logit}(\hat{s}) = 2.054 + 0.812 \times \text{age} - 0.086 \times \text{age}^2 + 0.003 \times \text{age}^3 - 0.006 \times \text{date} \quad (1)$$

We begin by asking the simple question, what is the period survival rate (from initiation to fledge) of a nest initiated on day j? To be successful, the nest must first survive day j as a 1-d-old nest, then survive day $(j + 1)$ as a 2-d-old nest, and so on until it survives day $(j + k - 1)$ as a k-d-old nest. Note that for ease of notation, we are considering a nest to be 1 d old during its first day of exposure. We can express this relation as follows:

$$P_j = S_{j1}\, S_{(j+1)\,2} \cdots S_{(j+k-1)\,k} \quad (2)$$

It is clear from (1) and (2) that estimates of P_j will be different for each value of j. Period survival of all nests is a weighted average of the individual period survival rates: $P = \sum(N_j/N)P_j$, where N_j is the number of nests initiated on day j and $N = \sum N_j$. Thus to estimate P, we require estimates of the N_j (or estimates of N_j/N) for all j. Grant et al. (2005) estimated the N_j by scaling the number of observed initiations on day j upward to account for nests that failed before they could be discovered. For example, if they discovered a 2-d-old nest that was initiated on day j, they considered that nest to represent $1 \div \hat{s}_{j1}$ initiated nests. Similarly, a nest found at 3 d of age was considered to represent

$$1 \div \left(\hat{s}_{j1}\, \hat{s}_{(j+1)2}\right)$$

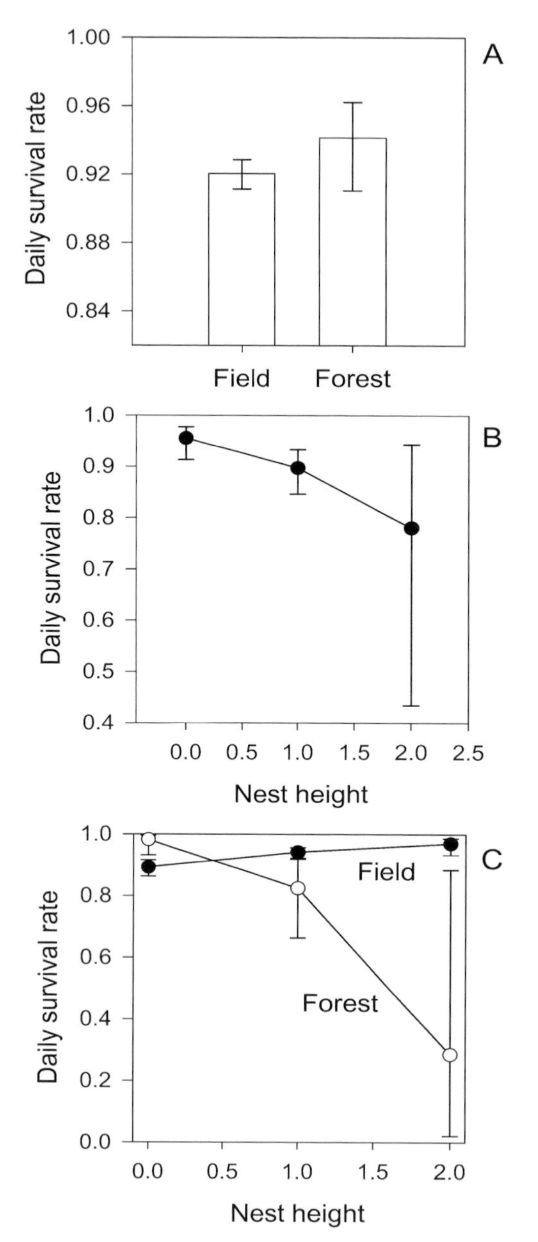

FIGURE 3. Effects of two covariates and their interaction from a logistic-exposure model of daily nest survival of Indigo Buntings (*Passerina cyanea*) in northeast Missouri. Data are from Peak et al. (2004).

initiated nests. These values were then summed by date of initiation to produce estimates of the N_j (Fig. 4).

This type of model-based estimator has received relatively little use, but appears to have potential for improving estimates of nest survival and nest density. However, properties of the estimator and situations under which it performs adequately have not been thoroughly investigated, and Grand et al. (2006) suggested caution in the use of the estimator because it is sensitive to errors in survival estimates. In addition, no straightforward method currently exists for computing estimates of precision. We expect the estimator to provide reasonable results when samples are large (N >100), when daily survival rates are not excessively low (>0.90), when nest searches are frequent and span the entire nesting season, and when the model fits the data and is not over-parameterized. The importance of a well-fitting model in model-based estimation can not be overstated, especially in this situation because the survival model is used to estimate both the daily survival rates and numbers of initiated nests. Thus errors in prediction from the survival model have the potential to be compounded. We consider the issue of model fit in greater detail later.

MODEL-AVERAGED ESTIMATES

We extend the above strategies for model-based estimation based on a single model to the multiple-model situation in which model averaging is necessary. In general, we produce a prediction based on a given set of covariate values from each model and then average the predictions using equations 4.1 (mean) and 4.9 (unconditional variance) from Burnham and Anderson (2002). We illustrate this with the Clay-colored Sparrow data from Grant et al. (2005). We consider four models for describing age-related patterns in survival (Fig. 5). The first is the cubic-age model reported by Grant et al. (2005) The estimated logit for a 10-d-old nest was 3.096 ± 0.144 (SE). The second model allowed for linear effects of age within laying, incubation, and nestling stages. The estimated logit from this model was 2.916 ± 0.126. The third model allowed survival to vary among stages but assumed that it was constant within a stage. The estimated logit from this model was 2.940 ± 0.125. The final model was based on the assumption of constant survival from initiation to fledging. The estimated logit from this model was 2.862 ± 0.087.

Model weights for the four models were 0.99, 0.01, <0.01, and <0.01, respectively, which indicates that the cubic-age model was vastly superior to the other models and that model averaging was unnecessary. For sake of illustration, however, the model-averaged prediction for a 10-d-old nest would be (0.99)(3.096) + (0.01)(2.916) + (0)(2.940) + (0)(2.862) = 3.093.

As the above example demonstrates, the process of generating model-averaged predictions is straightforward. In practice, however,

```
SAS code:

  data found;
  input initdate findage @@;
  cards;
  120 7 120 3 120 1 130 11 130 6 130 13 130 3
  run;

  data inits;
    retain b0 2.054 b1 0.812 b2 -0.086 b3 0.003 b4 -0.006; /* coeff. in logistic-
      exposure model */
    set found;
    f=1;
    do age = 1 to (findage-1);
      s = exp(b0 + b1*age + b2*age**2 + b3*age**3 + b4*(initdate
      + age - 1))/(1 + exp(b0 + b1*age + b2*age**2 + b3*age**3
      + b4*(initdate + age - 1)));
       f = f*s;
    end;
    found = 1;
    init = found / f;
    drop b0-b4 age s;
run;

  /* sum to determine no. nests found and to estimate no. nests initiated by date */
  proc means sum;
    class initdate;
    var found init;
  run;

  Output from proc means:

    Initdate    Nobs    Variable         Sum
       120        3       found       3.0000000
                           init       3.5839180


       130        4       found       4.0000000
                           init       5.7407344
```

FIGURE 4. SAS code for estimating numbers of initiated nests with a Horvitz-Thompson estimator that corrects for nests that failed before they could be discovered.

the coding of ESTIMATE statements in SAS can be very tedious and prone to error. The process quickly becomes unwieldy as the number and complexity of models or ESTIMATE statements increase. We developed SAS macro code (Shaffer 2004b) that greatly streamlines the process and reduces opportunities for error. The ESTIMATE statements are created by the macro at the time the model is run. The user controls the process by specifying the desired covariate values in a spreadsheet. Columns in the spreadsheet correspond to effects in the model, with column 1 being reserved for the label that identifies each ESTIMATE statement. Rows correspond to individual ESTIMATE statements, with row 1 containing the names of each effect in the model. Categorical covariates have a column for each category.

MODEL-BASED ESTIMATES OF PRECISION

A critical but sometimes overlooked aspect of estimating nest survival is deriving meaningful estimates of precision. Recall in our previous example that our sample under represents newly initiated nests, resulting in relatively few nest days corresponding to very young ages on which to base inferences. This is reflected in the cubic age and stage-specific linear models by the general narrowing of confidence intervals with increasing age (Figs. 5a, b). Less noticeable is the tendency for the confidence intervals to widen as survival decreases, reflecting the fact that the variance of the binomial distribution approaches its maximum value as the survival probability approaches 0.5. Our main point is that the precision estimates from these two

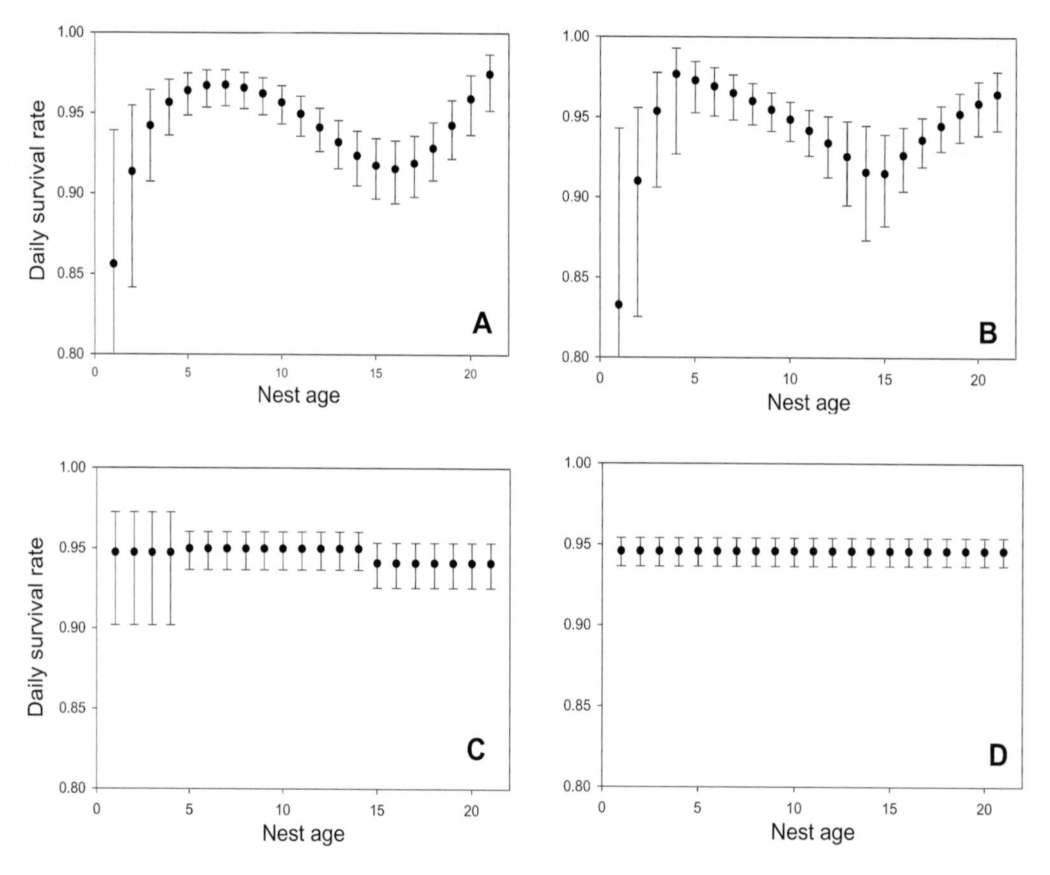

FIGURE 5. Four models of the effect of nest age on daily survival of Clay-colored Sparrow (*Spizella pallida*) nests: (A) cubic-age, (B) stage-specific linear, (C) stage-specific constant, and (D) constant survival. Data are from Grant et al. (2005).

models are intuitively reasonable given what we know about the distribution of nest ages from our sample.

In contrast, the stage-specific constant-survival model and especially the constant-survival model lead to precision estimates that seem unrealistic (Figs. 5c, d). For example, the number of intervals corresponding to 1-, 2-, 3-, and 4-d-old nests were 10, 17, 28, and 43, respectively. Yet, the stage-specific constant-survival model resulted in identical precision estimates for 1-, 2-, 3-, and 4-d-old nests. This is a consequence of the constant-survival assumption, and therefore the appropriateness of the precision estimates is highly dependent on the validity of that assumption.

IMPORTANCE OF A WELL-FITTING MODEL

Model-based estimates are only as good as the models on which they are based. Poorly constructed survival models can result in biased estimates of survival and precision. Unfortunately, no easy method exists to determine how well a model fits the data or to determine if overdispersion (extra-binomial variation) is present. Ideally we would like to have some sort of goodness-of-fit criterion that would allow us to assess model fit and adjust variance estimates for overdispersion. However, the usual goodness-of-fit tests based on the model deviance are not appropriate because the chi-square distribution provides a poor approximation to the sampling distribution of the deviance when sample sizes are small (McCullagh and Nelder 1989, Dinsmore et al. 2002). Small sample sizes are common when continuous covariates are present (i.e., N = 1 for many levels of the covariate). Model-selection results can indicate the relative support for a model compared to other models, and likelihood ratio tests can examine whether a particular model offers significant improvements over another model, but neither assesses how well a model fits the data. Instead, one must rely on ad hoc methods to assess model fit.

We use data from the previous example to illustrate a simple graphical method useful for investigating model fit. The method is analogous to comparing plots of observed and predicted values in ordinary linear regression. The method involves grouping observation intervals into discrete categories on the basis of the average age of the nest during the interval. For example, the first category might consist of intervals in which nests were 1- or 2-d old, the second category would include nests that were 3- or 4-d old, etc. One then estimates daily survival for each age category (treating age category as a CLASS variable) and visually compares the predictions from the best model to those estimates.

We grouped the Clay-colored Sparrow data into 11 age categories that included anywhere from 10 (age = 1–2 d) to 167 (age = 20–21 d) visitation intervals. Predicted values from the cubic age model showed close agreement with observed values of daily survival, except for the first age category (Fig. 6). This is not surprising given the small sample of very young nests. In fact, this situation might be a reasonable candidate for some sort of a weakly structured modeling approach (Heisey et al., *this volume*), such as a piecewise-polynomial spline. This approach would blend together a simple model, fit to the younger nests (where data are sparse), with a more complex model that applied to older nests. Regardless, the cubic age model seems to provide an adequate fit to these data.

Cross-validation (Snee 1977) is another method that can be used to judge the adequacy of a model. Sample sizes must be large enough to develop models first from a portion of the data and then evaluate those models by applying them to the remainder of the data. If cross validation does not reveal serious inadequacies with the structure of the model, then the model parameters can be re-estimated from the entire data set and model-based estimation can proceed from there.

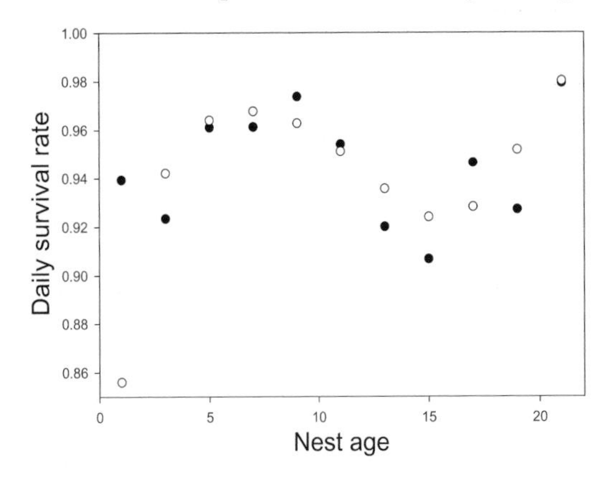

FIGURE 6. Observed (filled symbols) and predicted values (open symbols) of daily-survival rates of Clay-colored Sparrow nests (*Spizella pallida*). Observed values are logistic-exposure estimates based on grouping the data into intervals of age (i.e., 1–2 d, 3–4 d, etc.). Predicted values are based on the cubic-age model from Grant et al. (2005).

Neither of the above methods can guarantee that model-based estimates of survival will be unbiased. However, situations in which a model is clearly inadequate for making meaningful estimates of nest survival should become obvious. Models should also have some biological basis and not be derived purely from curve fitting. For example, Grant et al. (2005) argued that the cubic-age model was biologically reasonable because survival may vary among laying, incubation and/or nestling stages either in response to changes in predator numbers during the nesting season or by changes in cues that may allow predators to locate the nest. They offered several biologically based hypotheses that might explain patterns they observed.

PRESENTING RESULTS

We offer some suggestions for presenting results from studies of nest survival. We assume that through some process the investigator has arrived at a final model that has acceptable fit; other papers offer guidelines for presenting results from model selection or hypothesis testing (Anderson et al. 2001). We focus on presentation of model parameter estimates and estimates of nest survival derived from the model. The final model could be either a single best-fitting model or, in the case of multi-model inference, an average model. In addition to estimates discussed below we recommend reporting descriptive statistics for covariates because the range of variation observed provides the context for inferences that are made. We also suggest reporting descriptive information on visitation intervals and age when found, as that information can provide a gauge to the degree of interval-censoring and left-truncation (Heisey et al. *this volume*), and may be useful in comparisons with other studies.

MODEL PARAMETER ESTIMATES

Parameter estimates, which include the intercept (or constant term) and coefficients for each covariate, should be presented along with their standard errors in text or a table. In addition the number of nests and effective sample size (Rotella et al. 2004) should be reported. The coefficients can be difficult to interpret directly so we also recommend presenting odds ratios and their confidence intervals for covariates of particular interest. Odds ratios offer a more intuitive interpretation than the coefficients themselves (Allison 1999), and by simultaneously considering their magnitude and confidence interval, one can evaluate the strength of support for the effect.

Model-Based Estimates of Nest Survival

We assume that the investigator has generated some model-based survival estimates (and standard errors or confidence intervals) that are appropriate for the objectives. Estimates can be presented in tables or figures but figures often provide more insight, especially for continuous covariates or categorical covariates with several levels. Survival estimates should generally be calculated for the range of observed values of the covariate of interest while holding the values of other covariates in the model constant (see earlier sections on appropriate values for covariates), and provide the reader with specific values for variables that were held constant (as opposed to saying that the variable was held at its mean value). If interactions are present in the model, they should show the effects of one variable for a range of values of the other variable. Survival estimates should not be provided without estimates of precision. If figures are cluttered when estimates of precision are included, the analysis must clearly demonstrate that effects are real and properly documented in the text.

Although modeling is usually done in terms of daily survival rates (actually the logit of daily survival rates), we believe period-survival estimates are more intuitive and are therefore better suited for presentation in some cases. For example, in situations where daily survival is non-constant, period-survival rates can appropriately integrate effects of nest age or stage across the entire nesting cycle and simplify the presentation of other effects by reducing the number of variables in a biologically meaningful way (Fig. 2 in Grant et al. 2005). One must be sure to include information on the length of nest period or nest stages used to generate period-survival estimates. Daily survival estimates make sense when survival is constant (but so do period-survival rates) or when survival is non-constant and the goal is to illustrate effects of age (Fig. 5).

A question we often get is should I report Mayfield estimates too? The motivation behind this question is usually the desire for comparability with past studies that used Mayfield's method. Generally speaking, the answer to this question is no. Mayfield's estimator (including Mayfield logistic regression; Hazler 2004) is based on an approximate likelihood as a result of the midpoint assumption (Heisey et al., *this volume*). This results in a bias that can be either positive or negative depending on the lengths of the intervals between visits (and to a lesser degree on the survival rates themselves [Johnson 1979]). Although the bias is often small enough to be of little concern, it is nevertheless a bias that is unpredictable and inconsistent among data sets.

Johnson (1979) developed an alternative to Mayfield's estimator that was based on an exact likelihood and log link. Johnson's (1979) estimator did not receive much use because software was not readily available and because Mayfield's estimator generally performed well. The logistic-exposure model is also based on an exact likelihood, but uses a different link function than Johnson's (1979) estimator. However, a logistic-exposure model that assumes constant survival (day to day and nest to nest) will give results that are essentially identical to Johnson's estimator (Shaffer 2004a). We compared logistic-exposure and Mayfield estimates using data from several duck nesting studies on file at Northern Prairie Wildlife Research Center. We selected data sets to obtain a wide range in visitation intervals (6–25 d), numbers of nests (33–972), and 34-d-period survival rates (0.10–0.89). Under the assumption of constant-survival, logistic-exposure and Mayfield estimates were nearly identical (Table 1). Confidence intervals were similar when sample sizes were small ($N \leq 44$) or modest ($108 \leq N \leq 180$), and nearly identical when sample sizes were large ($N \geq 547$). We see no reason to report Mayfield estimates along with logistic-exposure estimates.

A more important issue is whether the constant-survival assumption can be justified. Further analysis of the above data sets revealed significant effects of age, date, or both age and date in data sets with $N \geq 132$. Thus, estimates based on the constant-survival assumption are likely biased to some unknown degree. An even bigger issue is how the sample of nests relates to the target population. To be meaningful, estimates of nest survival must be properly weighted to reflect the distribution of nests in the target population. Often practitioners new to modern nest survival methods develop a model and then fail to use that model to estimate nest survival. For example, the analysis might show that survival varied by X1, X2, and X3, but the method used to estimate overall nest survival is to pool all nests without regard to how the population of nests was distributed with respect to X1, X2, and X3. This mistake can lead to serious biases.

TABLE 1. COMPARISON OF LOGISTIC-EXPOSURE AND MAYFIELD PERIOD-SURVIVAL ESTIMATES (34 D) UNDER THE ASSUMPTION OF CONSTANT SURVIVAL FOR NINE DATA SETS

Species	N nests	Visitation interval (days)	Mayfield	Logistic-exposure
Mallard (*Anas platyrhynchos*)	33	6	0.27 (0.14–0.50) [a]	0.28 (0.12–0.45)
Blue-winged Teal (*A. discors*)	44	14	0.84 (0.72–0.98)	0.84 (0.66–0.93)
Gadwall (*A. strepera*)	35	23	0.71 (0.55–0.92)	0.71 (0.49–0.85)
Blue-winged Teal	108	9	0.27 (0.19–0.38)	0.27 (0.21–0.34)
Gadwall	132	19	0.89 (0.82–0.97)	0.89 (0.79–0.94)
Mallard	180	25	0.63 (0.54–0.74)	0.64 (0.54–0.73)
Mallard	547	7	0.10 (0.08–0.13)	0.11 (0.08–0.13)
Blue-winged Teal	553	9	0.39 (0.34–0.44)	0.39 (0.34–0.44)
Gadwall	972	21	0.32 (0.29–0.36)	0.33 (0.30–0.37)

[a] 95% confidence interval.

Therefore, we recommend that when reporting results of model-based estimation, practitioners be explicit about the assumptions they made and the evidence supporting those assumptions. If bias is likely, then potential sources should be reported and discussed.

Recent studies (Dinsmore et al. 2002, Nur et al. 2004, Grant et al. 2005) have demonstrated the importance of age as a covariate in nest-survival models. In most cases, effects of age could not be adequately represented by surrogates such as nest stage (laying, incubation, and brood rearing or, alternatively, egg and nestling). Yet, nest age is often not recorded in many nesting studies. We recommend that investigators whenever possible measure nest age, in addition to recording nest stage and date.

A goal of many nest-survival studies is to obtain an unbiased estimate of nest survival for some population of interest. One way of achieving this would be to base the survival estimate on a random sample of nests from the population. As we have discussed, random sampling of nests is seldom possible. Model-based methods described here offer a practical alternative, and when used properly provide meaningful estimates of nest survival.

ACKNOWLEDGMENTS

We are grateful to T. A. Grant, E. M. Madden, and R. G. Peak for use of their data in our examples. D. A. Buhl, D. E. Burhans, T. A. Grant, A. L. Holmes, and G. C. White provided comments that improved the manuscript. We thank G. R. Geupel and S. L. Jones for the opportunity to participate in the symposium.

Studies in Avian Biology No. 34:96–104

ANALYZING AVIAN NEST SURVIVAL IN FORESTS AND GRASSLANDS: A COMPARISON OF THE MAYFIELD AND LOGISTIC-EXPOSURE METHODS

JOHN D. LLOYD AND JOSHUA J. TEWKSBURY

Abstract. Several new methods for analyzing avian nest survival have been developed recently. To date, few tests have compared the performance of these new approaches with the traditional approach to nest survival analysis, the Mayfield method. To address this question, we used the Mayfield method to reanalyze data on avian nest survival from two published studies that employed the logistic-exposure approach, one of the Mayfield alternatives. We found that both approaches yielded nearly identical point estimates of daily nest survival, although the Mayfield estimates were less precise than estimates generated by the logistic-exposure models. Hypothesis tests conducted via the two different approaches also yielded generally similar results, although in one of the studies the Mayfield analysis failed to identify one of the significant covariates revealed by the logistic-exposure approach, apparently due to the imprecision of the Mayfield estimates. In sum, our results suggest that estimates of nest survival generated using the Mayfield estimator or its alternatives will be comparable, and that results of studies conducted using the Mayfield method should not be discounted. At the same time, our results reinforce the previously demonstrated advantages of alternatives such as the logistic-exposure approach: the ability to evaluate complex models of nest survival, consider individual and continuous covariates, and produce more precise estimates of daily nest survival.

Key Words: American Robin, *Calcarius ornatus*, Chestnut-collared Longspur, *Dendroica petechia*, grassland birds, logistic-exposure, Mayfield method, nest survival, riparian birds, *Turdus migratorius*, Yellow Warbler.

ANALIZANDO LA SOBREVIVENCIA DE NIDO EN BOSQUES Y PASTIZALES: UNA COMPARACIÓN DE LOS MÉTODOS MAYFIELD Y DE EXPOSICIÓN LOGÍSTICA

Resumen. Varios métodos para el análisis de la sobrevivencia de nidos de aves han sido desarrollados recientemente. A la fecha, pocas pruebas han comparado el funcionamiento de estos nuevos enfoques, con el enfoque tradicional de análisis de sobrevivencia de nido, el método Mayfield. Para tratar esta cuestión utilizamos el método Mayfield para reanalizar datos sobre sobrevivencia de nido, de dos estudios publicados que emplearon el enfoque de exposición logística, una de las alternativas Mayfield. Encontramos que ambos enfoques mostraron casi estimaciones de punto idénticas de sobrevivencia diaria de nido, a pesar de que las estimaciones Mayfield eran menos precisas que las estimaciones generadas por los modelos de exposición logística. Pruebas de hipótesis conducidas vía ambos enfoques también muestran en general los mismos resultados, a pesar que en uno de los estudios el análisis Mayfield falló al identificar una de las covarientes significativas revelada por el enfoque de exposición logística, aparentemente debido a la imprecisión de las estimaciones Mayfield. En resumen, nuestros resultados sugieren que estimaciones de sobrevivencia de nido generadas utilizando el estimador Mayfield o sus alternativas, serán comparables, y que los resultados de estudios conducidos utilizando métodos Mayfield no deberían ser descontinuados. De igual forma nuestros resultados refuerzan las ventajas anteriormente demostradas de alternativas tales como el enfoque de exposición logística: la habilidad de evaluar modelos complejos de sobrevivencia de nido, consideración de covariantes individuales y continuas, y la producción de estimaciones más precisas de sobrevivencia de nido diaria.

Most studies of avian nest survival address two distinct components: estimation of daily nest survival rates and tests of hypotheses about the causes of variation in daily nest survival. Until recently, the Mayfield (Mayfield 1961) method has been the de facto standard for estimating daily nest-survival rate, and was used widely in hypothesis testing. However, testing hypotheses with the Mayfield method requires making contrasts among groups of nests and thus the types of hypotheses that could be tested has been limited. Over the past several years, a handful of new methods for estimating and comparing rates of daily nest survival have been developed that address some of the limitations of the Mayfield method and offer the opportunity for more complex analyses of nest survival (Dinsmore et al. 2002, Nur et al. 2004, Rotella et al. 2004, Shaffer 2004a). Although the advantages of these new approaches have been well established, rarely addressed is the extent to which analyses conducted under these new approaches will yield results that differ from the Mayfield method (but see Jehle et al. 2004). Answering this question is important for at least two reasons.

First, although Mayfield's estimator of daily nest survival is ad hoc, it is an unbiased, maximum-likelihood estimator (Hensler and Nichols 1981) like the proposed alternatives. Furthermore, it is simple to calculate, as is the standard error of the estimator (Johnson 1979). In contrast, estimating daily nest survival under all of the proposed alternatives requires the use of more complex statistical tools (e.g., generalized linear modeling), an understanding of model-based inference, and may require the use of specialized software (e.g., program MARK; Dinsmore et al. 2002). Given that the Mayfield method is easier to implement, many investigators may wish to continue using it for estimation purposes or for hypothesis tests conducted on grouped data. Thus, it is useful to compare results and inferences gained through the Mayfield method and its alternatives. Do hypothesis tests conducted with the Mayfield method commonly yield equivalent results to more complex models evaluated using one of the alternative methods? Second, an extensive body of nest survival estimates generated using the Mayfield approach exists; understanding how estimates generated under the Mayfield method differ from estimates generated by alternative methods is important if results obtained under different analytic approaches are to be compared.

Several existing studies contain information that can be used to evaluate the similarity of estimates obtained under different approaches (Rotella et al. 2004; Shaffer 2004a; Winter et al. 2004, 2005a, b). Jehle et al. (2004) addressed this question explicitly by comparing site-, year-, and stage-specific estimates of Lark Bunting (*Calamospiza melanocorys*) nest survival generated by the Mayfield method, the nest-survival module in program MARK (Dinsmore et al. 2002), and the method described by Stanley (2000, 2004a), and found that the estimates generated by different methods were nearly identical. Here, we add to this existing information by comparing estimates of daily nest survival and the results of hypothesis testing completed under the Mayfield method and the logistic-exposure approach (Shaffer 2004a). We chose to evaluate the logistic-exposure approach in particular as an alternative to the Mayfield estimator for several reasons. First, it has been widely adopted in studies of avian nesting success (Peak et al. 2004; Winter et al. 2004, 2005a, b); second, it is identical or comparable to other linear-modeling approaches in terms of both the estimates it generates and the way in which it evaluates independent variables (Rotella et al. 2004, Shaffer 2004a); and finally, it has not been included in previous comparisons with the Mayfield estimator (but see results in Shaffer 2004a; Winter et al. 2004, 2005a, b).

The Mayfield method and the logistic-exposure approach are fundamentally different in how they treat estimation and comparison of daily nest survival rates. In particular, the logistic-exposure approach relies on evaluating the strength of support for linear combinations of variables assembled into a set of candidate models. The best-supported model is generally used for estimation purposes, and the strength of all variables considered is addressed by evaluating odds ratios, which can be averaged across all models. In contrast, the Mayfield method relies on categorical comparisons among variables rather than a model-based approach to inference. Thus, directly parallel contrasts of the two methods are difficult to obtain. To compare the two approaches, we reanalyzed data presented in two existing studies of avian nest survival with the goal not only of comparing estimates of nest survival generated by Mayfield and the logistic-exposure approach, but also of addressing in a more general fashion how methodological choices influence the results of hypothesis tests. Each study addressed a different question of importance to avian ecologists, and each study was conducted in a different environment. These two studies are also useful in that one (Lloyd and Martin 2005) was focused primarily on comparing a categorical variable (native vs. exotic habitat), whereas the independent variables of interest in the other (Tewksbury et al. 2006) were both categorical (presence of a habitat buffer) and continuous (percent of agriculture in the landscape). Lloyd and Martin (2005) compared nest survival of Chestnut-collared Longspurs (*Calcarius ornatus*) in native and exotic grasslands, and Tewksbury et al. (2006) addressed the influence of landscape features on nest survival of birds breeding in western riparian forests. Both studies used the logistic-exposure approach to analyze nest survival; we reanalyzed the data using the Mayfield estimator to examine how the choice of an analytical method might influence study results.

METHODS

Full methodological details can be found in the original studies (Lloyd and Martin 2005, Tewksbury et al. 2006). Both studies estimated daily nest survival (probability that a nest survives a given day) and tested hypotheses about the causes of variation in daily nest survival using the generalized-linear-modeling approach of Shaffer (2004a). Hypotheses regarding variation in nest survival were tested by examining support, as indicated by Akaike's information criterion (AIC), for a set of candidate models (Burnham and Anderson 2002) that reflected the authors' assessment of likely causes of variation in nest survival. Lloyd and Martin (2005) were interested primarily in estimating habitat-specific reproductive success of Chestnut-collared Longspurs breeding in native prairie and non-native grasslands dominated by crested wheatgrass (*Agropyron cristatum*). The goal of the research was to address the possible link between the spread of exotic grasses, the loss of native prairie, and the decline of grassland birds. However, in addition to examining the effect of breeding habitat, they also examined the influence of year, nest age, date of nest initiation, and clutch size on daily nest survival. The authors considered 15 different combinations of these variables.

Tewksbury et al. (2006) addressed the general question of how landscape features influence rates of nest predation and brood parasitism. They collected data at 22 study sites along two river systems in the western US (the Bitterroot River and Snake River). Study sites were patches of riparian forest that were embedded within an agricultural landscape. Some sites were buffered from agriculture by remnant woodlands, whereas other sites were immediately adjacent to various agricultural lands. Tewksbury et al. (2006) used the logistic-exposure approach to examine the effect of two landscape variables—buffering (whether a site was buffered from agriculture) and the percent of each 1 km landscape surrounding the study sites that was under active agriculture. In addition to these variables, they examined the effects of nest age and date of nest initiation. Based on combinations of these variables, they built a candidate set of nine models.

Nest Survival of Chestnut-collared Longspurs in Native and Exotic Habitat

To investigate how the logistic-exposure approach and the Mayfield method differ in a hypothesis-testing context, we calculated odds ratios for each of the parameters included in the best supported model of Lloyd and Martin (2005). The parameters in the best-supported model included all of the parameters that Lloyd and Martin (2005), using model-averaged estimates, found to be important predictors of nest survival. We calculated 95% confidence intervals around each odds ratio, and interpreted those that did not overlap 1 as having significant effects on nest survival. We then used chi-square tests, implemented by program CONTRAST (Hines and Sauer 1989), to conduct parallel comparisons using the Mayfield estimator.

To compare point estimates of daily nest survival obtained using the two analytical approaches, we first took the best-supported model from Lloyd and Martin (2005) and used it to estimate daily nest survival in each habitat. Because the best-supported model included effects of three covariates (nest age, year, and clutch size; see Results), we used an iterative process in which appropriate values were entered for each covariate (i.e., all possible combinations of nest age, year, and clutch size). Estimates of daily nest survival thus obtained were averaged to produce a single estimate for each habitat. We also estimated nest survival using a model that included only an effect of habitat, which, although unsupported by the data in the analysis of Lloyd and Martin (2005), provides the most direct comparison with the Mayfield method. We then compared these two estimates to estimates of daily nest survival obtained using the traditional Mayfield method (Mayfield 1961, Johnson 1979). We recognize that collapsing the information derived from the best-fitting model is somewhat contrived, yet we also feel that it adequately addresses our question and provides important information on how the two estimation methods perform.

Nest Survival of Riparian Birds

Tewksbury et al. (2006) were interested in estimating daily nest survival of riparian birds in habitat patches that were either buffered or unbuffered from adjacent agricultural lands and that were situated in landscapes that differed in the proportion of land under agricultural production. Because one of the main covariates of interest (percent agriculture in the landscape) was continuous, comparing the performance of the Mayfield and logistic-exposure approaches required a somewhat different approach than required for Lloyd and Martin (2005).

To address the question using the logistic-exposure approach, we reanalyzed the data presented in Tewksbury et al. (2006) by comparing a subset of their candidate set of models. We evaluated four models that included combinations of the following variables: presence/absence of a buffer, percent of agriculture in the landscape, age of the nest, date of nest initiation, and a term reflecting the interaction between buffers and the percent of agriculture in the landscape. We used data from two species, Yellow Warblers

(*Dendroica petechia*) and American Robins (*Turdus migratorius*). We calculated odds ratios for each parameter in the best-supported model, 95% confidence intervals around each odds ratio, and interpreted those that did not overlap 1 as having significant effects on nest survival.

To address the question using the Mayfield method, we first calculated Mayfield estimates (Mayfield 1961) with standard errors (Johnson 1979) for each species at each study site. We then used the Mayfield estimates in an ANCOVA, with the presence of a buffer as a fixed factor and the percent of agriculture in the landscape as a covariate. We also examined the interaction between the presence of a buffer and the percent of agriculture in the landscape. Non-significant interaction terms were eliminated from analysis.

In addition to comparing the results of hypothesis tests conducted with the Mayfield method and the logistic-exposure approach (Shaffer 2004a), we also compared point estimates of daily nest survival generated by the two methods. We calculated point estimates for each site by adding a site dummy variable to the best-fitting logistic-exposure model and using the LSMEANS command. Point estimates of daily nest survival calculated by both approaches were then compared using Pearson's correlation coefficient

RESULTS

Nest Survival of Chestnut-collared Longspurs in Native and Exotic Habitat

The best-fitting model in Lloyd and Martin (2005) contained all variables except for nest initiation date, and was strongly supported relative to all other models (Akaike weight = 0.67). The model that included only an effect of habitat, which is comparable to the Mayfield comparison of reproductive success in the two habitats, received virtually no support (ΔAIC_c = 94.7, Akaike weight = 0). The logistic-regression equation for the best model (one standard error in parentheses) was:

$$\text{Logit}(\hat{S}_i) = \underset{(0.09)}{3.20} - \underset{(0.07)}{0.18}\,(\text{habitat}) + \underset{(0.0001)}{0.0001}\,(\text{year}) + \underset{(0.10)}{0.27}\,(\text{clutch size}) - \underset{(0.005)}{0.04}\,(\text{nest age})$$

Based on odds ratios calculated from parameter estimates in the best-fitting model, clutch size had the strongest effect on nest success, with each additional egg producing a 30% increase in the odds of a nest surviving a given day (odds ratio = 1.3, CL = 1.1, 1.6). The odds of daily survival decreased 4% per day over the course of the nesting period (odds ratio = 0.96, CL = 0.95, 0.97). Finally, the odds of daily nest survival were 17% greater in native habitat than in exotic habitat (odds ratio = 0.83, CL = 0.72, 0.96). The odds of a year effect (odds ratio = 1.0, CL = 1.0, 1.0) did not differ from that expected by random chance alone.

Results obtained by re-analyzing the same data set using the Mayfield method were somewhat similar. Daily nest survival varied significantly between the two habitats (χ^2 = 3.19, P = 0.07), and daily nest survival varied among nesting stages (laying = 0.84, incubation = 0.96, nestling = 0.94; χ^2 = 16.16, P <0.001). However, unlike the best-fitting model in the logistic-exposure analysis, which predicted a linear decrease in daily nest survival as a function of age, the Mayfield analysis indicated highest survival during the incubation period with slightly lower survival during the nestling period and extremely low survival during the laying period. As with the logistic-exposure analysis, yearly variation in nest survival was discountable (χ^2 = 0.30, P = 0.58). Clutch size, which was the strongest predictor of variation in nest survival in the logistic-exposure analysis, did not have a significant effect on nest survival (χ^2 = 2.74, P = 0.25) when evaluated using the Mayfield estimator. In examining the point estimates produced by the Mayfield estimate, there was evidence that nests with a clutch size of three had lower rates of daily nest survival (0.934, CL = 0.910, 0.958) than did nests with either four eggs (0.956, CL = 0.946, 0.966) or five eggs (0.956, CL = 0.940, 0.972). The lack of a statistically significant result appears to stem from the broad confidence intervals, especially for daily survival estimates for three-egg clutches.

Both methods produced similar estimates of daily nest survival in native and exotic habitat with broadly overlapping 95% confidence intervals (Table 1). Although point estimates of daily nest survival were almost identical, the confidence interval around the Mayfield estimator was much broader than for either of the estimates generated by the logistic-exposure approach.

Nest Survival of Riparian Birds

The best-fitting models in the reanalysis of American Robin and Yellow Warbler data from Tewksbury et al. (2006) contained all variables, and in both cases the best-fitting model was heavily supported by the data relative to the other models (Tables 2 and 3). In neither case was there strong evidence for an interaction between the presence of a buffer and the

TABLE 1. DAILY SURVIVAL RATE (95% CONFIDENCE LIMITS) OF CHESTNUT-COLLARED LONGSPUR NESTS IN NATIVE AND EXOTIC HABITAT, AS ESTIMATED BY THE MAYFIELD METHOD AND THE LOGISTIC-EXPOSURE METHOD.

	Estimator		
Habitat	Mayfield	Logistic-exposure (habitat only model)	Logistic-exposure (best model)
Native	0.954 (0.933, 0.957)	0.957 (0.953, 0.960)	0.954 (0.950, 0.959)
Exotic	0.945 (0.944, 0.963)	0.946 (0.941, 0.951)	0.946 (0.941, 0.951)

TABLE 2. SUMMARY OF AKAIKE'S INFORMATION CRITERION (AIC_c) VALUES FOR CANDIDATE MODELS EXPLAINING NEST SURVIVAL OF AMERICAN ROBINS IN THE SNAKE AND BITTERROOT RIVERS, AS GENERATED BY THE LOGISTIC-EXPOSURE APPROACH. K IS THE NUMBER OF PARAMETERS ESTIMATED BY THE MODEL, ΔAIC_c IS THE DIFFERENCE BETWEEN A GIVEN MODEL AND THE MODEL WITH THE LOWEST ΔAIC_c SCORE[a], AND AIC_c WEIGHT REFLECTS THE RELATIVE SUPPORT FOR EACH MODEL.

Model	K	ΔAIC_c	AIC_c weight
$S_{buffer+ agriculture+age+start\ date}$	5	0	0.74
$S_{buffer*agriculture+age+start\ date}$	5	2.8	0.18
$S_{buffer+age+start\ date}$	4	4.7	0.07
$S_{agriculture+age+start\ date}$	4	15.3	0.01

[a] The lowest AIC_c score was 2,397.9.

TABLE 3. SUMMARY OF AKAIKE'S INFORMATION CRITERION (AIC_c) VALUES FOR CANDIDATE MODELS EXPLAINING NEST SURVIVAL OF YELLOW WARBLERS IN THE SNAKE AND BITTERROOT RIVERS, AS GENERATED BY THE LOGISTIC-EXPOSURE APPROACH. K IS THE NUMBER OF PARAMETERS ESTIMATED BY THE MODEL, ΔAIC_c IS THE DIFFERENCE BETWEEN A GIVEN MODEL AND THE MODEL WITH THE LOWEST ΔAIC_c SCORE[a], AND AIC_c WEIGHT REFLECTS THE RELATIVE SUPPORT FOR EACH MODEL.

Model	K	ΔAIC_c	AIC_c weight
$S_{buffer+ agriculture+age+start\ date}$	5	0	0.79
$S_{buffer*agriculture+age+start\ date}$	5	2.6	0.21
$S_{buffer+age+start\ date}$	4	32.6	0.00
$S_{agriculture+age+start\ date}$	4	69.5	0.00

[a] The lowest AIC_c score was 3,882.8.

percent of agriculture. The logistic-regression equation for the best model (one standard error in parentheses) of American Robin daily nest survival was:

$$\text{logit}(\hat{S}_i) = \underset{(0.623)}{3.49} - \underset{(0.143)}{0.633}\,(\text{buffer}) - \underset{(0.056)}{0.17}\,(\text{agriculture}) - \underset{(0.106)}{0.007}\,(\text{age}) + \underset{(0.003)}{0.005}\,(\text{start date})$$

The logistic-regression equation for the best model (one standard error in parentheses) of Yellow Warbler daily nest survival was:

$$\text{logit}(\hat{S}_i) = \underset{(0.671)}{1.10} - \underset{(0.109)}{0.916}\,(\text{buffer}) - \underset{(0.062)}{0.036}\,(\text{agriculture}) - \underset{(0.103)}{0.016}\,(\text{age}) + \underset{(0.004)}{0.023}\,(\text{start date})$$

For both species, site-specific point estimates of daily survival as estimated by the best-fitting model were highly correlated with point estimates generated using the Mayfield method (American Robin, $r^2 = 0.999$, $P < 0.001$; Yellow Warbler, $r^2 = 0.992$, $P < 0.001$; Fig. 1).

Odds ratios calculated from parameter estimates in the best-fitting model indicated a strong negative effect of natural habitat buffers in both species (American Robin, odds ratio = 0.53, CL = 0.40, 0.70; Fig. 2a; Yellow Warbler, odds ratio = 0.40, CL = 0.32, 0.50; Fig. 3a). Odds ratios also indicated a strong negative effect of the percentage of agriculture in the landscape on daily nest survival for American Robins (odds ratio = 0.84, CL = 0.76, 0.94), and a somewhat weaker negative effect for Yellow Warblers (odds ratio = 0.96, CL = 0.95, 0.98). The odds of an effect of the age of the nest were not different from that expected by random chance for either species. Start date had no effect on daily nest survival of American Robins, but did co-vary

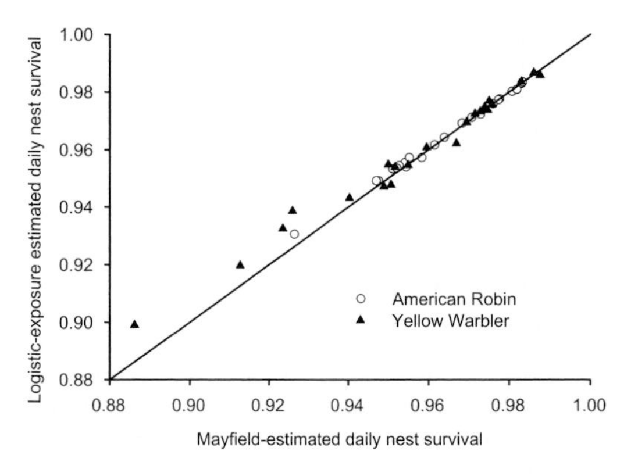

FIGURE 1. Estimates of daily nest survival generated by the Mayfield method and the logistic-exposure approach are nearly identical for both American Robin (r^2 = 0.999, P<0.001) and Yellow Warbler (r^2 = 0.992, P <0.001).

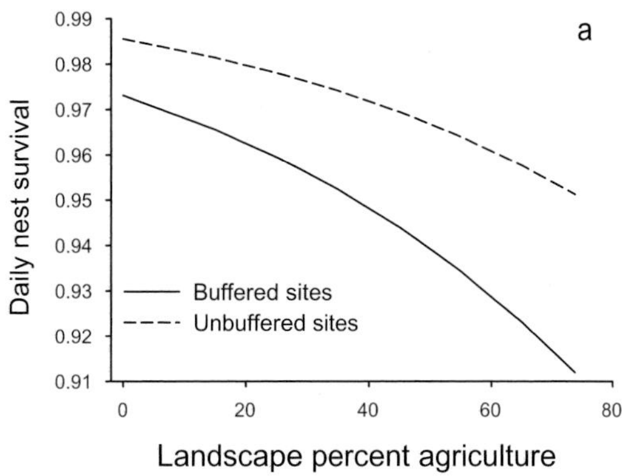

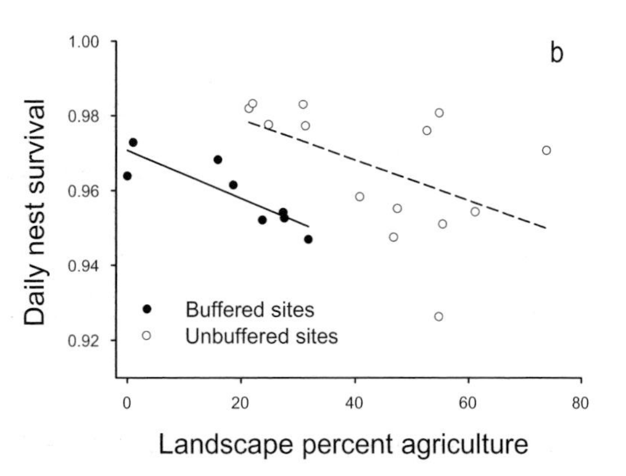

FIGURE 2. Both the best-fitting model from the logistic-exposure analysis (a) and the site-specific Mayfield estimates (b) indicated that daily nest survival of American Robins declined as the amount of agriculture in the landscape increased, and that daily nest survival was lower in sites buffered from surrounding agriculture by remnant woodland habitat. Mean population values for nest age and date of nest initiation were used to solve the logistic-regression equation and generate the curves.

positively with daily nest survival of Yellow Warblers (odds ratio = 1.02, CL = 1.02–1.03).

The ANCOVAs based on the Mayfield estimates for each site yielded somewhat different results. For American Robins, the presence of a natural habitat buffer (F = 8.2, df = 1, P = 0.01) and the percent of agriculture in the landscape (F = 8.6, df = 1, P = 0.01) both significantly affected daily nest survival (Fig. 2b). The interaction between buffer and agriculture was not significant (F = 0.05, df = 1, P = 0.84). For Yellow Warblers, the presence of a woodland buffer did not significantly affect daily nest survival (F = 1.24, df = 1, P = 0.28) but the percent of agriculture in the landscape had a significant negative effect on daily nest survival (F = 26.69, df = 1, P < 0.001; Fig. 3b). In addition, the interaction between agriculture and buffer was significant for Yellow Warblers (F = 10.16, df = 1, P = 0.005). The effect of woodland buffers appears to increase as the amount of agriculture in the landscape increases; buffers appeared to result in decreased daily nest survival at all sites except for those embedded in landscapes with a low percentage of agriculture. The ANOVA model of American Robins daily nest survival explained relatively little variation (adjusted r^2 = 0.28), whereas the Yellow Warbler ANOVA model explained substantially more (adjusted r^2 = 0.65).

DISCUSSION

In our reanalysis of two studies of avian nest survival, we compared the performance of the Mayfield method and the logistic-exposure approach, one of a class of similar methods that are based in generalized linear modeling, in estimating rates of daily nest survival and testing hypotheses about the causes of variation in these rates. In both studies, estimates of daily nest survival generated under the two approaches were nearly identical. This is not a surprising result as the Mayfield estimator, like the logistic-exposure approach, is a maximum-likelihood estimator. Several other studies also have reported little difference in daily nest survival as estimated by the Mayfield method and several of its alternatives, including the logistic-exposure approach (Shaffer 2004a; Winter et al. 2004, 2005a, b), the PROC NLMIXED model (Rotella et al. 2004), program MARK (Dinsmore et al. 2002), and the method developed by

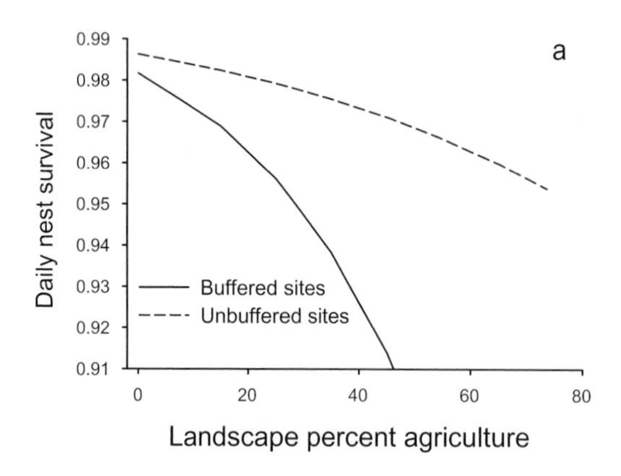

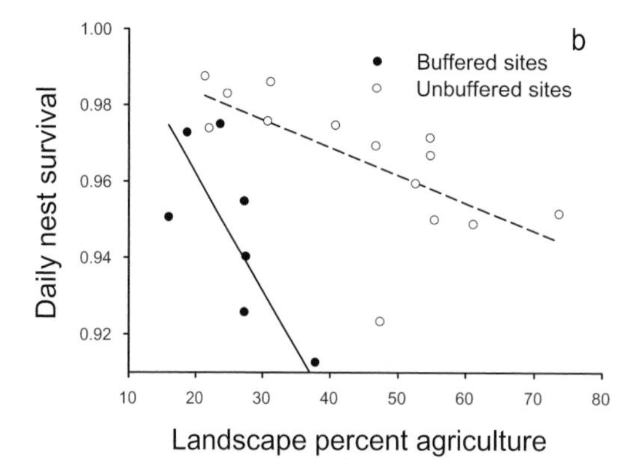

FIGURE 3. Both the best-fitting model from the logistic-exposure analysis (a) and the site-specific Mayfield estimates (b) indicated that daily nest survival of Yellow Warblers declined as the amount of agriculture in the landscape increased, and that daily nest survival was lower in sites buffered from surrounding agriculture by remnant woodland habitat. Mean population values for nest age and date of nest initiation were used to solve the logistic-regression equation and generate the curves.

Stanley (2000, 2004a, Jehle et al. 2004). However, an important caveat of our finding, and similar findings in the previously cited studies, is that the comparison of point estimates generated under the two approaches required collapsing large amounts of information from the logistic-exposure model to generate a single mean that could be compared to the point estimate generated by the Mayfield method. For example, to compare estimates of daily nest survival of Chestnut-collared Longspurs in native and exotic habitat, we had to calculate point estimates of daily nest survival for all possible combinations of habitat, clutch size, nest age, and year, the variables included in the best logistic-exposure model. We then averaged these values to arrive at a single estimate for each habitat for comparison with the Mayfield estimate. This effectively eliminates much of the additional information gained by using a generalized-linear-modeling approach. At the same time, the similarity of estimates of daily survival generated by the Mayfield method and the habitat-only model of Lloyd and Martin (2005) suggests that the Mayfield method and its alternatives will produce comparable estimates when the same covariates are considered. However, in this case, the Mayfield estimate was substantially less precise than estimates of daily nest survival generated from the logistic-exposure models.

Our comparison of hypothesis testing under the Mayfield method and the logistic-exposure approach yielded mixed results. In the re-analysis of Lloyd and Martin (2005), the principal finding was similar regardless of the method used to compare rates of daily nest survival—Chestnut-collared Longspurs in the exotic habitat had lower rates of daily nest survival. The Mayfield method and the logistic-exposure approach also indicated that daily nest survival varied depending upon the age of the nest. However, the two approaches differed in the predicted form of this relationship. The Mayfield analysis, which by its nature was limited to comparisons among stages of nesting, indicated that survival was lowest during egg laying, increased during incubation, and decreased slightly during the nestling period. In contrast, nest age was modeled as a linear function in the logistic-exposure analysis, and thus predicted a linear decline in nest survival from laying to fledging. This does not reflect an inherent flaw in the logistic-exposure approach, but rather points to the importance of including models that accurately reflect biological reality. For example, Lloyd and Martin (2005) might have better modeled the relationship between daily nest survival and nest age using a quadratic function, rather than the apparently over-simplistic linear model. Investigators who adopt the philosophy of model-based inference must keep in mind that the best model in a weak set of candidate models generates only weak inference.

Lloyd and Martin (2005) also reported that clutch size had the strongest effect on daily nest survival of Chestnut-collared Longspurs, with nests of larger clutch size having higher daily survival rates. In contrast, the re-analysis using the Mayfield method indicated that daily nest survival was constant among nests of different clutch size; this appeared to be a result of the large standard errors associated with the survival estimates for three-egg clutches. Although the failure to detect an effect of clutch size did not affect the conclusions drawn about the quality of the native and exotic habitats (clutch size is identical in both habitats), it does reveal how the reduced precision of Mayfield estimates can limit the power to detect differences among groups of nests. In this case, using the logistic-exposure approach revealed an interesting relationship that would have gone undetected with the Mayfield method.

The reanalysis of the data in Tewksbury et al. (2006) indicated broad similarities in the results of hypothesis tests conducted under the two approaches. The logistic-exposure approach suggested support for a negative effect of both natural habitat buffers and the percent of agriculture in the landscape on daily nest survival of American Robins and Yellow Warblers. These results lend support to the additive-predation model of Tewksbury et al. (2006), which suggests that nest predation rates are a product of both forest-dwelling predators close to the study site and generalist agricultural predators acting at larger spatial scales. The reanalysis of these data using site-specific Mayfield estimates of daily nest survival also suggested a significant negative effect of natural habitat buffers for both species, and a significant negative effect of agriculture. In the ANCOVA model for Yellow Warblers, buffers as a main effect were not significant, but the significant interaction between buffers and agriculture suggests a relationship similar to that predicted by the logistic-exposure analysis. In landscapes with little agriculture, buffers are relatively unimportant predictors of daily nest survival. However, as the amount of agriculture in the landscape increases, the effect of agriculture on daily nest survival increasingly depends upon the presence of a woodland buffer. Thus, for both species, the Mayfield method also provided support for the additive-predation model.

Several caveats should be kept in mind regarding our findings. First, we have not conducted a formal meta-analysis, and our results are based on a reanalysis of data presented in two studies, neither of which was chosen randomly. However, we felt these studies were useful for re-analysis because they addressed commonly asked questions in avian ecology, they were conducted in two different environments and with different species, and they were interested in the effect of fundamentally different covariates of daily nest survival (a categorical habitat variable in Lloyd and Martin [2005], and a mix of categorical and continuous variables in Tewksbury et al. [2006]). Second, although we found that both methods produced nearly identical point estimates of daily nest survival, comparing estimates from the best-fitting model in the logistic-exposure analysis with Mayfield estimates required collapsing much of the unique information obtained from the logistic-exposure approach. Finally, our comparison does not address instances in which the logistic-exposure and related methods are the only appropriate way to analyze data, e.g., modeling patterns of daily variation in nest survival (Grant et al. 2005).

Despite these caveats, we believe that the results presented here have important implications for the analysis of nest-survival data. First, they suggest that Mayfield estimates and estimates obtained under alternative approaches will be similar. This is important for analyses that seek to synthesize multiple existing estimates of daily nest survival from the literature, such as for meta-analyses or range-wide comparisons of reproductive success. Second, in some cases, the choice of an analytical method will not influence the results of hypothesis tests. In the studies presented here, both the Mayfield method and the logistic-exposure analysis yielded similar conclusions, although the results were not identical. The only substantive difference was that the analysis of the Mayfield estimates from Lloyd and Martin (2005) did not indicate a significant effect of clutch size on daily nest survival, whereas the logistic-exposure analysis revealed clutch size to be the strongest predictor of variation in nest survival. Also, the ANCOVA on Mayfield estimates from Tewksbury et al. (2006) suggested an interaction between buffers and agriculture for Yellow Warblers, whereas the interaction model tested with the logistic-exposure analysis received relatively little support. However, the significance of the interaction term had little bearing on the conclusions drawn: under both analytical approaches, American Robins and Yellow Warblers experienced lower daily nest survival rates in buffered sites and in landscapes dominated by agriculture. Nonetheless, the differences that we observed between results generated by the two methods suggest that, in some cases, conclusions may be dependent on the choice of an analytical method.

That the results of the Mayfield method and its alternatives are often comparable should not be construed as an argument for or against a particular mode of analysis. Other authors (Dinsmore et al. 2002, Nur et al. 2004, Rotella et al. 2004, Shaffer 2004a) have clearly established the drawbacks and limitations of both the Mayfield method and its alternatives. Many of the recently developed approaches for modeling avian nest survival offer the ability to test new hypotheses about avian nest survival or more robustly address existing hypotheses that have been limited to flawed tests using ad hoc approaches (see examples in Rotella et al. 2004). They also offer the opportunity to ask more interesting questions about nest survival, and to build models that may better reflect biological reality. The Mayfield alternatives, such as logistic exposure, allow more precise estimates of nest survival, and thus can offer increased power to detect patterns obscured by the chi-square tests used to compare Mayfield estimates. The linear-modeling process exploited by the Mayfield alternatives also allows investigators to estimate the effect of changes in one independent variable while holding all other independent variables constant. Thus, the Mayfield alternatives may allow better control over potentially confounding relationships among independent variables. At the same time, our results suggest that results obtained via the Mayfield method may not be substantively different from results obtained using one of the Mayfield alternatives. The Mayfield method, with its ease of application, remains a reasonable choice for estimation purposes or for the analysis of grouped data. Finally, with the increased flexibility offered by the Mayfield alternatives comes an increased obligation to carefully consider the variables that are included in candidate models. The questions asked concerning avian nest survival, and the variables measured to address those questions, must still come from theory and logic, and not from faith that more powerful analytical techniques alone will yield novel insights into causal relationships.

ACKNOWLEDGMENTS

This work was supported in part by the U.S. Prairie Pothole Joint Venture, a Sigma Xi Grant-in-Aid of Research to JDL, the Wildlife Biology Program at the University of Montana, and the USDA Forest Service, Bitterroot Ecosystem Management Research Project, Rocky Mountain Research Station, Missoula, Montana. We also thank Terry Shaffer for his assistance in implementing the logistic-exposure models; for critical reviews of earlier versions of this manuscript we thank Maiken Winter, Geoff Geupel, Stephanie Jones, and an anonymous reviewer. Finally, we thank Stephanie Jones and Geoff Geupel for organizing this symposium and offering us the opportunity to participate.

Studies in Avian Biology No. 34:105–116

COMPARING THE EFFECTS OF LOCAL, LANDSCAPE, AND TEMPORAL FACTORS ON FOREST BIRD NEST SURVIVAL USING LOGISTIC-EXPOSURE MODELS

MELINDA G. KNUTSON, BRIAN R. GRAY, AND MELISSA S. MEIER

Abstract. We studied the bird communities of Mississippi River floodplain and adjacent upland forests to identify factors associated with nest survival. We estimated daily nest survival for forest-nesting birds using competing logistic-exposure models, that will allow a comparison of multiple possible factors associated with nest survival, measured at different spatial or temporal scales. We compared models representing landscape (upland vs. floodplain and forest cover), edge (nest distance to edge and forest edge density), nest-site (nest height, canopy cover, nest concealment, and shrub density), Brown-headed Cowbird (*Molothrus ater*; parasitism rate and cowbird abundance), and temporal effects (year, nest stage, and Julian date of observations). We found that the temporal effects model had the strongest support, followed by the landscape effects model for most species. Nest survival tended to be highest early in the nesting season (May–June) and late in the nest cycle (nestling stage). For Eastern Wood-Pewees (*Contopus virens*) and Prothonotary Warblers (*Protonotaria citrea*), higher nest survival was associated with lower proportions of forest surrounding the plot. Significant effects of nest placement in upland vs. floodplain locations were not observed for any species. Models representing edge, nest-site, and cowbird effects had less statistical support, although higher nest survival was sometimes associated with dense shrubs and more concealment around the nest. Management implications may include timing management disturbances to avoid the early nesting season (May and June). For shrub nesting species, management to open the canopy and allow the shrub layer to develop may be beneficial.

Key Words: Brown-headed Cowbird, demographic monitoring, floodplain forest, information-theoretic, landbird, landscape, logistic-exposure model, Mississippi River, nest-site, nest survival.

COMPARACIÓN DE LOS EFECTOS DE FACTORES LOCALES, DE PAISAJE Y TEMPORALES EN SOBREVIVENCIA DE NIDOS DE AVES FORESTALES UTILIZANDO MODELOS DE EXPOSICIÓN LOGÍSTICA

Resumen. Estudiamos las comunidades de aves de las planicies inundadas del Río Mississippi y los bosques adyacentes de las tierras altas, para identificar factores asociados con la sobrevivencia de nido. Estimamos la sobrevivencia diaria del nido para aves anidadoras de bosque utilizando modelos competentes de exposición logística, que permitirán comparar posibles factores múltiples asociados a la sobrevivencia de nido medidos a distintas escalas espaciales y temporales. Comparamos modelos representando al paisaje (tierras altas vs. planicies inundadas y cobertura forestal), borde (distancia del nido al borde y la densidad del borde de bosque), sitio del nido (altura de nido, cubierta de dosel, ocultación de nido, y densidad de arbustos), el Tordo Cabeza Café (*Molothrus ater*); tasa de parasitismo o abundancia de tordo), y efectos temporales (año, etapa de nido, y fecha Julian de observaciones). Encontramos que el modelo de efectos temporales tiene el soporte más alto para casi todas las especies, seguido del modelo de efectos de paisaje. La sobrevivencia de nido tendía a ser la mayor en la estación temprana de anidación (Mayo–Junio) y tardía en el ciclo de nido (etapa de volantón). Para los Pibí Oriental (*Contopus virens*) y Chipe Dorado (*Protonotaria citrea*), estaba asociada mayor sobrevivencia de nido con menores proporciones de bosque rodeando el sitio. Efectos significativos de colocación de nido en tierras altas vs. localidades de planicies inundadas no fueron observadas por muchas especies. Modelos que representan efectos de borde, sitio de nido y tordo, tienen menor soporte estadístico a pesar de que la sobrevivencia de nido estaba algunas veces asociada con arbustos densos y más ocultación alrededor del nido. Las implicaciones en el manejo quizás incluyan la sincronización de disturbios de manejo para evitar el período de anidación temprana (Mayo y Junio). Para especies de anidación de arbusto quizás sea benéfico el manejo para abrir el dosel y para permitir que se desarrolle la capa arbustiva.

Successful landbird conservation requires that managers have an understanding of the major factors affecting nest survival in a region, while also acknowledging that such factors may not act independently. Survival models, including logistic-exposure models (Shaffer 2004a), permit factors associated with nest survival, possibly measured at different spatial or temporal scales; to be compared in a unified information-theoretic modeling framework (Dinsmore et al. 2002). A variety of factors have been shown to affect nest survival, ranging in scale from landscape variables to factors operating at the scale of a single nest (Faaborg 2002). At large spatial scales, nest survival may be influenced by landscape context, usually represented by the amount of forest in the landscape (Rodewald 2002). Landscapes with fewer edges and less fragmentation are often positively associated with nest survival (Donovan et al. 1997, Stephens et al. 2004). Nests placed near forest edges may have decreased success compared with those placed in the interior of large forests (Batary and Baldi 2004). Factors specific to the nest, such as placement height, canopy cover, vegetation concealment, and shrub density have variable associations with nest survival (Wilson and Cooper 1998, Siepielski et al. 2001). Finally, timing can be important; nest survival often varies annually, by nest-initiation date, or by nest age or stage (laying, incubation, or nestling) (Burhans et al. 2002, Peak et al. 2004, Winter et al. 2004).

We studied the bird community of Mississippi River floodplain and adjacent upland forests to identify factors associated with nest survival for purposes of informing managers of upland and floodplain forests in the region. Our objective was to examine the relative importance of models representing possible major factors affecting nest survival, including landscape, edge, nest-site, Brown-headed Cowbird (*Molothrus ater*), and temporal effects. We expected that temporal, landscape, and edge effects would have a generally stronger association with nest survival than nest-site or cowbird effects for most forest bird species in our study area. However, we also expected that factors affecting nest survival would vary by species or life-history group. Landscape and edge effects were expected to be stronger for area-sensitive species and life history groups. A cowbird-effects model was expected to explain variation in nest success for generalist species, and non-area-sensitive ground species and groups vulnerable to parasitism. Temporal or nest-site effects were expected to better explain variation in nest success for generalist species and non-area-sensitive ground and shrub nesters.

METHODS

The study area was located in the driftless area ecoregion, including portions of the states of Iowa, Minnesota, and Wisconsin (McNab and Avers 1994). Driftless area forests are dominated by oaks (*Quercus* spp.), sugar maple (*Acer saccharum*), and basswood (*Tilia americana*) (Curtis 1959, Cahayla-Wynne and Glenn-Lewin 1978). Forests are confined to steep slopes adjacent to streams and rivers and form a connected, dendritic pattern, while complex topography and erosive soils support a less intensive agriculture than in many parts of the Midwest (McNab and Avers 1994). Forests and agriculture comprise about 12–56% and 2–38% of the landscape, respectively, within 10 km of our study plots (Gustafson et al. 2002, Knutson et al. 2004). The Mississippi River floodplain in this region is unrestricted by levees; forests dominate most islands and main channel borders within the floodplain (Knutson et al. 1996). The floodplain forest-plant community is dominated by silver maple (*Acer saccharinum*), with elm (*Ulmus* spp.), green ash (*Fraxinus pennsylvanica*), swamp white oak (*Quercus bicolor*), cottonwood (*Populus deltoides*), hackberry (*Celtis occidentalis*), and river birch (*Betula nigra*) as subdominants (Knutson and Klaas 1997).

We assessed factors affecting the nest survival of six forest bird species—American Redstart (*Setophaga ruticilla*), Prothonotary Warbler (*Protonotaria citrea*), American Robin (*Turdus migratorius*), Eastern Wood-Pewee (*Contopus virens*), Blue-gray Gnatcatcher (*Polioptila caerulea*), and Rose-breasted Grosbeak (*Pheucticus ludovicianus*). We grouped 21 additional species according to similar life history-strategies; these species had insufficient sample sizes individually (Best et al. 1995). The groups were area-sensitive low nesters—Ovenbird (*Seiurus aurocapilla*) and Wood Thrush (*Hylocichla mustelina*); area-sensitive tree nesters—Acadian Flycatcher (*Empidonax virescens*), Red-eyed Vireo (*Vireo olivaceus*), Scarlet Tanager (*Piranga olivacea*), and Warbling Vireo (*Vireo gilvus*); ground or shrub nesters: Brown Thrasher (*Toxostoma rufum*), Eastern Kingbird (*Tyrannus tyrannus*), Gray Catbird (*Dumetella carolinensis*), Indigo Bunting (*Passerina cyanea*), Northern Cardinal (*Cardinalis cardinalis*), Song Sparrow (*Melospiza melodia*), and Yellow Warbler (*Dendroica petechia*); and cavity nesters—Black-capped Chickadee (*Poecile atricapillus*), Downy Woodpecker (*Picoides pubescens*), Great Crested Flycatcher (*Myiarchus crinitus*), Hairy Woodpecker (*Picoides villosus*), Red-bellied Woodpecker (*Melanerpes carolinus*), Red-headed Woodpecker (*Melanerpes erythrocephalus*), White-breasted Nuthatch (*Sitta carolinensis*), and Yellow-bellied Sapsucker (*Sphyrapicus varius*). Species with fewer than five nests were not modeled.

NEST SEARCHING AND MONITORING

We monitored nests from May–August on 10 floodplain and 10 upland plots from 1996–1998. We selected upland plots non-probabilistically from state forests that were not recently logged or grazed. In the floodplain, we randomly selected plots from federal land in the upper Mississippi River, based on forest inventory data (United States Army Corps of Engineers 1990–1997). Study plots were approximately 40 ha in size in the uplands and 20 ha in the floodplain; field effort was similar among all plots.

Nests were located following standard protocols (Martin and Geupel 1993) by following adults and flushing incubating and brooding birds. All active nests were monitored every 2–3 d until the outcome was determined. At each visit, we recorded date, time, parental behavior, nest stage, nest contents, and evidence of cowbird parasitism. Nests were considered successful if they fledged at least one host young. We relied on cues to assess nest success including fledglings seen or heard, adults in the vicinity of the nest with food or scolding, and no evidence of renesting. The location of each nest was defined using a global-positioning system.

We measured nest-site variables immediately after the fate of the nest was determined, including nest height, canopy cover, nest concealment, and shrub density. Nest height was the distance (meters) from the ground to the bottom of the nest cup; canopy cover was the total canopy cover above 5 m from the ground, estimated with a densiometer. Nest concealment was the percent of the nest hidden by vegetation 1 m from the nest in each direction, estimated from the side in four cardinal directions and from the top; the mean of the five estimates was used for analysis. Shrub density was the number of shrub stems <8 cm diameter at breast height (dbh) counted at 10 cm above the ground, within a 5-m circle (0.008 ha) centered on the nest.

We estimated Brown-headed Cowbird abundance from point-count data; cowbirds were counted on each plot between 20 May and 30 June at six points spaced ≥200 m apart. We recorded birds within 50 m of the observer during a 10-min time period (Ralph et al. 1993) and calculated relative abundance as the mean number of cowbirds per survey point, by plot and year.

Landscape Variables

U.S. Geological Survey gap-analysis program classifications were used to represent land cover (Scott et al. 1993). We calculated and summarized landscape metrics for each plot, including the percentage of the landscape in forest cover and forest edge density using a 5-km radius circle (7,854 ha) centered on the plot. The distance (meters) of each nest to the nearest forest edge was measured using land-cover maps of the study plots digitized from 1:15,000 scale aerial photographs taken in 1997 (Owens and Hop 1995). Edge density was defined as the linear distance of forest edge per unit area (meters per hectare) for each plot, represented by the 5-km radius circle (McGarigal and Marks 1995). A 5-km radius was selected because it approximates the home range of cowbirds (Thompson 1994) from breeding to feeding areas.

Statistical Analyses

We used survival analysis (Shaffer 2004a) to model nest survival as a function of nest-specific predictor variables and to estimate daily nest-survival rates. This logistic-exposure approach (Shaffer 2004a) accommodates varying exposure periods, continuous, categorical, and time-specific predictor variables, and random effects. We used a modified logit link function, ($\log_e(\theta^{1/t})/[1 - \theta^{1/t}]$), where θ is the interval survival rate and t is the interval length in days (Peak et al. 2004, Shaffer 2004a), and assumed survival and predictor variables to be constant within a nest-observation interval. Models were fitted using the SAS generalized linear modeling procedure (PROC GENMOD; SAS Institute 2003).

For each species and group we evaluated models representing landscape, edge, nest-site, cowbird, and temporal effects. Specifically, we evaluated a landscape-effects model with forest type (upland or floodplain) and percent forest cover; an edge-effects model with distance to forest edge and forest edge density; a nest-site-effects model with nest height, canopy cover, nest concealment, and shrub density; a cowbird-effects model with parasitism of the nest (parasitized or not parasitized) and cowbird relative abundance; and a temporal-effects model with year, nest stage, and Julian observation date (midpoint between two successive nest visits). We also evaluated a global model with all effects, and an intercept-only (null) model. We dropped the cowbird model for species not vulnerable to cowbird parasitism (American Robins and cavity nesters) and the nest-concealment model for cavity nesters and forest type for species found only in one forest type (Prothonotary Warblers, floodplain; Ovenbird and Wood Thrushs, uplands). For some species and groups, we combined laying and incubation stages because models with too few intervals failed to converge.

We evaluated the candidate models using a small sample variant of the Akaike information criterion (AIC_c) and the associated Akaike weight, w_i (Burnham and Anderson 2002). Akaike information criterion for small sample sizes is defined as –2 log likelihood + 2 × K (the number of estimated parameters) × (small sample correction factor), where the correction factor = N/(N – K – 1) and N = number of observation intervals (Hurvich and Tsai 1989). Differences between the AIC_c values for the ith model and that of the model with the smallest AIC_c value were denoted ΔAIC_{ci}; a ΔAIC_{ci} of 2–5 units was considered evidence of stronger support (Burnham and Anderson 2002). A given w_i indicates the weight of evidence in favor of model *i* being the best supported model (among those considered), and was defined as $e^{-\Delta AIC_{ci}/2}$. For convenience, ΔAIC_{ci} is hereafter denoted ΔAIC_c.

We presented odds ratios for predictor variables with confidence intervals that excluded 1 from the model with the smallest AICc value. To clarify the interpretation, an odds ratio of 1.5 for year 1996 vs. 1998 indicates that the odds of daily nest survival were 50% higher in 1996 than in 1998. A predictor was included in only one model per species or species group.

Daily nest survival for each species was estimated using the model with the smallest AICc value. The predicted probabilities represent the probability of a nest surviving 1 d, are comparable to Mayfield daily nest survival estimates (Mayfield 1961, Johnson 1979), and are conditional on median (continuous) or mean (categorical) covariate values. Conditional interval nest survival was estimated using the model with the smallest AICc value and the literature-based mean number of laying, incubation, and nestling days (Ehrlich et al. 1988). For the life history groups of species, we used a weighted average of the appropriate number of laying, incubation, and nestling days (Baicich and Harrison 1997). Nest survival was estimated for all species in the study. For species in the life-history groups, nest-survival estimates were conditional on temporal effects (day, stage, and year) only.

RESULTS

We monitored 1,142 nests among all the species. Nests tended to be located in areas with relatively high canopy cover (79%), high stem counts of shrubs, and 50–110 m from an edge (Table 1). Predictor means often varied substantially by species (Table 2). For example, Prothonotary Warbler nests were found closer to the forest edge (24 m) than other species; in contrast, area-sensitive low nesters placed their nests in forest interiors (263 m from an edge; Table 2).

As expected, the models with strongest support varied among the species and life history groups (Table 3). The temporal model had the most general support in explaining nest survival across species; it was the best supporting model for American Redstarts, Rose-breasted Grosbeaks, and cavity nesters and had moderate support ($\Delta AIC_c < 10$) for all other species and groups (Table 3). The landscape model was the best supporting model for Eastern Wood-Pewees and had moderate support for American Robins, Blue-gray Gnatcatchers, area-sensitive low nesters, area-sensitive tree nesters, and ground and shrub nesters.

The edge-, nest-site-, and cowbird-effects models received less support among the species and groups we studied (Table 3). The global model was the best model for Prothonotary Warblers and ground and shrub nesters and had moderate support for American Redstarts, Eastern Wood-Pewees, and Rose-breasted Grosbeaks (Table 3). American Robins, Blue-gray Gnatcatchers, area-sensitive low nesters, and area-sensitive tree nesters had the null model as their best model. In each case, a second

TABLE 1. PREDICTOR VARIABLES USED TO EVALUATE NEST SURVIVAL OF BIRDS BREEDING IN FLOODPLAIN AND UPLAND FORESTS OF THE DRIFTLESS AREA, 1996–1998.

Variable[a]	Scale	N	Mean	SD	Median	Min	Max
Day	day	5,507	169.5[b]	15.3	169.5[b]	130.0[c]	223.8[d]
Edge (meters)	nest	1,142	109.1	132.0	50.2	0.2	794.5
Nest height (meters)	nest	1,142	7.2	5.6	5.7	0.0	31.5
Canopy cover (percent)	nest	1,142	78.6	22.1	86.0	0.0	100.0
Concealment	nest	1,142	66.3	28.4	70.0	0.0	100.0
Shrub	nest	1,142	76.1	105.9	41.0	0.0	914.0
Forest (percent)	plot	20	41.0	11.9	45.0	12.0	56.1
Edge density (meters/hectare)	plot	20	56.2	15.2	54.3	19.7	75.2
Cowbird abundance	plot	20	0.5	0.3	0.3	0.0	1.0

[a] Day = Julian day midpoint between two successive nest visits; Edge = distance in meters from nest to forest edge; Nest height = nest height in meters; Canopy cover = percent total canopy cover >5m in height; Concealment = nest concealment calculated as the mean of side cover and overhead cover values; Shrub = number of shrub stems >10 cm above the ground and <8 cm dbh within a 5-m radius circle centered on the nest; Forest = percentage of landscape made up of forest within a 5-km radius circle centered on the plot; Edge density = forest-edge density measured in meters/hectare within a 5-km radius circle centered on the plot; Cowbird abundance = mean relative abundance of cowbirds per survey point, across all plots.

[b] Corresponds to approximately June 18.

[c] Corresponds to approximately May 10.

[d] Corresponds to approximately August 11.

TABLE 2. PREDICTOR VARIABLES (MEAN ± SE) AND COUNTS OF CATEGORICAL VARIABLES USED TO EVALUATE NEST SURVIVAL, BY SPECIES AND LIFE-HISTORY GROUPINGS OF BIRDS NESTING IN FLOODPLAIN AND UPLANDS FOREST OF THE DRIFTLESS AREA, 1996–1998.

Variable[a]	American Redstart (*Setophaga ruticilla*)	American Robin (*Turdus migratorius*)	Blue-gray Gnatcatcher (*Polioptila caerulea*)	Eastern Wood-Pewee (*Contopus virens*)	Prothonotary Warbler (*Protonotaria citrea*)	Rose-breasted Grosbeak (*Pheucticus ludovicianus*)	Area-sensitive tree nesters	Area-sensitive low nesters	Cavity nesters	Ground/shrub nesters
Day	167.8 (0.5)	168.1 (0.8)	163.2 (0.8)	184.8 (0.5)	168.3 (0.5)	164.2 (0.6)	171.6 (0.6)	169.7 (1.1)	165.5 (0.6)	168.4 (0.6)
Edge (meters)	121.0 (7.7)	81.6 (10.4)	82.7 (12.9)	168.3 (14.0)	23.5 (2.2)	164.3 (20.5)	146.0 (13.7)	263.0 (33.7)	109.2 (12.2)	73.4 (7.2)
Nest height (meters)	6.0 (0.2)	6.3 (0.5)	13.5 (0.6)	14.7 (0.4)	2.9 (0.2)	8.3 (0.7)	9.4 (0.4)	2.2 (0.5)	8.3 (0.4)	3.2 (0.3)
Canopy cover (percent)	85.3 (1.1)	82.4 (1.7)	79.9 (2.0)	87.5 (1.0)	71.7 (2.3)	72.2 (3.2)	83.7 (1.3)	88.4 (1.7)	79.6 (1.7)	63.5 (2.4)
Concealment	56.6 (1.4)	58.7 (2.1)	50.8 (2.6)	25.8 (2.3)	96.5 (0.6)	67.2 (2.1)	59.8 (2.1)	51.4 (4.8)	97.2 (0.8)	69.1 (1.9)
Shrub	64.9 (6.0)	59.0 (6.1)	62.2 (13.9)	62.2 (6.6)	19.1 (4.2)	111.8 (13.4)	73.1 (9.5)	87.4 (11.8)	69.7 (9.0)	152.6 (11.9)
Forest (percent)	39.1 (0.7)	34.5 (1.2)	43.2 (1.0)	42.2 (1.0)	42.1 (0.6)	39.0 (1.4)	43.3 (1.0)	46.6 (1.0)	38.4 (0.9)	31.7 (1.2)
Edge density (meters/hectare)	59.1 (0.8)	53.9 (1.7)	61.3 (1.3)	57.7 (1.3)	64.2 (0.8)	53.6 (1.8)	59.9 (1.4)	53.6 (1.7)	54.7 (1.1)	47.7 (1.5)
Cowbird abundance	0.8 (0.1)	1.0 (0.1)	1.1 (0.1)	1.2 (0.1)	0.9 (0.1)	1.2 (0.1)	1.1 (0.1)	1.2 (0.1)	0.9 (0.1)	1.0 (0.1)
Floodplain/upland	164/32	91/18	32/34	37/63	134/0	20/53	39/82	0/34	89/59	116/45
1996/1997/1998	31/79/86	22/35/52	7/32/27	11/39/50	39/44/51	9/39/25	16/54/51	9/19/6	25/50/73	21/62/78

[a] Day = Julian day midpoint between two successive nest visits; Edge = distance in m from nest to forest edge; Nest height = nest height in m; Canopy cover = percent total canopy cover >5 m in height; Concealment = nest concealment calculated as the mean of side cover and overhead cover values; Shrub = number of shrub stems >10 cm above the ground and <8 cm dbh within a 5-m radius circle centered on the nest; Forest = percentage of landscape made up of forest within a 5-km radius circle centered on the plot; Edge density = forest edge density measured in meters/hectare within a 5-km radius circle centered on the plot; Cowbird abundance = relative abundance of cowbirds on plot within a year; numbers of nests by treatment (floodplain and upland) and year (1997, 1997, 1998).

TABLE 3. CANDIDATE MODELS EXPLAINING NEST SURVIVAL IN FLOODPLAIN AND UPLAND FORESTS OF THE DRIFTLESS AREA, 1996–1998, BY SPECIES AND LIFE-HISTORY GROUP.

Species	Model	K	ΔAIC_c	w_i
American Redstart	Temporal effects	6	0.0	0.98
(*Setophaga ruticilla*) (N = 825)	Global	16	9.3	0.01
American Robin	Null	1	0.0	0.66
(*Turdus migratorius*) (N = 512)	Landscape effects	3	3.1	0.14
	Edge effects	3	3.4	0.12
	Nest-site effects	5	5.3	0.05
	Temporal effects	6	7.2	0.02
	Global	14	7.5	0.02
Prothonotary Warbler	Global	14	0.0	0.79
(*Protonotaria citrea*) (N = 629)	Temporal effects	5	2.8	0.20
	Nest-site effects	5	8.8	0.01
Eastern Wood-Pewee	Landscape effects	3	0.0	0.90
(*Contopus virens*) (N = 622)	Temporal effects	6	6.8	0.03
	Null	1	7.1	0.03
	Edge effects	3	7.6	0.02
	Global	16	9.1	0.01
	Nest-site effects	5	9.4	0.01
Blue-gray Gnatcatcher	Null	1	0.0	0.38
(*Polioptila caerulea*) (N = 354)	Temporal effects	5	0.4	0.31
	Cowbird effects	3	2.3	0.12
	Edge effects	3	2.4	0.12
	Landscape effects	3	3.7	0.06
	Nest-site effects	5	6.5	0.02
Rose-breasted Grosbeak	Temporal effects	6	0.0	0.96
(*Pheucticus ludovicianus*) (N = 318)	Null	1	8.5	0.01
	Edge effects	3	9.0	0.01
	Global	16	9.0	0.01
Area-sensitive low nesters (N = 146)	Null	1	0.0	0.44
	Landscape effects	2	0.8	0.30
	Edge effects	3	2.7	0.11
	Cowbird effects	3	2.8	0.11
	Temporal effects	5	5.2	0.03
	Nest-site effects	5	7.9	0.01
Area-sensitive tree nesters (N = 565)	Null	1	0.0	0.33
	Temporal effects	6	0.1	0.32
	Landscape effects	3	1.5	0.16
	Nest-site effects	5	2.5	0.09
	Cowbird effects	3	3.7	0.05
	Edge effects	3	3.8	0.05
Ground and shrub nesters (N = 714)	Global	16	0.0	0.45
	Nest-site effects	5	0.9	0.29
	Edge effects	3	2.8	0.11
	Temporal effects	6	3.8	0.07
	Landscape effects	3	4.8	0.04
	Null	1	5.7	0.03
	Cowbird effects	3	7.2	0.01
Cavity nesters (N = 702)	Temporal effects	5	0.0	0.99

Notes: Models are ranked by ΔAIC_c; K = number of parameters including the intercept, N = number of observation intervals. For the sake of brevity, models with $\Delta AIC_c > 10$ are not shown.

model was a close competitor (within 1 ΔAICc unit and model weight >30%), with the exception of American Robins, a generalist species.

Among the predictor variables associated with nest survival, those representing temporal, landscape, and nest-site effects had the most support (Table 4; Fig. 1a–s). Nest concealment and shrub density were supported for Prothonotary Warblers and nest height and concealment were supported for ground and shrub nesters (Table 4; Fig. 1a–s). Nest stage, year, or Julian day were supported for seven species and groups. Daily nest-survival estimates from the best model for each species ranged from a low of 0.938 for Song Sparrows to a high of 0.994 for Red-headed Woodpeckers (Table 5).

DISCUSSION

The logistic-exposure modeling approach allowed us to evaluate a variety of factors that could influence nest survival in the driftless area

TABLE 4. CONDITIONAL ODDS RATIOS AND 95% CONFIDENCE INTERVALS (CI) FOR SELECTED PREDICTOR VARIABLES FROM MODELS WITH SMALLEST AIC_C VALUES FOR INDIVIDUAL SPECIES AND LIFE HISTORY GROUPINGS FOR BIRDS NESTING IN FLOODPLAIN AND UPLAND FORESTS OF THE DRIFTLESS AREA, 1996–1998.

Species	Predictor variable[a]	Odds ratio	CI
American Redstart[b]	Laying + incubation vs. nestling	0.477	0.309, 0.734
(*Setophaga ruticilla*)	1996 vs. 1998	1.871	1.003, 3.492
	1997 vs. 1998	1.518	1.014, 2.271
Prothonotary Warbler[b]	Day	0.955	0.929, 0.982
(*Protonotaria citrea*)	Laying + incubation vs. nestling	0.401	0.209, 0.769
	Concealment	1.059	1.016, 1.104
	Shrub	1.015	1.001, 1.029
	Forest	0.828	0.712, 0.962
Eastern Wood-Pewee[b] (*Contopus virens*)	Forest	0.940	0.901, 0.980
Blue-gray Gnatcatcher	Day	0.970	0.944, 0.996
(*Polioptila caerulea*)	1996 vs. 1998	5.478	1.049, 28.606
Rose-breasted Grosbeak[b]	Day	0.939	0.906, 0.974
(*Pheucticus ludovicianus*)	Laying + incubation vs. nestling	0.380	0.179, 0.805
	Shrub	1.004	1.000, 1.008
Area-sensitive tree nesters	Day	0.969	0.944, 0.994
	Incubation vs. nestling	0.489	0.270, 0.886
Cavity nesters[b]	Day	0.972	0.946, 0.999
	1997 vs. 1998	0.345	0.156, 0.765
Ground-shrub nesters	1996 vs. 1998	2.714	1.092, 6.744
	Concealment	1.015	1.006, 1.024
	Nest height	1.103	1.022, 1.191

Note: for the sake of brevity, values are shown only for species and variables with CI's that exclude 1, the null value.
[a] Day = Julian day midpoint between two successive nest visits; Nest height = nest height in meters; Concealment = nest concealment calculated as the mean of side cover and overhead cover values; Shrub = number of shrub stems >10 cm above the ground and <8 cm dbh within a 5-m radius circle centered on the nest; Forest = percentage of landscape made up of forest within a 5-km radius circle centered on the plot.
[b] For these species, intervals for the nesting stage of laying were included with incubation intervals for analysis.

ecoregion. Many a priori expectations were supported by the data. For example, temporal and, to a lesser extent, landscape factors were confirmed as having strong support across species, but edge effects appeared less important than expected. We also confirmed that factors affecting nest survival varied by species or life history group and that none of the models were supported for a generalist species like American Robins.

The strong support for the temporal-effects model across species suggests that nest survival in general varies more by year, nest stage, and timing during the nesting season than by any of the other modeled sets of factors. Our observation that nest survival tended to be higher early in the nesting season and late in incubation is in agreement with other studies of temporal effects on nest survival (Pescador and Peris 2001, Dinsmore et al. 2002, Peak et al. 2004, Winter et al. 2004). The strong annual variation in nest survival that we observed is commonly identified in nesting studies (Fauth 2000, Sillett et al. 2000, Winter et al. 2005a).

Species with the strongest support for landscape effects had higher nest survival with less forest cover in the landscape, not more, contrary to our expectations (Hartley and Hunter 1998). Our finding that Eastern Wood-Pewees had higher nest survival in plots with less landscape forest cover fits with general habitat associations for the species; it is not known to be sensitive to forest fragmentation (Rodewald and Smith 1998). Our finding that Prothonotary Warblers also benefited from less landscape forest cover was unexpected; this species is heavily dependent upon large floodplain and wetland forests (Hoover 2006). This apparent contradiction remains unexplained. We found only weak support for our expectation that landscape effects would be important for area-sensitive species like Blue-gray Gnatcatchers and Rose-breasted Grosbeaks (Best et al. 1996, Burke and Nol 2000), as well as area-sensitive low nesters and tree nesters. Others have also observed Blue-gray Gnatcatchers breeding in narrow floodplains (Kilgo et al. 1998). We were surprised to find little support for differences in nest survival between floodplain and upland plots for species that nested in both habitats. Tree species composition, humidity, and other environmental factors are quite different between these two habitat types; bird relative abundances are twice as high in the floodplain as in the uplands (Knutson et al. 1996, Knutson et al. 2006).

The nest-site-effects model had more support than we expected for most species, although it failed to rank as the best model for any species or group. Eastern Wood-Pewees tend to respond positively to management that opens the canopy

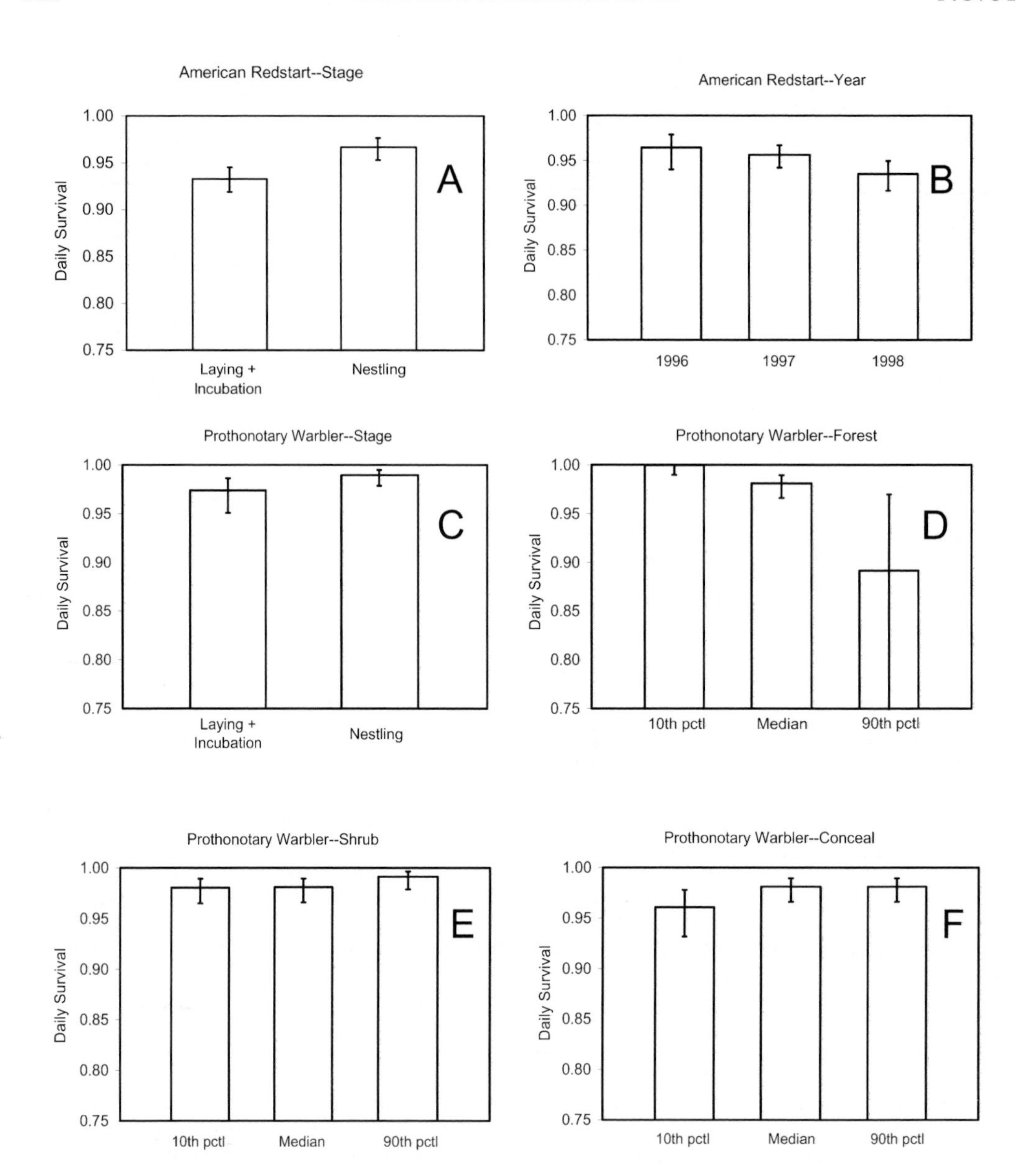

FIGURE 1A–F. Effects of predictor variables on daily survival rates of individual species and groups of birds nesting in floodplain and upland forests of the driftless area, 1996–1998. Day = Julian day midpoint between two successive nest visits; Nest height = nest height in m; Conceal = nest concealment calculated as the mean of side cover and overhead cover values; Shrub = number of shrub stems >10 cm above the ground and <8 cm dbh within a 5-m radius circle centered on the nest; Forest = percentage of landscape made up of forest within a 5-km radius circle centered on the plot; Year = 1996, 1997, 1998; Stage = laying, incubation, nestling. For continuous variables, survival rates are estimated at their 10th, 50th (median) and 90th percentiles. *Figure 1 is continued on the next page.*

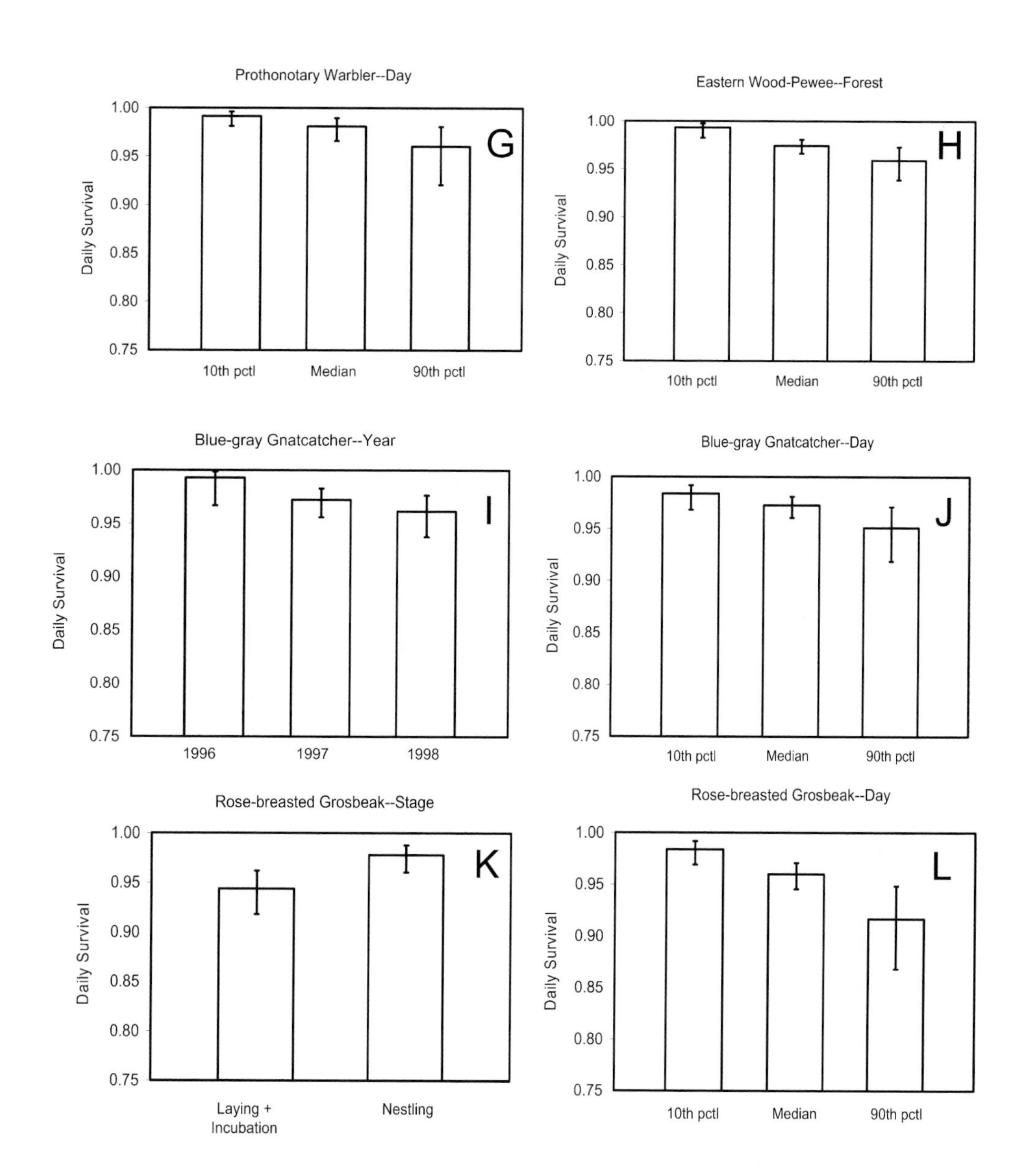

FIGURE 1G–L. *Continued.* Effects of predictor variables on daily survival rates of individual species and groups of birds nesting in floodplain and upland forests of the driftless area, 1996–1998. Day = Julian day midpoint between two successive nest visits; Nest height = nest height in m; Conceal = nest concealment calculated as the mean of side cover and overhead cover values; Shrub = number of shrub stems >10 cm above the ground and <8 cm dbh within a 5-m radius circle centered on the nest; Forest = percentage of landscape made up of forest within a 5-km radius circle centered on the plot; Year = 1996, 1997, 1998; Stage = laying, incubation, nestling. For continuous variables, survival rates are estimated at their 10th, 50th (median) and 90th percentiles. *Figure 1 is continued on the next page.*

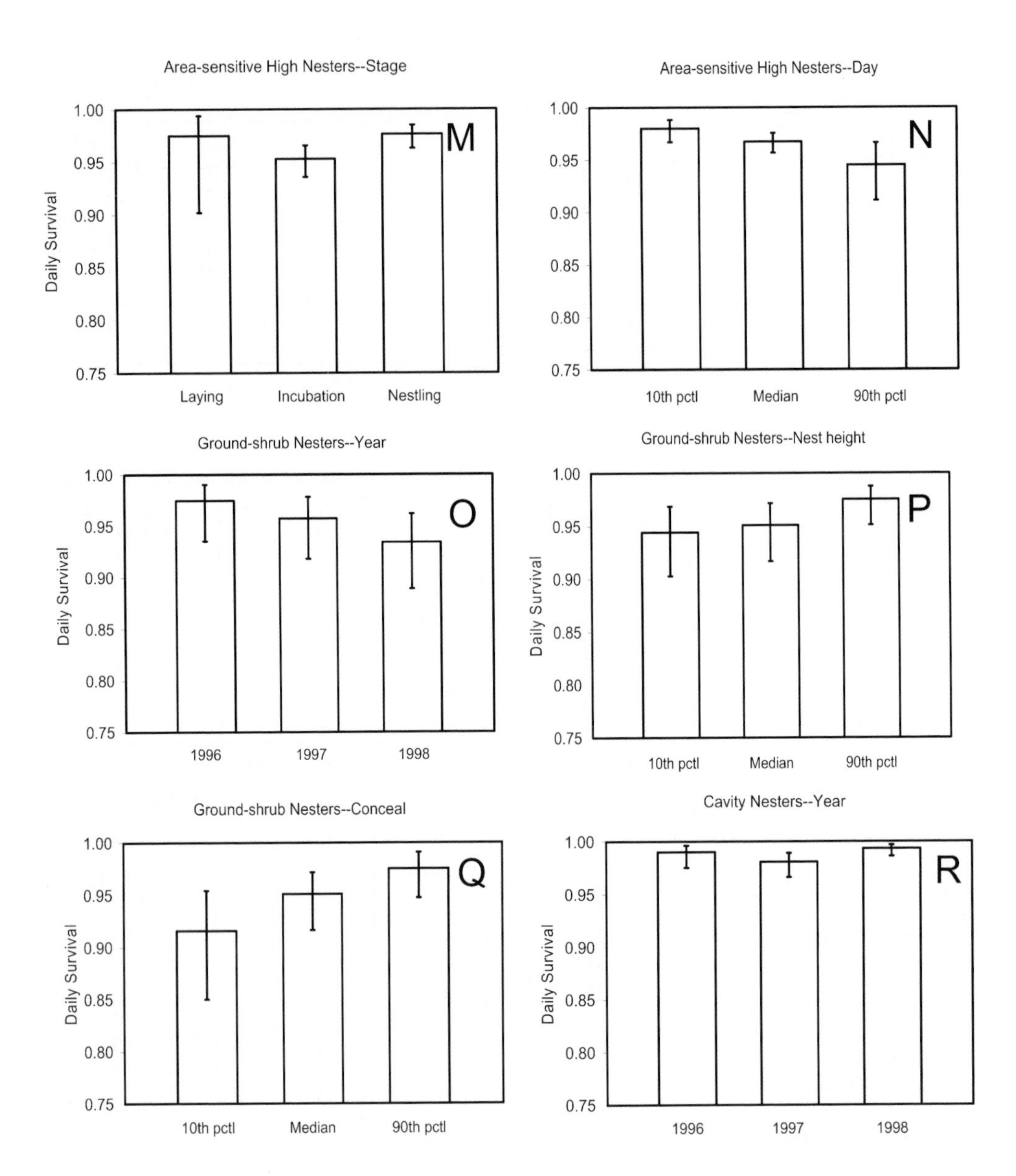

FIGURE 1M–R. *Continued.* Effects of predictor variables on daily survival rates of individual species and groups of birds nesting in floodplain and upland forests of the driftless area, 1996–1998. Day = Julian day midpoint between two successive nest visits; Nest height = nest height in m; Conceal = nest concealment calculated as the mean of side cover and overhead cover values; Shrub = number of shrub stems >10 cm above the ground and <8 cm dbh within a 5-m radius circle centered on the nest; Forest = percentage of landscape made up of forest within a 5-km radius circle centered on the plot; Year = 1996, 1997, 1998; Stage = laying, incubation, nestling. For continuous variables, survival rates are estimated at their 10th, 50th (median) and 90th percentiles. *Figure 1 is continued on the next page.*

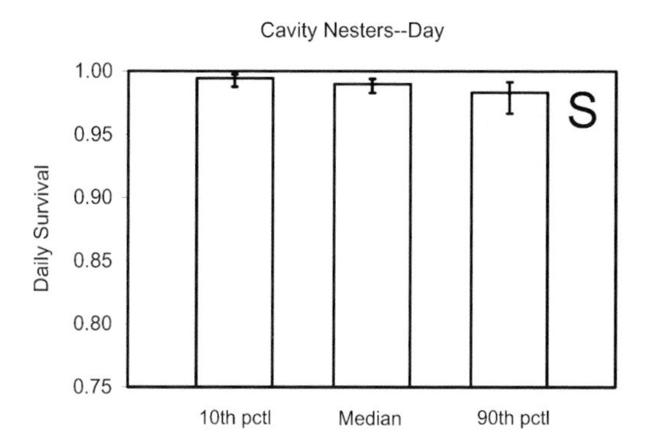

FIGURE 1S. *Continued.* Effects of predictor variables on daily survival rates of individual species and groups of birds nesting in floodplain and upland forests of the driftless area, 1996–1998. Day = Julian day midpoint between two successive nest visits; Nest height = nest height in m; Conceal = nest concealment calculated as the mean of side cover and overhead cover values; Shrub = number of shrub stems >10 cm above the ground and <8 cm dbh within a 5-m radius circle centered on the nest; Forest = percentage of landscape made up of forest within a 5-km radius circle centered on the plot; Year = 1996, 1997, 1998; Stage = laying, incubation, nestling. For continuous variables, survival rates are estimated at their 10th, 50th (median) and 90th percentiles.

and understory (Rodewald and Smith 1998, Artman et al. 2001), but we found only weak support for nest-site effects for this species. Ground and shrub nesters showed moderate support for nest-site effects, as expected, but the global model was their best model, indicating that this group of birds is responding to multiple factors across all the models. Our finding that concealment was supported for ground and shrub nesters is in agreement with previous studies of shrub-nesting species (Murphy 1983, Weidinger 2002, Albrecht 2004), while nest height for ground-shrub nesters has also been observed as a factor in nest survival of roadside bird communities (Shochat et al. 2005b) and Bell's Vireos (*Vireo bellii*) (Budnik et al. 2002). To our knowledge, concealment and shrub density has not been previously reported in association with nest survival for Prothonotary Warblers.

The two models with relatively weak support in our study (cowbird and edge effects) have been intensively studied in dozens of other research studies with mixed results. Comprehensive reviews indicate that cowbirds and landscape edges are factors that can affect nest survival in biologically important ways; however, negative effects are not observed in every study (Thompson et al. 2000, Batary and Baldi 2004, Lloyd et al. 2005). The relatively weak support we observed for the cowbird-effects model suggests that parasitism was not a major factor affecting nest survival in our study. Low rates of parasitism are unusual for the midwestern US, although the heaviest cowbird effects typically come from landscapes with even lower forest cover than our study area (Fauth 2000). Species-specific comparative data on edge effects is difficult to find because much of the literature is based on artificial nest studies or focuses on general effects on the bird community rather than species-specific vulnerability (Batary and Baldi 2004, Moore and Robinson 2004). However, other studies in the midwestern U.S. have identified negative effects of fragmented (high-edge) landscapes on landbird nest survival (Donovan et al. 1997).

The ability to directly assess the relative importance of a wide variety of factors that may affect nest survival, measured at multiple-spatial scales, has major implications for the management of bird populations. With this information, managers will be able to allocate resources more efficiently and identify when the major factors associated with nest survival are beyond their control. For example, landscape-scale factors respond to changes in public policy and economics, whereas local-scale variables associated with the nest site itself are modified by silvicultural methods and other site-scale habitat management (Duguay et al. 2000, Bettinger et al. 2005).

ACKNOWLEDGMENTS

We thank T. J. Fox, R. K. Hines, C. Sveum, E. Anderson, S. Anderson, G. Amsrud, D. Baker, C. Fylling, S. Hoffman, S. Houdek, W. Klouda, C. E. Korschgen, J. E. Lyon, K. Max, D. McClellan, L. McColl, M. Mullaney, J. C. Nelson, T. Nolan, L. R. Robinson, K. Skroch, G. Stern, L. Thomas, B. Tomica, and L. Zebehazy for their assistance. T. L. Shaffer, F. R. Thompson, III, and R. G. Peak provided consultation on the analyses. Four anonymous reviewers provided helpful comments that improved the paper. Project support was provided by the U.S. Geological Survey, Breeding Biology Research Database (BBIRD) program; the USDI Fish and Wildlife Service, Region 3 Nongame Bird Program; the Minnesota Department of Natural Resources; the Wisconsin Department of Natural Resources; and the Iowa Department of Natural Resources. Identification of commercial equipment and software in the text does not imply endorsement by the U.S. government.

TABLE 5. CONDITIONAL MEDIAN DAILY NEST-SURVIVAL ESTIMATES AND INTERVAL-SURVIVAL ESTIMATES WITH ASSOCIATED 95% CONFIDENCE INTERVALS (CI) FROM BEST MODELS FOR SPECIES AND LIFE-HISTORY GROUPINGS OF BIRDS NESTING IN FLOODPLAIN AND UPLAND FORESTS OF THE DRIFTLESS AREA, 1996–1998.

Species	Nests found	Nests successful	Exposure days	Nesting cycle (N of days)	Daily survival estimate (CI)	Interval survival estimate (CI)
American Redstart (*Setophaga ruticilla*)	196	66	2,488.5	24	0.949 (0.940, 0.958)	0.262 (0.182, 0.348)[a]
American Robin (*Turdus migratorius*)	109	68	1,785.5	30	0.974 (0.966, 0.981)	0.458 (0.352, 0.559)
Blue-gray Gnatcatcher (*Polioptila caerulea*)	66	26	1,315.0	28	0.973 (0.961, 0.981)	0.460 (0.326, 0.585)
Eastern Wood-Pewee (*Contopus virens*)	100	50	2,131.5	33	0.975 (0.966, 0.981)	0.428 (0.323, 0.528)
Prothonotary Warbler (*Protonotaria citrea*)	134	82	2,095.0	28	0.981 (0.966, 0.990)	0.558 (0.325, 0.740)[b]
Rose-breasted Grosbeak (*Pheucticus ludovicianus*)	73	33	1,063.0	27	0.960 (0.946, 0.971)	0.300 (0.157, 0.458)[c]
Area-sensitive low nesters	34	18	474.0	29	0.968 (0.947, 0.981)	0.388 (0.208, 0.565)
Ovenbird (*Seiurus aurocapilla*)	12	7	174.5	26	0.971 (0.932, 0.988)	0.463 (0.160, 0.727)
Wood Thrush (*Hylocichla mustelina*)	22	11	299.5	30	0.966 (0.938, 0.982)	0.356 (0.147, 0.574)
Area-sensitive tree nesters	121	58	1,890.5	29	0.968 (0.957, 0.976)	0.446 (0.128, 0.672)[d]
Acadian Flycatcher (*Empidonax virescens*)	15	11	225.5	32	0.982 (0.953, 0.993)	0.559 (0.214, 0.804)
Red-eyed Vireo (*Vireo olivaceus*)	24	10	339.5	28	0.957 (0.929, 0.975)	0.294 (0.127, 0.485)
Scarlet Tanager (*Piranga olivacea*)	43	21	676.0	28	0.967 (0.950, 0.978)	0.391 (0.240, 0.539)
Warbling Vireo (*Vireo gilvus*)	39	16	649.5	29	0.961 (0.942, 0.973)	0.312 (0.179, 0.456)
Cavity nesters	148	132	2,453.5	40	0.990 (0.983, 0.994)	0.661 (0.500, 0.782)
Black-capped Chickadee (*Poecile atricapillus*)	27	23	341.5	35	0.982 (0.961, 0.992)	0.531 (0.246, 0.753)
Downy Woodpecker (*Picoides pubescens*)	20	18	270.0	37	0.989 (0.966, 0.996)	0.658 (0.275, 0.874)
Great Crested Flycatcher (*Myiarchus crinitus*)	20	15	461.5	33	0.985 (0.968, 0.993)	0.601 (0.345, 0.785)
Hairy Woodpecker (*Picoides villosus*)	21	21	231.0	46	0.969 (0.936, 0.985)	0.232 (0.048, 0.500)
Red-bellied Woodpecker (*Melanerpes carolinus*)	14	12	332.5	42	0.988 (0.968, 0.995)	0.599 (0.257, 0.825)
Red-headed Woodpecker (*Melanerpes erythrocephalus*)	6	5	170.5	44	0.994 (0.956, 0.999)	0.772 (0.162, 0.964)
White-breasted Nuthatch (*Sitta carolinensis*)	5	4	90.5	46	0.989 (0.925, 0.998)	0.597 (0.028, 0.930)
Yellow-bellied Sapsucker (*Sphyrapicus varius*)	35	34	556.0	44	0.989 (0.976, 0.995)	0.619 (0.344, 0.806)
Ground-shrub nesters	161	66	2338.5	26	0.951 (0.917, 0.972)	0.271 (0.104, 0.474)
Brown Thrasher (*Toxostoma rufum*)	9	5	167.0	28	0.976 (0.937, 0.991)	0.504 (0.163, 0.774)
Eastern Kingbird (*Tyrannus tyrannus*)	6	4	178.5	37	0.983 (0.948, 0.995)	0.528 (0.140, 0.815)
Gray Catbird (*Dumetella carolinensis*)	53	21	797.5	27	0.962 (0.946, 0.973)	0.347 (0.221, 0.478)
Indigo Bunting (*Passerina cyanea*)	17	7	217.0	27	0.953 (0.914, 0.974)	0.271 (0.089, 0.496)
Northern Cardinal (*Cardinalis cardinalis*)	22	7	283.5	25	0.945 (0.912, 0.967)	0.246 (0.099, 0.431)
Song Sparrow (*Melospiza melodia*)	7	3	67.5	27	0.938 (0.846, 0.977)	0.178 (0.011, 0.528)
Yellow Warbler (*Dendroica petechia*)	47	19	627.5	24	0.954 (0.935, 0.968)	0.325 (0.197, 0.461)

[a] Assuming 4-, 11-, and 9-d laying, incubation, and nestling period, respectively.
[b] Assuming 5-, 13-, and 10-d laying, incubation, and nestling period, respectively.
[c] Assuming 4-, 13-, and 10-d laying, incubation, and nestling period, respectively.
[d] Assuming 4-, 13-, and 12-d weighted average laying, incubation, and nestling period, respectively.

Studies in Avian Biology No. 34:117–123

THE RELATIONSHIP BETWEEN PREDATION AND NEST CONCEALMENT IN MIXED-GRASS PRAIRIE PASSERINES: AN ANALYSIS USING PROGRAM MARK

STEPHANIE L. JONES AND J. SCOTT DIENI

Abstract. Nest predation is the principle cause of nest failure in most upland avian communities. In this paper, we explore the relationship between nest predation and nest-site concealment for six passerine species that co-occur in mixed-grass prairie of north-central Montana (1997–2002). Since ground-nesting passerines are susceptible to a wide range of predators, we hypothesized that selection processes would favor nest sites with more vegetative concealment to minimize the probability of nest detection. Although nests in our study were generally well concealed, concealment estimates were variable within and among species. We estimated daily nest-survival rates using the program MARK and covariates that were modeled included mean percent concealment, site, and year; models were evaluated within an information-theoretic framework. Nest concealment was negatively related to daily nest survival in Savannah Sparrows (*Passerculus sandwichensis*), Baird's (*Ammodramus bairdii*) Sparrows, and Chestnut-collared Longspurs (*Calcarius ornatus*) across all years, and Grasshopper Sparrows (*Ammodramus savannarum*) during some years. In the dome-nesting species, Sprague's Pipits (*Anthus spragueii*) and Western Meadowlarks (*Sturnella neglecta*), our results suggest that daily nest-survival rates increased with greater nest concealment. Although our precision was relatively poor, our results indicate that predation rates may actually increase with greater concealment for the four cup-nesting species, in some years, providing contradictory evidence that concealment deters predation for some grassland bird species of the northern plains.

Key Words: daily survival rate, grassland passerines, mixed-grass prairie, Montana, nest predation, nest concealment, nest success, program MARK.

LA RELACIÓN ENTRE DEPREDACIÓN Y OCULTACIÓN DE NIDO EN COLORINES DE PASTOS MIXTOS DE PRADERA: UN ANÁLISIS UTILIZANDO PROGRAMA MARK

Resumen. La depredación de nidos es la principal causa del fracaso de nidos en la mayoría de las comunidades de aves de tierras altas. En este artículo exploramos la relación entre depredación de nido y ocultación de nido de sitio para seis especies de colorines que co-ocurren en praderas mixtas de pasto, del norte central de Montana (1997–2002). Debido a que los colorines que anidan en el suelo son susceptibles a un amplio rango de depredadores, nuestra hipótesis es que procesos de selección favorecerían a sitios de nidos con mayor ocultación de vegetación, para minimizar la probabilidad de detección de nido. A pesar de que los nidos en nuestro estudio se encontraban en su mayoría bien conectados, las estimaciones de ocultación fueron variables dentro y entre las especies. Estimamos las tasas diarias de sobrevivencia de nido utilizando el programa MARK, así como las covariantes que fueron modeladas, incluyendo el porcentaje de la media de ocultación, sitio, y año; los modelos fueron evaluados dentro de un marco teórico de información. La ocultación de nido estuvo negativamente relacionada a la sobrevivencia diaria de nido en Gorrión Sabanero (*Passerculus sandwichensis*), Gorriones de Baird (*Ammodramus bairdii*), Escribano Collar Castaño (*Calcarius ornatus*) durante todos los años; y en Gorrión Chapulín (*Ammodramus savannarum*) durante algunos años. En las especies anidadoras de domo, Bisbita Llanera (*Anthus spragueii*) y en Pradero Occidental (*Sturnella neglecta*) nuestros resultados sugieren que las tasas diarias de sobrevivencia de nido incrementaron con mayor ocultación de nido. A pesar de que nuestra precisión fue relativamente pobre, nuestros resultados indican que las tasas de depredación de hecho quizás incrementen con mayor ocultación para las cuatro especies anidadoras de tasa en algunos años, mostrando evidencia contradictoria de que la ocultación disuade la depredación en algunas especies de aves de tierras de prados de las planicies del norte.

Nest predation is typically the most significant factor affecting productivity in ground-nesting passerines, regardless of taxon, habitat, or geographic area (Ricklefs 1969, Murphy 1983; Martin 1993, 1998), and is considered the primary cause of nest failure in grassland passerines of North America (Johnson and Temple 1990, Vickery et al. 1992, Winter 1999; Davis 2003, 2005). Although a number of other factors contribute to nest failure, nest predation should exert a major evolutionary force on nest-site selection and be a dominant factor directing nest-site-selection patterns (Martin 1998). As in other landscapes, nonrandom nest-site placement has been documented in grasslands (Clark and Shutler 1999, Dieni and Jones 2003; Davis 2003, 2005). Most species have evolved several anti-predator strategies, including direct effects, e.g., parental behavior and nest defense, and indirect effects, including nest-site selection, timing of nesting, double brooding, length of incubation, and nestling periods (Weidinger 2002). A well-concealed nest appears to be an obvious response to nest predation since high cover reduces the communication of auditory, visual, and olfactory cues from the nest to potential predators (Martin 1993). By selecting safe sites, birds can reduce nest failure either by decreasing the nest encounter rate for incidental nest predation or by decreasing nest detectability for actively searching predators (Weidinger 2002). The relative importance of nest-site characteristics to other nest-defense strategies is crucial to understanding the evolution of life-history traits and population limitations (Cresswell 1997).

The nest-concealment hypothesis predicts decreased predation risk for nests with greater surrounding vegetation (Martin 1993). Indeed, some cup-nesting passerines select nest sites that have higher vegetation densities than surrounding areas (Petit and Petit 1996, Dieni and Jones 2003) and, in some cases, predation rates have been found to be lower at nests with greater concealment (Martin and Roper 1988, Clark and Shutler 1999, Schmidt and Whelan 1999, Davis 2005). However, other studies have found no relationship between nesting success and nest concealment (Filliater et al. 1994, Clark and Shutler 1999, Davis 2005). The lack of a relationship between concealment and nest success has led to other hypotheses to explain how birds avoid nest predation including, nest-defense (parental compensation) hypothesis, potential-prey-site hypothesis, trade-off hypothesis, and others.

Active nest defense may compensate for poorly concealed nests through parental behavior which may include direct attacks, mobbing, nest guarding, vocalizations, e.g., alarm calls, injury feigning and distraction displays (Cresswell 1997, Martin and Menge 2000, Remes 2005). Passive nest-defense strategies include crypsis, e.g., camouflaging the nest contents while sitting on the nest (Weidinger 2002). The potential-prey-site hypothesis is based on the premise that search efficiency of a predator declines as the number of potential nest sites increases (Liebezeit and George 2002), and it predicts that nests surrounded by many potential nest sites should have a lower probability of depredation than those surrounded by few nest sites (Liebezeit and George 2002). The trade-off hypothesis states that nest-site choice is often a trade-off between the need for concealment and the need for individuals to maintain some view of the surrounding, to reduce the risk of predation on the adults (Götmark et al. 1995).

We tested the hypothesis that nest-site-selection strategies in the grasslands of the northern prairie may maximize vegetative concealment to minimize the probability of detection by predators. If nest concealment affects nest-predation rates, then poorly concealed nests should have a higher probability of being depredated, provided that significant variation occurs in concealment values. In the undisturbed arid grasslands of north-central Montana, structurally homogeneous graminoids are the dominant vegetation, while woody vegetation is limited. The predator community here is diverse using a variety of techniques to locate nests, including visual, olfactory, and random-search strategies. Nest placement is restricted to the ground, which makes the nests accessible to all potential predators.

To determine if nest predation varies in relation to nest concealment, we modeled daily nest survival as a function of vegetative nest concealment using the nest-survival model in program MARK (Dinsmore et al. 2002, White 2005). Six common grassland species that co-occur in north-central Montana were studied: Sprague's Pipit (*Anthus spragueii*), Savannah (*Passerculus sandwichensis*), Grasshopper (*Ammodramus savannarum*), and Baird's (*A. bairdii*) sparrows, Chestnut-collared Longspur (*Calcarius ornatus*), and Western Meadowlark (*Sturnella neglecta*).

METHODS

Study Area

During 1997–2002, we conducted this study at Bowdoin National Wildlife Refuge in Phillips County, north-central Montana (48°25′N, 107°39′W; ~700 m in elevation). The study area consisted of four permanent plots (26–59 ha), situated 1.6–3.8 km apart and comprising 183 ha of flat to gently rolling native northern mixed-grass prairie. The climate is continental and semiarid, characterized by strong winds and high evaporation rates. Long-term annual and seasonal (May–July) precipitation totals are 33.7 and 18.2 cm, respectively. Annual and seasonal precipitation totals averaged 31.0 and 16.6 cm, respectively during the study period. Western wheatgrass (*Pascopyrum smithii*), needle-and-thread (*Stipa comata*), blue grama (*Bouteloua gracilis*), dense clubmoss (*Selaginella densa*), and fringed sagewort (*Artemisia frigida*) were the dominant herbaceous species. Shrubs (*Sarcobatus vermiculatus, Artemisia cana, Ceratoides lanata*) were sparse and trees largely absent, except Russian olive (*Elaeagnus angustifolia*) and cottonwood (*Populus deltoides occidentalis*), which occurred sporadically along the edges of two study sites. The study area had not been grazed by cattle for ≥29 yr. A 3-ha portion of one study site burned in 1994; otherwise no burning events have occurred since refuge documentation began in 1936.

Potential or suspected terrestrial nest predators included badger (*Taxidea taxus*), long-tailed weasel (*Mustela frenata*), red fox (*Vulpes vulpes*), coyote (*Canis latrans*) (Peitz and Granfors 1998), mice and voles (*Zapus, Reithrodontomys, Peromyscus,* and *Microtus*), ground squirrels (*Spermophilus tridecemlineatus* and *S. richardsonii*), bull snake (*Pituophis melanoleucus*), garter snake (*Thamnophis* spp.), and western rattlesnake (*Crotalus viridis*). Avian predators such as Northern Harrier (*Circus cyaneus*), gulls (*Larus* spp.), Short-eared Owl (*Asio flammeus*), Loggerhead Shrikes (*Lanius ludovicianus*), Black-billed Magpie (*Pica hudsonia*) and Western Meadowlark have been observed on or within the immediate vicinity of the study sites. Sprague's Pipit and Baird's Sparrow nests (N = 13) monitored with micro-cameras (Pietz and Granfors 2000) documented garter snake, Northern Harrier, Short-eared Owl, Western Meadowlark, and deer mouse depredation of nestlings within the study area (P. J. Gouse and S. L. Jones, unpubl. data).

Nest Searching and Monitoring

Sites were searched for nests 3–5 times per week from mid-May through mid-August in an attempt to locate all active nests each year (Dieni and Jones 2003). Search techniques included behavioral observation (Martin and Geupel 1993), foot surveys, and rope dragging (Davis 2003). Once located, nests were marked for relocation by placing a discreet strip of plastic flagging on the ground approximately 2.5 m on either side of the nest. Nests were monitored every 2–4 d thereafter. Nesting outcomes were: (1) successful fledging (at least one young of the host species), (2) complete depredation, (3) abandonment (eggs or nestlings left permanently unattended), or (4) outcome unknown. Observations of fledglings within 3 d of expected fledging, minimal nest disturbance, the presence of feces and feather scales in the nest, fledglings near the nest, or adults uttering alarm calls nearby or feeding new fledglings within 50 m of the nest were treated as evidence of success. Depredation was assumed when the nest, eggs or nestlings too young to fledge disappeared or were destroyed.

Within 2–4 d following nest termination, we estimated percent cover from directly above the nest and in the four cardinal directions. Five ocular estimates of percent concealment of the constructed nest (not nest contents) were obtained for each nest, as viewed from a distance of 1 m in the four cardinal directions at ground level, and from directly above (Dieni and Jones 2003). The arithmetic mean of those five measurements was used as the concealment value for each nest.

Analysis

We estimated daily survival rates (DSR) for nests using the survival model in program MARK (White 2005). Program MARK uses a generalized linear approach to modeling daily nest-survival rates, using maximum likelihood estimation to estimate regression coefficients (Rotella et al. 2004). Our objective was to determine if mean vegetative concealment of the nest was inversely related to nest predation rates, and if so, estimate the strength of that relationship. All nests that failed from reasons other than predation (e.g., inclement weather, parasitism, or unknown) were excluded from the analysis to focus on concealment using only those nests with known fates, either depredated or successful. Estimates of DSR in this context served also as an inverse measure of nest depredation rates.

Analyses were conducted independently for the six dominant passerine species found on the study area. Six linear-regression models predicting daily nest survival were constructed and evaluated for each bird species, using a combination of explanatory variables—constant DSR (intercept-only model), nest concealment, and nest concealment—while simultaneously controlling for the effects of site and year, with and without their respective interactions. Nest concealment was the parameter of interest; however, site and year were also used in the models because of the plausibility that nest fates were not independent within sites or years (Winter et al. 2005a), a fundamental assumption of the nest-survival model in program MARK (Dinsmore et al. 2002). Regression models were constructed using the logistic transformation (logit) as the link function, using natural logs.

Encounter histories are constructed in program MARK, which required the following data for each nest (Rotella 2005): (1) the day the nest was found, (2) the last day the nest was checked when still active, (3) the last day that the nest was checked, and (4), the fate of the nest. For successful nests, an attempt was made to estimate the actual day that the nest fledged young, rather than simply using the last day checked. The latter, if different, would unjustifiably add survival days to a nest when failure was no longer possible (Rotella 2005). Days were standardized so that the earliest date across all years when a nest (or nests) was first found was coded as day 1, with subsequent dates numbered sequentially relative to the first day (Rotella 2005). Analyses were conducted independently for each bird species, thus each species potentially had a different standardized earliest date. Since we had 6 yr of data for each species, the earliest date across all years was standardized as day 1, thus subsequent dates were numbered relative to this date, regardless of year.

Model covariates included mean concealment, year, and site. Mean concealment was treated as a proportion in the analysis and reported as such in the results. Site and year variables were treated as categorical (four and six levels, respectively), with each level introduced into the regression model as an artificial explanatory variable with the usual 0 or 1 coding scheme. Cross-product terms were also added accordingly for concealment and site-year interactions.

Each set of candidate models was evaluated within an information-theoretic framework (Burnham and Anderson 2002). For each model within a set, program MARK calculated Akaike's information criterion corrected for small sample sizes (AIC_c), and ranked each model in ascending order of AIC_c values (Burnham and Anderson 2002). Models with lower AIC_c values indicate greater empirical support, which can be roughly interpreted as a compromise between explaining more variance and limiting the number of parameters (Cooch and White 2005).

Our goal was not to determine the best model per se, but rather to make a general estimate of the direction and magnitude of the effects of concealment on DSR. We considered this relationship both in a bivariate context, and while controlling for the simultaneous effects of year and site. Models with and without interaction terms were judged to have received similar support from the data if their AIC_c values were within two units of each other: in which case, we viewed the evidence of an interaction as weak and consequently dropped the interaction from further consideration. We then used the model-averaging approach (Burnham and Anderson 2002) for the remaining models to estimate an average regression coefficient for concealment for each bird species, with an unconditional estimate of the variance. Coefficient estimates were weighted according to that model's likelihood in the set (Akaike's weights; w_i). Model-averaged coefficients may provide better estimates of precision because the variance component dealing with model-selection uncertainty is included in the variance estimator (Burnham and Anderson 2002). Intercept-only models (where the regression coefficient for concealment is set to 0) were included in the set of models to be averaged, which serves to reduce model-selection bias of the estimate (Burnham and Anderson 2002). The magnitude of the estimated regression coefficient can be interpreted in terms of its effect on the odds of daily nest survival. This is achieved by taking the antilog of both sides of the logistic equation. The right-hand side of the equation has the exponential form, e^{BX}, which gives the estimated factor change in DSR for every unit increase in nest concealment (Agresti and Finlay 1986).

RESULTS

From 1997–2002, 1,014 nests of 19 species (excluding waterfowl) were discovered and monitored; here we report on the six dominant passerines species that composed >90% (N = 919) of the total nests located (Table 1). Predation accounted for 82% of all known nest failures; among abandoned nests (N = 89), 33% were directly attributed to severe weather events (e.g., heavy rain and hailstorms). Only a small number of nests had nesting fates that were unknown (N = 11; Table 1).

Mean nest concealment varied within and among bird species. Across all nests, Chestnut-collared Longspurs had the least concealed nests, with the most variability ($\overline{x}$ = 58%, CV = 38%), while mean nest-concealment estimates for the five remaining species were higher but less variable ($\overline{x}$ = 83–89%, CV = 13–22%).

Except for Grasshopper Sparrows, nest-survival models that included interaction terms between nest concealment and site or year variables received little empirical support, suggesting that the relationship between nest concealment and daily nest survival varied little across sites or years. Constant-survival models (y-intercept only) and models including bivariate relationships between DSR and nest concealment all had substantial support for all bird species (Table 2). Models controlling for site and year all had reasonable empirical support (ΔAIC_c <8) for all species (Table 2).

Model-averaged regression coefficients are presented in Table 3. Both Sprague's Pipits and Western Meadowlarks showed a positive relationship between nest concealment and DSR, although the precision of those estimates was

TABLE 1. RELATIVE FREQUENCIES (NUMBER OF NESTS WITH BROWN-HEADED COWBIRD [*MOLOTHRUS ATER*] PARASITISM) OF NESTING OUTCOMES FOR THE DOMINANT BIRD SPECIES AT BOWDOIN NATIONAL WILDLIFE REFUGE (1997–2002).

Species	Abandoned	Depredated	Successful	Unknown	N
Sprague's Pipit (*Anthus spragueii*)	8.7 (1)	52.2 (2)	39.1 (0)	0.0	69
Savannah Sparrow (*Passerculus sandwichensis*)	17.6 (3)	40.0 (16)	41.8 (4)	0.6	170
Grasshopper Sparrow (*Ammodramus savannarum*)	12.5 (0)	29.7 (4)	56.3 (1)	1.6	64
Baird's Sparrow (*Ammodramus bairdii*)	10.2 (0)	47.5 (3)	42.4 (0)	0.0	59
Chestnut-collared Longspur (*Calcarius ornatus*)	5.3 (2)	45.2 (7)	47.5 (2)	1.9	469
Western Meadowlark (*Sturnella neglecta*)	15.9 (3)	45.5 (15)	38.6 (11)	0.0	88
Total	89 (9)	403 (47)	416 (18)	11	919

TABLE 2. SELECTION RESULTS MODELING DAILY SURVIVAL RATES USING PROGRAM MARK FOR SIX GRASSLAND PASSERINE SPECIES. SIX LINEAR CANDIDATE MODELS WERE CONSIDERED FOR EACH BIRD SPECIES, WHICH INCLUDED THE FOLLOWING VARIABLES: CONSTANT DAILY SURVIVAL (Y-INTERCEPT = B_0), MEAN NEST CONCEALMENT ALONE AND CONTROLLING FOR SITE AND YEAR, AND THEIR RESPECTIVE INTERACTIONS. MODELS ARE LISTED IN ORDER OF DESCENDING AIC_C, BY BIRD SPECIES. NUMBER OF PARAMETERS (*K*) VARIED AMONG SPECIES FOR IDENTICAL MODELS, SINCE SPECIES OCCURRENCE VARIED BY YEAR AND SITE.

Species	Model	ΔAIC_c	w_i	*K*
Sprague's Pipit (*Anthus spragueii*)	b_0 + bconceal + byear	0.0	0.45	7
	b_0	0.7	0.32	1
	b_0 + bconceal	2.6	0.12	2
	b_0 + bconceal + byear+ bint	3.5	0.08	11
	b_0 + bconceal + bsite	6.8	0.02	5
	b_0 + bconceal + bsite + bint	8.1	0.01	8
Savannah Sparrow (*Passerculus sandwichensis*)	b_0	0.0	0.39	1
	b_0 + bconceal + bsite	0.7	0.27	5
	b_0 + bconceal	1.3	0.21	2
	b_0 + bconceal + bsite + bint	3.6	0.06	8
	b_0 + bconceal + byear	4.5	0.04	7
	b_0 + bconceal + byear + bint	5.4	0.03	12
Grasshopper Sparrow (*Ammodramus savannarum*)	b_0 + bconceal + byear + bint	0.0	0.98	8
	b_0	10.1	0.01	1
	b_0 + bconceal + bsite + bint	11.0	0.00	6
	b_0 + bconceal + bsite	11.9	0.00	4
	b_0 + bconceal	12.1	0.00	2
	b_0 + bconceal + byear	15.5	0.00	6
Baird's Sparrow (*Ammodramus bairdii*)	b_0 + bconceal + byear	0.0	0.35	6
	b_0	0.5	0.28	1
	b_0 + bconceal	0.7	0.24	2
	b_0 + bconceal + bsite + bint	3.1	0.07	8
	b_0 + bconceal + bsite	4.2	0.04	5
	b_0 + bconceal + byear + bint	6.2	0.02	10
Chestnut-collared Longspur (*Calcarius ornatus*)	b_0 + bconceal	0.0	0.51	2
	b_0	1.3	0.27	1
	b_0 + bconceal + bsite	2.0	0.19	5
	b_0 + bconceal + bsite + bint	6.6	0.02	8
	b_0 + bconceal + byear	7.4	0.01	7
	b_0 + bconceal + byear + bint	13.3	0.00	12
Western Meadowlark (*Sturnella neglecta*)	b_0	0.0	0.52	1
	b_0 + bconceal	1.1	0.30	2
	b_0 + bconceal + bsite	2.9	0.12	5
	b_0 + bconceal + byear	5.6	0.03	6
	b_0 + bconceal + bsite + bint	6.5	0.02	8
	b_0 + bconceal + byear + bint	9.0	0.01	10

TABLE 3. REGRESSION COEFFICIENTS FOR MEAN NEST CONCEALMENT ESTIMATED USING A WEIGHTED AVERAGE ACROSS ALL MODELS, BY BIRD SPECIES. BECAUSE OF STRONG EVIDENCE OF AN INTERACTION BETWEEN YEAR AND CONCEALMENT FOR GRASSHOPPER SPARROW, COEFFICIENTS WERE AVERAGED BETWEEN INTERCEPT-ONLY AND BIVARIATE MODELS FOR EACH EYAR SEPARATELY. GENERALLY LOW PRECISION OF ALL ESTIMATES IS REFLECTED BY THE RELATIVELY WIDE 95% CONFIDENCE INTERVALS. THE MAGNITUDE OF THE ESTIMATED REGRESSION COEFFICIENT CAN BE INTERPRETED IN TERMS OF ITS EFFECT ON THE ODDS OF DAILY NEST-SURVIVAL, WHICH GIVES THE ESTIMATED FACTOR CHANGE IN DAILY SURVIVAL RATE FOR EVERY 0.1 UNIT (10%) INCREASE IN NEST CONCEALMENT.

Species	$b_{conceal}$	Upper 95% CI	Lower 95%CI	$e^{b(\Delta 10\%)}$
Sprague's Pipit (*Anthus spragueii*)	0.6	2.2	-1.1	1.1
Savannah Sparrow (*Passerculus sandwichensis*)	-0.4	0.5	-1.3	1.0
Grasshopper Sparrow				
(*Ammodramus savannarum*) – 1997	-0.5	1.5	-2.5	1.0
– 1998	20.2	37.6	2.8	7.5
– 2000	5.8	13.9	-2.3	1.8
– 2002	-1.9	3.3	-7.0	0.8
Baird's Sparrow (*Ammodramus bairdii*)	-0.9	1.3	-3.2	0.9
Chestnut-collared Longspur (*Calcarius ornatus*)	-0.4	0.1	-1.0	1.0
Western Meadowlark (*Sturnella neglecta*)	0.8	2.4	-0.8	1.1

low (CV = 141% and 107%, respectively). Strong evidence was found of an interaction between nest concealment and year for Grasshopper Sparrows (Table 3). The relationship between nest concealment and DSR was positive for 1997 and 2002, while negative for 1998 and 2000. The three other species studied showed a negative relationship between nest concealment and DSR.

DISCUSSION

Nest predation was the primary cause of nest failure, which is largely consistent with other reports for grassland passerines (Johnson and Temple 1990, Vickery et al. 1992; Davis 2003, 2005; Winter et al. 2005a). While nest-concealment values varied among species, it was generally high except for Chestnut-collared Longspurs. In this study, if nest concealment did lessen nest predation as predicted the effect was extremely weak or difficult to detect. In the four cup-nesting species, nest concealment had a weak inverse relationship with DSR for Savannah and Baird's sparrows and Chestnut-collared Longspurs, or varied substantially across years in Grasshopper Sparrows, with poor within-year precision. In contrast, both dome-nesting species, Western Meadowlarks and Sprague's Pipits, showed a weak positive relationship between concealment and DSR, but again with relatively low precision.

A number of studies on passerines have also shown a lack of association between nesting success and nest concealment (Filliater et al. 1994, Clark and Shutler 1999, Davis 2005). If nesting songbirds recognize micro-sites that are more susceptible to predation, we would expect strong selection for specific nest-site micro-habitats. However, the predator community in the mixed-grass prairie is diverse with diverse strategies to locate nests, depending on visual or olfactory cues and random-search methods. This predator diversity may preclude the existence of safe nest sites for ground-nesting songbirds (Filliater et al. 1994, Wilson and Cooper 1998). In addition, the avian community in the northern mixed-grass prairie may be adapted to a suite of predators that differs from what is now present.

Small mammals, considered the primary threat to ground nests in the northern Great Plains (Pietz and Granfors 2000, Davis 2003) opportunistically find grassland bird nests while foraging for invertebrates (Howlett and Stutchbury 1996, Dion et al. 2000). This may eliminate the predictability of successful nest sites (Filliater et al. 1994) since rodents take eggs or nestlings opportunistically from unattended nests (Weidinger 2002). In addition, small mammals may avoid foraging in areas with less vegetative cover to reduce the risk of avian predation on themselves, which may explain why concealed nests were somewhat more likely to be depredated (Howlett and Stutchbury 1996). Moreover, nest defense may actually be more effective on poorly concealed nests, as there may be a trade-off between increased nest cover and the ability of parents on the nest to detect an approaching predator (Götmark et al. 1995).

Avian predators generally rely on visual cues for detecting active nests (Filliater et al. 1994, Dion et al. 2000), and therefore high nest cover should be more effective against avian predators. We documented avian predators (N = 5) depredating nests during the nestling stage, and it is plausible that they located nests in response to increased parental activity or begging calls by nestlings, typical of the late nestling stage (Liebezeit and George 2002).

If nest-site concealment is not effective in reducing nest failure due to diverse predator strategies, adult behavior may be important in nest predator deterrence (Murphy et al. 1977). The effects of parental behavior on nest survival differ among species, generally being either positive or neutral (Weidinger 2002), although increased adult activity at nests could be negative (Halupka 1998, Martin and Menge 2000, Remes 2005). Strong adult nest defense (Murphy et al. 1977), re-nesting, and double-brooding (Murphy 1983, Schmidt and Whelan 1999), faster nestling growth, and early fledging (Ricklefs 1969, Murphy et al. 1977) may all contribute more to nest success than micro-site selection. We suggest that the three species studied that showed a weak negative relationship between concealment and DSR had behavior consistent with the parental compensation, nest-defense, and trade-off hypotheses.

Chestnut-collared Longspurs have high rates of re-nesting and double-brooding, shortened time for nestling development, and commonly exhibit distraction displays when flushed from the nest (Hill and Gould 1997; S. L. Jones and P. J. Gouse, unpubl. data). Chestnut-collared Longspurs and Sprague's Pipits are also noted for their distraction-flight displays when off the nest (Hill and Gould 1997, Robbins 1998). Savannah Sparrows do show nest-site selection patterns that favor nest sites with greater vegetation structure (Dieni and Jones 2003); however, in this analysis no positive relationship was found from concealment to DSR. Conversely, both Davis (2005) in the mixed-grass prairie of southern Saskatchewan and Winter et al. (2005a) in the northern tall-grass prairie of Missouri documented a positive relationship between nest concealment and nest success in Savannah Sparrows, although the latter study did not discount abandoned nests from the analysis. Savannah Sparrows do demonstrate active nest-defense behavior, particularly using alarm calls and distraction displays.

Birds can also increase investment in one nesting attempt by adapting more secretive behavior when visiting the nests (Cresswell 1997). Sprague's Pipits and the *Ammodramus* sparrows are not generally double-brooded (Sutter 1997, Green et al. 2002, Davis 2003) and did not flush until the searcher was extremely close to the nest. Adults of these species are typically quiet and unobtrusive around the nest, using foliage to conceal movements. They return by flying to the vicinity of the nest, but typically travel the last few meters discreetly on foot. This may mimic a running rodent and serve to divert predators from the nest (Morton et al. 1993). Cryptic alternate plumages are typical for the species studied here; their plumages are particularly cryptic when the incubating or brooding individual is on the nest. Therefore, these species may rely more on crypsis than nest concealment to avoid visually oriented predation and may be under strong directional selection from nest predators to choose nest sites that allow them to blend into the background.

Nest-site selection is likely a trade-off among several competing constraints, and may not primarily reflect an anti-predation strategy. However, the fact that no functional relationships were uncovered between predation rates and nesting concealment is striking, particularly given the wide variation in concealment values observed within and across the bird species studied here. Our failure to uncover a relationship between nest concealment and nest-predation rates may be a function of the local predator community, in conjunction with adult behavioral strategies. Indeed, parental behavior at the nest may lead to complex relationships between nest concealment and survival and the accumulating evidence is in support of multiple and interactive effects on nest predation (Weidinger 2002). However, micro-site characteristics, in conjunction with adult behavioral adaptations, may still serve to conceal nests through crypsis.

ACKNOWLEDGMENTS

This project was funded by the USDI Fish and Wildlife Service, Nongame Migratory Bird Program, Region 6. Field support and resources were provided by J. E. Cornely, C. R. Luna, D. M. Prellwitz, and the staff at Bowdoin National Wildlife Refuge. We are indebted to P. J. Gouse for her capable direction in the field. We thank all the field assistants who worked on this project during 1997–2002: B. Adams, A. C. Araya, B. S. Atchley, R. R. Conover, M. Friederhick, B. D. Gouse, J. Hammond, J. Hinz, B. G. Larson, S. N. Luttich, K. Payne, H. Sauls, C. Stahala, V. Trabold, P. N. Wiederrick, and J. K. Wood. This project also benefited from the support and assistance of M. T. Green, G. R. Geupel and the staff at Caffe Di Lucca. J. J. Rotella provided advice on several analytical design questions using program MARK, while J. Bart, S. K. Davis, G. R. Geupel, M. Herzog, D. R. Petit, D. L. Reinking, J. J. Rotella, J. M. Ruth, J. A. Sedgwick, and several anonymous reviewers provided helpful comments on earlier versions of this manuscript.

Studies in Avian Biology No. 34:124–135

THE INFLUENCE OF HABITAT ON NEST SURVIVAL OF SNOWY AND WILSON'S PLOVERS IN THE LOWER LAGUNA MADRE REGION OF TEXAS

Sharyn L. Hood and Stephen J. Dinsmore

Abstract. Snowy Plovers (*Charadrius alexandrinus*) and Wilson's Plovers (*Charadrius wilsonia*) are two shorebird species that nest along the Gulf Coast of the US. We modeled the daily nest survival of both species in the lower Laguna Madre region of Texas during the 2003 and 2004 breeding seasons as a function of nest age, year, day in the season, maximum daily temperature, daily precipitation, and habitat features at three spatial scales (microhabitat, a 25-m radius of the nest, and landscape). Daily survival of Snowy Plover nests increased with nest age ($\hat{\beta}_{Age}$ = 0.03, 95% confidence limits were -0.01, 0.07, on a logit scale), but did not vary between years. Nests inland had substantially lower daily survival than nests on the coast ($\hat{\beta}_{Inland}$ = -0.18, 95% confidence limits were -1.03, 0.67, on a logit scale). The presence of a conspicuous object at the nest site increased daily nest survival. A quadratic trend occurred on the coefficient of variation (CV) for low vegetation (CV used as an index of low vegetation spatial heterogeneity) at the 25-m scale for Snowy Plover nests. Daily nest survival of Wilson's Plovers was best explained by a combination of two habitat metrics at the microhabitat scale. Less vegetation at the immediate nest site increased daily survival ($\hat{\beta}_{Veg}$ = -1.35, 95% confidence limits were -2.28, -0.42, on a logit scale) while daily nest survival was higher for nests with lower contagion at the microhabitat scale ($\hat{\beta}_{Contagion}$ = -0.87, 95% confidence limits were -1.65, -0.10, on a logit scale). We found no evidence for yearly differences or an effect of weather on the daily nest survival of either species. Our results illustrate the role that selected habitat features play in the nest survival of Snowy and Wilson's plovers and further our understanding of their nesting ecology. We anticipate that our results will assist in the identification and protection of habitats critical to breeding populations of these and other shorebird species.

Key Words: *Charadrius alexandrinus, C. wilsonia,* Laguna Madre, nest success, nest survival, program MARK, Snowy Plover, Texas, Wilson's Plover.

LA INFLUENCIA DEL HÁBITAT EN LA SOBEVIVENCIA DE NIDO DE CHORLO NEVADO Y CHORLO PICOGRUESO EN LA REGIÓN BAJA DE LA LAGUNA MADRE DE TEXAS

Resumen. El Chorlo Nevado (*Charadrius alexandrinus*) y el Chorlo Picogrueso (*Charadrius wilsonia*) son dos especies de ave de orilla que anidan a lo largo de la Costa del Golfo de EU. Modelamos sobrevivencia diaria de nido para ambas especies en la región baja de la Laguna Madre de Texas durante el 2003 y el 2004, estaciones de reproducción como función de la edad de nido, año, día en la estación, temperatura máxima diaria, precipitación diaria, y características de hábitat en tres escalas espaciales (microhabitat, un radio de 25-m del nido, y paisaje). La sobrevivencia diaria de nidos de Chorlo Nevado incrementó con la edad del nido ($\hat{\beta}_{edad}$ = 0.03, 95% de los límites de confidencia fueron -0.01, 0.07 en escala logit), pero no variaron entre los años. La anidación en tierra tuvo substancialmente una sobrevivencia menor que los nidos en la costa ($\hat{\beta}_{Inland}$ = -0.18, 95% de los límites de confidencia fueron -1.03, 0.67 en escala logit). La presencia de un objeto visible en el sitio del nido incrementó la sobrevivencia diaria del nido. Una tendencia cuadrática ocurrió en el coeficiente de variación (CV) para la vegetación baja (CV utilizado como un índice de heterogeneidad especial de baja vegetación) a la escala de 25-m para nidos de Chorlo Nevado. La sobrevivencia de nido diaria de Chorlo Picogrueso fue mejor explicada por una combinación de dos métricas de hábitat a la escala de microhabitat. Menor vegetación en la parte inmediata del nido incrementó la sobrevivencia diaria ($\hat{\beta}_{Veg}$ = -1.35, 95% de límites de confidencia fueron -2.28, -0.42 en escala logit), mientras que la sobrevivencia diaria de nido fue más alta para los nidos con menor contagio a la escala de microhábitat ($\hat{\beta}_{Contagion}$ = -0.87, 95% de límites de confidencia fueron -1.65, -0.10 en escala logit). No encontramos evidencia para diferencias anuales, o algún efecto del clima en la sobrevivencia diaria de nido para ninguna de las especies. Nuestros resultados ilustran el papel que juegan ciertas características del hábitat en la sobrevivencia de nido de Chorlos Nevado y Picogrueso, y mejora nuestro entendimiento de su ecología de anidación. Anticipamos que nuestros resultados ayudarán a la identificación y protección de hábitats críticos para poblaciones reproductoras de estas y otras especies de aves costeras.

The study of nest survival is an important and frequently used tool in investigations of breeding bird population dynamics. Several recently developed analytical approaches (Rotella et al. 2004) enable researchers to go beyond the traditional Mayfield method (Mayfield 1961) and model nest survival as a function of a wide range of factors of interest. Such detailed studies of nest survival have the potential not only to provide estimates of nest-survival probabilities, but also to examine the possible influence of various biological factors on these survival probabilities. Elucidating these biological factors and how they relate to avian reproduction is critical for taking the appropriate management or conservation actions in an attempt to improve nest survival of a declining species.

Snowy Plovers (*Charadrius alexandrinus*) and Wilson's Plovers (*Charadrius wilsonia*) are two shorebirds that depend on coastal habitats along the Gulf Coast of the U.S. for breeding, wintering, and migration stopover areas. The amount and quality of coastal habitat available to these and other shorebirds continues to decline as human activity and development in these coastal areas increase. This anthropogenic pressure is undoubtedly having a negative impact on shorebird populations, particularly those that rely on coastal areas for breeding (Gore and Chase 1989, Page et al. 1995, Corbat and Bergstrom 2000).

In North America, Snowy Plovers breed along the Gulf Coast, the Pacific Coast, and in the Great Basin and southern Great Plains. The North American populations of Snowy Plovers are listed as highly imperiled (Prioritization Category 5) by the United States Shorebird Conservation Plan (Brown et al. 2001). The USDI Fish and Wildlife Service listed the Pacific Coast population of the Snowy Plover as threatened in 1993 (United States Department of the Interior 1993); Gulf Coast and interior populations are not listed. Primary threats to the species along the Pacific and Gulf coasts are habitat degradation and increased recreational use of beaches (Page et al. 1995).

The nesting ecology of Snowy Plovers along the Pacific Coast and inland in the Great Basin and Great Plains has been well studied (Boyd 1972, Wilson-Jacobs and Meslow 1984, Page et al. 1995, Paton 1995), but less information is available for the birds that nest along the western Gulf Coast of the U.S. (Rupert 1997). Snowy Plovers nest on barren to sparsely vegetated sand and alkaline flats of coastal areas, and inland along river channels and shorelines of saline lakes (Page et al. 1995). Nests are often located near clumps of vegetation or conspicuous objects such as debris, rocks, or large shells, on small elevated areas, or on an area of high shell or pebble concentration relative to the surrounding area (Boyd 1972, Purdue 1976, Hill 1985, Page et al. 1985, Stern et al. 1990, Paton 1995). Clutch size is typically three eggs, with the average length of incubation ranging from 25–28 d (Page et al. 1995). Several studies have estimated apparent nest success for Snowy Plovers, ranging from 13% on the Oregon coast (Wilson-Jacobs and Meslow 1984) to 87% along the California coast (Wehtje and Baron 1993). Page et al. (1995) calculated an average apparent nest success of 53% based on 17 studies in North America. Rupert (1997) reported apparent nest success for Snowy Plovers in the lower Laguna Madre region of Texas at 23% and 25% during two nesting seasons.

Wilson's Plovers occur only in the Americas and are uncommon breeders along the southern Atlantic, southern Pacific and Gulf coasts. They are listed as a species of high concern (Prioritization Category 4) by the United States Shorebird Conservation Plan (Brown et al. 2001). The primary threats to the species in the United States are habitat destruction as a result of coastal development and increased recreational use of beaches (Corbat and Bergstrom 2000).

Wilson's Plovers have been less well studied than Snowy Plovers, and relatively little is known about many aspects of the species' ecology. Bergstrom (1982, 1988) and Corbat (1990) provide information on the breeding biology of this species in Texas and Georgia, respectively. Wilson's Plovers nest on sparsely to moderately vegetated sand and mud flats in saline areas, including the front and back sides of primary dune lines and the edges of coastal bays and lagoons (Corbat and Bergstrom 2000). Corbat (1990) reported nest initiation to begin in mid-April in Georgia, and Bergstrom (1988) the first week in April in Texas, although nesting may begin as early as late March in this region (Hood 2006). Clutch size is typically three eggs, and the incubation period is estimated at 25 d (Tomkins 1965, Bergstrom 1988, Corbat 1990). Previous estimates of apparent nest success for Wilson's Plovers were 25% and 54% at two sites in Texas (Bergstrom 1988), and ranged from 11–55% for sites in Georgia (Corbat 1990).

For many shorebird species, including Snowy and Wilson's plovers, features of the nest site (e.g., the presence of a conspicuous object or the amount of vegetation near the nest cup) are often theorized to influence nest survival (Bergstrom 1982, Wilson-Jacobs and Meslow 1984, Page et al. 1985, Corbat 1990). The scale of interest is often the immediate nest site, and few investigations have examined the influence of habitat at larger scales (Knetter et al.

2002). In some cases, plover nesting success and nest-site selection have been correlated with the presence or absence of such features (Wilson-Jacobs and Meslow 1984). More often, habitat features are recorded and simply compared between successful and unsuccessful nests. In these cases, the hypothesized relationship between these habitat characteristics and the survival of the nest remains conjecture because the relationship is not quantified.

Given this context, the objective of our study was to estimate nest survival of Snowy and Wilson's plovers as a function of several external biological variables, and to test hypotheses concerning the effect of selected habitat features on nest survival. Biological variables of interest included temporal variation within year, nest age, temperature, precipitation, and habitat features measured at three spatial scales: (1) microhabitat-nest site (0.5-m radius buffer around nest), (2) macrohabitat (25-m radius buffer), and (3) landscape (800-m radius buffer). We illustrate the use of program MARK for modeling avian nest survival as a function of these variables, and the study results have important implications for the management of both species.

METHODS

STUDY AREA

The study area comprised the lower Laguna Madre region of southern Texas within portions of Cameron, Willacy, and Hidalgo counties. The area primarily included USDI Fish and Wildlife Service tracts within the Lower Rio Grande Valley National Wildlife Refuge complex, as well as some public and private lands. Study sites covered roughly 415 km^2 and included Laguna Atascosa National Wildlife Refuge, La Sal del Rey, East Lake, Brazos Island, Boca Chica-South Bay area, and South Padre Island (Fig. 1). La Sal del Rey and East Lake are hypersaline lakes located about 70 km inland which are used as breeding sites by Snowy Plovers. Birds use lake shorelines, areas surrounding salt evaporation ponds, and man-made limestone gravel, or caliche causeways for nesting. The shorelines are relatively bare but contain sparse patches of vegetation. The area immediately surrounding and slightly elevated from the shoreline is composed of a strip of grasses, shrubs, and succulents ranging from 5–30 m wide, leading into thorn-scrub woodland dominated by mesquite (*Prosopis* sp.).

The remaining study areas were the shorelines and associated flats of coastal bays (Laguna Madre and South Bay), and barrier island flats of Brazos Island and South Padre Island. In the barrier island habitats, both Snowy and Wilson's plovers nested in the area between the vegetated flats and the bayshore (the bay side of the island). A vegetated barrier flat extends from the fore dunes (or back dunes, if present) toward the tidal flats, and ranges in width from a few meters to a few kilometers before the vegetation becomes sparse and the barrier flats begin. Birds nested on these barrier flats, which typically contain tidal flats, high sand flats, algal flats, washover flats with channels, and/or active back-island dunes (Britton and Morton 1989). The flats surrounding South Bay closely resembled the habitat on the barrier islands. Mean annual precipitation near the center of the study area was approximately 71 cm for both coastal and inland sites (National Climatic Data Center 2003, 2004).

LOCATING AND MONITORING NESTS

We conducted field work from 8 March to 15 July 2003 and from 14 March to 14 July 2004. Nests were located by systematically driving a vehicle (truck or all-terrain vehicle) through suitable breeding habitat and periodically stopping to scan for plovers. We were careful to remain on makeshift roads or existing tire paths to minimize disturbance to the birds and their nesting areas. When we located an adult bird, we watched it return to its nest to pinpoint the exact location of the nest. In smaller areas or areas unsuitable for vehicles, we searched for nests on foot.

Upon locating a nest, we recorded its position with a hand-held global positioning system (GPS) unit (Magellan SporTrak Pro) and identified it with a small numbered wooden craft stick approximately 1–3 m from the nest. A circle with a 0.5-m radius (constructed of semi-rigid PVC pipe) was then centered over the nest and the area was photographed using a 2.1 megapixel digital camera. These photos were later used in microhabitat data interpretation.

We checked nests every 3–7 d until the eggs hatched or the nest failed. We considered a nest successful if ≥1 egg hatched. We assumed an incubation period of 26 d for Snowy Plovers (Boyd 1972, Page et al. 1983, Hill 1985, Warriner et al. 1986) which is also the mean incubation length for Snowy Plovers nesting in Florida (Gore and Chase 1989), an area of similar latitude. We assumed an incubation period of 25 d for Wilson's Plovers (Tomkins 1965, Bergstrom 1988, Corbat 1990). Sustained incubation does not begin in either species until the last egg in a clutch is laid (Bergstrom 1988, Page et al. 1995), so we estimated daily nest survival from the beginning of sustained incubation. We

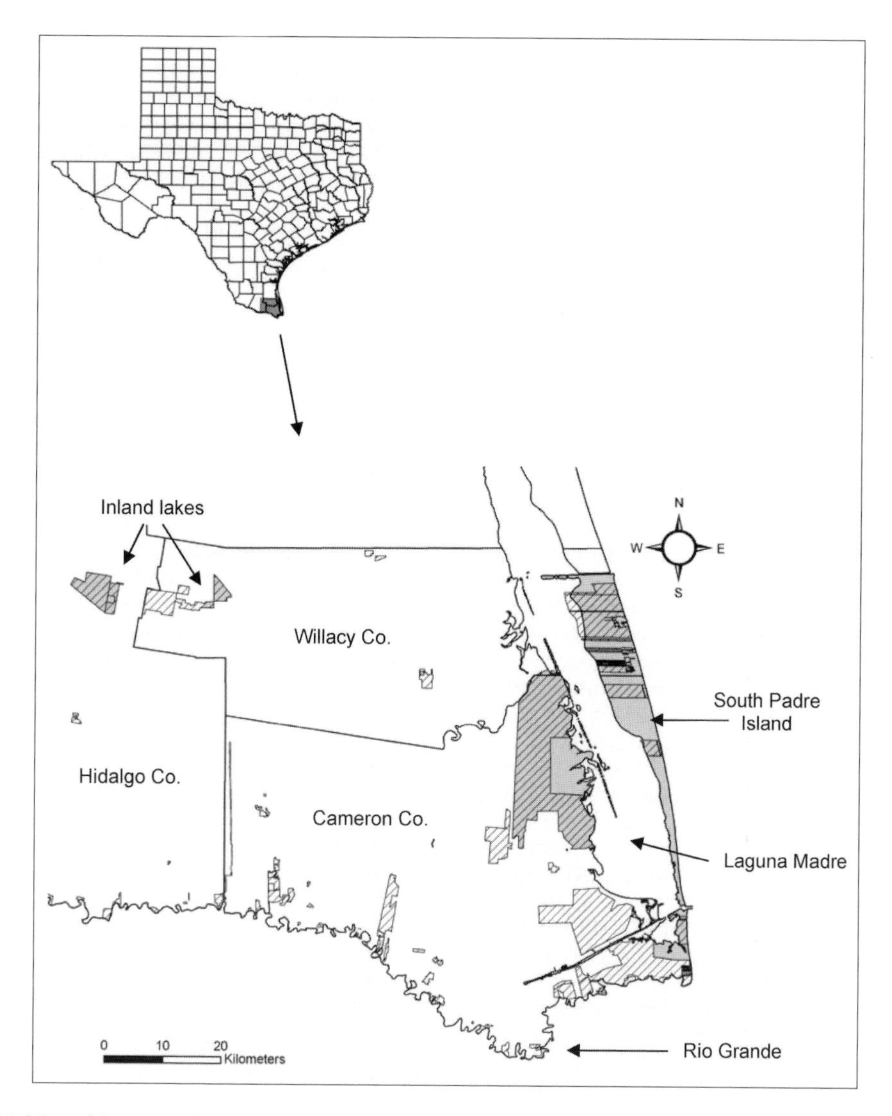

FIGURE 1. Map of Snowy and Wilson's plover study areas in the lower Laguna Madre region of Texas, 2003–2004. Study areas are shown in gray, USDI Fish and Wildlife Service properties are designated by hatch marks.

determined nest age for each species using egg flotation (Hood 2006). Using this float information we could correctly age most nests to within 1–2 d. For the small number of nests that failed between the day they were found and the day they were next checked, we assigned them the mean age of their incubation stage when they were found (Dinsmore et al. 2002). We determined nest fate using eggshell evidence (Mabee 1997) and hatch date using egg flotation or by finding young in or near the nest.

Microhabitat Scale Data

Photographs of the 0.5-m radius buffer area around each nest were digitized using ArcView GIS (version 3.2), and areas within each circle were placed into one of three classes: vegetation, bare ground, and objects or debris. We classified conspicuous objects and debris as any shell or rock larger than the nest cup, any nonliving woody debris, or any other non-natural item such as pieces of glass, plastic, and metal. The digitized images were then analyzed using FRAGSTATS (McGarigal and Marks 1995) to obtain metrics describing the proportions and distribution of these three classes within each buffered area. Metrics of interest were: percent vegetation (%vegM), presence or absence of a conspicuous object or debris (objectM), and contagion index. Contagion is a metric calculated in FRAGSTATS that describes the extent to which patch types are clumped within a landscape.

MACROHABITAT/25-M RADIUS DATA

We used line-intercept sampling (Canfield 1941) to measure various aspects of vegetation, substrate, and debris arrangement within a 25-m radius of each nest. We centered a 50-m measuring tape over the nest cup in a randomly chosen direction, and placed a second line perpendicular to the first, resulting in four 25-m transects radiating outward from the nest. By randomly placing these four transects, we collected data that were representative of a 25-m radius around the nest. These data were collected soon after the nest hatched or failed to reduce disturbance and to standardize measures between nests.

Continuous measurements were taken along each line, and the distance covered by each of the following variables was measured: (1) high (>30 cm, %highveg25) and low (<30 cm, %lowveg25) vegetation, (2) heterogeneity in low vegetation patch size (both linear and quadratic trends), indexed by the coefficient of variation for low vegetation (lowvegCV25) (Roth 1976), (3) bare ground (bare25), (4) substrate mixed with shells or gravel (shell/gravel25), (5) debris (debris25), and (6) roads (road25) and vehicle tracks (tracks25) as indicators of disturbance. We defined roads as well-established, regularly traveled pathways, and tracks as any marks left behind when a vehicle left the established roads and traveled over the sand flats. Roads were recorded as either present or absent within 25-m of a nest, and the number of vehicle tracks intersecting the measuring tape was recorded as an additional measure of disturbance.

LANDSCAPE-SCALE DATA

Using GPS coordinates collected for each nest, we placed nests onto a Landsat Enhanced Thematic Mapper 7 satellite image of the south Texas area from March 2003 (path 26, row 42). We buffered each nest by a radius of approximately 800 m (resulting in a circle 2 km^2 in area) using ESRI ArcMap (version 8.3). Using the supervised classification procedure in ERDAS IMAGINE (version 8.7) we classified areas as vegetation, water, or bare ground. We used high-resolution aerial photography (2004 1:24,000 Digital Ortho Quarter-Quads) as reference data to assess classification accuracy. Average overall classification accuracy was 67.0% for bare ground, 85.7% for vegetation, and 83.7% for water.

We then ran each classified and buffered nest area through FRAGSTATS to obtain metrics describing the landscape composition and configuration within 800 m of each nest. Metrics of interest were: percent bare ground (%bareL), percent vegetation (%vegL), total edge of water (total edge waterL), percent water (%waterL), and contagion index (contagionL). At the landscape scale, contagion index describes whether the landscape around the nest is composed of a few large patches or many smaller patches.

ADDITIONAL SOURCES OF VARIATION

In addition to the above habitat covariates specific to each nest, we examined the influence of five additional variables that were not related to habitat. These were: year, temporal variation within years (evaluated using a constant daily nest-survival model as well as linear (T) and quadratic (TT) trends), nest age (age), location (site), and maximum daily temperature, and daily precipitation. We monitored Snowy Plover nests at two very different locations—coastal areas and two inland lakes. We included location as a covariate because we believed differences in size and in densities of nesting birds between coastal and inland locations would result in differential nest survival. Wilson's Plovers were not present at the two inland lakes, so models for this species did not include a location effect. We obtained all weather data from the National Oceanic and Atmospheric Administration (National Climatic Data Center 2003, 2004). We used data from the Raymondville, Texas, weather station for inland Snowy Plover nests and averaged data from the South Padre Island and Brownsville, Texas, weather stations for all nests along the coast.

MODELING APPROACH

We used the nest-survival model in program MARK (White and Burnham 1999) to model the daily survival rates of Snowy and Wilson's plover nests. We standardized 19 March as day one of the nesting season for Snowy Plovers, and 31 March as day one for Wilson's Plovers. For Snowy Plovers, year and location were combined and modeled as groups, resulting in four groups (lakes and coast in both years). For Wilson's Plovers, only two groups were used, one for each year, because Wilson's Plovers did not nest at East Lake or La Sal del Rey. Snowy Plover nests were monitored from 19 March to 9 July (113 d) and Wilson's Plover nests from 31 March to 15 July (107 d) in both years.

We selected the best approximating model for inference in a three-stage, hierarchical modeling process using AIC$_c$ model selection

(Burnham and Anderson 2002). Our approach was the same for both Snowy and Wilson's plovers, but each species was analyzed separately. In the first stage, we evaluated possible sources of temporal variation in daily nest survival rates within years by constructing models with constant daily nest survival (analogous to a Mayfield estimate), a logit-linear time trend, and a logit-quadratic time trend. To the model that best described temporal variation within year, we added the other non-habitat, or main effects, singly. These included year, location (Snowy Plovers only), nest age, maximum daily temperature, and daily precipitation. If more than one of these effects emerged as competing models ($\Delta AIC_c \leq 2.0$), we combined those effects into an additive model to test the hypothesis that two (or more) variables together performed better than they had separately. To the best model from stage two we added each habitat covariate from the three spatial scales singly. For each species, we also included a model that combined the best performing covariate from each spatial scale into one additive model. We hypothesized that features from different spatial scales working in concert might be more important in explaining variation in nest survival than one feature at any single scale. We also developed three models for each species that reflected specific a priori hypotheses representing combinations of two covariates at each spatial scale that we thought might influence daily nest survival rates.

Snowy Plover

1. An additive model combining the presence or absence of an object and percent vegetation present at the microhabitat scale. We hypothesized that the presence of an object near the nest cup would have a positive effect on nest survival, and increasing amounts of vegetation would have a negative effect on nest survival.
2. An additive model combining the amount of shell or gravel and a quadratic trend on the heterogeneity index for low vegetation at the 25-m buffer scale. We hypothesized that a large amount of shell or gravel and a moderate level of heterogeneity would both have a positive effect on nest survival.
3. An additive model combining percent bare ground and percent water at the landscape scale. We hypothesized that nest survival would be positively influenced by large amounts of bare ground and large amounts of water at the landscape scale.

Wilson's Plover

1. An additive model combining percent vegetation and contagion index at the microhabitat scale. We hypothesized that smaller amounts of vegetation and low contagion values would result in higher daily nest survival rates, as this species seemed to prefer areas in which the vegetation present occurred in small patches and was spread out in a diffused manner.
2. An additive model combining percent low vegetation and the heterogeneity index for low vegetation at the 25-m buffer scale. As with the microhabitat scale, we hypothesized that low to moderate amounts of vegetation occurring in variably-sized patches (moderate coefficient of variation) would result in higher nest survival. If the amount of vegetation present around the nest is too great or it occurs in very large patches, the ability of the incubating adult to scan for predators and to quickly escape from the nest may be hindered.
3. An additive model combining percent water and percent bare ground at the landscape level. We hypothesized that larger amounts of bare ground and water at the landscape scale would result in higher daily nest survival.

We evaluated the strength of evidence for model variables included in our research hypotheses using the approach of Burnham and Anderson (2002). To illustrate the effects of the most important explanatory variables, we also predicted their influence on nest survival using the best model and reasonable ranges of a particular variable while keeping other variables constant.

RESULTS

We monitored 105 Snowy Plover nests and 94 Wilson's Plover nests during this 2-yr study with average apparent nest success being 55% and 69% for Snowy Plovers and Wilson's Plovers, respectively.

Snowy Plover Nest Survival

We averaged five competing models with $\Delta AICc \leq 2.0$ across all candidate models to obtain estimates of any covariate effects and of daily nest survival rates (Table 1). The daily survival of Snowy Plover nests varied temporally and was a function of both location and nest age. A negative linear time trend was found in survival ($\hat{\beta}_T = -0.016$, SE = 0.006, 95% CI = 0.027, –0.005 on

TABLE 1. MODEL SELECTION RESULTS FOR THE NEST SURVIVAL OF SNOWY PLOVERS IN THE LOWER LAGUNA MADRE REGION OF TEXAS, USA, 2003–2004.

Model[a]	AIC_c[b]	ΔAIC_c	w_i[c]	K[d]	Deviance
S_T + age + site + objectM + low vegCV^{2}25 +% waterL	257.01	0.00	0.14	8	240.86
S_T + age + site + low vegCV^{2}25	258.48	1.47	0.07	6	246.39
S_T + age + site + % high veg25	258.53	1.52	0.07	5	248.47
S_T + age + site + objectM	258.62	1.61	0.06	5	248.56
S_T + age + site	258.97	1.96	0.05	4	250.93
S_T + age + site + % shell/gravel25	259.02	2.01	0.05	5	248.95
S_T + age + site + objectM + % vegM	259.10	2.09	0.05	6	247.01
S_T + site	259.11	2.10	0.05	3	253.08
S_T + age + site + % waterL	259.49	2.48	0.04	5	249.43
S_T + age + site + % vegM	259.50	2.49	0.04	5	249.44
S_T + age + site + low vegCV25	259.87	2.85	0.03	5	249.80
S_T + age + site + tracks25	260.11	3.10	0.03	5	250.05
S_T + age + site + debris25	260.17	3.16	0.03	5	250.10
S_T + age + site + low vegCV^{2}25 + % shell/gravel25	260.22	3.21	0.03	7	246.10
S_T + age + site + % bareL	260.30	3.28	0.03	5	250.23
S_T + age + site + road25	260.33	3.32	0.03	5	250.26
S_T + age + site + contagionL	260.56	3.55	0.02	5	250.49
S_T + age + site + % bare25	260.91	3.89	0.02	5	250.84
S_T + age + site + % vegL	260.93	3.92	0.02	5	250.86
S_T + age	260.95	3.94	0.02	3	254.92
S_T + age + site + contagionM	260.99	3.98	0.02	5	250.92
S_T + age + site + % lowveg25	260.99	3.98	0.02	5	250.93
S_T + age + site + total edge waterL	260.99	3.98	0.02	5	250.93
S_T + age + site + % bareL + % waterL	261.34	4.33	0.02	6	249.25
S_T + year	261.35	4.33	0.02	3	255.32
S_T	262.04	5.03	0.01	2	258.03
S_{TT}	262.76	5.75	0.01	3	256.74
S_T + temp	263.09	6.08	0.01	3	257.07
S_T + precip	263.20	6.19	0.01	3	257.18

[a] Models are ranked by ascending ΔAIC_c.
[b] Akaike's information criteria adjusted for small sample size.
[c] AIC model weight.
[d] Number of parameters.

a logit scale), indicating that daily nest survival rates decline slightly over the nesting season. The best overall model included age effects; the coefficient on age was positive but small ($\hat{\beta}_{age}$ = 0.03, SE = 0.02 on a logit scale) and its confidence interval contained zero, indicating the possibility of a weak effect of nest age on daily nest survival rates. Snowy Plover nests at the inland lakes had lower daily survival than those at coastal sites (Fig. 2).

The best approximating model contained habitat covariates at each of the three spatial scales measured. Nests that contained an object or debris at the immediate nest site had higher daily survival than those that did not. The estimate for the additive effect of an object within 0.5 m of the nest was $\hat{\beta}_{objectM}$ = 0.62 (SE = 0.30, 95% CI = 0.03, 1.21) on a logit scale. To illustrate the effects of nest age, location, and the presence or absence of an object, we plotted predicted daily survival rates using the logistic-regression equation with selected values of each variable. For nests early (nest age = 1) and late (nest age = 26) in incubation, we plotted daily survival of nests at the inland lakes (site = 1) and at coastal sites (site = 0) for nests with (object = 1) and without (object = 0) an object or debris within 0.5 m of the nest (Fig. 2).

The best approximating model also included a quadratic trend on the coefficient of variation (CV) for low vegetation at the 25-m radius scale. Daily nest survival decreased with increasing variability in low vegetation patch size, but then increased slightly at very high levels of vegetation patch size heterogeneity. This effect also appeared as the only habitat covariate in the second best model (ΔAIC_c = 1.47; w_i = 0.07), providing further support for the influence of this factor on daily nest survival. Using the logistic-regression equation from the best approximating model, we plotted daily survival of nests with selected low vegetation CV values. We held nest age and site constant (nest age = 1, site = 0, or coast) and varied the low vegetation CV value to predict daily nest survival rates at three levels of spatial heterogeneity of low vegetation within 25 m of the nest cup. The values 0, 200, and 400 that we chose for low vegetation

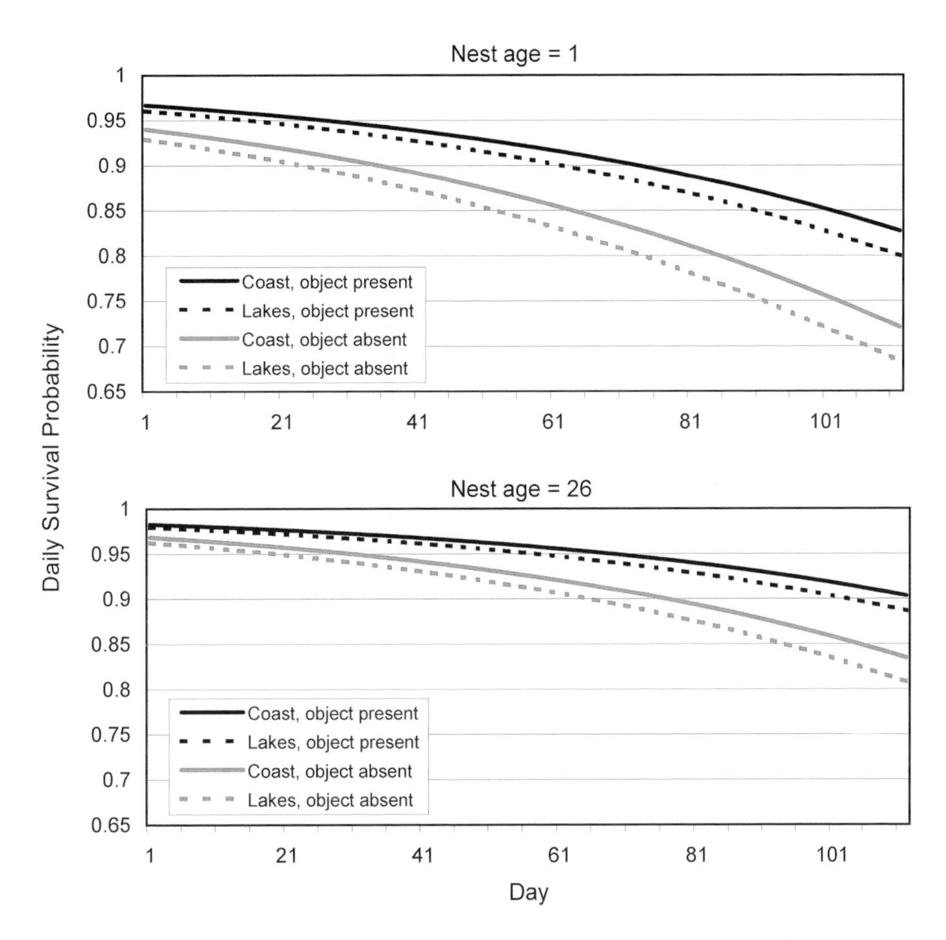

FIGURE 2. The effects of nest age (1- and 26-d-old nests), location (coast versus inland lakes), and the presence of an object within 0.5 m of the nest on the daily survival rates of Snowy Plover nests in south Texas, 2003–2004. Day one corresponds to 19 March, and day 112 corresponds to 9 July.

CV reflect the actual range of values observed in the field (range 0–385). Daily nest survival rates are lowest at medium levels of spatial heterogeneity of low vegetation, and highest at both low and high levels of heterogeneity (Fig. 3).

The landscape-level habitat covariate in the best approximating model was the percentage of water contained within 800 m of a nest. This effect was negative ($\hat{\beta}_{waterL}$ = -0.02, SE = 0.01, 95% CI = -0.04, 0.01 on a logit scale), suggesting that daily nest-survival rates decreased as the proportion of water in the surrounding landscape increased. This effect is likely confounded by location, however, as nests at the inland lakes were surrounded by more water (mean = 35%, range = 7–56%) than those at coastal sites (mean = 10%, range = 0–36%) but also had lower nest survival than at coastal sites.

The remaining five competing models were three single-scale habitat models containing the same three effects present in the top model, a model with no habitat effects, and a single-scale habitat model including the amount of high vegetation present at the 25-m radius scale. The latter model ranked third, and the effect of high vegetation was negative ($\hat{\beta}_{high\ veg25}$ = -0.08, SE = 0.05, 95% CI = -0.17, 0.02 on a logit scale), suggesting that daily nest survival is lower for nests with large amounts of high vegetation within 25 m. No statistical support was found for year effects or for the influence of daily precipitation or maximum daily temperature on Snowy Plover nest survival.

We used the logistic-regression equation from the best model to predict period survival (the probability of a nest surviving the 26-d incubation period) for Snowy Plovers at both the inland lakes and coastal nesting sites. We incorporated age and time effects, and held the effects of habitat covariates constant by multiplying the coefficients of each habitat covariate by the mean value of that covariate.

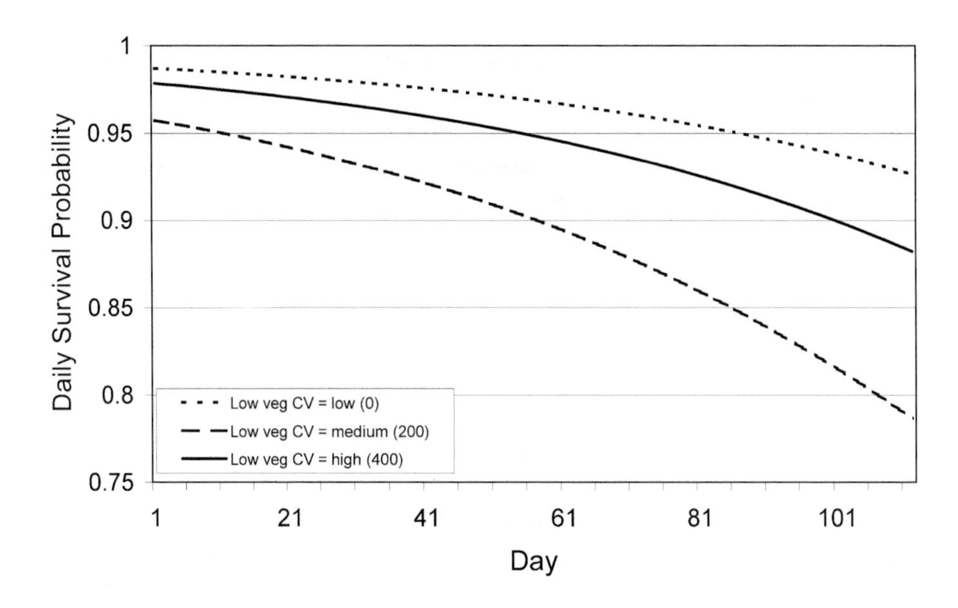

FIGURE 3. The effect of selected values of low vegetation heterogeneity (indexed by low vegetation CV) on the daily survival rates of Snowy Plover nests in south Texas, 2003–2004. Day one corresponds to 19 March, and day 112 corresponds to 9 July.

The covariate object was a categorical variable, however, and so we held its effect constant at 1, or present. The probability of a nest at each location surviving the entire 26-d incubation period (following initiation on day x of the nesting season) is illustrated in Fig. 4.

Wilson's Plover Nest Survival

The nest survival of Wilson's Plovers was a function of both the amount and spatial structure of vegetation present at the microhabitat scale (Table 2). The model best describing temporal variation within the nesting season was the constant nest-survival model. Although the addition of several habitat covariates substantially improved the constant-survival model, only one model had $\Delta AIC_c \leq 2.0$ and it included the effects of percent vegetation and contagion at the microhabitat scale. Nests with less vegetation within a 0.5-m radius had higher survival than those with greater amounts. From the best overall model (w_i = 0.82), the coefficient on the effect of vegetation at the microhabitat scale was $\hat{\beta}_{\%\ vegM}$ = –1.35 (SE = 0.47, 95% CI = –2.28, –0.42) on a logit scale. To demonstrate this effect, we used the logistic-regression equation from the best approximating model to predict daily nest survival at three different values of percent vegetation (10, 40, and 70%, chosen to reflect the range we observed in our study). When holding the effect of contagion constant, the predicted survival of a Wilson's Plover nest containing 10% vegetation within 0.5 m of the nest was 0.97 and this decreased to 0.50 at 40% vegetation and 0.03 at 70% vegetation.

Daily nest survival was higher for Wilson's Plover nests with low contagion at the microhabitat level. From the best model, the slope estimate for contagion at the microhabitat level was negative ($\hat{\beta}_{contagionM}$ = –0.87, SE = 0.39, 95% CI = –1.65, –0.10 on a logit scale). To demonstrate this effect, we used the same approach as with vegetation (above), this time varying only the contagion values (50, 75, and 100%, again chosen to reflect the range we observed in our study) and keeping percent vegetation constant at the mean observed value. Predicted daily nest survival of a Wilson's Plover nest with 50% contagion at the microhabitat scale was 0.998 and this decreased to 0.987 at 75% and 0.930 at 100%.

No statistical support existed for year or age effects or for the influence of daily precipitation or maximum daily temperature on Wilson's Plover nest survival. We used the logistic-regression equation from the best model to compute the best estimate of nest survival for this species. We held the effects of habitat covariates constant by multiplying the coefficients of each habitat covariate by the mean value of that covariate. The predicted probability of a Wilson's Plover nest surviving the 25-d incubation period was 0.58, regardless of the date of nest initiation.

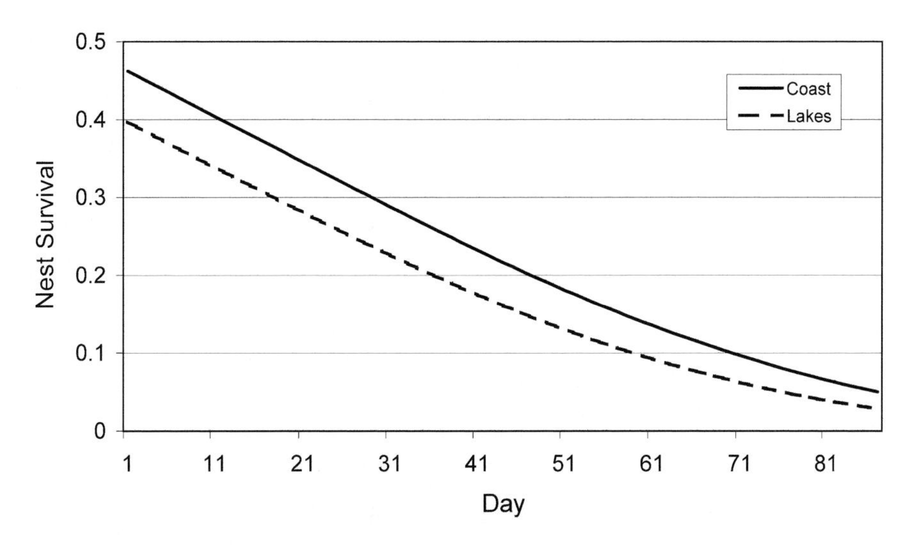

FIGURE 4. Predicted nest survival (the probability that a nest initiated on day *x* of the season survives the 26-d incubation period) for Snowy Plovers nesting at inland and coastal sites in south Texas, 2003–2004. Day one corresponds to 19 March, and day 87 corresponds to 13 June.

TABLE 2. MODEL SELECTION RESULTS FOR THE NEST SURVIVAL OF WILSON'S PLOVERS IN THE LOWER LAGUNA MADRE REGION OF TEXAS, USA, 2003–2004.

Model[a]	AIC_c[b]	ΔAIC_c	w_i[c]	K[d]	Deviance
$S_{\text{\% vegM + contagionM}}$	202.18	0.00	0.82	3	196.16
$S_{\text{\% vegM}}$	206.21	4.03	0.11	2	202.20
$S_{\text{\% vegM + \% high veg25 + \% vegL}}$	210.15	7.97	0.02	4	202.12
$S_{\text{\% vegL}}$	212.25	10.07	0.01	2	208.24

[a] Models are ranked by ascending ΔAIC_c.
[b] Akaike's information criteria adjusted for small sample size.
[c] AIC model weight.
[d] Number of parameters.

DISCUSSION

SNOWY PLOVER

In the lower Laguna Madre region, Snowy Plover daily nest survival was influenced by location, the daily age of the nest, nest-initiation date, and habitat features at each of three spatial scales. At the inland lakes, nest survival over the 26-d incubation period ranged from 40% for a nest initiated on day one of the nesting season to 3% for a nest initiated on day 87 of the season (Fig. 4). Period survival at coastal sites ranged from 46% for nests initiated on day 1–5% for nests initiated on day 87 (Fig. 4). This supports our hypothesis that nest survival of Snowy Plovers was lower at the inland lake sites than at coastal sites. This location effect is likely due to differences in size and habitat structure between the two areas, and how these features affect the vulnerability of a nest to predation. During this study, the primary predator of nests of both Snowy and Wilson's plovers appeared to be the coyote (*Canis latrans*), based on observations of tracks leading directly to depredated nests. A potential mammalian predator might more easily locate plover nests while walking the narrow shoreline of a lake than while traversing the expansive sand and mud flats of a large barrier island or other coastal site. This arrangement of nesting habitat at the lakes also results in higher nest densities than in the coastal areas, which may also increase predation risk (Page et al. 1983).

The temporal trend reported in this study suggests a slight decline in daily nest survival during the nesting season. This trend may be the result of older, more experienced adults returning to the breeding grounds first. These individuals might be more likely to have successful nests because they are more experienced breeders or because they arrive early and occupy the best nesting sites (Nisbet et al. 1978). Other reasons for a decrease in nest survival during a season include a decrease in body condition of nesting adults as the season progresses (especially if females put significant energy into multiple re-nesting attempts) or a change in predator feeding preferences or behavior as a result of the birth and development of their young (Klett and Johnson 1982).

Our results indicate that nests further along in incubation may have higher survival; this pattern is similar to results observed in other plover species (Dinsmore et al. 2002). This relationship likely exists because these older nests have already been exposed to a risk period to which younger nests have not (Klett and Johnson 1982).

The strongest habitat effect we found for Snowy Plovers was the presence of a conspicuous object or debris within 0.5 m of the nest, which resulted in increased nest survival. Placement of nests next to conspicuous objects is a well-documented behavior in Wilson's and Snowy plovers, and may confer some advantage in survival of the nest (Bergstrom 1982, Winton et al. 2000). Our results provide quantitative evidence in support of this hypothesis. Page et al. (1985), however, found that Snowy Plover nests next to objects were more likely to fail than those under objects or in the open. They speculated that nest predators may use conspicuous objects as part of their search image, but acknowledged that this technique may benefit predators only where objects are not common. On the coastal beaches where the majority of nests in our study were located, debris and objects such as large shells are probably too numerous to be used in locating nests.

Beyond the immediate nest site, it is likely that the spatial structure and composition of the vegetation and other features also play a role in nest survival. The amount of high vegetation within 25 m of the nest received weak support as a predictor of daily nest survival, and Snowy Plover nest survival decreased with increasing amounts of high vegetation within 25 m of the nest. Although Snowy Plovers typically locate their nests in areas devoid of vegetation, some type of vegetation is usually located in the larger surrounding area, probably for use as a foraging area or brood-rearing habitat (Rupert 1997). This vegetation is usually <30 cm (considered high vegetation in this study) in height, however, probably because higher vegetation may conceal mammalian predators and reduce an incubating adult's ability to scan for potential predators.

When low vegetation is present within 25 m of the nest site, the structure of that vegetation may also influence nest survival. Nest survival was highest at very low levels of variation in low vegetation patch size, and generally decreased with increasing variation. At very high levels of heterogeneity, however, nest survival increased slightly. Heterogeneity in vegetation patch size translates into areas containing both very large and very small patches of vegetation. Most Snowy Plover nests in this study were not located within 25 m of vegetation, and it was these nest sites devoid of vegetation that were responsible for most of the values of low vegetation CV equal to or near zero. Those nests that were located near vegetation were typically on an area of sand or mud flat adjacent to an expanse of vegetated barrier flat. Vegetation present in these areas typically occurred along a gradient moving from very sparse on the margin of the sand flat to dense within the vegetated barrier flat, resulting in a very heterogeneous vegetation profile. Our results suggest that Snowy Plover nests located on bare sand flats or near the transition zone between vegetated and sand flats have higher nest survival than those in other vegetated areas. Nesting in or adjacent to open areas may offer incubating adults easier escape routes from the nest upon the approach of a predator. A Snowy Plover's low, crouched run and accompanying distraction display probably functions less efficiently if the incubating bird is forced to flee into vegetation where it may not be seen or which may impede its escape if the predator decides to pursue the adult.

The amount of water at a landscape scale was present in the top model, although we suspect that this effect was confounded with location. Nests at inland lakes all contained a large amount of water at the landscape scale ($\bar{x}$ = 35%, range = 7–56%) because they were all located around the edge of a lake. These nests also had lower daily survival rates than those along the coast. Nests in coastal areas contained, on average, much lower proportions of water ($\bar{x}$ = 10%, range = 0–36%). Because obvious differences in nest survival occurred in these two locations, we do not believe the amount of water present on a landscape level to be a true habitat effect, but rather a redundant effect of location.

Wilson's Plover

Wilson's Plover daily nest survival in the lower Laguna Madre region was a function of the amount of vegetation present and the spatial distribution of the features around the nest, both at the microhabitat scale. Nest survival was higher when the vegetation at the immediate nest site was present in relatively small amounts. Greater amounts of vegetation can restrict the line of sight for an incubating bird scanning for predators, may impede rapid escape from the nest with the approach of a predator, and may also provide cover for potential predators.

Our results also showed strong evidence of the effect of contagion at the microhabitat level on nest survival of Wilson's Plovers. This metric describes the extent to which patch types are aggregated, or clumped within a landscape—in this case within a 0.5-m buffer area around the nest. High contagion values reflect the presence of a few large patches and low values indicate many small patches. Three patch types were measured for each nest (bare ground, vegetation, and object/debris), but the majority of nests (N = 58, 62% of total) did not contain an object or debris. For nests that did contain objects or debris, these features comprised only a small portion (usually only one patch) of the overall landscape. Taking this into consideration, the contagion metric essentially refers to the structure or clumpiness of vegetation and bare ground components at the nest site. Nest survival was higher for lower values of contagion, or for nests at which vegetation patches were spread out in a diffuse manner rather than present in large clumps. This supports our hypothesis that although Wilson's Plovers may place their nests in or near vegetation, the vegetation would be present in a smaller proportion than bare ground and in small diffuse patches rather than in large contiguous ones.

Study Implications

Our study has important implications for illustrating the use of contemporary nest-survival modeling approaches, and also for providing information needed for the conservation of Snowy and Wilson's plovers.

Our nest-survival modeling for Snowy and Wilson's plovers in program MARK illustrates the many advantages of this approach over traditional constant-nest-survival methods like those of Mayfield (1961). In particular, we were able to (1) rigorously test multiple models of nest survival using information-theoretic approaches, (2) fit complex models that included seasonal variation in nest survival and the effects of covariates at multiple spatial scales, and (3) use this information to predict how specific factors would be expected to influence the nest survival of these species. Ultimately, we hope our approach here provides a general example for the use of program MARK for a nest-survival analysis.

An understanding of the habitats needed for the continued survival and reproduction of a given species is a critical component of conservation planning. Our study provides the first estimates of nest survival for Snowy and Wilson's plovers in the lower Laguna Madre region of Texas as well as some important baseline information on how habitat characteristics may influence the nest survival of two plover species of conservation concern. Continued efforts to further our understanding of their habitat requirements and breeding ecology are necessary in order to develop effective methods for conservation of these and other shorebird species.

ACKNOWLEDGMENTS

We are grateful to Bill Howe of the USDI Fish and Wildlife Service, Office of Migratory Bird Management, for providing financial support for this study. We would like to thank the entire staff at both Laguna Atascosa and Santa Ana National Wildlife refuges for providing logistical support, particularly D. Blankinship, M. Maxwell, M. Perez III, J. Rupert, and J. Wallace. M. D. Smith provided instruction and assistance with spatial data during several phases of the study, and we are extremely grateful for his patience and expertise. We thank M. Sternberg, T. Shearer, and J. Wallace for providing maps and GIS assistance. We also thank M. Zdravkovic of the National Audubon Society, Coastal Bird Conservation Program, for cooperation and assistance in the field, and A. Leggett for assistance with data entry. We are grateful to B. Howe, B. Andres, S. L. Jones, and three anonymous reviewers for their constructive reviews of this manuscript.

Studies in Avian Biology No. 34:136–144

BAYESIAN STATISTICS AND THE ESTIMATION OF NEST-SURVIVAL RATES

ANDREW B. COOPER AND TIMOTHY J. MILLER

Abstract. Bayesian statistical approaches have received little attention in the nest-survival literature despite the growing usage in other fields of ecology. Appealing aspects of Bayesian statistics are that they allow the researcher to quantitatively account for prior knowledge when analyzing data and they calculate the probability of a hypothesis being true or of a parameter taking on a certain range of values given the collected data. While attempting to keep the discussion accessible to non-statisticians, we give an overview of the theory of Bayesian statistics, including discussions of prior distributions, likelihoods, and posterior distributions. We briefly discuss some of the advantages and disadvantages of Bayesian methods relative to alternative approaches. Finally, we describe how Bayesian methods have been applied to estimating age-specific nest survival rates.

Key Words: age-specific, Bayes, hypothesis testing, likelihood, parameter estimation, posterior, prior, survival.

ESTADÍSITICAS BAYESIANAS Y LA ESTIMACIÓN DE TASAS DE SOBREVIVENCIA DE NIDO

Resumen. Enfoques de estadísticas Bayesianas han recibido poca atención en la literatura sobre sobrevivencia de nido, a pesar de su creciente utilización en otros campos de la ecología. Algunos de los motivos por los cuales son atractivas las estadísticas Bayesianas es porque al analizar los datos permiten al investigador a contar cuantitativamente para el conocimiento previo, y también calculan si la probabilidad de que una hipótesis sea verdad o un parámetro, tomando un cierto rango de valores segun los datos colectados. Mientras tratamos de mantener la discusión accesible a no estadistas, proporcionamos un panorama de la teoría de las estadísticas Bayesianas incluyendo discusiones de distribuciones previas, probabilidades, y distribuciones posteriores. Discutimos brevemente algunas de las ventajas y desventajas de los métodos Bayesianos en relación a métodos alternativos. Finalmente, describimos cómo los métodos Bayesianos han sido aplicados en la estimación de tasas de sobrevivencia de nido específicas de edad.

While growing in popularity in many fields of ecology, Bayesian statistics have received only scant attention in the nest-survival literature. Bayesian statistics allow the researcher to formally incorporate prior knowledge into the analysis and then provide results that give the probability of a hypothesis being true or of a parameter taking on a certain range of values. No other statistical approach permits such statements, despite the fact that they are crucial for decision making. This paper gives an overview of the theory and application of Bayesian statistics and then describes one way in which they have been applied to estimating age-specific nest survival rates when the age of the nest is not known.

BAYESIAN STATISTICAL INFERENCE

Based purely on the calculus of probabilities (Casella and Berger 1990), Bayes rule (also known as Bayes theorem) describes the relationship between two conditional probabilities and can be used to calculate the probability of one event occurring given (or conditional on) another event having already occurred. In equation form, we use a vertical line, |, to represent this conditioning. As such, the probability of event A occurring given event B has already occurred would be written as, $P(A \mid B)$. For two events, A and B, Bayes rule is written as:

$$P(A \mid B) = \frac{P(B \mid A) * P(A)}{P(B)}$$

Where $P(A)$ and $P(B)$ are the probabilities of event A and event B occurring under all possible conditions, respectively; and $P(A \mid B)$ and $P(B \mid A)$ are the conditional probabilities of event A occurring given event B has already occurred and event B occurring given event A has already occurred, respectively. Bayes rule is considered to be a mathematical fact when it refers to generic events. Controversy, however, arises over the application of Bayes rule to statistical inference. For Bayesian statistical inference, the hypothesis in question (i.e., that a parameter Θ, equals a specific value, θ) is treated as one event (A), and observation of data (y) is treated as another event (B). In order to distinguish between a random variable and a specific realization of that random variable, we use Θ to represent the parameter (which is treated as a random variable) but θ to represent the specific value of that parameter, and we use Y to represent data that have not yet been observed (i.e., before the study takes place), and y to represent the actual data in hand. When applying Bayes rule to statistical inference, and using these new symbols to describe events A and B, the equation for Bayes rule appears as:

$$P(\Theta \mid y) = \frac{P(Y \mid \theta) * P(\Theta)}{P(Y)}$$

Bayes rule has four main components when applied to statistical inference, each of which will be explained in greater detail: (1) the prior probability distribution of the parameter values, P(Θ); (2) the probability distribution of the data before it is actually observed given a hypothesized value for the parameter, P(Y | θ); (3) the marginal probability distribution of the data, P(Y); and (4) the posterior probability distribution of the parameter values given the observed data, P(Θ | y).

When the prior probability distribution for the parameter values is assumed to take a parametric form (i.e., normal, lognormal, beta), Bayes rule becomes more complex because we now must condition on the parameter values, known as hyperparameters, which govern the shape of the prior distribution and are symbolized by ω. For example, if one used a normal distribution as a prior, then the mean and variance would be the hyperparameters. If one used a uniform distribution, then the maximum and minimum values would be the hyperparameters. To emphasize the dependency on these hyperparameters, we write Bayes rule as:

$$P(\Theta \mid y,\omega) = \frac{P(Y \mid \theta) * P(\Theta \mid \omega)}{P(Y \mid \omega)}$$

Where P(Θ | ω) represents the prior probability distribution of the parameter values given the values for the hyperparameters, P(Y | θ) represents the probability distribution of the data before they are actually observed given a hypothesized value for the parameter, P(Y | ω) represents the marginal probability distribution of the data given the values for the hyperparameters, and P(Θ | y,ω) represents the posterior probability distribution of the parameter values given the observed data and hyper parameters. Using a parametric prior distribution often decreases the difficulty in computing the posterior distribution and is commonly used for Bayesian mark-recapture and nest-survival studies (Dupis 1995, 2002; He et al. 2001, He 2003). We use this version of Bayes rule throughout the rest of the manuscript.

When the data have not yet been observed (Y) but we have a hypothesis about a specific parameter value, θ, we can describe the probability of the not-yet-observed data occurring given the hypothesized parameter value with the probability distribution, P(Y | θ). However, once we have data in hand (y) and are interested in the potential set of values of the parameter, Θ, we use a different nomenclature and refer to the likelihood, L(Θ | y). The likelihood is commonly used instead of P(Y | θ) in Bayes rule. The likelihood measures how likely different parameter values are given the observed data, and the maximum likelihood estimate (MLE) for a parameter is the parameter value that yields the highest likelihood value. However, it is important to note that the likelihood as a function of the parameter given observed, fixed data is not a probability distribution for the parameter values. In other words, it does not tell us the probability of the parameter taking on specific values. Indeed, this is the reason for using Bayes rule.

The likelihood serves as the basis for many statistical methods used in ecological research today, including testing a null hypothesis of some parameter equaling zero or comparing models that make different assumptions about the parameters (i.e., constant survival rates versus time-varying survival rates). Generalized linear regression models (of which normal and logistic regression are subsets) rely on likelihoods (McCullagh and Nelder 1989). Mark-recapture models are often estimated using likelihoods (Lebreton et al. 1992) as are the nest survival models of Heisey and Nordheim (1995), Dinsmore et al. (2002), and Shaffer (2004). The information-theoretic approaches to model selection (AIC, AIC_c, $QAIC_c$) described in Burnham and Anderson (2002) are based on likelihoods. It is the combining of likelihoods and prior probability distributions which causes much of the controversy between Bayesian and frequentist statisticians.

The prior probability distribution of the parameter values (also less formally called the prior): P(Θ | ω), describes any knowledge or assumptions about the model parameters, and ideally the model structure itself, that exists before the data are observed. The functional form of a prior is usually chosen to match the range of sensible values of the parameters, and the hyperparameters (ω) specify, among other things, the shape, average, and variability of the parameter values before the data are observed.

As such, $P(\Theta \mid \omega)$ can be read as the prior probability of the parameter taking on a range of values given the choice of hyperparameters. Bayesian analysis requires that the knowledge or assumptions about model parameters be explicitly and quantitatively stated (Gelman et al. 1995, Ellison 1996) and the hyperparameters are chosen to reflect this. For example, with nest-survival models, priors must be stated for both the probability that a nest is encountered and the probability that a nest survives from one observation point to the next. Models such as those described by Heisey and Nordheim (1995), He et al. (2001), He (2003), and Cao et al. (in press) explicitly model the encounter probabilities in order to account for the fact that some nests do not enter the study because they did not survive (a form of truncation bias) and that the encounter probability may change as a function of time or nest age. A prior on a survival or encounter probability parameter may be that the probability is bounded between zero and one, inclusive, and no value is more probable than another. This could be modeled using the uniform distribution, though beta or Dirichlet distributions, which include the uniform distribution as special cases, are more common for survival and encounter probabilities (Dupis 1995, 2002; He et al. 2001, He 2003). When a prior states only very limited or imprecise knowledge of the potential values of the parameter, they are often described as being diffuse, vague, or flat; when they represent no knowledge, they are called non-informative. A Jeffreys' prior (Jeffreys 1961) is a specific type of non-informative prior and is mentioned here only so that readers may recognize the term if it is encountered in other readings. A subset of Bayesian methods called objective Bayesian methods use only such priors (Link et al. 2002). However, researchers must be careful in that what may at first appear to be a non-informative prior on one parameter may convey a great deal of information about other parameters (Walters and Ludwig 1994). Berger et al. (2001) and Hobert and Casella (1996) discuss some of the difficulties in using diffuse priors.

When warranted, priors may contain more detailed information. For example, one could base the priors on a formal synthesis of previous studies focused on the same or similar species in the same or similar habitats. The priors could be based on a survey of the opinions from a range of experts (Wolfson et al. 1996). In some cases, the priors are based on the subjective belief of the investigator, which in turn, should be based on an understanding of the biological system in question (Cooper et al. 2003). In any case, the specific form of the prior and the justification for this form should be stated in any presentation of the research to ensure the underlying assumptions are transparent to the reader (Link et al. 2002). As will be discussed later, researchers should also assess the sensitivity of their results to the choice of priors.

The marginal probability of the data, $P(Y \mid \omega)$, is obtained by integrating the joint probability distribution of the data and the hypotheses over all possible hypotheses (i.e., that $\Theta = \theta$ for all possibly values of θ), where the joint probability distribution is the product of the prior and the likelihood. As such, $P(Y \mid \omega)$ does not depend upon the particular hypothesis in question, but is dependent upon the hyperparameters (ω) in the prior probability distribution, (i.e., $P(\Theta \mid \omega)$). In practice, $P(Y \mid \omega)$ is treated as a scaling constant because the data are already observed and the hyperparameters are chosen a priori (Ellison 1996).

The final component of Bayes rule is the posterior probability distribution (less formally called the posterior), $P(\Theta \mid y,\omega)$. The posterior can be thought of as a compromise between, or a weighted average of, the prior distribution and the information contained in the data (Gelman et al. 1995). The posterior specifically describes the probabilities associated with possible values (for discrete distributions) or ranges of values (for continuous distributions) for the parameters in question given the data in hand and the prior knowledge of those parameters as defined by the hyperparameters (Link et al. 2002). So, unlike a confidence interval, the posterior distribution permits such concepts as a specific probability that the parameter of interest lies within a specific range, called the Bayesian credibility interval. For example, a 95% credibility interval implies a 95% chance that the true value of the parameter lies within the stated range. It is important to note that the posterior distribution describes only the uncertainty in the parameter estimate, not its variability over spatio-temporal scales (Clark 2005) unless such variability is explicitly incorporated by adding parameters to the model (i.e., time-specific survival rather than constant survival). With non-informative, vague, or flat priors, the mode of the posterior distribution will occur at the same value as the maximum likelihood estimate obtained under the purely likelihood-based methods (Link et al. 2002, Clark 2005).

If the model has more than one parameter, then the posterior distribution actually describes the joint probability of the parameters taking on sets of values, fully accounting for the correlation between the parameter estimates (e.g., the probability of survival falling within some range and encounter probability falling within another range). In many cases, however, the researcher is only interested in one or a few of the many parameters. For example, even though care is taken in modeling the encounter probabilities (e.g., constant over time or ages versus variable over time or ages), the real questions of interest typically center on the survival rate estimates. A similar situation exists with regard to the recapture probabilities in a mark-recapture model designed to estimate survival rates. In these cases, the encounter or recapture probabilities would be called nuisance parameters because they are unknown and must be estimated, but the real interest (and the hypothesis in question) lies elsewhere. The marginal posterior distribution allows one to make statements about the parameter of interest alone and is calculated by integrating over the nuisance parameters (Gelman et al. 1995, Ellison 1996, Hobbs and Hilborn 2006). To calculate the marginal probability of survival falling within a specific range, we would integrate over all possible values for the encounter probabilities, essentially incorporating the uncertainty of the encounter probabilities and their correlation with survival directly into the probability statement for survival alone.

To determine the posterior can be rather challenging. One issue is that few programs are available to perform these analyses. WinBUGS (Spiegelhalter et al. 1995) is one user-friendly program applicable to many Bayesian analyses, but one must still have a familiarity with likelihoods and Bayesian methods in order to use it. The program MARK (White and Burnham 1999) can perform Bayesian estimation of nest survival for the Dinsmore et al. (2002) model, but it only allows for normally distributed priors for the parameters in the logit model for the covariates which define the survival probabilities. Another related issue is that even with such user-friendly packages as WinBUGS, computing the posterior distributions for some models can take on the order of hours for a standard desktop computer (Hobbs and Hilborn 2006). The posteriors are often approximated using an approach called Markov chain Monte Carlo (MCMC) and, in particular, the Metropolis-Hastings algorithm, of which Gibbs sampling is a special case. Readers will come across these terms when reading about Bayesian methods, but the details of these methods are beyond the scope of this manuscript. See Casella and George (1992), Kass et al. (1998), and especially Link et al. (2002) for more complete descriptions.

The computational burden of determining the posterior distribution can be greatly decreased by using priors that are conjugate distributions (or more simply conjugates) for the likelihood. When the prior is a conjugate for the likelihood, the posterior distribution will, by definition, have the same functional form as the prior. For example, a beta-distributed prior is a conjugate for the binomial likelihood. Most mark-recapture and nest-survival models, whether Bayesian or not, use a binomial likelihood. When the prior for survival is defined using a beta distribution, the posterior distribution will always follow a beta distribution because of this conjugacy. This is one reason why the beta distribution or its multivariate relative, the Dirichlet distribution, is often used to define the priors for survival in Bayesian mark-recapture and nest-survival studies (Dupis 1995, 2002; He et al. 2001, He 2003). Another reason is that both these distributions are flexible enough to be used for both informative and non-informative priors (Fig. 1). Although using a beta (or Dirichlet) distribution for the prior with a binomial likelihood will ensure that the posterior is also beta-distributed, the specific shape of beta-distributed posterior will depend on both the prior and the data.

When applying Bayesian methods, it is important to examine the posteriors' sensitivity to the choice of priors. Specifically, it may be useful to apply a range of priors, all of which still conform to the researchers a priori knowledge of the parameters, and examine the changes these different priors cause in the posterior (Link et al. 2002). If the posterior is sensitive to changes in the prior, then the currently available data contain relatively little information about the parameter of interest, possibly due to small sample size (Ellison 1996, Ludwig 1996, Link et al. 2002). In such cases, the posterior is determined mostly by the prior information, and therefore great care must be taken in interpreting the meaningfulness of the posterior. However, it is not uncommon for the data from a well-designed study to overwhelm the information contained in the priors and produce posteriors robust to changes in these priors (Clark 2005).

WHY BOTHER WITH BAYESIAN METHODS?

A long-running discussion concerns the pros and cons of frequentist versus Bayesian methods in both the statistical and ecological journals. The discussion often focuses on the philosophical underpinnings of each (Clark 2005) such as the definition of probability (Ludwig 1996) and whether variables are fixed but unknown as opposed to random (Ellison 1996). Rather than delving into these discussions once again, we refer readers to Dixon and Ellison (1996) and

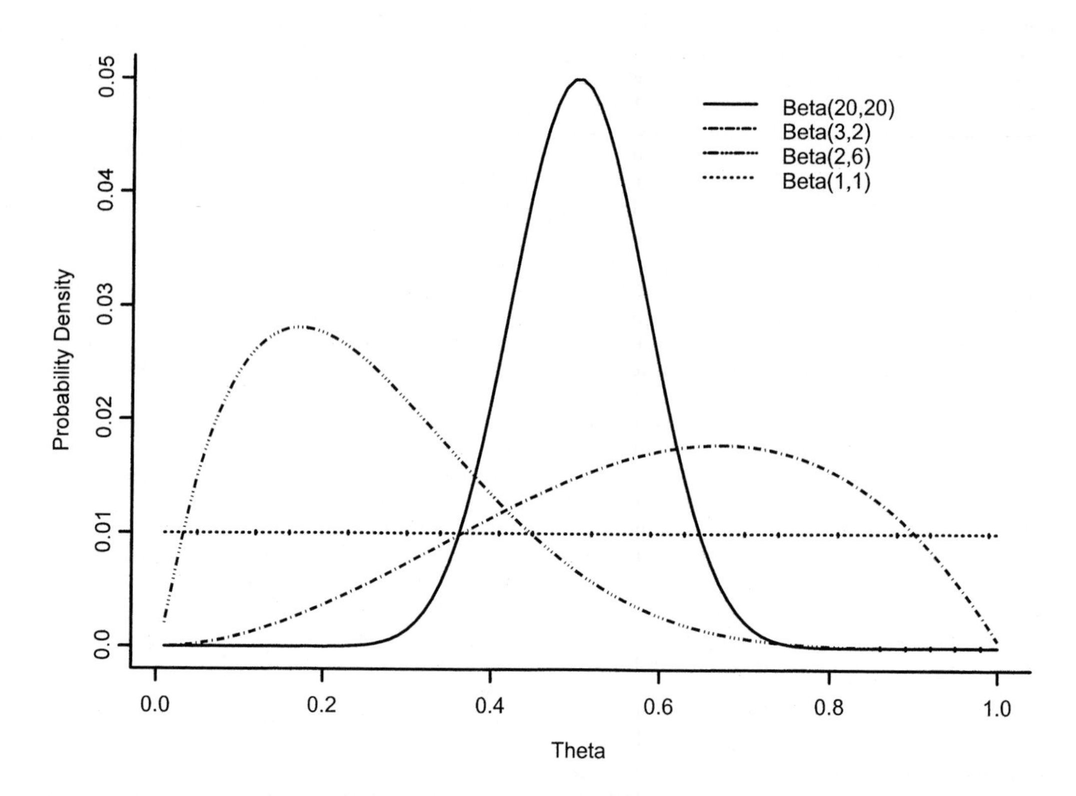

FIGURE 1. The beta-distribution can take on a range of shapes depending on the values of the hyperparameters.

the other papers immediately following it in that issue of *Ecological Applications*. Here, we will focus solely on those points we feel are of practical importance with respect to estimating nest survival rates.

The primary outputs from a frequentist analysis are typically the P-value, the parameter estimate (or effect size), and a confidence interval for the parameter value. The P-value gives the probability of obtaining a value for a test statistic (which is based on both the data and the parameter value) as or more extreme than the one observed, given the null hypothesis is true (i.e., that a given parameter equals zero). If the P-value is small, usually <0.05, then the null hypothesis is rejected because it is unlikely that the value would be observed if the null hypothesis were true. It is important to remember, and often forgotten (as argued by Johnson 2002), that failure to reject the null hypothesis does not translate into support for the null hypothesis (Kass and Raftery 1995, Ellison 1996, Johnson 2002). Similarly, a small P-value does not describe the level of support for the specific estimated parameter value, only that it is unlikely to be the value defined in the null hypothesis (Ellison 1996).

In order to move away from strict hypothesis testing, some (Robinson and Wainer 2002) are advocating more frequent use of confidence intervals for the estimated parameter values. A k% confidence interval (e.g., a 95% confidence interval) implies that if the experiment were repeated ad infinitum, and a k% confidence interval was estimated for each experiment, then k% of those intervals would contain the true value of the parameter. This also implies that 100–k% of those intervals would not contain the true value of the parameter; and for a single experiment, there is no way to determine whether the estimated confidence interval actually contains the true value. Despite continued confusion on this point, as mentioned by Hobbs and Hilborn (2006), the confidence interval does not mean that a k% probability exists that the true value for the parameter lies within the interval, nor does it describe the probability distribution for the parameter (Ellison 1996). A k% Bayesian credibility interval, however, does imply that there is a k% chance that the true value of the parameter lies within the stated range.

Another way in which frequentist methods have moved away from null hypothesis testing is through the use of information theoretic approaches such as AIC and AIC-based model averaging (Burnham and Anderson 2002). These approaches allow researchers to estimate the relative support the data provide for competing models and then make predictions that incorporate the uncertainty as to which is the best model. These approaches, as with P-values and confidence intervals, do not allow researchers to make statements about the relative probability of a parameter (e.g., survival rate) taking on one value or another value or the relative probability of a predicted outcome. Only Bayesian statistics, and the posterior distribution in particular, allow researchers to make probabilistic statements concerning the validity of the null or alternative hypothesis, about specific values of the parameters in question, or about predicted outcomes based on the fitted model (Reckhow 1990, Ellison 1996, Wade 2000, Hobbs and Hilborn 2006). It should also be noted that model averaging is possible in a Bayesian context using what are called Bayes factors (Gelman et al. 1995, Kass and Raftery 1995).

The benefit of being able to make probabilistic statements regarding hypotheses is crucial when it comes to applying the results of research to management decision making. It is not likely to be good enough to simply state that some land-use practice effects nest survival (i.e., the null hypothesis of no effect has been rejected). Managers will wish to know how much survival may be affected. What is the probability that survival will decrease by >5%, by >10%, or by >30%? Rather than knowing that one management option is better than another at increasing nest-survival rates (rejecting the null hypothesis of two management actions producing equal survival rates), managers wish to have an estimate of how much better one management option is over another, and their associated probabilities (e.g., option A has a 75% chance of increasing survival rates by more than 1% compared to option B, but only a 10% chance of increasing survival rates by more than 5% compared to option B). Answering such questions requires a Bayesian framework. If one wishes to use the output of a nest-survival study in a population dynamics model, then one needs to know the relative probability of survival taking on a range of values. Mean effect sizes, standard errors, and the associated confidence intervals from frequentist analyses do not give you this, even when based on AIC model averages. Only the posterior distribution gives you this information.

One of the more subtle differences between the output from a frequentist analysis and a Bayesian analysis centers on the treatment of nuisance parameters, such as the encounter probabilities in the models of Heisey and Nordheim (1995), He et al. (2001), He (2003), and Cao et al. (in press) or the recapture probabilities in mark-recapture models. In a frequentist framework, the maximum likelihood estimate and the standard error of that estimate for the parameter of interest (e.g., the survival rate) is calculated by maximizing the likelihood of all parameters, including the nuisance parameters. Though in practice, nuisance parameters are often removed from the likelihood equation prior to maximization by the use of either sufficient statistics or integration. In the Bayesian framework, however, we can calculate marginal posterior distributions for our parameters of interest as mentioned above. The uncertainty associated with the parameter of interest is assessed by integrating across the posterior distribution of the nuisance parameters (Gelman et al. 1995, Ellison 1996, Hobbs and Hilborn 2006). As such, the uncertainty in the nuisance parameters is propagating directly into the posterior distribution for the parameter of interest. In the case of nest-survival or mark-recapture models, any uncertainty in the encounter or recapture probabilities is propagated directly into the posterior distribution of survival. This may make little difference for simple models (Hobbs and Hilborn 2006), but for more complex models, the differences can be startling (Reckhow 1990:2053) and this difference will be especially noticeable when the parameter of interest is non-linearly correlated with the nuisance parameters (Ludwig 1996).

In addition to the ability to make probability statements about the parameters of interest and propagate the uncertainty in nuisance parameters, Bayesian methods are often touted because of a range of other desirable features. First, unlike frequentist methods, inference from Bayesian methods is not based on asymptotic assumptions. The results from Bayesian methods are valid even for small sample sizes, assuming the models for the data and priors are both correct. Uncertainty will increase with decreasing sample sizes, but the posterior distributions and credibility intervals remain valid. Second, Bayesian methods can be used to estimate a wide class of hierarchical models (e.g., mixed-effects models with random effects that have non-normal distributions) because the conditional structure and computational methods do not require that certain parameters be removed from the likelihood via sufficient statistics or integration, as is often required with non-Bayesian methods. And third, because of the requirement of explicitly stating assumptions in the form of prior distributions and the conditional structure of Bayesian models, increasing the complexity of these models can often be accomplished without decreasing the transparency to the reader

APPLICTION OF BAYESIAN STATISTICS TO NEST-SURVIVAL STUDIES

Despite the fact Bayesian statistics have been applied extensively to mark-recapture models (Dupis 1995, Brooks et al. 2002, Johnson and Hoeting 2003) and band-recovery models (Vounatsou and Smith 1995; Brooks et al. 2000, 2002), Bayesian nest-survival models have been largely unexplored. Any nest-survival model based on a likelihood equation (Bart and Robson 1982, Heisey and Nordheim 1995, Dinsmore et al. 2002, Shaffer 2004, Stanley 2004a) could be analyzed in a Bayesian framework. A review of each of these methods is beyond the scope of this manuscript, but is included elsewhere in this volume (Johnson, *this volume*), but with the careful application of prior knowledge, each of them could be adapted so as to produce formal posterior distributions for survival and the effects of covariates on survival, when applicable. The program MARK (White and Burnham 1999) can, in fact, perform Bayesian estimation of the Dinsmore et al. (2002) model, but only allows prior distributions for the parameters for the covariates in the logit model, and these priors must be normal distributions. Except for the Dinsmore et al. (2002) model in MARK, all applications of Bayesian statistics to nest-survival models have focused on estimating age-specific survival rates, especially when nest age is not known.

Several frequentist techniques exist for estimating age-specific survival. The models described by Dinsmore et al. (2002) and Shaffer (2004) are able to estimate age-specific survival, but only when ages are known, such as through egg floating (Westerskov 1950) or egg candling (Weller 1956, Lokemoen and Koford 1996), and they are unable to accommodate age-specific encounter probabilities (Rotella et al. 2004). The method of Heisey and Nordheim (1995) is able to estimate age-specific nest-survival rates when nest ages are unknown, but the algorithm to solve the likelihood equations often has difficulty converging on an estimate when the incubation period (the number of days between the time when the first egg is laid and the first nestling fledges) is long (He 2003). The solution to the estimation problem for the Heisey and Nordheim (1995) model has been to group ages together and assume constant survival and encounter probabilities for each group. If, however, the interval lengths for the groups are not chosen properly or too many ages are grouped together, this solution can produce biased estimators of survival (Heisey and Nordheim 1990, He et al. 2001, He 2003). The algorithms used for Bayesian models, such as MCMC, do not tend to have such difficulties estimating large numbers of parameters and can therefore successfully estimate age-specific survival rates when nest age is unknown without having to make assumptions about certain ages having equal probabilities.

He et al. (2001) were the first to publish a Bayesian nest-survival model that could estimate age-specific survival rates without knowing nest age. This model makes many of the typical nest-survival model assumptions (i.e., nests are independent, nest fate is independent of nest encounter and visits to the nest, and nest fate is correctly determined). The key differences in the assumptions behind the He et al. (2001) model are that nests of the same age have the same survival and encounter probabilities, nests of different ages may have different survival and encounter probabilities, and nest age need not be known. This model does, however, require that nests be visited daily once they are encountered.

He et al. (2001) were able to estimate age-specific survival and encounter probabilities without knowing age because they assume nests are visited daily and the incubation period is constant and known (i.e., each nest requires the same fixed number of days between the day the first egg is laid and the first nestling fledges, and that number is known a priori). The latter assumption was also used by Heisey and Nordheim (1995). When encountered nests are visited daily and the incubation period is known, the age of a successful nest at first encounter can be deduced. For example, if the incubation period is 26 d, and the nest was determined to be successful on day 10 of observation, then the nest must have been 17-d old when it was discovered (first day of observation). For species with multi-stage nests, age at first encounter might be able to be determined based on the day on which it transitioned from one stage to the next, regardless of whether the nest fails or succeeds.

If the nest is unsuccessful, then nest age at first encounter and at failure can still be placed within a range of values when the nest is not directly aged. For example, if the incubation period is 26 d, and the nest failed on day 22 of observation, then the following scenarios could have occurred: the nest was discovered at age 1, survived from ages 1–21, and failed at age 22; the nest was discovered at age 2 and failed at age 23; the nest was discovered at age 3 and failed at age 24; the nest was discovered at age 4 and failed at age 25. The uncertainty as to which scenario actually occurred can be incorporated directly into the likelihood equation in much the same way as unknown fates are incorporated into mark-recapture models (Lebreton et al. 1992). It is this uncertainty, however, which causes problems for the method of Heisey and Nordheim (1995) when incubation times are long. If a species has clearly defined nesting stages and the researcher knows the stage in which the nest failed but is unable to determine an exact age at first encounter, then this stage information can be included in the model below by limiting the range of possible age at failure to those ages within the observed stage at failure.

The likelihood equation in He et al. (2001) can be constructed by writing the observation history for each nest in probabilistic terms and then multiplying them together, just as one can do with mark-recapture models. We will use the same variables as in He et al. (2001)—δ_i equals the probability that a nest of age i is encountered, q_i equals the probability that a nest of age i fails (note that this is a failure rate rather than a survival rate), and the probability that a nest succeeds equals one minus the sum of all the age-specific failure probabilities. For the following example, assume the incubation period is 26 d as above. For nests that succeeded, we calculate their ages at discovery, so the equation for their contribution to the likelihood, with the actual age substituted for the subscript i would be:

$$\delta_i * (1 - (q_1 + q_2 + q_3 + \ldots + q_{26}))$$

For nests that failed, rather than writing a general equation, we will simply give examples. If a nest failed on the day 22 of observation (as above), that nest's contribution to the likelihood would equal:

$$\delta_1 q_{22} + \delta_2 q_{23} + \delta_3 q_{24} + \delta_4 q_{25}$$

If the nest failed on day five of observation, then that nest's contribution to the likelihood would equal:

$$\delta_1 q_5 + \delta_2 q_6 + \delta_3 q_7 + \ldots + \delta_{19} q_{23} + \delta_{20} q_{24} + \delta_{21} q_{25}$$

The above equation would be read as the probability of the nest being discovered at age 1 (the first observation) and failing at age 5 (the fifth observation) plus the probability of being discovered at age 2 and failing at age 6, all the way up to the probability of being discovered at age 21 and failing at age 25. When nest ages are determined at first encounter but fail, the uncertainty in the age at discovery and failure is removed, and only a single term is required to model that nest's history, $\delta_i q_j$ with the actual ages substituted for the subscripts i and j. Similar equations would be written for every single nest and then multiplied together. The model is flexible enough to be applied to situations when all, some, or no nests are aged at first encounter. The full likelihood equation, as described in He et al. (2001), is the product of all the nests' contributions to the likelihood divided by a scaling variable that equals the sum of all possible combinations of encounter at age and either failure at age or survival to first fledging.

The next component of the Bayesian model in He et al. (2001) is the set of priors. He et al. (2001) use non-informative priors for both the age-specific survival and encounter probabilities. In particular, they use the Dirichlet distribution, which is a multivariate version of the beta distribution with hyperparameters equal to one as depicted in Fig. 1. A problem with this is that the Dirichlet distribution induces a correlation between the age-specific parameters (i.e., survival probabilities are correlated across ages or encounter probabilities are correlated across ages). He (2003), however, uses independent beta distributions for each age-specific survival and encounter probability, thus removing the correlation issue.

With the likelihood and priors now defined as above, He et al. (2001) use the Gibbs sampler to produce the marginal posterior for the age-specific encounter and failure probabilities. The likelihood equation as described above was manipulated by substituting and transforming some variables so that the Gibbs sampler would solve for all the parameters more efficiently, but the details of these substitutions and transformations are beyond the scope of this manuscript. He et al. (2001) demonstrate this method working well with both simulated and real data.

A number of refinements to the He et al. (2001) model have been made. Along with relaxing the assumption of correlated priors on the age-specific encounter and survival probabilities, He (2003) also relaxed the assumption that each nest was visited daily, thus allowing for irregular visits and censoring of failure events (i.e., when the timing of failure events is not known exactly). The model in He (2003), however, can underestimate the age 1 survival probabilities under certain irregular visiting schedules, and Cao and He (2005) present three solutions to this. Cao et al. (in press) extends the He (2003) irregular visit model by incorporating categorical covariates into the survival probabilities. Finally, Cao and He (unpubl. data) expand on Cao et al. (in press) by allowing for both categorical and continuous nest-specific covariates for the survival probabilities. All the above models are currently written as FORTRAN programs, but work is underway to make them more user-friendly (C. Z. He, pers. comm.).

CONCLUSION

Bayesian statistics provide a powerful tool for formally incorporating prior knowledge and allow researchers to make probabilistic statements about the realized outcomes. Being able to calculate the probability of a hypothesis being true or a parameter taking on a range of values is crucial for applying research to management and decision-making.

The algorithms used for Bayesian analysis perform well with even very complex models, which is in large part why the age-specific survival models with unknown age work as well as they do. Computer programs such as WinBUGS and those under development by He and colleagues (C. Z. He, pers. comm.) will make Bayesian methods far more accessible than they have been in the past. Even though writing code in WinBUGS is relatively straight forward for those comfortable with other programming languages (Visual Basic, C++, or even scripts in Splus or R), developing one's own model based on the work of He and colleagues would be no small feat. Developing less complicated models in WinBUGS such as when the age of each nest is known exactly, could be achieved if one has a firm understanding of likelihoods and probability distributions, is comfortable with programming, and understands the wide array of diagnostics (Kass et al. 1998, Link et al. 2002) necessary to examine the adequacy of the posterior distribution. The program MARK has the capability of performing a Bayesian analysis of the Dinsmore et al. (2002) model, however the way in which the priors are required to be defined (i.e., as normal distributions and only on the parameters for the covariates in the logit model, and not the survival rate itself) may limit researchers' ability to adequately incorporate the full range of prior knowledge. If one wishes to use only non-informative priors, the formulation in MARK for the Dinsmore et al. (2002) should be more than adequate. As both science and statistical theory move forward, Bayesian methods hold great promise for helping researchers find solutions to complex problems and provide managers and decision-makers the tools they need to make wise choices.

ACKNOWLEDGEMENTS

We would like the thank Stephanie Jones for giving us the opportunity to participate in this special issue and Chong Z. He for introducing us to this topic. The manuscript was greatly improved by the comments of Stephanie Jones, Brian Dennis, Jay Rotella, Micheal Wunder, and five anonymous reviewers.

Studies in Avian Biology No. 34:145–148

MODELING NEST-SURVIVAL DATA: RECENT IMPROVEMENTS AND FUTURE DIRECTIONS

JAY ROTELLA

Abstract. Studies of nesting birds commonly seek to estimate nest success and to evaluate relationships between nest-survival rates and hypothesized influential factors. Recently, a number of advances have been made with regard to the analysis of nest-survival data, and improved methods now exist for relaxing assumptions and accounting for potentially important sources of variation in nest-survival data. Methods have been developed that allow diverse covariates of nest-survival rate to be incorporated into analyses of either discrete survival data or failure times. Analysis of binomial data for nest fates over discrete periods has dominated the nest-survival literature and been the subject of many recent advances that extend possible analyses beyond that of the Mayfield method. Recent papers that describe the use of generalized linear mixed models to incorporate covariate effects on nest survival, including some examples that employed a random-effects framework, illustrate the benefits that can be gained from using such models when they are appropriate. Noteworthy examples of the use of analysis of failure times also exist and illustrate the key elements of this type of analysis, which can accommodate censoring, heterogeneity in survival, staggered entry of subjects into the study, and continuous and categorical covariates of survival times. The new analytical approaches should allow avian ecologists to evaluate a broad variety of competing models. By using the various methods interchangeably, future analyses should provide new insights into the nesting ecology of birds.

Key Words: daily survival rate, logistic regression, mixed models, Mayfield, nest success, nest survival.

MODELANDO DATOS DE SOBREVIVENCIA DE NIDO: MEJORAS RECIENTES Y DIRECCIONES FUTURAS

*Resumen.*Comúnmente los estudios de anidación de aves buscan estimar el éxito de anidación y evaluar las relaciones entre las tasas de sobrevivencia de nido, así como hipotetizar los factores que influyen. Recientemente un número de avances han sido desarrollados respecto al análisis de datos de sobrevivencia de nido, y existen ahora métodos mejorados para suavizar las suposiciones, así como el conteo de potenciales fuentes importantes de variación en datos de sobrevivencia de nido. También han sido desarrollados métodos los cuales permiten que diversas tasas de covariantes de sobrevivencia de nido sean incorporadas ya sea a análisis de datos discretos de sobrevivencia, como a veces fallidas. El análisis de datos binomiales para destino de nido sobre periodos discretos ha dominado la literatura respecto a sobrevivencia de nido, y ha sido el tema de varios avances recientes que amplían posibles análisis más allá del método de Mayfield. Artículos recientes los cuales describen la utilización de modelos generalizados lineares mezclados para incorporar efectos covariables en sobrevivencia de nido, incluidos algunos ejemplos que emplearon un marco de efectos al azar, ilustran los beneficios que pueden ser obtenidos al utilizar dichos modelos cuando son apropiados. Existen ejemplos significativos de la utilización de análisis de veces fallidas que ilustran los elementos clave de este tipo de análisis, los cuales pueden adecuar la censura, heterogeneidad en la sobrevivencia, escalonar la entrada de temas en el estudio, y continuas y categóricas covariantes de veces de sobrevivencia. Los nuevos enfoques deberían permitir a los ecólogos de aves evaluar una amplia variedad de modelos competentes. Al utilizar los métodos intercambiablemente, análisis futuros deberían proveer nuevas incursiones en la ecología de anidación de aves.

Studies of nesting birds are widespread in the avian literature. For example, several hundred such papers were published in the year 2004 alone. Studies commonly seek to estimate nest success (the probability that a nest survives from initiation to completion and has at least one offspring leaves the nest) and to evaluate relationships between nest-survival rates and hypothesized influential factors. Accordingly, methods for estimating nest-survival rate have received considerable attention (Mayfield 1961, Johnson 1979, Bart and Robson 1982, Natarajan and McCulloch 1999, Farnsworth et al. 2000, Dinsmore et al. 2002). Williams et al. (2002), Johnson (*this volume*), and Heisey et al. (*this volume*) provided recent and useful reviews of historical development, available approaches, and estimation programs.

The Mayfield method, either in its original form or as expanded by Johnson (1979) and Bart and Robson (1982), requires the assumption of a constant daily survival rate for all nests in a sample over the time period being considered (for further details of the method, its assumptions, and history, see Johnson, *this volume*). However, heterogeneity in daily survival rates among members of the study population can cause estimates of nest success and, in some cases, daily survival rate to be biased (Johnson 1979). Thus, nest-survival data are frequently divided into groups for analysis with the Mayfield method, e.g., stratified by stage of the nesting cycle, season, and habitat conditions (Heisey and Fuller 1985). But, stratification can commonly lead to small samples for many strata if multiple covariates are used to classify data, because most nesting studies investigate how daily survival rates of nests vary in relation to multiple explanatory variables.

To allow greater flexibility in modeling nest-survival data in the presence of heterogeneity, numerous publications have presented methods for relaxing assumptions and accounting for potentially important sources of variation (Dinsmore et al. 2002). Some of the recent improvements have received considerable attention in the avian ecology literature (Dinsmore et al. (2002) had already been cited by 21 publications by the end of 2005, while other advances have received less attention; He et al. (2001) had only been cited twice by the end of 2005). Such differences may have to do with the ease with which new approaches can be implemented in readily available software: Dinsmore et al.'s (2002) approach is implemented in program MARK (White and Burnham 1999) with excellent supporting materials; whereas the approach developed by He et al. (2001) allows great flexibility in modeling but has not yet been accompanied by readily accessible software or code for implementation. Still other methods are simply too new to have yet received attention by the majority of avian ecologists, (Nur et al. 2004, Etterson and Bennett 2005).

Given the diversity of important developments that have recently been made with respect to analysis of nest-survival data, the goal of this paper is to briefly review the latest advances and to comment on areas of future research that would further improve analysis of nest-survival data. The excellent and detailed reviews by Johnson (*this volume*), Heisey et al. (*this volume*) provide much greater detail on the plethora of analysis options that are currently available.

GENERAL APPROACHES

Many of the recent advances can be placed into several broad analytical categories. Here, following the recent treatment of the topic by Williams et al. (2002), two broad classes are used: the analysis of discrete survival data and the analysis of failure times. Heisey et al. (*this volume*) examine these two classes in detail and discuss how they relate to one another.

ANALYSIS OF DISCRETE SURVIVAL DATA

Analysis of binomial data for nest fates over discrete periods has dominated the nest-survival literature and been the subject of many recent advances. Specifically, generalized linear models have been used in a number of recent publications that have extended the analysis of nest-survival data beyond that of the Mayfield method (Dinsmore et al. 2002, Rotella et al. 2004, Shaffer 2004a). As used for nest-survival data, generalized linear models usually employ a logit link between daily survival rate and the covariates of interest, while allowing visitation intervals to vary among observations and making no assumptions about when nest failure occurs.

The recent use of generalized linear mixed models to incorporate covariate effects on nest survival in a random-effects framework takes further advantage of modeling advances (Natarajan and McCulloch (1999); also see reviews by Rotella et al. (2004, *this volume*). Shaffer (2004a), Winter et al. (2005a), and Stephens et al. (2005) employed methods that allow incorporation of random effects along with fixed effects, i.e., mixed models. Several benefits can be gained from using mixed models when they are appropriate. In some situations, the precision of estimates will be increased. Further, when models containing random effects are supported by data, impetus is provided for considering what is responsible for the overdispersion being modeled by the random effect. Such an effort can improve future studies if it leads to the inclusion of new covariates in the fixed effects that reduce the overdispersion. Finally, incorporation of random effects can allow one to make broader inferences, e.g., to a population of study sites rather than just the specific study sites used.

However, one must be cautious with interpretation of estimates obtained in the presence of random effects. In typical studies of nest survival, data are left-truncated because some nests that fail early are not included in the sample (Heisey et al., *this volume*). Under these circumstances, the usual assumption that the mean of a random effect is zero is inappropriate if the design is not balanced (Rotella et al., *this volume*), i.e., if sample sizes are unequal across levels of the covariate being treated as a random factor (e.g., study sites). All else being equal, if care is not taken to balance the sampling design, sample sizes will be larger for those covariate levels (e.g., study sites) that are associated with higher survival rates simply because nests in such settings are expected to survive longer and thus, have a greater chance of entering the sample. When the sample sizes are positively correlated with survival rates, estimates of survival will be biased high to some extent because nests in the sample over represent nests with higher underlying survival rates (Heisey et al., *this volume*). Simulation work completed to date indicates that balanced designs (equal numbers of nests found across levels of the covariate being treated as a random factor) effectively deal with this potential problem (Rotella et al., *this volume*). Thus, given that one will not typically know prior to data analysis whether or not random effects will exist in the data, it seems prudent to adjust search effort such that balanced samples are achieved. The issue of bias from left truncation has received little attention, and more work is needed to determine the magnitude of the problem under typical sampling scenarios.

More information on the use of generalized linear mixed models for nest-survival data can be found in Natarajan and McCulloch (1999), Rotella et al. (2004, *this volume*), and Heisey et al. (*this volume*). Also, the statistics literature contains numerous in-depth treatments of the topic from a more fundamental perspective. As succinctly stated by Williams et al. (2002: 349), the complexity of the computations may limit the ability of many biologists to apply a random-effects approach. However, random-effects modeling is a reasonable and natural way to view nest survival. Williams et al. (2002) believe that the approach will see increasing use, especially when computations are simplified or made more accessible with, for example, Markov chain Monte Carlo methods. The prediction of increasing use may prove correct quite quickly. Biologists are becoming more aware of the benefits of such models and the use of Markov chain Monte Carlo methods due to recent articles explaining the benefits of the approach (Link et al. 2002). Further, Bayesian approaches to modeling nest survival (He et al. 2001, He 2003), which have also recently been extended to include diverse spatio-temporal covariates (J. Cao and C. He, pers. comm.), have proved useful for obtaining parameter estimates.

Although the linear-logistic-modeling approach makes no assumption about the timing of nest failures that occur between two nest visits (but see Aebischer 1999), it is important to consider that the method does require the assumption that nests can be aged correctly. Implicit in this is the assumption that the day of hatching, or fledging, can also be determined correctly. In some studies, uncertainty will exist about nest ages and when transitions among nest stages occur (Williams et al. 2002). For some species, nest age will be a covariate of interest but be unknown for many nests (Stanley 2004a). Also, typical assumptions about the distributions of hatching and fledging events may be violated in some studies (for details, see Etterson and Bennett 2005). Under such circumstances, it will also be difficult to know the exact fledging date for nests and to time final nest checks such that nest fates can be unambiguously determined (Manolis et al. 2000). Several publications have presented methods for dealing with ambiguities in aging and determining fate (Manolis et al. 2000; Stanley 2000, 2004a; Etterson and Bennett 2005). However, these advances have not yet been integrated into models containing complex sets of covariates despite the fact that these circumstances will occur regularly for some species of interest.

Analysis of Failure Times

In contrast to the general analysis approach described above, which focuses on the number of nests surviving over a fixed time period, this approach focuses on time until failure (nest loss) or censoring (Williams et al. 2002). The analysis of failure times has been used in many fields, notably medical science and engineering, and thus, has received a great deal of statistical development and can readily be executed in many statistical packages. Accordingly, diagnostics for analysis of failure times are quite extensive (Nur et al. 2004). Analysis of failure times is compared and contrasted with analysis of discrete survival data by Williams et al. (2002) and Heisey et al. (*this volume*). Analysis of failure times can accommodate censoring (ultimate nest fate need not be known), heterogeneity in survival, staggered entry of subjects into the study, and continuous and categorical covariates of survival times. Accordingly, it should not be surprising that the method was recently applied to the analysis of nest survival by Renner and Davis (2001) and Nur et al. (2004). Nur et al. (2004), Heisey et al. (*this volume*), and Johnson (*this volume*) provide excellent treatments of the subject with respect to the analysis of nest survival. Non-parametric (Kaplan-Meier estimation), semi-parametric (proportional hazards model), and parametric (e.g., Weibull regression) alternatives to analysis of failure time exist. However, for reasons given in Heisey et al. (*this volume*), non-parametric methods have limited utility in most studies of nest survival. Both the semi-parametric and parametric analyses allow continuous and categorical covariates of survival times to be incorporated. Shochat et al. (2005a, b) recently used the proportional-hazards model to successfully analyze nest-survival data of diverse species as functions of multiple covariates. Further, Pankratz et al. (2005) recently provided methods for conducting variance component analyses under general random-effects proportional-hazards models, which makes it feasible to handle correlated time-to-event data, but the applicability of their approach to nest-survival data has not yet been fully evaluated.

As explained by Nur et al. (2004), it is important to realize that estimates of the age of a nesting attempt upon discovery are required for survival-time analysis. However, this requirement exists for the discrete time analyses discussed above as well, unless the analyst is willing to assume constant survival. A further assumption of the analysis of failure times as presented by Nur et al. (2004), although not a general assumption for the method and one that is not necessary with discrete time analysis, is that the date of nest failure is accurately obtained. Thus, short intervals between nest visits are necessary with this method.

Future Directions

The methods discussed here that allow complex sets of covariates to be incorporated in models of nest-survival data do not consider detection probability for nests with different characteristics as do some other methods (Pollock and Cornelius 1988, Bromaghin and McDonald 1993a, McPherson et al. 2003). Accordingly, the methods reviewed here provide estimates that are conditional on the data set. That is, they only represent the population of interest to the extent that the sample of nest data is representative of the population of nest data. A better understanding of how well samples represent populations of interest under various circumstances is needed, e.g., see discussion of random effects above. Information on age-specific nest encounter probabilities can provide information about survival probabilities prior to encounter. The utility of such information has been presented by Williams et al. (2002) and McPherson et al. (2003), and it would be useful if encounter probability could be incorporated into regression models of nest survival. Given the flexibility of the Bayesian approaches (He et al. 2001, He 2003), it would be beneficial if analysis programs and supporting documentation for implementing Bayesian analyses could be made readily available.

Goodness-of-fit tools now exist for models of discrete survival data that include individual covariates and/or random effects (Sturdivant et al., *this volume*) and are available in diverse forms for parametric and semi-parametric analysis of failure times (Lawless 1982). However, estimation of overdispersion remains problematic for analyses of discrete survival data unless random effects are incorporated (see Rotella et al., *this volume*). Further work on this topic would be helpful, but it should be readily apparent that goodness-of-fit and overdispersion are much lesser issues for the complex models now available than they were for simple Mayfield analyses where survival rate is assumed constant over all observations analyzed.

It is clear that new analytical tools allow avian ecologists to evaluate a broader variety of covariates and competing models than was previously possible. The available approaches can be used interchangeably as best suits a particular problem. However, to take full advantage of the approaches, sizeable samples of nests across gradients relevant to the hypotheses of interest will be needed. Interesting questions and well-thought-out sampling designs should, when combined with recent analytical advances, provide new insights into the nesting ecology of birds.

ACKNOWLEDGMENTS

I thank S. L. Jones and G. R. Geupel for organizing the symposium and inviting my participation. This paper benefited from my interactions with S. J. Dinsmore, D. H. Johnson, S. L. Jones, T. L. Shaffer, M. L. Taper, and G. C. White.

LITERATURE CITED

AEBISCHER, N. J. 1999. Multi-way comparisons and generalised linear models of nest success: extensions of the Mayfield method. Bird Study 46: S22–S31.

AGRESTI, A., AND B. FINLAY. 1986. Statistical methods for the social sciences. 2nd ed. Dellen Publishing Company, San Francisco, CA

AKAIKE, H. 1973. Information theory and an extension of the maximum likelihood principle. Pp. 267–281 *in* B. N. Petran, and F. Csaki (editors). International symposium on information theory, 2nd ed. Budapest, Hungary.

ALBRECHT, T. 2004. Edge effect in wetland-arable land boundary determines nesting success of Scarlet Rosefinches (*Carpodacus erythrinus*) in the Czech Republic. Auk 121:361–371.

ALDRIDGE, C. L., AND R. M. BRIGHAM. 2001. Nesting and reproductive success of Greater Sage-Grouse in a declining northern fringe population. Condor 103:537–543.

ALLISON, P. D. 1999. Logistic regression using the SAS system, theory and application. SAS Institute, Cary, NC.

ANDERSON, D. R., AND K. P. BURNHAM. 2002. Avoiding pitfalls when using information-theoretic methods. Journal of Wildlife Management 66:912–918.

ANDERSON, D. R., W. A. LINK, D. H. JOHNSON, AND K. P. BURNHAM. 2001. Suggestions for presenting the results of data analyses. Journal of Wildlife Management 65:373–378.

ANDERSON, P. K., O. BORGAN, R. D. GILL, AND N. KEIDING. 1992. Statistical models based on counting processes. Springer-Verlag, New York, NY.

ANDERSON, P. K., J. P. KLEIN, K. M. KNUDSEN, AND R. T. PALACIOS. 1997. Estimation of variance in Cox's regression model with shared gamma frailties. Biometrics 53:1475–1484.

ANONYMOUS. 1981. Correction. Ibis 123:595.

ARMSTRONG, D. P., E. H. RAEBURN, R. G. POWLESLAND, M. HOWARD, B. CHRISTENSEN, AND J. G. EWEN. 2002. Obtaining meaningful comparisons of nest success: data from New Zealand Robin (*Petroica australis*) populations. New Zealand Journal of Ecology 26:1–13.

ARTMAN, V. L., E. K. SUTHERLAND, AND J. F. DOWNHOWER. 2001. Prescribed burning to restore mixed-oak communities in southern Ohio: effects on breeding-bird populations. Conservation Biology 15: 1423–1434.

BAICICH, P. J., AND J. O. HARRISON. 1997. A guide to the nests, eggs, and nestlings of North American birds, 2nd ed. Academic Press, San Diego, CA.

BANERJEE, S., M. M. WALL, AND B. P. CARLIN. 2003. Frailty modeling for spatially correlated survival data, with application to infant mortality in Minnesota. Biostatistics 4:123–142.

BART, J., AND D. S. ROBSON. 1982. Estimating survivorship when the subjects are visited periodically. Ecology 63:1078–1090.

BATARY, P., AND A. BALDI. 2004. Evidence of an edge effect on avian nest success. Conservation Biology 18:389–400.

BEAUCHAMP, W. D., R. R. KOFORD, T. D. NUDDS, R. G. CLARK, AND D. H. JOHNSON. 1996. Long-term declines in nest success of prairie ducks. Journal of Wildlife Management 60:247–257.

BELETSKY, L. D. 1996. The Red-winged Blackbird. The biology of a strongly polygynous songbird. Academic Press, San Diego, CA.

BERGER, J. O., V. DE OLIVEIRA, AND B. SANS. 2001. Bayesian analysis of spatially correlated data. Journal of the American Statistical Association 96:1361–1374.

BERGSTROM, P. W. 1982. Ecology of incubation in Wilson's Plover (*Charadrius wilsonia*). Ph.D. dissertation, University of Chicago, Chicago, IL.

BERGSTROM, P. W. 1988. Breeding biology of Wilson's Plovers. Wilson Bulletin 100:25–35.

BEST, L. B., K. E. FREEMARK, J. J. DINSMORE, AND M. CAMP. 1995. A review and synthesis of habitat use by breeding birds in agricultural landscapes of Iowa. American Midland Naturalist 134:1–29.

BEST, L. B., K. E. FREEMARK, B. S. STEINER, AND T. M. BERGIN. 1996. Life history and status classifications of birds breeding in Iowa. Journal of the Iowa Academy of Science 103:34–45.

BETTINGER, P., M. LENNETTE, K. N. JOHNSON, AND T. A. SPIES. 2005. A hierarchical spatial framework for forest landscape planning. Ecological Modelling 182:25–48.

BISHOP, Y. M. M., S. E. FIENBERG, AND P. W. HOLLAND. 1975. Discrete multivariate analysis. MIT Press, Cambridge, MA.

BOYD, R. L. 1972. Breeding biology of the Snowy Plover at Cheyenne Bottoms Waterfowl Management Area, Barton County, Kansas. M.S. thesis, Emporia State University, Emporia, KS.

BRESLOW, N. 1974. Covariance analysis of censored survival data. Biometrics 30:89–99.

BRESLOW, N. E., AND D. G. CLAYTON. 1993. Approximate inference in generalized linear mixed models. Journal of the American Statistical Association 88:9–25.

BRITTON, J. C., AND B. MORTON. 1989. Shore ecology of the Gulf of Mexico. University of Texas Press, Austin, TX.

BROMAGHIN, J. F., AND L. L. MCDONALD. 1993a. Weighted nest survival models. Biometrics 49:1164–1172.

Bromaghin, J. F., and L. L. McDonald. 1993b. A systematic-encounter-sampling design for nesting studies. Auk 110:646–651.

Brooks, S. P., E. A. Catchpole, B. J. T. Morgan, and S. C. Barry. 2000. On the Bayesian analysis of ring-recovery data. Biometrics 56:951–956.

Brooks, S. P., E. A. Catchpole, B. J. T. Morgan, and M. P. Harris. 2002. Bayesian methods for analyzing ringing data. Journal of Applied Statistics 29:187–206.

Brown, S., C. Hickey, B. Harrington, and R. Gill (editors). 2001. The U.S. Shorebird Conservation Plan, 2nd ed. Manomet Center for Conservation Sciences, Manomet, MA.

Budnik, J. M., F. R. Thompson III, and M. R. Ryan. 2002. Effect of habitat characteristics on the probability of parasitism and predation of Bell's Vireo nests. Journal of Wildlife Management 66:232–239.

Burhans, D. E., D. Dearborn, F. R. Thompson III, and J. Faaborg. 2002. Factors affecting predation at songbird nests in old fields. Journal of Wildlife Management 66:240–249.

Burke, D. M., and E. Nol. 2000. Landscape and fragment size effects on reproductive success of forest-breeding birds in Ontario. Ecological Applications 10:1749–1761.

Burnham, K. P., and D. R. Anderson. 2002. Model selection and multi-model inference: a practical information-theoretic approach, 2nd ed. Springer-Verlag, New York, NY.

Burnham, K. P., and D. R. Anderson. 2004. Multimodel inference—understanding AIC and BIC in model selection. Sociological Methods and Research 33: 261–304.

Burnham, K. P., D. R. Anderson, G. C. White, C. Brownie, and K. H. Pollock. 1987. Design and analysis experiments for fish survival experiments based on capture-recapture. American Fisheries Society Monograph No. 5.

Caccamise, D. F. 1976. Nesting mortality in the Red-winged Blackbird. Auk 93:517–534.

Caccamise, D. F. 1977. Breeding success and nest site characteristics of the Red-winged Blackbird. Wilson Bulletin 89:396–403.

Caccamise, D. F. 1978. Seasonal patterns of nesting mortality in the Red-winged Blackbird. Condor 80:290–294.

Cahayla-Wynne, R., and D. C. Glenn-Lewin. 1978. The forest vegetation of the driftless area, northeast Iowa. American Midland Naturalist 100:307–319.

Cai, T., and R. A. Betensky. 2003. Hazard regression for interval-censored data with penalized spline. Biometrics 59:570–579.

Cam, E., W. A. Link, E. G. Cooch, Y.-A. Monnat, and E. Danchin. 2002. Individual covariation in life-history traits: seeing the trees despite the forest. American Naturalist 159:96–105.

Canfield, R. H. 1941. Application of the line interception method in sampling range vegetation. Journal of Forestry 38:388–394.

Cao, J., and C. Z. He. 2005. Bias adjustment in Bayesian estimation of bird nest age-specific survival rates. Biometrics 61:877–878.

Cao, J., C. Z. He, and T. D. McCoy. In press. Bayesian estimation of age-specific bird nest survival rates with categorical covariates. Environmental and Ecological Statistics.

Carey, J. R. 1989. The multiple decrement life table: a unifying framework for cause-of-death analysis in ecology. Oecologia 78:131–137.

Casella, G., and R. L. Berger. 1990. Statistical inference. Duxbury Press, Belmont, CA.

Casella, G., and E. I. George. 1992. Explaining the Gibbs sampler. American Statistician 46:167–174.

Chiang, C. L. 1968. Introduction to stochastic process in biostatistics. Wiley, New York, NY.

Clark, J. S. 2005. Why environmental scientists are becoming Bayesians. Ecology Letters 8:2–14.

Clark, R. G., and D. Shutler. 1999. Avian habitat selection: pattern from process in nest-site use by ducks. Ecology 80:272–287.

Cooch, E., and G. C. White. 2005. Program MARK: a gentle introduction. 4th ed. <http://www.phidot.org/software/mark/docs/book/> (15 November 2006).

Cooper, A. B., R. Hilborn, and J. W. Unsworth. 2003. An approach for population assessment in the absence of abundance indices. Ecological Applications 13: 814–828.

Copas, J. B. 1989. Unweighted sum of squares test for proportions. Applied Statistics 38:71–80.

Corbat, C. A. 1990. Nesting ecology of selected beach-nesting birds in Georgia. Ph.D. dissertation, University of Georgia, Athens, GA.

Corbat, C. A., and P. W. Bergstrom. 2000. Wilson's Plover (*Charadrius wilsonia*). *In* A. Poole, and F. Gill (editors). The Birds of North America, No. 516. The Academy of Natural Sciences, Philadelphia, PA and The American Ornithologists' Union, Washington, DC.

Coulson, J. C. 1956. Mortality and egg production of the Meadow Pipit with special reference to altitude. Bird Study 3:119–132.

Cox, D. R. 1972. Regression models and life tables (with discussion). Journal of the Royal Statistical Society, Series B 34:187–220.

Cox, D. R. 1983. Some remarks on overdispersion. Biometrika 70:269–274.

Cresswell, W. 1997. Nest predation: the relative effects of nest characteristics, clutch size and parental behaviour. Animal Behaviour 53:93–103.

Crumpton, W. G. 1993. Establishment of an experimental wetland research complex. Leopold Center Progress Reports 2:9–12.

Curtis, J. T. 1959. The vegetation of Wisconsin: an ordination of plant communities. University of Wisconsin Press, Madison, WI.

Davis, S. K. 2003. Nesting ecology of mixed-grass prairie songbirds in southern Saskatchewan. Wilson Bulletin 115:119–130.

DAVIS, S. K. 2005. Nest-site selection patterns and the influence of vegetation on nest-survival of mixed-grass prairie passerines. Condor 107:605–616.

DEMPSTER, A. P., N. M. LAIRD, AND D. B. RUBIN. 1977. Maximum likelihood from incomplete data via the EM algorithm. Journal of the Royal Statistical Society, Series B 39:1–38.

DIENI, J. S., AND S. L. JONES. 2003. Grassland songbird nest site selection patterns in north-central Montana. Wilson Bulletin 115:388–396.

DINSMORE, S. J., G. C. WHITE, AND F. L. KNOPF. 2002. Advanced techniques for modeling avian nest survival. Ecology 83:3476–3488.

DION, N., K. A. HOBSON, AND S. LARIVIRE. 2000. Interactive effects of vegetation and predators on the success of natural and simulated nests of grassland songbirds. Condor 102:629–634.

DIXON, P., AND A. M. ELLISON. 1996. Bayesian inference. Ecological Applications. 6:1034–1035.

DO, K. 2002. Biostatistical approaches for modeling longitudinal and event time data. Clinical Cancer Research 8:2473–2474.

DONOVAN, T. M., P. W. JONES, E. M. ANNAND, AND F. R. THOMPSON III. 1997. Variation in local-scale edge effects: mechanisms and landscape context. Ecology 78:2064–2075.

DOW, D. D. 1978. A test of significance for Mayfield's method of calculating nest success. Wilson Bulletin 90:291–295.

DUGUAY, J. P., P. B. WOOD, AND G. W. MILLER. 2000. Effects of timber harvests on invertebrate biomass and avian nest success. Wildlife Society Bulletin 28:1123–1131.

DUPIS, J. A. 1995. Bayesian estimation of movement and survival probabilities from capture-recapture data. Biometrika 82:761–772.

DUPIS, J. A. 2002. Prior distributions for stratified capture-recapture models. Journal of Applied Statistics 29:225–237.

DYER, M. I., J. PINOWSKI, AND B. PINOWSKA. 1977. Population dynamics. Pp. 53–105 *in* J. Pinowski, and S. C. Kendeigh (editors). Granivorous birds in ecosystems, their evolution, populations, energetics, adaptations, impact, and control. Cambridge University Press, Cambridge, UK.

EFRON, B. 1988. Logistic regression, survival analysis, and the Kaplan-Meier curve. Journal of the American Statistical Association 83:414–425.

EFRON, B. 1995. Business statistics center interviews. Irwin/McGraw-Hill Company. <http://www.mhhe.com/business/opsci/bstat/efron.mhtml> (11 April 2006).

EHRLICH, P. R., D. S. DOBKIN, AND D. WHEYE. 1988. The birder's handbook. Simon and Schuster, New York, NY.

ELLISON, A. M. 1996. An introduction to Bayesian inference for ecological research and environmental decision-making. Ecological Applications 6:1036–1046.

ENNIS, D. M. 1998. The beta-binomial model: accounting for inter-trial variation in replicated difference and preference tests. Journal of Sensory Studies 13:389–412.

ETHERIDGE, B., R. W. SUMMERS, AND R. E. GREEN. 1997. The effects of illegal killing and destruction of nests by humans on the population dynamics of the hen harrier *Circus cyaneus* in Scotland. Journal of Applied Ecology 34:1081–1105.

ETTERSON, M. A., AND R. S. BENNETT. 2005. Including transition probabilities in nest survival estimation: a Mayfield Markov chain. Ecology 86: 1414–1421.

ETTERSON, M., AND R. BENNETT. 2006. The effects of uncertainty about age of transition on bias in the Mayfield family of estimators. Ecological Modelling 199:253–260.

ETTERSON, M. A., L. R. NAGY, AND T. RODDEN-ROBINSON. 2007. Partitioning risk among different causes of nest failure. Auk 124:432–443.

FAABORG, J. 2002. Saving migrant songbirds: developing strategies for the future. University of Texas Press, Austin, TX.

FAN, X., A. FELSOVALYI, S. A. SIVO, AND S. C. KEENAN. 2003. SAS for Monte Carlo studies: a guide for quantitative researchers. SAS Institute, Inc., Cary, NC.

FARNSWORTH, G. L., K. C. WEEKS, AND T. R. SIMONS. 2000. Validating the assumptions of the Mayfield method. Journal of Field Ornithology 71:658–664.

FAUTH, P. T. 2000. Reproductive success of Wood Thrushes in forest fragments in northern Indiana. Auk 117:194–204.

FILLIATER, T. S., R. BREITWISCH, AND P. M. NEALEN. 1994. Predation on Northern Cardinal nests: does choice of nest-site matter? Condor 96:761–768.

FITZMAURICE, G. M. 1997. Model selection with overdispersed data. Statistician 46:81–91.

FLINT, P. L., K. H. POLLOCK, D. THOMAS, AND J. S. SEDINGER. 1995. Estimating prefledging survival: allowing for brood mixing and dependence among brood mates. Journal of Wildlife Management 59:448–455.

FOWLKES, E. B. 1987. Some diagnostics for binary logistic regression via smoothing methods. Biometrika 74:503–515.

GELMAN, A., J. B. CARLIN, H. S. STERN, AND D. B. RUBIN. 1995. Bayesian data analysis. Chapman and Hall, London, UK.

GILMER, D. S., I. J. BALL, L. M. COWARDIN, AND J. H. RIECHMANN. 1974. Effects of radio packages on wild ducks. Journal of Wildlife Management 38: 243–252.

GOC, M. 1986. A new method of estimating nest success in birds. Vår Fågelvarld (Supplement) 11: 33–34.

GÖRANSSON, G., AND J. LOMAN. 1976. Predation på konstgjorda fasanreden (predation on simulated pheasant's nests). Anser 15:195–200.

GORE, J. A., AND C. A. CHASE III. 1989. Snowy Plover breeding distribution. Final performance report. Nongame Wildlife Section, Florida Game and Fresh Water Fish Commission, Tallahassee, FL.

GÖTMARK, F. 1992. The effects of investigator disturbance on nesting birds. Current Ornithology 9:63–104.

GÖTMARK, F., D. BLOMQUIST, O. C. JOHANSSON, AND J. BERGKVIST. 1995. Nest site selection: a trade-off between concealment and view of the surroundings? Journal of Avian Biology 26:305–312.

GRAND, J. B., T. F. FONDELL, D. A. MILLER, AND R. M. ANTHONY. 2006. Nest survival in Dusky Canada Geese (*Branta canadensis occidentalis*): use of discrete-time models. Auk 123:198–210.

GRANT, T. A., T. L. SHAFFER, E. M. MADDEN, AND P. J. PIETZ. 2005. Time-specific variation in passerine nest survival: new insights into old questions. Auk 122:661–672.

GRAY, R. J. 1992. Flexible methods for analyzing survival data using splines, with applications to breast cancer prognosis. Journal of the American Statistical Association 87:942–951.

GREEN, M. T., P. E. LOWTHER, S. L. JONES, S. K. DAVIS, AND B. C. DALE. 2002. Baird's Sparrow (*Ammodramus bairdii*). *In* A. Poole, and F. Gill (editors). The Birds of North America, No. 638. Academy of Natural Sciences, Philadelphia, PA and The American Ornithologists' Union, Washington, DC.

GREEN, R. E. 1989. Transformation of crude proportions of nests that are successful for comparison with Mayfield estimates of nest success. Ibis 131: 305–306.

GREEN, R. F. 1977. Do more birds produce fewer young? A comment on Mayfield's measure of nest success. Wilson Bulletin 89:173–175.

GREENBERG, R. 2003. The use of nest departure calls for surveying Swamp Sparrows. Journal of Field Ornithology 74:12–16.

GREENBERG, R., C. ELPHICK, J. C. NORDBY, C. GJERDRUM, H. SPAUTZ, G. SHRIVER, B. SCHMELING, B. OLSEN, P. MARRA, N. NUR, AND M. WINTER. 2006. Flooding and predation: trade-offs in the nesting ecology of tidal-marsh sparrows. Studies in Avian Biology 32:96–109.

GROSS, A. J., AND V. A. CLARK. 1975. Survival distributions: reliability applications in the biomedical sciences. Wiley, New York, NY.

GUSTAFSON, E. J., M. G. KNUTSON, G. J. NIEMI, AND M. A. FRIBERG. 2002. Evaluation of spatial models to predict vulnerability of forest birds to brood parasitism by cowbirds. Ecological Applications 12:412–426.

HALUPKA, K. 1998. Vocal begging by nestlings and vulnerability to nest predation in Meadow Pipits *Anthus pratensis*: to what extent do predation costs of begging exist? Ibis 140:144–149.

HAMMOND, M. C., AND W. R. FORWARD. 1956. Experiments on causes of duck nest predation. Journal of Wildlife Management 20:243–247.

HARDLE, W. 1990. Applied nonparametric regression. Cambridge University Press, Cambridge, UK.

HARTLEY, M. J., AND M. L. HUNTER, JR. 1998. A meta-analysis of forest cover, edge effects, and artificial nest predation rates. Conservation Biology 12: 465–469.

HAZLER, K. R. 2004. Mayfield logistic regression: a practical approach for analysis of nest survival. Auk 121:707–716.

HE, C. Z. 2003. Bayesian modeling of age-specific survival in bird nesting studies under irregular visits. Biometrics 59:962–973.

HE, C. Z., D. SUN, AND Y. TRA. 2001. Bayesian modeling of age-specific survival in nesting studies under Dirichlet priors. Biometrics 57:1059–1066.

HEISEY, D. M. 1991. Applications of survival analysis in animal ecology. Ph.D. dissertation, University of Wisconsin, Madison, WI.

HEISEY, D. M., AND A. P. FOONG. 1998. Modelling time-dependent interaction in a time-varying covariate and its application to rejection episodes and kidney transplant failure. Biometrics 54:712–719.

HEISEY, D. M., AND T. K. FULLER. 1985. Evaluation of survival and cause-specific mortality-rates using telemetry data. Journal of Wildlife Management 49:668–674.

HEISEY, D. M., AND E. V. NORDHEIM. 1990. Biases in the Pollock and Cornelius method of estimating nest survival. Biometrics 46:855–862.

HEISEY, D. M., AND E. V. NORDHEIM. 1995. Modeling age-specific survival in nesting studies, using a general approach for doubly-censored and truncated data. Biometrics 51:51–60.

HENSLER, G. L. 1985. Estimation and comparison of function of daily nest survival probabilities using the Mayfield method. Pp. 289–301 *in* B. J. T. Morgan, and P.M. North (editors). Statistics in ornithology. Springer-Verlag, Berlin, Germany.

HENSLER, G. L., AND J. D. NICHOLS. 1981. The Mayfield method of estimating nesting success: a model, estimators and simulation results. Wilson Bulletin 93:42–53.

HILL, D. P., AND L. K. GOULD. 1997. Chestnut-collared Longspur (*Calcarius ornatus*). *In* A. Poole, and F. Gill (editors). The Birds of North America, No. 288. Academy of Natural Sciences, Philadelphia, PA and The American Ornithologists' Union, Washington, DC.

HILL, L. A. 1985. Breeding ecology of interior Least Terns, Snowy Plovers, and American Avocets at Salt Plains National Wildlife Refuge. M.S. thesis, Oklahoma State University, Stillwater, OK.

HINDE, J., AND C. G. B. DEMETRIO. 1998. Overdispersion: models and estimation. Computational Statistics and Data Analysis 27:151–170.

HINES, J. E., AND J. R. SAUER. 1989. Program CONTRAST: a general program for the analysis of several survival or recovery rate estimates. USDI Fish and Wildlife Service Technical Report 24. Washington, DC.

HOBBS, N. T., AND R. HILBORN. 2006. Alternatives to statistical hypothesis testing in ecology: a guide to self teaching. Ecological Applications 16:5–19.

HOBERT, J. P., AND G. CASELLA. 1996. The effect of improper priors on Gibbs sampling in hierarchical linear mixed models. Journal of the American Statistical Association 91:1461–1473.

HOEKMAN, S. T., L. S. MILLS, D. W. HOWERTER, J. H. DEVRIES, AND I. J. BALL. 2002. Sensitivity analyses of the life cycle of midcontinent Mallards. Journal of Wildlife Management 66:883–900.

HOLFORD, T. R. 1976. Life tables with concomitant information. Biometrics 32:587–597.

HOLFORD, T. R. 1980. The analysis of rates and survivorship using log-linear models. Biometrics 36: 299–306.

HOOD, S. L. 2006. Nesting ecology of Snowy and Wilson's plovers in the lower Laguna Madre region of Texas. M.S. thesis, Mississippi State University, Mississippi State, MS.

HOOVER, J. P. 2006. Water depth influences nest predation for a wetland-dependent bird in fragmented bottomland forests. Biological Conservation 127: 37–45.

HOOVER, J. P., AND M. C. BRITTINGHAM. 1998. Nest-site selection and nesting success of Wood Thrushes. Wilson Bulletin 110:375–383.

HORVITZ, D. G., AND D. J. THOMPSON. 1952. A generalization of sampling without replacement from a finite universe. Journal of the American Statistical Association 47:663–685.

HOSMER, D. W., T. HOSMER, S. LE CESSIE, AND S. LEMESHOW. 1997. A comparison of goodness-of-fit tests for the logistic regression model. Statistics in Medicine 16:965–980.

HOWLETT, J. S., AND B. J. STUTCHBURY. 1996. Nest concealment and predation in Hooded Warblers: experimental removal of nest cover. Auk 113: 1–9.

HUBER-CAROL, C., AND I. VONTA. 2004. Frailty models for arbitrarily censored and truncated data. Lifetime Data Analysis 10:369–388.

HURVICH, C. M., AND C. L. TSAI. 1989. Regression and time series model selection in small samples. Biometrika 76:297–307.

HYDE, J. 1977. Testing survival under right censoring and left truncation. Biometrika 64:225–230.

IBRAHIM, J. G., M. H. CHEN, AND D. SINHA. 2001. Bayesian survival analysis. Springer, New York, NY.

JEFFREYS, H. 1961. Theory of probability. 3rd ed. Oxford University Press, Oxford, UK.

JEHLE, G., A. A. YACKEL ADAMS, J. A. SAVIDGE, AND S. K. SKAGEN. 2004. Nest survival estimation: a review of alternatives to the Mayfield estimator. Condor 106:472–484.

JIANG, H., J. FINE, AND R. J. CHAPPELL. 2005. Semiparametric analysis of survival data with left truncation and dependent right censoring. Biometrics 61:567–575.

JOHNSON, D. H. 1979. Estimating nest success: the Mayfield method and an alternative. Auk 96:651–661.

JOHNSON, D. H. 1990. Statistical comparison of nest success rates. Proceedings of the North Dakota Academy of Science 44:67. <http://www.npwrc.usgs.gov/resource/2000/statcomp/statcomp.htm> (9 June 2006)

JOHNSON, D. H. 1991. Further comments on estimating nest success. Ibis 133:205–207.

JOHNSON, D. H. 2002. The role of hypothesis testing in wildlife science. Journal of Wildlife Management 66:272–276.

JOHNSON, D. H., AND A. T. KLETT. 1985. Quick estimates of success rates of duck nests. Wildlife Society Bulletin 13:51-53.

JOHNSON, D. H., J. D. NICHOLS, AND M. D. SCHWARTZ. 1992. Population dynamics of breeding waterfowl. Pp. 446-485 *in* B. D. J. Batt, A. D. Afton, M. G. Anderson, C. D. Ankney, D. H. Johnson, J. A. Kadlec, and G. L. Krapu (editors). Ecology and management of breeding waterfowl. University of Minnesota Press, Minneapolis, MN.

JOHNSON, D. H., A. B. SARGEANT, AND R. J. GREENWOOD. 1989. Importance of individual species of predators on nesting success of ducks in the Canadian prairie pothole region. Canadian Journal of Zoology 67:291–297.

JOHNSON, D. H., AND T. L. SHAFFER. 1990. Estimating nest success: when Mayfield wins. Auk 107:595–600.

JOHNSON, D. S., AND J. A. HOETING. 2003. Autoregressive models for capture-recapture data: a Bayesian approach. Biometrics 59:341–350.

JOHNSON, R. G., AND S. A. TEMPLE. 1990. Nest predation and brood parasitism of tallgrass prairie birds. Journal of Wildlife Management 54:106–111.

KALBFLEISCH, J. D., AND R. L. PRENTICE. 1980. The statistical analysis of failure time data. Wiley, New York, NY.

KAPLAN, E. L., AND P. MEIER. 1958. Nonparametric estimation from incomplete observations. Journal of the American Statistical Association 53:457–481.

KASS, R. E., B. P. CARLIN, A. GELMAN, AND R. M. NEAL. 1998. Markov chain Monte Carlo in practice: a roundtable discussion. American Statistician 52: 93–100.

KASS, R. E., AND A. E. RAFTERY. 1995. Bayes factors. Journal of the American Statistical Association 90:773–795.

KILGO, J. C., R. A. SARGENT, B. R. CHAPMAN, AND K. V. MILLER. 1998. Effect of stand width and adjacent habitat on breeding bird communities in bottomland hardwoods. Journal of Wildlife Management 62:72–83.

KIM, D. K. 1997. Regression analysis of interval-censored survival data with covariates using log-linear models. Biometrics 53:1274–1283.

KLETT, A. T., H. F. DUEBBERT, C. A. FAANES, AND K. F. HIGGINS. 1986. Techniques for studying nest success of ducks in upland habitats in the prairie pothole region. Resource Publication 158. USDI Fish and Wildlife Service, Washington, DC. <http://www.npwrc.usgs.gov/resource/tools/nest/nest.htm> (20 March 2006).

KLETT, A. T., AND D. H. JOHNSON. 1982. Variability in nest survival rates and implications to nesting studies. Auk 99:77–87.

KNETTER, J. M., R. S. LUTZ, J. R. CARY, AND R. K. MURPHY. 2002. A multi-scale investigation of Piping Plover productivity on Great Plains alkali lakes, 1994–2000. Wildlife Society Bulletin 30:683–694.

KNIGHT, R. L., S. KIM, and S. A. TEMPLE. 1985. Predation of Red-winged Blackbird nests by mink. Condor 87:304–305.

KNUTSON, M. G., J. P. HOOVER, AND E. E. KLAAS. 1996. The importance of floodplain forests in the conservation and management of neotropical migratory birds in the Midwest. Pp. 168–188 *in* F. R. THOMPSON (editor). Management of midwestern landscapes for the conservation of neotropical migratory birds. USDA Forest Service General Technical Report NC-GTR-187. USDA Forest Service, North Central Research Station. St. Paul, MN.

KNUTSON, M. G., AND E. E. KLAAS. 1997. Declines in abundance and species richness of birds following a major flood on the upper Mississippi River. Auk 114:367–380.

KNUTSON, M. G., G. J. NIEMI, W. E. NEWTON, AND M. A. FRIBERG. 2004. Avian nest success in midwestern forests fragmented by agriculture. Condor 106: 116–130.

KNUTSON, M. G., L. A. POWELL, M. A. FRIBERG, G. J. NIEMI, AND R. K. HINES. 2006. An assessment of bird habitat quality using population growth rates. Condor 108:301–314.

KORSCHGEN, C. E., K. P. KENOW, W. L. GREEN, D. H. JOHNSON, M. D. SAMUEL, AND L. SILEO. 1996. Survival of radiomarked Canvasback ducklings in northwestern Minnesota. Journal of Wildlife Management 60:120–132.

LAIRD, N., AND D. OLIVER. 1980. Covariance analysis of censored survival data using log-linear analysis techniques. Journal of the American Statistical Association 86:899–909.

LAWLESS, J. F. 1982. Statistical models and methods for lifetime data. Wiley, NY.

LE CESSIE, S., AND J. C. VAN HOUWELINGEN. 1991. A goodness-of-fit test for binary regression models, based on smoothing methods. Biometrics 47: 1267–1282.

LEBRETON, J. D., K. P. BURNHAM, J. COLBERT, AND D. R. ANDERSON. 1992. Modeling survival and testing biological hypotheses using marked animals: a unified approach with case studies. Ecological Monographs 62:67–118.

LEE, Y., AND J. A. NELDER. 2000. Two ways of modeling overdispersion in non-normal data. Journal of the Royal Statistical Society Series C-Applied Statistics 49:591–598.

LELE, S., AND M. L. TAPER. 2002. A composite likelihood approach to estimation of (co)variance components. Journal of Statistical Planning and Inference 103:117–135.

LIEBEZEIT, J. R., AND T. L. GEORGE. 2002. Nest predators, nest-site selection, and nesting success for the Dusky Flycatcher in a managed ponderosa pine forest. Condor 104:507–517.

LINDGREN, B. W. 1976. Statistical theory. 3rd ed. MacMillan Publishing Co., Inc. New York, NY.

LINDSEY, J. C., AND L. M. RYAN. 1998. Tutorial in biostatistics: methods for interval-censored data. Statistics in Medicine 17:219–238.

LINK, C. L. 1984. Confidence intervals for the survival function using Cox's proportional hazards model with covariates. Biometrics 40:601–609.

LINK, W. A., E. CAM, J. D. NICHOLS, AND E. G. COOCH. 2002. Of BUGS and birds: Markov chain Monte Carlo for hierarchical modeling in wildlife research. Journal of Wildlife Management 66: 277–291.

LITTELL, R. C., G. A. MILLIKEN, W. W. STROUP, AND R. D. WOLFINGER. 1996. SAS system for mixed models. SAS Institute Inc., Cary, NC.

LLOYD, J. D., AND T. E. MARTIN. 2005. Reproductive success of Chestnut-collared Longspurs in native and exotic grassland. Condor 107:363–374.

LLOYD, P., T. E. MARTIN, R. L. REDMOND, U. LANGNER, AND M. M. HART. 2005. Linking demographic effects of habitat fragmentation across landscapes to continental source-sink dynamics. Ecological Applications 15:1504–1514.

LOKEMOEN, J. T., AND R. R. KOFORD. 1996. Using candlers to determine the incubation stage of passerine eggs. Journal of Field Ornithology 67:660–668.

LONGFORD, N. T. 1993. Random coefficient models. Clarendon Press, Oxford, UK.

LUDWIG, D. 1996. Uncertainty and the assessment of extinction probabilities. Ecological Applications 6:1067–1076.

LUNN, D. J., A. THOMAS, N. BEST, AND D. SPIEGELHALTER. 2000. WinBUGS—a Bayesian modeling framework: concepts, structure, and extensibility. Statistics and Computing 10:325–337.

LYNDEN-BELL, D. 1971. A method of allowing for known observational selection in small samples applied to 3CR quasars. Monthly Notices of the Royal Astronomy Society 155:95–118.

MABEE, T. J. 1997. Using eggshell evidence to determine nest fate of shorebirds. Wilson Bulletin 109: 307–313.

MANLY, B. F. J., AND J. A. SCHMUTZ. 2001. Estimation of brood and nest survival: comparative methods in the presence of heterogeneity. Journal of Wildlife Management 65:258–270.

MANOLIS, J. C., D. E. ANDERSEN, AND F. J. CUTHBERT. 2000. Uncertain nest fates in songbird studies and variation in Mayfield estimation. Auk 117: 615–626.

MARTIN, T. E. 1993. Nest predation among vegetation layers and habitat types: revising the dogmas. American Naturalist 141:897–913.

MARTIN, T. E. 1998. Are microhabitat preferences of coexisting species under selection and adaptive? Ecology 79:656–670.

MARTIN, T. E., AND G. R. GEUPEL. 1993. Nest-monitoring plots: methods for locating nests and monitoring success. Journal of Field Ornithology 64:507–519.

MARTIN, T. E., AND J. J. ROPER. 1988. Nest predation and nest-site selection of a western population of the Hermit Thrush. Condor 90:51–57.

MARTIN, T. E., AND S. J. MENGE. 2000. Nest predation increases with parental activity: separating nest site and parental activity effects. Proceedings Royal Society London B 267:2287–2293.

MATHWORKS. 2004. MATLAB, Version 7.0, R14. The Mathworks, Inc., Natick, MA.

MAYFIELD, H. 1960. The Kirtland's Warbler. Cranbrook Institute of Science, Bloomfield Hills, MI.

MAYFIELD, H. 1961. Nesting success calculated from exposure. Wilson Bulletin 73:255–261.

MAYFIELD, H. F. 1975. Suggestions for calculating nest success. Wilson Bulletin 87:456–466.

MCCULLAGH, P., AND J. A. NELDER. 1989. Generalized linear models, 2nd ed. Chapman and Hall, New York, NY.

MCGARIGAL, K., AND B. J. MARKS. 1995. FRAGSTATS: spatial pattern analysis program for quantifying landscape structure. USDA Forest Service General Technical Report PNW-GTR-351. USDA Forest Service, Pacific Northwest Research Station. Portland, OR.

MCNAB, W. H., AND P. E. AVERS. 1994. Ecological subregions of the United States. USDA Forest Service WO-WSA-5. USDA Forest Service, Washington, DC. <http://www.fs.fed.us/land/pubs/ecoregions/index.html> (15 November 2006).

MCPHERSON, R. J., T. W. ARNOLD, L. M. ARMSTRONG, AND C. J. SCHWARZ. 2003. Estimating the nest-success rate and the number of nests initiated by radiomarked Mallards. Journal of Wildlife Management 67:843–851.

MEIER, P., T. KARRISON, R. CHAPPELL, AND H. XIE. 2004. The price of Kaplan-Meier. Journal of the American Statistical Association 99:890–896.

MILLER, H. W., AND D. H. JOHNSON. 1978. Interpreting the results of nesting studies. Journal of Wildlife Management 42:471–476.

MILLER, R. G. JR. 1981. Survival analysis. Wiley, New York, NY.

MILLER, R. G. JR. 1983. What price Kaplan-Meier? Biometrics 39:1077–1081.

MOORE, R. P., AND W. D. ROBINSON. 2004. Artificial bird nests, external validity, and bias in ecological field studies. Ecology 85:1562-1567.

MORRISON, M. L., W. M. BLOCK, M. D. STRICKLAND, AND W. L. KENDALL. 2001. Wildlife study design. Springer-Verlag, New York, NY.

MORTON, M. L., K. W. SOCKMAN, AND L. E. PETERSON. 1993. Nest predation in the Mountain White-crowned Sparrow. Condor 95:72–82.

MURPHY, M. T. 1983. Nest success and nesting habits of Eastern Kingbirds and other flycatchers. Condor 85:208–219.

MURPHY, M. T., C. L. CUMMINGS, AND M. S. PALMER. 1977. Comparative analysis of habitat selection, nest site and nest success by Cedar Waxwings (*Bombycilla cedrorum*) and Eastern Kingbirds (*Tyrannus tyrannus*). American Midland Naturalist 138:344–356.

NATARAJAN, R., AND C. E. MCCULLOCH. 1999. Modeling heterogeneity in nest survival data. Biometrics 55: 553–559.

NATIONAL CLIMATIC DATA CENTER. 2003. Climatological data, Texas: March–July. National Oceanic and Atmospheric Administration. <http://www.ncdc.noaa.gov/oa/ncdc.html> (6 November 2006).

NATIONAL CLIMATIC DATA CENTER. 2004. Climatological data, Texas: March–July. National Oceanic and Atmospheric Administration. <http://www.ncdc.noaa.gov/oa/ncdc.html> (6 November 2006).

NICHOLS, J. D., H. F. PERCIVAL, R. A. COON, M. J. CONROY, G. L. HENSLER, AND J. E. HINES. 1984. Observer visitation frequency and success of Mourning Dove nests: a field experiment. Auk 101:398–402.

NISBET, I. C. T., K. J. WILSON, AND W. A. BROAD. 1978. Common Terns raise young after death of their mates. Condor 80:106–109.

NUR, N., A. L. HOLMES, AND G. R. GEUPEL. 2004. Use of survival time analysis to analyze nesting success in birds: an example using Loggerhead Shrikes. Condor 106:457–471.

OAKES, D. 1972. Discussion of the paper by D. R. Cox. Journal of the Royal Statistical Society, Series B 34:208.

OWENS, T., AND K. D. HOP. 1995. Long term resource monitoring program standard operating procedures: photointerpretation. LTRMP 95-P008-1. (NTIS # PB95-264610) National Biological Service, Environmental Management Technical Center, Onalaska, WI.

PAGE, G. W., J. S. WARRINER, J. C. WARRINER, AND P. W. C. PATON. 1995. Snowy Plover (*Charadrius alexandrinus*). *In* A. Poole, and F. Gill (editors). The Birds of North America, No. 154. The Academy of Natural Sciences, Philadelphia, PA and The American Ornithologists' Union, Washington, DC.

PAGE, G. W., L. E. STENZEL, AND C. A. RIBIC. 1985. Nest site selection and clutch predation in the Snowy Plover. Auk 102:347–353.

PAGE, G. W., D. W. WINKLER, AND C. W. SWARTH. 1983. Spacing out at Mono Lake: breeding success, nest density and predation in the Snowy Plover. Auk 100:13–24.

PAN, W., AND R. CHAPPELL. 1999. A note on inconsistency of NPMLE of the distribution function from left truncated and case I interval censored data. Lifetime Data Analysis 5:281–291.

PAN, W., AND R. CHAPPELL. 2002. Estimation in the Cox proportional hazards model with left-truncated and interval-censored data. Biometrics 58:64–70.

PAN, Z., AND D. Y. LIN. 2005. Goodness-of-fit methods for generalized linear mixed models. Biometrics 61:1000–1009.

PANKRATZ, V. S., M. DE ANDRADE, AND T. M. THERNEAU. 2005. Random-effects Cox proportional hazards model: general variance components methods for time-to-event data. Genetic Epidemiology 28: 97–109.

PATON, P. W. C. 1995. Breeding biology of Snowy Plovers at Great Salt Lake, Utah. Wilson Bulletin 107:275–288.

PEAK, R. G, F. R. THOMPSON III, AND T. L. SHAFFER. 2004. Factors affecting songbird nest survival in riparian forests in a midwestern agricultural landscape. Auk 121:726–737.

PEAKALL, D. B. 1960. Nest records of the Yellowhammer. Bird Study 7:94–102.

PESCADOR, M., AND S. PERIS. 2001. Effects of land use on nest predation: an experimental study in Spanish croplands. Folia Zoologica 50:127–136.

PETIT, L. J., AND D. K. PETIT. 1996. Factors governing habitat selection by Prothonotary Warblers: field test of the Fretwell-Lucas models. Ecological Monographs 66:367–387.

PIETZ, P. J., AND D. A. GRANFORS. 2000. Identifying predators and fates of grassland passerine nests using miniature video cameras. Journal of Wildlife Management. 64:71–87.

PINHEIRO, J. C., AND D. M. BATES. 2000. Mixed-effects models in S and S-plus. Springer-Verlag, New York, NY.

POLLOCK, K. H., AND W. L. CORNELIUS. 1988. A distribution-free nest survival model. Biometrics 44: 397–404.

POLLOCK, K. H., S. R. WINTERSTEIN, C. M. BUNCK, AND P. D. CURTIS. 1989. Survival analysis in telemetry studies: the staggered entry design. Journal of Wildlife Management 53:7-15.

PRENTICE, R. L., AND L. A. GLOECKLER. 1978. Regression analysis of grouped survival data with application to breast cancer data. Biometrics 34:57–67.

PURDUE, J. R. 1976. Thermal environment of the nest and related parental behavior in Snowy Plovers, *Charadrius alexandrinus*. Condor 78:180–185.

RABE-HESKETH, S., A. SKRONDAL, AND A. PICKLES. 2002. Reliable estimation of generalized linear mixed models using adaptive quadrature. Stata Journal 2:1–21.

RALPH, C. J., G. R. GEUPEL, P. PYLE, T. E. MARTIN, AND D. F. DESANTE. 1993. Handbook of field methods for monitoring landbirds. USDA Forest Service General Technical Report PSW-GTR-144. USDA Forest Service, Pacific Southwest Research Station, Albany, CA.

RECKHOW, K. H. 1990. Bayesian inference in non-replicated ecological studies. Ecology 71:2053–2059.

REMES, V. 2005. Nest concealment and parental behaviour interact in affecting nest survival in the Blackcap (*Sylvia atricapilla*): an experimental evaluation of the parental compensation hypothesis. Behavioral Ecology and Sociobiology 58:326–332.

RENNER, M., AND L. S. DAVIS. 2001. Survival analysis of Little Penguin *Eudyptula minor* chicks on Motuara Island, New Zealand. Ibis 143:369–379.

RICKLEFS, R. E. 1969. An analysis of nesting mortality in birds. Smithsonian Contributions in Zoology No. 9. Washington, DC.

ROBBINS, M. B. 1998. Display behavior of male Sprague's Pipits. Wilson Bulletin 110:435–438.

ROBEL, R. J., J. N. BRIGGS, A. D. DAYTON, AND L. C. HULBERT. 1970. Relationships between visual obstruction measurements and weights of grassland vegetation. Journal of Range Management 23:295–298.

ROBINSON, D. H., AND H. WAINER. 2002. On the past and future of null hypothesis significance testing. Journal of Wildlife Management 66:263–271.

RODEWALD, A. D. 2002. Nest predation in forested regions: landscape and edge effects. Journal of Wildlife Management 66:634–640.

RODEWALD, P. G., AND K. G. SMITH. 1998. Short-term effects of understory and overstory management on breeding birds in Arkansas oak-hickory forests. Journal of Wildlife Management 62: 1411–1417.

RODRIGUEZ, G., AND N. GOLDMAN. 1995. An assessment of estimation procedures for multilevel models with binary responses. Journal of the Royal Statistical Society A 158:73–89.

ROTELLA, J. J. 2005. Nest survival models. Chapter 14 *in* E. Cooch, and G. C. White (editors). Program MARK: a gentle introduction. 4th ed. <http://www.warnercnr.colostate.edu/~gwhite/mark/mark.htm> (15 November 2006).

ROTELLA, J. J., S. J. DINSMORE, AND T. L. SHAFFER. 2004. Modeling nest-survival data: a comparison of recently developed methods that can be implemented in MARK and SAS. Animal Biodiversity and Conservation 27:187–205.

ROTELLA, J. J., M. L. TAPER, AND A. J. HANSEN. 2000. Correcting nesting-success estimates for observer effects: maximum-likelihood estimates of daily survival rates with reduced bias. Auk 117:92–109.

ROTELLA, J. J., M. L. TAPER, S. E. STEPHENS, AND M. L. LINDBERG. 2006. Code for extending methods for modeling heterogeneity in nest-survival data using generalized mixed models. Montana State University, Bozeman, MT. <http://www.montana.edu/rotella/nestsurv> (28 November 2006).

ROTH, R. R. 1976. Spatial heterogeneity and bird species diversity. Ecology 57:773–782.

ROYAMA, T. 1981. Evaluation of mortality factors in insect life table analysis. Ecological Monographs 51:495–505.

RUPERT, J. R. 1997. The brood-rearing habitat, brood home range, and fecundity of the Snowy Plover (*Charadrius alexandrinus*) in coastal southern Texas. M.S. thesis, University of Texas–Pan American, Edinburg, TX.

SAS INSTITUTE INC. 2004. SAS onlinedoc 9.1.2. SAS Institute Inc., Cary, NC. <http://support.sas.com/onlinedoc/912/docMainpage.jsp> (12 January 2007).

SAUER, J. R., AND B. K. WILLIAMS. 1989. Generalized procedures for testing hypotheses about survival or recovery rates. Journal of Wildlife Management 53:137–142.

SAWIN, R. S., M. W. LUTMAN, G. M. LINZ, and W. J. BLEIER. 2003. Predators on Red-winged Blackbird nests in eastern North Dakota. Journal of Field Ornithology 74:288–292.

SCHMIDT, K. A., AND C. J. WHELAN. 1999. Nest placement and mortality: a random event in space and time. Condor 101:916–920.

SCOTT, J. M., F. DAVIS, B. CSUTI, R. NOSS, B. BUTTERFIELD, C. GROVES, H. ANDERSON, S. CAICCO, F. D'ERCHIA, T. C. EDWARDS, JR., J. ULLIMAN, AND R. G. WRIGHT. 1993. Gap analysis: a geographic approach to protection of biological diversity. Wildlife Monographs 123:1–41.

SEARCY, W.A., AND J. YASUKAWA. 1995. Polygyny and sexual selection in Red-winged Blackbirds. Princeton University Press, Princeton, NJ.

SEBER, G. A. F. 1982. The estimation of animal abundance and related parameters. 2nd ed. Macmillan, New York, NY.

SEDINGER, J. S. 1990. Effects of visiting Black Brant nests on egg and nest survival. Journal of Wildlife Management 54:437–443.

SERVICE, P. M. 2000. Heterogeneity in individual mortality risk and its importance for evolutionary studies of senescence. American Naturalist 156:1–13.

SHAFFER, T. L. 2004a. A unified approach to analyzing nest success. Auk 121:526–540.

SHAFFER, T. L. 2004b. Logistic-exposure analyses of nest survival. Northern Prairie Wildlife Research Center, Jamestown, ND. <http://www.npwrc.usgs.gov/resource/birds/nestsurv/index.htm> (27 November 2006).

SHOCHAT, E., M. A. PATTEN, D. W. MORRIS, D. L. REINKING, D. H. WOLFE, AND D. K. SHERROD. 2005a. Ecological traps in isodars: effects of tallgrass prairie management on bird nest success. Oikos 111:159–169.

SHOCHAT, E., D. H. WOLFE, M. A. PATTEN, D. L. REINKING, AND S. K. SHERROD. 2005b. Tallgrass prairie management and bird nest success along roadsides. Biological Conservation 121:399–407.

SIEPIELSKI, A. M., A. D. RODEWALD, AND R. H. YAHNER. 2001. Nest site selection and nesting success of the Red-eyed Vireo in central Pennsylvania. Wilson Bulletin 113:302–307.

SILLETT, T. S., R. T. HOLMES, AND T. W. SHERRY. 2000. Impacts of a global climate cycle on population dynamics of a migratory songbird. Science 288: 2040–2042.

SIMPSON, E. H. 1951. The interpretation of interaction in contingency tables. Journal of the Royal Statistical Society, Series B 13:238–241.

SNEE, R. D. 1977. Validation of regression models: methods and examples. Technometrics 19: 415–428.

SNIJDERS, T. A. B., AND R. J. BOSKER. 1999. Multilevel analysis: an introduction to basic and advanced multilevel modeling. Sage Publications, London, UK.

SNOW, D.W. 1955. The breeding of Blackbird, Song Thrush and Mistle Thrush in Great Britain, Part III. nesting success. Bird Study 2:169–178.

SPIEGELHALTER, D. J., A. THOMAS, N. G. BEST, AND W. R. GILKS. 1995. BUGS: Bayesian inference using Gibbs Sampling. MRC Biostatistics Unit and Imperial College of Science, Technology and Medicine, Cambridge, UK.

STANLEY, T. R. 2000. Modeling and estimation of stage-specific daily survival probabilities of nests. Ecology 81:2048–2053.

STANLEY, T. R. 2004a. Estimating stage-specific daily survival probabilities of nests when nest age is unknown. Auk 121:134–147.

STANLEY, T. R. 2004b. When should Mayfield model data be discarded? Wilson Bulletin 116:267–269.

STEPHENS, S. E. 2003. The influence of landscape characteristics on duck nesting success in the Missouri Coteau Region of North Dakota. Ph.D. dissertation, Montana State University, Bozeman, MT.

STEPHENS, S. E., D. N. KOONS, J. J. ROTELLA, AND D. W. WILLEY. 2004. Effects of habitat fragmentation on avian nesting success: a review of the evidence at multiple spatial scales. Biological Conservation 115:101–110.

STEPHENS, S. E., J. J. ROTELLA, M. S. LINDBERG, M. L. TAPER, AND J. K. RINGELMAN. 2005. Duck nest survival in the Missouri Coteau of North Dakota: landscape effects at multiple spatial scales. Ecological Applications 15:2137–2149.

STERN, M. A., K. A. KRISTENSEN, AND J. F. MORAWSKI. 1990. Investigations of Snowy Plovers at Albert Lake, Lake Co., Oregon. The Nature Conservancy, Portland, OR.

STURDIVANT, R. X. 2005. Goodness-of-fit in hierarchical logistic regression models. Ph.D. dissertation, University of Massachusetts, Amherst, MA.

STURDIVANT, R. X., AND D. W. HOSMER. In press. A smoothed residual based goodness-of-fit statistic for logistic hierarchical regression models. Computational Statistics and Data Analysis.

STURDIVANT, R. X., J. J. ROTELLA, AND R. E. RUSSELL. 2006. Code for a smoothed residual based goodness-of-fit statistic for nest-survival models. Montana State University, Bozeman, MT. <http://www.montana.edu/rotella/nestsurv/> (30 November 2006).

Sutter, G. C. 1997. Nest-site selection and nest-entrance orientation in Sprague's Pipit. Wilson Bulletin 109:462–469.

Taper, M. L., and S. R. Lele. 2004. The nature of scientific evidence: a forward-looking synthesis. Pp. 527–551 *in* M. L. Taper, and S. R. Lele (editors). The Nature of Scientific Evidence: Empirical, Statistical, and Philosophical Considerations. University of Chicago Press, Chicago, IL.

Tewksbury, J. J., L. Garner, S. Garner, J. D. Lloyd, V. Saab, and T. E. Martin. 2006. Tests of landscape influence: nest predation and brood parasitism in fragmented ecosystems. Ecology 87:759–768.

Therneau, T. M., and P. M. Grambsch. 2000. Modeling survival data: extending the Cox model. Springer, New York, NY.

Thompson, F. R., III. 1994. Temporal and spatial patterns of breeding Brown-headed Cowbirds in the midwestern United States. Auk 111:979–990.

Thompson, F. R., and D. E. Burhans. 2004. Differences in predators of artificial and real songbird nests: evidence of bias in artificial nest studies. Conservation Biology 18:373–380.

Thompson, F. R., III, S. K. Robinson, T. M. Donovan, J. R. Faaborg, D. R. Whitehead, and D. R. Larsen. 2000. Biogeographic, landscape, and local factors affecting cowbird abundance and host parasitism levels. Pp. 271–279 *in* J. N. M. Smith, T. L. Cook, S. I. Rothstein, S. K. Robinson, and S. G. Sealy (editors). Ecology and management of cowbirds and their hosts. University of Texas Press, Austin, TX.

Thompson, W. A. 1977. On the treatment of grouped observations in life studies. Biometrics 33: 463–470.

Tomkins, I. R. 1965. Wilson's Plover: some egg weights. Oriole 30:67–68.

Townsend, G. H. 1966. A study of waterfowl nesting on the Saskatchewan River delta. Canadian Field-Naturalist 80:74–88.

Trent, T. T., and O. J. Rongstad. 1974. Home range and survival of cottontail rabbits in southwestern Wisconsin. Journal of Wildlife Management 38: 459–472.

Tsai, W. Y., N. P. Jewell, and M. C. Wang. 1987. A note on the product-limit estimator under right-censoring and left truncation. Biometrika 74: 883–886.

Turnbull, B. W. 1976. The empirical distribution function with arbitrarily grouped, censored and truncated data. Journal of the Royal Statistical Society, Series B 38:290–295.

United States Army Corps of Engineers. 1990–1997. Forest inventory field data for Corps fee title lands of the Mississippi River 9-foot channel navigation project. U.S. Army Corps of Engineers, St. Paul District, La Crescent, MN.

United States Department of the Interior. 1993. Endangered and threatened wildlife and plants: determination of threatened status for the Pacific coast population of the western Snowy Plover. Federal Register 58:12864–12874.

Vickery, P. D., M. L. Hunter, and J. V. Wells, Jr. 1992. Evidence of incidental nest predation and its effects on nests of threatened grassland birds. Oikos 63:281–288.

Vounatsou, P., and A. F. M. Smith. 1995. Bayesian analysis of ring-recovery data via Markov chain Monte Carlo simulation. Biometrics 51:687–708.

Wade, P. R. 2000. Bayesian methods in conservation biology. Conservation Biology 14:1308–1316.

Walters, C., and D. Ludwig. 1994. Calculations of Bayes posterior probability distributions for key population parameters. Canadian Journal of Fisheries and Aquatic Sciences 51:713–722.

Wand, M. P., and M. C. Jones. 1995. Kernel smoothing. Chapman and Hall/CRC, Boca Raton, FL.

Warriner, J. S., J. C. Warriner, G. W. Page, and L. E. Stenzel. 1986. Mating system and reproductive success of a small population of polygamous Snowy Plovers. Wilson Bulletin 98:15–37.

Wehtje, W., and T. Baron. 1993. Population size and breeding success of the Western Snowy Plover on San Nicholas Island, 1993. Western Foundation for Vertebrate Zoology, Camarillo, CA.

Weidinger, K. 2002. Interactive effects of concealment, parental behaviour and predators on the survival of open passerine nests. Journal of Animal Ecology 71:424–437.

Weller, M. W. 1956. A simple field candler for waterfowl eggs. Journal of Wildlife Management 20: 111–113.

Westerskov, K. 1950. Methods for determining the age of game bird eggs. Journal of Wildlife Management 14:56–67.

Westerkov, K. 1956. Age determination and dating nesting events in the Willow Ptarmigan. Journal of Wildlife Management 20:274–279.

White, G. C. 2005. Program MARK. Mark and recapture survival rate estimation. (Version 4.2). <httpa: //www.warnercnr.colostate.edu/~gwhite/ mark/mark.htm> (15 November 2006).

White, G. C., and K. P. Burnham. 1999. Program MARK: survival estimation from populations of marked animals. Bird Study 46 (Supplement):120–138.

Williams, B. K., J. D. Nichols, and M. J. Conroy. 2002. Analysis and management of animal populations: modeling, estimation, and decision making. Academic Press, San Diego, CA.

Willis, E. O. 1973. Survival rates for visited and unvisited nests of Bicolored Antbirds. Auk 90:263–267.

Willis, E. O. 1981. Precautions in calculating nest success. Ibis 123:204–207.

Wilson, R. R., and R. J. Cooper. 1998. Acadian Flycatcher nest placement: does placement influence reproductive success? Condor 100:673–679.

Wilson-Jacobs, R., and E. C. Meslow. 1984. Distribution, abundance, and nesting characteristics of Snowy

Plovers on the Oregon Coast. Northwest Scientist 58:40–48.

WINTER, M. 1999. Nesting biology of Dickcissels and Henslow's Sparrows in southwestern Missouri prairie fragments. Wilson Bulletin 111:515–527.

WINTER, M., S. E. HAWKS, J. A. SHAFFER, AND D. H. JOHNSON. 2003. Guidelines for finding nests of passerine birds in tallgrass prairie. Prairie Naturalist 35:197–211.

WINTER, M., D. H. JOHNSON, AND J. A. SHAFFER. 2005a. Variability in vegetation effects on density and nesting success of grassland birds. Journal of Wildlife Management 69:185–197.

WINTER, M., D. H. JOHNSON, J. A. SHAFFER, AND W. D. SVEDARSKY. 2004. Nesting biology of three grassland passerines in the northern tallgrass prairie. Wilson Bulletin 116:211–223.

WINTER, M., J. A. SHAFFER, D. H. JOHNSON, T. M. DONOVAN, W. D. SVEDARSKY, P.W. JONES, AND B. R. EULISS. 2005b. Habitat and nesting of LeConte's Sparrows in the northern tallgrass prairie. Journal of Field Ornithology 76:61–71.

WINTON, B. R., D. M. LESLIE, JR., AND J. R. RUPERT. 2000. Breeding ecology and management of Snowy Plovers in north-central Oklahoma. Journal of Field Ornithology 71:573–584.

WOLFINGER, R. D., AND M. O'CONNELL. 1993. Generalized linear mixed models: a pseudo-likelihood approach. Journal of Statistical Computation and Simulation 48:233–243.

WOLFSON, L. J., J. B. KADANE, AND M. J. SMALL. 1996. Bayesian environmental policy decisions: two case studies. Ecological Applications 6:1056–1066.

WOODROOFE, M. 1985. Estimating the distribution function with truncated data. Annals of Statistics 13: 163–177.

YASUKAWA, J., AND W. A. SEARCY. 1995. Red-winged Blackbird (*Agelaius phoeniceus*). *In* A. Poole, and F. Gill, editors. The birds of North America, No. 184 The Academy of Natural Sciences, Philadelphia, PA and The American Ornithologists' Union, Washington, DC.